Holocaust vs. Popular Culture

Holocaust vs. Popular Culture debates and deconstructs the binary responses to the representation of the Holocaust in European and non-European forms of Popular Culture.

The binary is defined in terms of "incompatibility" between the Holocaust and Popular Culture on the one hand and the "universalization" of the Holocaust memory through Popular Culture on the other. The book does emphasize the anti-representation argument. Nevertheless, the authors make a case for a productive understanding of "Holocaust Popular Culture" as contributing to the expansion of Holocaust studies as well as cultural studies in the transnational context. The book theorizes Popular Culture in broad terms and highlights the diversity of Holocaust Popular Culture mainly but not exclusively produced in the twenty-first century. This interdisciplinary collection covers a wide variety of Popular Culture genres including language, literature, films, television shows, soap operas, music, dance, social media, advertisements, comics, graphic novels, videogames, and museums. It studies the (mis)representation of the Holocaust trauma, not only across genres but also across nations (Western and Asian) and generations (from testimonial remembrance to post-memory).

This book will be of interest to students and scholars from a wide range of disciplines and subjects, including Popular Culture, Holocaust studies, cultural studies, genocide studies, postcolonial and transnational studies, media and film studies, visual culture, games studies, race and ethnicity studies, memory studies, and Jewish studies.

Mahitosh Mandal is Assistant Professor of English at Presidency University, Kolkata, India.

Priyanka Das is Assistant Professor of English at Presidency University, Kolkata, India.

Holocaust vs. Popular Culture
Interrogating Incompatibility
and Universalization

**Edited by Mahitosh Mandal
and Priyanka Das**

LONDON AND NEW YORK

First published 2024
by Routledge
4 Park Square, Milton Park, Abingdon, Oxon OX14 4RN

and by Routledge
605 Third Avenue, New York, NY 10158

Routledge is an imprint of the Taylor & Francis Group, an informa business

© 2024 selection and editorial matter, Mahitosh Mandal and Priyanka Das; individual chapters, the contributors

The right of Mahitosh Mandal and Priyanka Das to be identified as the authors of the editorial material, and of the authors for their individual chapters, has been asserted in accordance with sections 77 and 78 of the Copyright, Designs and Patents Act 1988.

All rights reserved. No part of this book may be reprinted or reproduced or utilised in any form or by any electronic, mechanical, or other means, now known or hereafter invented, including photocopying and recording, or in any information storage or retrieval system, without permission in writing from the publishers.

Trademark notice: Product or corporate names may be trademarks or registered trademarks, and are used only for identification and explanation without intent to infringe.

British Library Cataloguing-in-Publication Data
A catalogue record for this book is available from the British Library

Library of Congress Cataloging-in-Publication Data
Names: Mandal, Mahitosh, editor. | Das, Priyanka, editor.
Title: Holocaust vs. popular culture : interrogating incompatibility and
    universalization / edited by Mahitosh Mandal, Priyanka Das.
Other titles: Holocaust versus popular culture
Description: 1. | New York, NY : Routledge, 2024. | Includes
    bibliographical references and index.
Identifiers: LCCN 2023009557 (print) | LCCN 2023009558 (ebook) |
    ISBN 9781032169736 (hardback) | ISBN 9781032169774 (paperback) |
    ISBN 9781003251224 (ebook)
Subjects: LCSH: Holocaust, Jewish (1939–1945), in popular culture. |
    Popular culture—Social aspects.
Classification: LCC D804.3 .H665 2024 (print) | LCC D804.3 (ebook) |
    DDC 940.53/18—dc23/eng/20230531
LC record available at https://lccn.loc.gov/2023009557
LC ebook record available at https://lccn.loc.gov/2023009558

ISBN: 978-1-032-16973-6 (hbk)
ISBN: 978-1-032-16977-4 (pbk)
ISBN: 978-1-003-25122-4 (ebk)

DOI: 10.4324/9781003251224

Typeset in Times New Roman
by Apex CoVantage, LLC

Dedicated to the memory of the millions who fell victim to Nazi atrocities

Contents

Acknowledgment	*x*
Holocaust Versus Popular Culture: A Critical Introduction MAHITOSH MANDAL AND PRIYANKA DAS	1

PART I
Explicating Incompatibility — 35

1 Popular Fiction, Literary Culture, and Artistic Truth: Thane Rosenbaum's *The Golems of Gotham* and Twenty-First Century Holocaust Representation — 37
CRAIG SMITH

2 Playing With the Unspeakable: The Holocaust and Videogames — 48
IKER ITOIZ CIÁURRIZ

3 Representation, Appropriation, and Popular Culture: Food and the Holocaust in Roman Polanski's *The Pianist* — 60
VED PRAKASH

4 Nazi Linguistics and Mass Manipulation: An Analysis of Holocaust Primary Sources Vis-à-vis Popular Culture — 69
SARAH SPINELLA

PART II
Rethinking Universalization — 81

5 Hitler's Popularity and the Trivialization of the Holocaust in India — 83
NAVRAS J. AAFREEDI

viii *Contents*

6 Decoding Holocaust Narratives in Japanese Pop Culture: Through the Lens of *Anne no Nikki* (1995) and *Persona Non Grata* (2015) 101

JOSÉ RODOLFO AVILÉS ERNULT AND ASTHA CHADHA

7 Holocaust Representations Through Popular Music: Ferramonti di Tarsia Amidst Documentation, Commemoration, and Mystification 113

SILVIA DEL ZOPPO

8 Holocaust Museums: A Study of the Memory Policies of the USA and Poland 126

ADRIANA KRAWIEC

9 Trace and Trauma: Early Holocaust Remembrance in American and Canadian Popular Culture 140

ROGER CHAPMAN

PART III
In Defense of Popular Culture 151

10 Mothers, Daughters, and the Holocaust: A Study of Miriam Katin's Graphic Memoirs 153

SUCHARITA SARKAR

11 Superheroes and the Holocaust in American Comics 164

MICHAELA WEISS

12 Unearthing the Real in the Magical: Holocaust Memory and Magic Realism in Select Post-Holocaust Fictions 175

TIASA BAL

13 "Once-upon-a-very-real-time": Fairy Tales and Holocaust in Jane Yolen's Novels 188

ANISHA SEN

14 Retelling the Holocaust With Children: A Pedagogic Study of Stephen King's *Apt Pupil* and Jane Yolen's *The Devil's Arithmetic* 202

DIGANTA RAY

Contents ix

15 **"Is It Safe?":** *Marathon Man* **as Holocaust Drama** 214
DOUGLAS C. MACLEOD, JR.

16 **Child's Play, Fantasy, and the Holocaust in** *Jojo Rabbit*
and *The Boy in the Striped Pajamas* 227
MEDHA BHADRA CHOWDHURY

17 *In*correctamundo?: **Holocaust, Humor, and Anti-Hate Satire**
in the Works of Brooks and Waititi 238
KYLE BARRETT

Notes on Contributors 252
Index 255

Acknowledgment

It is not easy to gather courage and engage with as important, serious, and vast a subject as the Holocaust. Acknowledging our debt to each and every one who believed in us is, thus, imperative.

We would like to express our gratitude to Emily Ross and Hannah Rich of Routledge for their constant support in the course of the preparation of the manuscript. We are indebted to the three anonymous reviewers for their critical feedback on our book proposal as well as the editorial board of Routledge for their comments and encouragement. It has been a thrilling journey to read the works of our contributors hailing from various parts of the world. We thank them sincerely for their cooperation and patience and for satisfactorily and promptly responding to our comments and queries on their manuscripts.

We have been teaching Holocaust literature at the Department of English, Presidency University, Kolkata for some years now and had the unique opportunity of introducing an entire module on Holocaust literature at the master's level. We are grateful to our colleague Shanta Dutta, who has been a constant source of kindness and encouragement, and to Navras J. Aafreedi, our colleague from the Department of History, for his friendship. We thank our students, who have been enthusiastic to learn about the Holocaust. Thanks to Prabal Bhowmik, our student, who promptly arranged a few e-books we needed at the last moment.

One of us had the opportunity of attending the 6th Bergen-Belsen International Summer School on the Holocaust and Transnational Memory held in 2019 at the Bergen-Belsen Memorial in Lower Saxony, Germany. We thank the organizers and mentors associated with the memorial, particularly Tessa Bouwman, Maximilian Vogel, and Stephanie Billib for their guidance.

Namrata Das has been a wonderful comrade and companion, frequently making witty and comic interventions and, thereby, motivating us to take things lightly when required. We would like her to stay like this always.

Our parents have always been supportive and understanding even if the work pressure and deadlines did not permit us to spend time with them. We remain in their debt.

Holocaust Versus Popular Culture

A Critical Introduction

Mahitosh Mandal and Priyanka Das

The Versus Thesis

Two parallel facts can be observed in the continued response to the Holocaust—the condemnation of its artistic and cultural representation and the increasing globalization of the Holocaust memory through Popular Culture. This volume is an attempt to renegotiate these binary tendencies defined, respectively, as "incompatibility" and "universalization." To claim that the Holocaust and Popular Culture are incompatible is to primarily emphasize that the Holocaust is an event that is unique, unspeakable, unrepresentable, irreproducible, and non-sellable (not-for-sale, as opposed to being unsellable). To claim that Popular Culture contributes to the universalization of the Holocaust memory is to highlight how it plays a role, however flawed, in keeping that memory alive across national and transnational audiences and forcing us to start renewed conversations on the Holocaust. These two claims, to be elaborated following, are oppositional, and critics are divided, either siding with the incompatibility argument or advocating the cause or the defense and justification of Popular Culture. This volume brings together both the views, argued freshly by 17 contributors, to not only make sense of the binary between the Holocaust and Popular Culture but also open up a fresh possibility to "deconstruct" it, without being unethical and irresponsible.

Deconstruction is a critical commonplace today. To deconstruct, in this context, is primarily to suspect, interrogate, decompose, de-hierarchize, de-essentialize, and decenter. Since both sides of the argument are vehemently presented and equally contested, at least in this post-memory world, time is ripe to deconstruct each of them. This does not mean we negate either of the arguments. To deconstruct is not to negate. This does not imply, more significantly, that such deconstructive gesture might end up making this volume just another covert act of trivialization of the Holocaust. By Jacques Derrida's own admission, while the notion that deconstruction is "a-historical and a-political" is popular among the Anglo-American philosophers, an equally common notion, exactly the opposite, is that "deconstruction is a political radicalism, that it is too political" (Ben-Naftali). We argue that the radical possibilities that deconstruction entails is not only antiestablishment but also useful for the cause of oppressed "other." Deconstruction, thus, involves, as Richard Kearney reminded us years back, "the question of ethical responsibility." For him,

DOI: 10.4324/9781003251224-1

2 Mahitosh Mandal and Priyanka Das

"deconstruction's obsession with alterity is compatible with the ethics of 'increased responsibility'" (Kearney quoted in Sarukkai 1407). According to Sundar Sarukkai, who develops on the concept of otherness via Derrida and Kearney:

> Deconstruction, unlike many mistaken accounts of it, partakes a responsibility which in its foundational sense is a search for the other. The continued onslaught on the reduction and representation of the other impels the ethical directedness of deconstruction which above all becomes "an openness towards the other"
>
> (Sarukkai 1407)

The possibilities of reading the responses to the Holocaust in conjunction with deconstruction were initiated by Derrida himself. It is true that Derrida, who experienced antisemitism and expulsion from school due to his Jewish identity, did not have to face the Nazi atrocities because he was born and, during the Holocaust was based, in Algeria. Nevertheless, his interrogation, but not rejection, of a certain absolutist approach to the Holocaust involving an exclusive reading of it in terms of its uniqueness and Jewish specificity can be an important direction to follow. As Derrida observes, "I have no cut-and-dry answer to this question [the question of Holocaust's Jewish specificity], but this is *the question I try to ask myself*" (Ben-Naftali, italics added). To interrogate, more than to answer, seems to be the implication. This volume is placed before the reader in the spirit of questioning the bifurcated responses to the relation between the Holocaust and Popular Culture. This is what explains the word "interrogating" included in the subtitle of the book.

The "versus thesis" is quite simply the idea that Popular Culture and the Holocaust constitute a binary and are incommensurable. It implies that the expression "Holocaust Popular Culture" is a contradiction in terms. The binary implies that the Holocaust is a sacred subject and it must not be trivialized through Popular Culture understood in whatever sense. Nobody would deny the fact that every act of commemorating the Holocaust must involve an ethical responsibility toward the victims. The question is, is Popular Cultural response to the Holocaust necessarily devoid of such responsibility? In what follows, both sides of the argument are fleshed out to make better sense of this question and to develop ways to deconstruct the binary at stake.

This binary, one could mention at the outset, needs to be historicized. The initial responses to the representation of the Holocaust in Popular Culture, in the immediate aftermath of the Holocaust, were marked by vehement condemnation. However, with the proliferation of Popular Cultural representations of the Holocaust, a kind of defense of Popular Culture has also emerged slowly but strongly. The more we move temporally away from the Holocaust, one could argue, the more the defense and justification of Popular Culture seems to have been bolstered. This does not mean the incompatibility argument has been completely overshadowed by the argument about universalization. From a structuralist point of view, one could argue that the fundamental structures of the conflict between the Holocaust and Popular Culture are somewhat ahistorical because they still persist and, one could say, shall persist in the future. Both sides of the argument, therefore, need to be explored at length to properly locate the "versus thesis." This is why this volume takes into consideration various points of intersection between the Holocaust and Popular Culture across a broader time frame from the 1940s to 2021.

The conflicting responses to the representation of the Holocaust have already been defined, albeit using standpoints and terminology different from those used in the current volume, by some Holocaust studies scholars. Two scholars can be mentioned here, although others like Peter Novick are also equally important. Alan Mintz theorizes what he calls the "two models in the study of the Holocaust culture"—the "exceptionalist" model and the "constructivist" model. The exceptionalist model is described as "a conception of the Holocaust as an unprecedented event that transformed our understanding of the world and produced a literature [testimonies, predominantly] that can be understood only internally and by reference to itself." The constructivist model, on the contrary, is understood as "the cultural lens through which the Holocaust is perceived" because "the cultural systems of particular societies are slow to absorb such an event and do so only within the terms of that particular culture" (Mintz xi). While Mintz's theorization is important for us, he does not delve into a) absolute incompatibility, implying a total ban on any representation of the Holocaust and b) the contrast that is specific to the complex and comprehensive relation between the Holocaust and various forms of Popular Culture. He discusses literature by the survivors, which can be difficult to categorize as Popular Culture, and three American films, which are read emphatically from the perspective of defense of cinematic representation. In other words, the "versus thesis," although touched upon through a different terminological framework in Mintz, is far from being comprehensively problematized with specific reference to Popular Culture, not just "culture," and with reference to the global, not just American, context.

A similar theorization is found in a relevant work by Matthew Boswell as he contrasts the so-called "Holocaust piety," a term coined by Gillian Rose in *Mourning Becomes the Law*, with what he describes as "Holocaust impiety." Whereas the former tends to reject all forms of artistic representation considering the Holocaust as "ineffable," the latter justifies the value of some, if not all, forms of artistic and cultural representation of the Holocaust. Boswell names a range of literary, musical, and cinematic works that accomplish an "impious" approach to the Holocaust: the poetry of Sylvia Plath and W. D. Snodgrass, the American and English punk and post-punk rock, and the films like *Nuit et brouillard* (*Night and Fog*), *Shoah*, *The Grey Zone,* and *Inglorious Basterds*. According to Boswell, such works "deliberately engineer a sense of crisis in readers, viewers or listeners by attacking the cognitive and cultural mechanisms that keep our understanding of the Holocaust at a safe distance from our understanding of ourselves." These works comprise "qualities such as representational excess, anti-sentimentalism, avant-garde experimentalism or overt historical irreverence" (Boswell 3). According to Boswell, "such impieties are rarely directed at the dead; they are more usually meant as an affront to the living, attacking those who see no connection between historical atrocity and their own values, political systems and day-to-day lives" (Boswell 4).

4   Mahitosh Mandal and Priyanka Das

Boswell's focus on specific, experimental, and anti-sentimental forms of representation of the Holocaust is different from the focus of the current volume that deals with Popular Culture in general and, in some respect, launches a defense of Popular Culture. With reference to Rose's formulation of Holocaust piety, one might reject all of Popular Culture as blasphemous misrepresentation of the Shoah. This volume aims to deconstruct such a view.

Explicating Incompatibility, Interrogating Universalization

Artistic representation of the Holocaust in general and Popular Cultural representations of the Holocaust in particular have been criticized and even condemned by many. In order to make sense of the incompatibility between the Holocaust and Popular Culture, some of these criticisms are mentioned next.

First, Theodor Adorno famously claimed that "writing poetry after Auschwitz is barbaric" (*Prisms* 33). He later clarified that writing poetry was barbaric but not impossible and that "perennial suffering has as much right to expression as a tortured man has to scream" (*Negative Dialectics* 362). Arguably, Adorno implied that one needed to reconsider aesthetics when it came to the representation of the Holocaust. Conventional frameworks of representation would completely fail to capture the Holocaust trauma. Adorno's statement had a tremendous impact not only on Holocaust scholars but also on a survivor and poet like Paul Celan, who shifted his entire poetics from the lyrical and the comprehensible (for example, in a poem like "The Fugue of Death") to the cryptic and the obscure (for example, the later poetry of Celan including a poem like "Speak You Too"). As John Felstiner has indicated, the later poetry of Celan is marked by an implicit acknowledgment of the limits of language in capturing the Holocaust trauma, alongside fragmentation and incoherence faced while articulating the same (Felstiner 139, 188–89).

Second, some Holocaust survivors feel that the experience of the Holocaust is "untransmutable" because it happened in a place and time that seem to be outside our usual sense of the chronotope. The Holocaust survivor Yehiel Dinur, for instance, while presenting himself as a witness at the Eichmann trial in 1961, described his experiences as having occurred in a different planet, "the Auschwitz planet," which operated following its unique laws quite distinct from those of ours (Crim 1). Dinur's parabolic approach to define Auschwitz within a courtroom triggered the judges to urge him to be precise in his response to their specific queries. But perhaps that was the only way Dinur could express his thoughts. Dinur's loss of consciousness at this point sent a shock wave, turning it into a crucial moment in an otherwise, to use Arendt's word, "banal" trial. The alien way of living that Dinur stresses finds echoes in Elie Wiesel's words: "Auschwitz and Treblinka seem to belong to another time; perhaps they are on the other side of time. They can be explained only in their own terms" (Wiesel quoted in Crim 2). Wiesel even described the Holocaust as ahistorical because "the Holocaust transcends history" (Wiesel quoted in Rothberg, *Multidirectional Memory* 8).

Third, according to some survivors and scholars, the testimony of the survivors is the only authentic way to learn about the Holocaust, and Popular Cultural (re) presentation of the Holocaust is blasphemous and transgressive. Wiesel, a staunch advocate of this position, was outraged at the American television series *Holocaust* (1978) for its vulgarization of the Holocaust memory and trivialization of the sufferings of the victims (Mintz 24–25). He also claimed that "any survivor has more to say than all the historians combined about what happened" in the Holocaust (Cargas 5). The literary and cultural representations of the Holocaust are, for him, a blasphemy. This is what he says, in *Dimensions of the Holocaust: Lectures at Northwestern University*, on this issue:

> "The Holocaust as Literary Inspiration" is a contradiction in terms. As in everything else, Auschwitz negates all systems, destroys all doctrines. . . . Ask any survivor and he will tell you, and his children will tell you. He or she who did not live through the event will never know it. And he or she who did live through the event will never reveal it. Not entirely. Not really. Between our memory and its reflection there stands a wall that cannot be pierced. The past belongs to the dead and the survivor does not recognize himself in the words linking him to them. We speak in code, we survivors, and this code cannot be broken, cannot be deciphered, not by you no matter how much you try. A novel about Treblinka is either not a novel or not about Treblinka. A novel about Majdanek is about blasphemy. Is blasphemy.
>
> (Wiesel et al. 7)

Similar to Wiesel, Art Spiegelman criticized Popular Culture as suffering from "the problem of (re)creation for the sake of the audience's recreation" (Spiegelman quoted in Mintz 146). He condemned Popular Cultural representations of the Holocaust, marked by sensationalism, by describing them as "Holokitsch" (Chute 260–261). In a similar vein, Claude Lanzmann, the director of the documentary *Shoah*, argued against certain artistic transgressions very much applicable in the context of Popular Culture. He asserted:

> The Holocaust is unique because it created a circle of flame around itself, a boundary not to be crossed, since horror in the absolute degree cannot be communicated. To pretend that one has done so is to commit the gravest of transgressions.
>
> (30)

Fourth, Popular Culture shifts the attention from the testimony of the survivors to fictionalization of the Holocaust, thus misrepresenting the Holocaust and doing injustice to the Holocaust memory. This line of argument is articulated fully by Sophia Marshman, who argues that the increase in Popular Cultural engagement with the Holocaust has happened at the cost of sidelining the testimonies of the survivors and commodification of the Holocaust, causing a great damage to the Holocaust memory. She contends that the Holocaust and Popular Culture are incompatible at all levels and that the latter always misrepresents and misuses the former. For her, Popular Culture "sanitizes" the Holocaust because ultimately "popular media tampers with history to make it more acceptable to the audience" (14). She further argues:

> Without testimony we can never know the Holocaust. Testimony urges medi-tation and contemplation rather than encouraging us to consume an image of the Holocaust in the manner of *Schindler's List*. Through testimony, we come to understand the inaccuracies of most Holocaust films and novels. The distortions of the culture industry have been such that, with testimony increasingly marginalized, many people do not realise that the "Holocausts" on offer are mere reproductions substituted for the real thing.
>
> (17)

Therefore, the only way to approach the Holocaust, according to her, is to revive the survivors' testimony. A similar argument is developed in Tim Cole's tellingly titled book *Selling the Holocaust: From Auschwitz to Schindler: How History is Bought, Packaged, and Sold*. For Cole, "Tourists in Krakow, Poland, do not visit the ghetto area because that is where the Holocaust ghetto was located. Rather, they visit the ghetto area because that is where Spielberg filmed his movie" (Cole quoted in Kaźmierczak 101). According to Cole, Popular Cultural representations of the Holocaust "skirt the horrors of the Holocaust and offer us something much more palatable in its place," and it uses "cunning, goodness and ingenuity" to "defeat the Holocaust and bring about salvation" (Cole quoted in Kaźmierczak 107). Cole demonstrates this point with reference to some of the most popular Holocaust films:

> *Schindler's List* shows us the exceptional story of 1,100 Polish Jews who were saved, rather than killed, during the Holocaust. *Life Is Beautiful* shows us the exceptional story of a boy who survived a concentration camp, rather than being killed. *Jakob the Liar* shows us the exceptional story of a ghetto that was liberated, rather than liquidated. *Train of Life* shows us the exceptional story of a "deportation" train that took Jews to freedom, rather than to a death camp.
>
> (Cole qtd. in Kaźmierczak 107)

For Kaźmierczak, through the "mechanisms" of "standardization, repetition, unification, mediatization and substitution through analogy," Popular Culture "creates the conviction that the Holocaust happened in the far, far, 'far-gotten' past and is real only in the fictional worlds" (107). This, combined with the "mythologiza-tion" of the Holocaust, has been reductive of the Holocaust memory and has led to unthinking, mechanical "performing" of the Holocaust memory. In Kaźmierczak's translation of a poem titled "Origami" by Julian Kornhauser, one finds how Holo-caust tourism is marked by the tourist's boredom and superficial interest:

> On the train from Cracow to Auschwitz
> The three young Japanese

are folding origami
killing the time.
We go past hills and forests,
and a paper
swan sleepily glances at the blazing
grass.

(Kaźmierczak 104)

In Popular Culture, it is not enough to represent the Holocaust; one must make a product that can be sold profitably. This is why not all episodes of the Holocaust qualify as worth representing in Popular Culture. Only few that are "spectacular," "worth watching," and have "commodity" value do. As Cole remarks, Popular Culture, thus, generates "a sugarcoated Holocaust" to be "swallowed" by its consumers (Cole qtd. in Kaźmierczak 109). Therefore, Kaźmierczak writes, "The reception of the Holocaust [in Popular Culture] is synonymous with the reception of the controlled ignorance" (109). In this sense, the YOLOCAUST project, which involved the German-Israeli artist Shahak Shapira juxtaposing tourist selfies in Berlin's Holocaust memorial with actual images from the concentration camps and posting such "hard-hitting images" on social media sites, exposed "at best, unthinking, at worst disrespectful attitude of tourists who take selfies for self-publicizing reasons without thinking about where exactly they are taking them and what that site represents" (Berberich 8). As Kaźmierczak puts it succinctly:

Popular culture is a system of possible and autopoietic substitutions: nostalgia instead of knowledge, visiting instead of exploring, watching instead of thinking, beauty instead of death, Eros instead of death, mythologization instead of interest and silence, analogy instead of discourse, sentiments instead of discussion, demagogy instead of dialogue, present instead of past and future.

(110)

Fifth, Popular Culture tends to universalize the Holocaust and, thereby, destroys its Jewish uniqueness—Holocaust being considered as a unique Jewish event—and, thus, ends up committing the "de-Judaization" of the Holocaust, which many survivors, including Wiesel, object to. As Manfred Gerstenfeld remarks, de-Judaization in this context is "not to be confused with the laudable effort to draw conclusions for all humanity from the genocidal catastrophe caused to the Jewish people." Instead, de-Judaization of the Holocaust involves the attempt "to rob the Jews of their painful memories or to weaken their perceived hold on the memory of this genocide" (Gerstenfeld quoted in Gray 74). To de-Judaize is to consider the Jews as "accidental victims" or to refuse to accept the fact that "the collective treatment of the Jews was uniquely different [compared] to other victims of Nazi persecution" (Gray 74). When works of Popular Culture, in an attempt "to market a product to a wider audience," "revolve around non-Jewish protagonists or marginalise the Jewishness of the characters" (Gray 75), they may be accused of de-Judaization of the Holocaust. *Schindler's List*, with a leading German protagonist, and *Sophie's Choice,* where the victim is a Polish Catholic, are examples of de-Judaization, according to Gray. The case of Anne Frank stands out in this context. As Gray adds:

> Within the representations of Anne Frank, her Jewish culture and religion has normally been overlooked. It is particularly the use of Anne Frank as a symbol of generalised rather than Jewish suffering which has characterised both the universalisation and the consequent de-Judaisation of the Holocaust.
>
> (Gray 75)

Here, one could emphasize that blatant misrepresentation of the Jews and the Holocaust memory and the continuation of antisemitism keeps happening in the field of Popular Culture, even in the context of America, and this might put into question some of the views of Alan Mintz, elaborated in the next section, who claims that Popular Culture has been instrumental in sensitizing the Americans about the Holocaust. Among many instances, two American sitcoms may be mentioned in this context, indicating the latest forms of Holocaust representations in television series, an important development in contemporary Popular Culture: CBS's *The Big Bang Theory* and Netflix's *Never Have I Ever*. Both the sitcoms have fictional Jewish characters as main leads, played by actors of Jewish origin, and can thus be viewed as empowering but they contain problematic Jewish portrayals too. Howard Wolowitz of *The Big Bang Theory* is a lustful degenerate who by default objectifies every woman he encounters. Howard's innate sexual perversion is projected such as to resonate with the Nazi antisemitic propaganda including the perception of "Jewish (and black) men as sexual predators, insatiable in their lust for white women" (Bergen 11). Antisemitic humor transgresses friendly banters and gets cemented in Sheldon's devout-Christian mother's frequent jokes on Howard's Jewish identity. Throughout the series, Howard is depicted as the staple fodder of laughter, both to the viewers and to the other characters. Both inwardly and outwardly, Howard is a creepy deviant, an embarrassing "other," who is morally questionable and, hence, is distinct from the other politically correct nerds in the sitcom.

Mindy Kaling's *Never Have I Ever* (2020–2021) has been applauded for celebrating diversity because of its focus on diasporic and immigrant culture. Though it goes beyond tokenism toward sexual and racial minorities, certain features of the sitcom have raised controversies, especially from Jewish viewers. Ben Gross, played by Jaren Lewison, is initially depicted as a racist, sexist, and highly insensitive teenager who is mercilessly competitive. Ben's materialist worldview, affluent background, and dysfunctional family fall in line with the unidimensional portrayal of Jewish characters in the media. While Mira Fox highlights how Ben's character is "glaringly clichéd" and is subjected to "pernicious stereotypes," Meena Venkataraman labels the show antisemitic for its Jewish caricatures (Venkataraman). What deserves more critical intervention is the obvious allusion to Nazism and the Holocaust. Mr. Shapiro, the history teacher at Sherman Oaks High, is another Jewish caricature, "clownish" and "detach[ed] from reality," who approaches the subject of fascism and Holocaust with utter lack of seriousness (Forman). The gravity and sensitivity required, both on the part of the instructor and the learner, to address the Holocaust within a classroom space, is entirely absent in the show. The Holocaust is generalized in a collective understanding of the war trauma, and more offensively discarded, when Paxton's Japanese ethnicity is waged against Ben's Jewishness. On another occasion, Devi, a diasporic Hindu teenager, aggressively tells Ben that she wished the Nazis killed him too. This demonstrates how an American school might shield its students against the ugly naked truths of the Holocaust. The humor that this scene is clouded with manifests that though antisemitism in America is constitutionally punishable, it is not discouraged behind closed doors.

Sixth, the understanding of the Holocaust in conjunction with other genocides has been condemned because such "relativization" of the Holocaust fails to consider its uniqueness as a Jewish suffering caused by the Nazis. Deborah Lipstadt, for instance, indicates that relativization is tantamount to Holocaust denial. According to her, comparisons and analogies relativize the Holocaust and this, similar to denying that Holocaust ever happened, leads to blurring of "boundaries between fact and fiction and between persecuted and persecutor" (Lipstadt qtd. in Rothberg 9).

These are some of the crucial instances of advocating the incompatibility between the Holocaust and Popular Culture and condemning the universalization of the Holocaust through Popular Culture. We have not aimed at offering a complete survey of criticism here but only some of the representative ones which can establish the argument at stake. Overall, the representation of the Holocaust in Popular Culture has been variously condemned as a misrepresentation involving trivialization, sensationalization, and de-Judaization of the Holocaust.

Advocating Universalization, Interrogating Incompatibility

There are many scholars who oppose the incompatibility argument and claim that Popular Culture can productively contribute to the representation of the Holocaust and continued Holocaust remembrance. They also support the so-called relativization of the Holocaust in transnational contexts. Some of their arguments can be explained as in the following.

First, Popular Culture, given its appeal to the masses, is instrumental in spreading awareness about the Holocaust. The best example is, perhaps, the Americanization of the Holocaust through a television series like *Holocaust* or a film like *Schindler's List* or the publication of *The Diary of Anne Frank* and its film and stage adaptations. All these, according to Mintz, contributed to a nationwide interest in the genocide, leading to the establishment of the United States Holocaust Memorial Museum. As Mintz argues at length, it is remarkable how a European genocide eventually became a "salient" aspect of American consciousness and how Popular Culture contributed to this process (3–35).

Second, some scholars argue that the continuous mystification of the Holocaust as the unspeakable and incomprehensible may prevent any fruitful investigation of and engagement with the Holocaust. Giorgio Agamben, who does not deny the uniqueness of the Holocaust asks, "But why unsayable? Why confer

10   *Mahitosh Mandal and Priyanka Das*

on extermination the prestige of the mystical?" (Agamben 32). Agamben rather advocates confronting the "unsayable" even if it means confronting the evil in ourselves. In a similar vein, Peter Hayes, in a book titled *Why?: Explaining the Holocaust*, argues that the Holocaust, like any other historical event, can and must be "explained." He defines the Holocaust, explains the Nazi justifications for it, and answers why the Jews could not launch an effective attack. Thus, drawing on Hayes, it can be stated that the Holocaust was the combined product of an age-old idea—that the Jew is the benighted, backward, and bacterial "other" who is, therefore, to be hated, penalized, converted, segregated, degraded, dehumanized, and murdered—and of a particular political event—the advent of Nazi Germany, which had the power, mechanism, and apparent ideological justifications to annihilate the Jewish community as a whole. In this vein, it is possible to argue the Popular Culture contributes to a fruitful demystification of the Holocaust by attempting to represent it on the screen or on the page, thereby generating self-critical, politically informed, and ethically responsible discussions on the subject in contemporary times.

Third, the concept of the survivor and testimony needs to be reconsidered, some scholars feel. For example, Agamben refers to the heterogeneity of the survivors and their testimonies. He groups the survivors under three categories: a) those who prefer complete silence and have decided to "never speak of Auschwitz," b) those who ensure the survival of witness, and c) those, like Primo Levi, who "speak of it incessantly," feeling an "unrestrainable need" to tell their stories (Agamben 15). The very dependence on testimony is questioned by Agamben through his reading of Levi. He refers to an integral lacuna at the core of the testimonies: "The survivors bore witness to something it is impossible to bear witness to." Levi, who bears survivors' guilt, calls the survivors a privileged category and distinguishes them from the "Muslims [who] did not speak" (Levi qtd. in Agamben 33). As Levi notes:

> I must repeat, we the survivors are not the true witnesses. . . . We survivors are not only an exiguous but also an anomalous minority: we are those who by their prevarications or abilities or good luck did not touch bottom . . . the Muslims, the submerged, the complete witness, the ones whose deposition would have a general significance. They are the rule, we are the exception.
>
> (Levi qtd. in Agamben 33)

The term "Muslim" or the "Muselmann" could be annotated here. According to the Yad Vashem website, it is a

> German term widely used among concentration camp inmates to refer to prisoners who were near death due to exhaustion, starvation, or hopelessness. . . . Some scholars believe that the term originated from the similarity between the near-death prone state of a concentration camp *Muselmann* and the image of a Muslim prostrating himself on the ground in prayer.
>
> ("Muselmann")

Admittedly, the equating of Muslims and the starving Jews can be problematic and offensive to the Muslim community. At the same time, this also indicates the usual human habit of comparison, describing one human group in terms of another. Be that as it may, the Muslim of the concentration camp could be easily recognized in terms of their "physical and psychological decline" and the fact that they "could not stand up for more than a short period of time" ("Muselmann"). Other prisoners feared they might contract the condition from the Muslims and thus maintained distance. The Nazis, on the other hand, considered them "undesirable" because they were not fit for work or able to endure the camp rules and because they "had no chance for survival" and "would not live for more than a few days or weeks." The Muslims, therefore, were "the first to be sentenced to death" ("Muselmann"). The survivor may not offer us the most horrible testimonies, as both Levi and Agamben seem to imply. Nor could the dead testify. And the Muslims who lived between the dead and the living were the true witness but they were not in a condition to testify. As Levi notes, "Weeks and months before being snuffed out, they [the Muslims] had already lost the ability to observe, to remember, to compare and express themselves. We speak in their stead, by proxy" (Levi quoted in Agamben 34). Thus, the survivor testimonies may, in some cases, run the risk of being incomplete and lacking. Therefore, Agamben makes the pertinent observation: "The value of testimony lies in essentially what it lacks; at its center it contains something that cannot be borne witness to and that discharges the survivors of authority" (Agamben 34). Similar arguments have been made by Jean-François Lyotard, Shoshana Felman, and Dori Laub. Lyotard considers the impossibility of bearing witness. According to him, the very text of the informant's testimony is problematic "either because he or she should have disappeared or else because he or she should remain silent" (Lyotard quoted in Agamben 35). Felman and Laub described the Shoah as an "event without witnesses . . . since no one can bear witness from the inside of death . . . and from the outside—since the 'outsider' is by definition excluded from the event" (Felman and Laub quoted in Agamben 35). Derrida goes on to problematize the testimony further. He points to the dangerous possibility that one could always argue that "there is no living testimony, either because those who experienced this have disappeared in the crematoria, or because—as these are testimonies which appeal to faith, to belief—it may always be considered that the witnesses lie." For him such horrible forms of negationism and revisionism are "inscribed in the very structure of extermination" (Ben-Naftali). Aaron Kerner, on the other hand, observes that "making the Holocaust exclusive property [of the survivors] is not only dubious but also short-sighted if the intention is to preserve a *vital* memory" (Kerner 8).

Fourth, the incompatibility between the Holocaust and its artistic and cultural representations can be refuted at several levels. In a unique rejoinder to positions taken by the likes of Wiesel, Slavoj Žižek claims that "the holocaust [sic] can *only* be represented by the arts" ("On Holocaust and Art," italics in the original). This is because "when truth is too traumatic to be confronted directly, it can only be accepted in the guise of a fiction." Žižek states that "a direct documentary about the holocaust [sic] would be obscene, even disrespectful towards the victims" (Žižek,

12 Mahitosh Mandal and Priyanka Das

"On Holocaust and Art"). He also counters Adorno by saying that "it is not poetry that is impossible after Auschwitz, but rather *prose*. Realistic prose fails, where the poetic evocation of the unbearable atmosphere of a camp succeeds" (Žižek, "On Holocaust and Art," italics in the original). Adorno's "impossibility," for Žižek, is "an enabling impossibility" because "poetry is always, by definition, about something that cannot be addressed directly, only alluded to" (Žižek, "On Holocaust and Art"). Categorizing films such *Life Is Beautiful, Jakob the Liar*, and *The Train of Life* as "Holocaust comedies," Žižek further argues that comedy is an effective way-out from the impasse of representation because it "accepts in advance its failure to render the horror of the holocaust [sic]" (Žižek, "Laugh Yourself to Death"). After all, "we cannot directly talk about a trauma, describe it, but this traumatic excess can be 'shown' in the distortion of our speech about the trauma, in its elliptic repetitions and other distortions" (Žižek, "On Holocaust and Art"). From a slightly different point of view, it can also be argued that the mimetic critique of Popular Culture as something that sidelines the survivor's testimony is somewhat misplaced if one considers the fact that the objective of Popular Culture might not necessarily be an authentic representation of history but a reflection on the contemporaneity of history (i.e., the possibilities of genocide looming large around us and our own implicit participation in the same). In other words, the audience's introspection rather than reproduction of a historical truth might be the primary goal of the Popular Culture representations of the Holocaust. The objective of Popular Culture is humble insofar as it evokes the interest of the audience in the Holocaust and inspires them to study more about the same even if it involves deconstructing Popular Culture itself. As a matter of fact, art works and artifacts of Popular Culture are used as pedagogic tools across the world, and it is through these tools, albeit flawed, that the discussion and research of the Holocaust is initiated. One could agree with Kerner, who remarks that a (re)presentation of the Holocaust, whether a documentary or feature film, "is always already an imperfect narrative construct" (5), and with Hilene Flanzbaum, who observes, "Let's all agree right now that no artistic representation of the Holocaust will ever sufficiently depict the horrors of that event—and move on to more explicit and meaningful discussion" (Flanzbaum qtd. in Kerner 5).

Fifth, the uniqueness of the Holocaust has been criticized by many and the demystification of the Holocaust through Popular Culture has been deemed necessary. Such an approach has not only been undertaken by literary scholars but also by historians such as Dirk Moses or Donald Bloxham. The idea that the Holocaust is a unique Jewish event, it can be argued, is problematic because many other minority groups were also victimized during the Holocaust. By (re)presenting the Holocaust and, thereby, triggering debates and discussions and analysis surrounding the Holocaust, one opens up the possibility of historicizing and intellectualizing the Holocaust albeit moving away, some claim justifiably, from abstraction of the Holocaust as a unique, singular, particularistic, and ahistorical Jewish event. Derrida, for instance, interrogates the claim that every other genocide has to be interpreted by reference to the Shoah. What does it mean, he asks, to "think . . . any genocide . . . any crime against humanity, as crime against the Law, against the

Holocaust Versus Popular Culture   13

Torah, against the commandment 'Thou shalt not kill'"? Such stance, according to him, implies that "the Jewish people are chosen [in biblical sense]" even in "its infinite disaster" and that it is supposed to grant them "absolute privilege" even in regard to genocides whether these happened in South Africa or in Cambodia or at any other place in the world. Derrida, therefore, expresses his deep apprehension that the Shoah might eventually, "in two or three generations," be relativized by being "classed" and categorized and "find its place as one episode, among so many others, of the murderous violence within humanity" (Ben-Naftali). Michael Rothberg, however, does not have any such apprehension. Rothberg theorizes memory as "multidirectional" and opposes the adherence to the uniqueness of Holocaust. Instead, he observes:

> The emergence of Holocaust memory on a global scale has contributed to the articulation of other histories—some of them predating the Nazi genocide, such as slavery, and others taking place later, such as the Algerian War of Independence (1954–62) or the genocide in Bosnia during the 1990s.
>
> (6)

While it is true that "in the first postwar decades there was a necessity to assertions of the Holocaust's specificity," continuing to do so even now "is intellectually and politically dangerous" (8–9). "The dangers of the uniqueness discourse," Rothberg points out, echoing others, "are that it potentially creates a hierarchy of suffering (which is morally offensive) and removes that suffering from the field of historical agency (which is both morally and intellectually suspect)" (9). For Rothberg, "the ever-increasing interest in the Nazi genocide distracts from the consideration of other historical tragedies" (9). As David Stannard argues, "the uniqueness argument 'willingly provides a screen behind which opportunistic governments today attempt to conceal their own past and ongoing genocidal actions"' (Stannard quoted in Rothberg 9). Holocaust, thus, functions, according to Rothberg, as "screen memory" in an extended and slightly modified Freudian sense whereby highlighting it by the state bodies helps in suppressing and remaining silent about other localized genocides and atrocities. Instead of treating the Holocaust as unique, Rothberg suggests looking at memories as cross-referencing, interacting, and spiraling. Such a multidirectional approach to memory shows "how memory is . . . as often a spur to unexpected acts of empathy and solidarity" and can become "the very ground on which people construct and act upon visions of justice" (19). This is particularly true in a transnational age where the Holocaust memory is glocalized, that is, it is both global as well as local. As Sierp and Wüstenberg argue, "Memories are (trans) formed, displayed, shared, and negotiated through transnational channels, while maintaining their local rootedness" (324). One, therefore, needs to study the "tension between local and the supranational" (Sierp and Wüstenberg 324) not only at the level of the European continent, one can argue, but, in fact, globally.

Sixth, a mechanical adherence to the Holocaust metanarrative, based only on testimonies, can lead to a mere ritualized commemoration of the Holocaust. Popular Cultural representations, on the other hand, can prevent us from a collective

14   Mahitosh Mandal and Priyanka Das

amnesia about the Holocaust. As John Gross argues, "Holocaust denial may or may not be a major problem in the future, but Holocaust ignorance, Holocaust forgetfulness, and Holocaust indifference are bound to be" (Gross quoted in Mintz 131). For Gross, a film like *Schindler's List* can "dispel" such ignorance and ensure that the Holocaust never fades into amnesia. As Alan Rosenbaum argues, "There is certainly an abiding wisdom in the recognition that the Holocaust has seared into the collective historical consciousness of humanity a new, indefeasible standard of evil" (7). Rosenbaum reminds us of the observation of George Santayana, "Those who cannot remember the past are condemned to repeat it" (Santayana 172). The genocidists must recollect the "barbaric Nazi methods" accordingly, and "we must be ever vigilant about the warning signs of a possible turn towards genocide" (Rosenbaum 21). A similar warning is given in the documentary *Nuit et brouillard* (*Night and Fog*), which ends on this ominous note from the narrator (as per the English subtitles):

> Somewhere among us there are still Kapos, reinstated officers and anonymous informers. There are those who refused to believe, or only now and then. We survey these ruins with a heartfelt gaze certain that the old monster lies crushed beneath the rubble. We pretend to regain hope, as the image recedes, as though we have cured of that plague. We tell ourselves it was all confined to one country to one point in time. We turn a blind eye to what surrounds us and a deaf ear to the never-ending cries.
>
> (*Nuit et brouillard*)

Similarly, Berberich argues against the ritualized Holocaust commemoration as she quotes the following lines spoken by the protagonist of Rachel Seiffert's novel *The Dark Room* (2002) (albeit some may claim reliance on a novel to make such an argument is not unproblematic): "Every year it's the fucking same. The students read survivors' accounts. Everyone cries these 'we didn't do it' tears. Then the essays get marked, the displays are packed away, and we move right on with the next project" (Seiffert qtd. in Berberich 6). Annual Holocaust commemoration, thus, is ritualized, as if "a box has been ticked—and the next item on the curriculum has to be covered" and thereby loses its meaning. Such commemoration "ultimately lacks the critical and continuous engagement that is necessary to meaningfully engage with the past" (Berberich 6). Genres like Holocaust fiction, Holocaust perpetrator fiction, and Holocaust comedies, Berberich argues, challenge "the sanctioned narrative" or the metanarrative of the Holocaust. But these must not be dismissed as "acts of commemorative sabotage" because these:

> Works do not question the Holocaust, nor do they doubt the importance of remembering. What they do challenge is an over-simplified, ritualized, unreflective act of remembering merely for the sake of remembering. What these works of literature seek to do is to find new and meaningful ways of engagement with the past that make their readers think and reflect.
>
> (Berberich 6)

In a similar vein, Demsky argues that: "As memory of the Nazis' crimes against European Jewry becomes increasingly removed from contemporary life, embracing the growing array of complicating and attention-grabbing intersections may help ensure that this past is remembered at all" (1). For him, Popular Culture can "rejuvenate" (2) the Holocaust memory, "invigorating the memorialization as much as they vulgarize it" (4). He demonstrates this through diverse kinds of "bastardized representations" (3) including American sitcoms and social media memes (particularly the meme of the Pepe Frog). By extension, the debates on social media, for instance, about the tourist selfies at the Holocaust memorials or about Holocaust-themed ice-dance by Tatyana Navka paradoxically keep the discussions about the Holocaust going.

The list of scholars who support the incompatibility argument as well as those who advocate the universalization argument is much longer. Holocaust scholarship is unimaginably vast, and, in a short introduction like this, we cannot include every scholar or every survivor testimony or every aspect of the arguments. However, as the above points indicate, both the arguments are strong in themselves while at the same time both can be subjected to interrogation. It is also clear that Popular Cultural representations of the Holocaust, although problematic at many levels, can contribute to the revitalization of the Holocaust memory. However, rather than taking any side, this volume is more interested in interrogating both the standpoints and exploring the possibilities of de-hierarchizing the binaries at stake without being ethically irresponsible. The contributions in this volume are an effort at helping the reader to develop a critical understanding of the interface between the Holocaust and Popular Culture and carry forward the Holocaust memory in a more meaningful manner.

Location of the Volume

This volume is written by contributors from across the globe, and the target audience is also global. However, the idea of this volume emerged from within an Indian context. Even though there is an increasing proliferation of Holocaust literature and Holocaust Popular Culture, the literature and cultural studies departments in Indian and South Asian universities do not substantially engage with this vast body of literature and Popular Culture. To address this lacuna, we launched a master's level course on Holocaust and literature at the Department of English, Presidency University, Kolkata, perhaps a first of its kind in the literature departments in India. Navras J. Aafreedi began a course on Holocaust history approximately at the same time at the Department of History of the same University to address a similar gap in history departments of South Asian universities. The attempt was to carve out a greater space within Indian and South Asian academia for Holocaust studies.

Over the last few years, we have also been witnessing how the Holocaust and Nazism are being evoked in the Indian context. In recent times, in India, the right wing Hindutva-based political party, which is infamous for its antiminority policies and whose leader, Narendra Modi, has occasionally been compared to Adolf Hitler by opposition parties, has initiated a citizenship act whereby those who do

16   Mahitosh Mandal and Priyanka Das

not qualify as Indian citizens (basically people who are Muslims) would be segregated and put into detention camps. The protesters in India have frequently compared these camps with the Holocaust concentration camps and have described the Muslims as the "new Jews" and the whole situation as having the potential of leading to a "Muslim holocaust." Irfan Raja draws attention to how Modi shares common characteristics with Hitler and has "Hitler's mindset." The leaders of the Modi-led Bhartatiya Janata Party keep suggesting that they are Aryans; therefore, they are superior to the Muslims of India. Raja states, "A tragic and horrible past is turning into a reality in India. Seriously, we are at the threshold of a probable Indian Muslim's Holocaust" ("Is India sleepwalking toward a Muslim holocaust?"). Mahua Moitra, a member of the Indian Parliament, in her maiden speech in office, slammed the right-wing party by explaining how its treatment of the citizens manifested "all signs of early fascism." While doing so, she mentioned a poster on "early warning signs of fascism" put up in the lobby of the United States Holocaust Memorial Museum in 2017 (Geeta Pandey). Whereas there are several examples of transnational representation and remembrance of the Holocaust, this specific Indian example goes on to show how, in the twenty-first century, a country far away from Europe, with no substantial connection with the genocide, takes recourse to Nazi history and Holocaust memory to make sense of contemporary nationalist politics. However, even though the Holocaust and Nazism have become terms of reference in contemporary political analysis and discourse in India, most of these discourses, we noticed, use the term Holocaust in an uninformed way and run the risk of trivializing it. Thus, the initial objective of the volume was to produce debates about the inevitable evocation of Nazi rhetoric in non-European contexts and the need to be aware of the question of trivialization.

As we delved deeper, we found that while trivialization of the Holocaust could happen in the transnational and non-Western context, a comparative study of the Holocaust and genocides in the Indian context was also possible, at least at the level of debates. At least two instances of atrocities emerged from Indian history and contemporary reality (apart from the present-day ghettoization of the Muslims, not just in Kashmir but across the country) as capable of being debated in conjunction with Nazism and the Holocaust. The first instance would be the 1947 Partition of India, and the second instance would be the centuries-old, and currently on the rise, caste-based atrocities against the Dalits (a political term adopted by the outcastes of India, earlier known as Untouchables and constitutionally designated as Scheduled Castes).

At multiple levels, there exists an incongruity between Partition historiography and Holocaust historiography. Partition of India and Pakistan involved the phenomenal physical and psychological devastation and the helplessness of individuals, irrespective of whether they were Hindus (meant to stay in India) or Muslims (asked to move to Pakistan). At least one million people died and fifteen million were displaced due to the Partition (Brocklehurst; Shashkevich). However, Partition as a political decision was not necessarily condemned at all levels. As Gyanendra Pandey argues, Partition historiography, by "justifying, or eliding" the violence, has rather moved away from recognizing it as a collective history (4). He insists that violence, if not anything else, is a shared experience between the Pakistanis and Indians. But in the case of the Holocaust, the violence was not two-directional. The violence that originated from one group deciding the fate of an entire community along with a few others, is anything but shared. Therefore, it can be argued that while Partition violence was horizontal, Holocaust violence was vertical. Nevertheless, there are comparative possibilities of reading the Partition in conjunction with the Holocaust. For instance, Gyanendra Pandey's analysis of liberal states detesting plural societies in a post-Smithian, economically competitive world may be extended to study the preconditions of both the Holocaust and the Indian Partition. However, a more interesting work, in this context, is Madhav Godbole's *The Holocaust of Indian Partition*. Evoking the fact that Auschwitz-Birkenau Liberation Day is regarded as Holocaust Remembrance Day, Godbole suggested that India as a nation was in dire need of one such special day. He welcomes Prime Minister Narendra Modi's declaration of August 14 as Partition Horrors Remembrance Day. However, one cannot miss the tint of right-wing sadism here in deciding the date and in the terminology. August 14 is celebrated as Pakistan's Independence Day, and although the actual Partition and the accompanying horrors spread across months, there is perhaps no better way of vilifying the rival state than ascribing the word "horror" with this date. Godbole's text, which attempts to equate the 1947 Indian Partition and the Holocaust, paradoxically, glorifies the very political ideology of fascism involving a celebration of Hindutva at the expense of Muslims.

Atrocities against Dalits in India, caused by the same rightist, Brahminical, and casteist ideologues for centuries, constitute another possible point of transnational engagement with the Holocaust memory. In today's India, every 10 minutes a crime is committed against a Dalit and every day 8 Dalit women are subjected to sexual abuse (Jyoti; GoNews Desk). Massacres of Dalit families and lynching and murder of Dalits are daily phenomena. Anand Teltumbde, while analyzing the naked parading, mutilation, and murder of four Dalits in the village of Khairlanji in the Indian state of Maharashtra, offers a glimpse of the amount of atrocities suffered by the Dalits:

Keezhvenmani (in Tamil Nadu state; forty-four dalits burnt alive in 1968), Belchi (in the state of Bihar; fourteen dalits burnt alive in 1977), Morichjhanpi (an island in the Sundarban mangrove forest of West Bengal where hundreds of dalit refugees from Bangladesh were massacred during a government eviction drive in 1978), Karamchedu (Andhra Pradesh; six dalits murdered, three dalit women raped and many more wounded in 1984), Chunduru (also Andhra Pradesh; nine dalits slaughtered and their bodies dumped in a canal in 1991), Melavalavu (Tamil Nadu; an elected dalit panchayat leader and five dalits murdered in 1997), Kambalapalli (in the state of Karnataka; six dalits burnt alive in 2000) and Jhajjar (in Haryana state, adjoining the capital, New Delhi, where five dalits were lynched outside a police station in 2002). The incidents listed here will never figure in any history of contemporary India. Most Indians may never even have heard of these places.

(40)

18 *Mahitosh Mandal and Priyanka Das*

Atrocities against the Dalits have been and can be analyzed in conjunction with various other forms of atrocity and genocide. For instance, Teltumbde, in *Persistence of Caste,* describes caste atrocities as "India's hidden apartheid," and Mandal compares the specific Dalit massacre at Marichjhapi (alternative spelling of Morichjhanpi) coordinated by a communist government in West Bengal in conjunction with the violence and genocide that occurred at the Soviet Gulag camps (Mandal, "Liars"). But other possible comparative studies can also be attempted for understanding the genocide from various perspectives. If the term Holocaust etymologically means "burning of everything," then is it possible to describe casteist hatred leading to burning and shooting and massacres of Dalits as some kind of caste-based holocaust (with a lowercase "h") or Dalit holocaust or even, to use a neologism, a kind of "holocaste"? If one can think of Black holocaust or Muslim holocaust, would it be possible, in a similar vein, to theorize "holocaste"? (Mandal, "Holocaste?"). It was the Indian thinker and Dalit icon Bhimrao Ramji Ambedkar (1891–1956) who opened up the possibility of studying Nazism, by extension the Holocaust, in conjunction with casteism or Brahmanism. It may be noted that Ambedkar was perhaps the only strong voice against Nazism from India during Hitler's lifetime. Pointing out how Hitler opposed the British government for giving Indians political and educational liberty, Ambedkar stated, "The Nazi ideology is a direct menace to the liberty and freedom of Indians. Given this fact, there is the strongest reason why Indians should come forward to light Nazism" (Ambedkar, "Why Indian Labour" 38). Drawing on Ambedkar, one can state that Brahmanism is the ideology of Brahminical supremacy, meaning that, among all Hindus, the Brahmans are the superior and that every other Hindu from other castes (Kshatriya or the military class, Vaishya or the mercantile class, and Shudra or the "servile" class) must serve the Brahmins. The Untouchables, or the Dalits, who did not have a place within the fourfold Varna system and who were excluded as outcastes from a more rigid caste system, became the worst victims of Brahmanism. Their sufferings continue, as the previous data shows, with the rise in right-wing Hindutva politics, which is just another form of Brahmanism. In his interesting comparative analysis of Brahmanism and Nazism, which cannot be elaborated here due to constraints on word length, Ambedkar demonstrated how Brahmans were projected as the supermen of India much like Hitler's obsession with the Nazis who were to become, what Friedrich Nietzsche called, *Übermensch.* Ambedkar described Hitler as Nietzsche's philosophy in action and compared the philosophy of Manu, the Hindu lawgiver who codified the *Übermensch* status of the Brahmin in *Manu-Smriti*, with that of Nietzsche (Ambedkar, "Ranade, Gandhi and Jinnah" 205–240; Ambedkar, "Philosophy of Hinduism" 3–92). He compared the ghettoization of the Jews in medieval times as being similar to the ghettoization of the Untouchables and pointed out that: "Like the Hindus [who do not consider the problem of the Untouchables as a Hindu or Brahmanical problem] the Gentiles also do not admit that the Jewish problem is in essence a Gentile problem" (Ambedkar, "Untouchability: Its Source" 3). Although Ambedkar also discussed the differences between the conditions of the Dalit and the Jew, his observations may be developed further to study the atrocities against the Dalits in conjunction with the Holocaust.

The aforementioned political and academic contexts of India prompted us to conceive of a volume that would debate the question of trivialization of the Holocaust and also the productive use and expansion of the Holocaust memory. This volume is the final result of such initial thoughts.

Annotating the Key Terms

This volume uses the term "antisemitism" instead of "anti-Semitism;" prefers the term "Holocaust," not without problematizing it, instead of "Shoah;" and roots for an open-ended and comprehensive understanding of the term "Popular Culture."

We acknowledge that the debates around the term "antisemitism" are ongoing as the differences between International Holocaust Remembrance Alliance (IHRA)'s definition and Jerusalem Declaration on Antisemitism's demonstrate ("The Politics of Defining"). Nevertheless, in the context of our volume, we consider "anti-Semite," with a hyphen, as somewhat of an incorrect term. In philology, "Semite" refers to a group of languages including Hebrew, Arabic, and Aramaic. A Semite person would imply someone speaking any one of these languages and "anti-Semite" (with hyphen) would imply an opposition to anybody speaking any of these languages. But antisemitism is widely understood as a form of hatred directed particularly at the Jews, whose language is predominantly Hebrew. Therefore, "anti-Semite," with hyphen, runs the risk of generalizing this hatred as being something aimed at all the Semites and, thus, dilute the specificity of the Jewish sufferers. Furthermore, as Peter Hayes notes, the hyphenated term "anti-Semitism" implies a prior existence of something called "Semitism." This is incorrect. The original German term is *Antisemitismus*, "all one word" (Hayes, chapter 1). Taking all these into consideration, this volume has done away with the hyphen and has used the following spellings: "antisemite," "antisemitic," and "antisemitism."

"Shoah" is a Hebrew term meaning "catastrophe." It has "its biblical root in the term 'shoah u-meshoah' (wasteness and desolation) that appears in both the Book of Zephaniah (1:15) and the Book of Job (30:3)" ("What Is the Difference"). Insofar as the Nazi atrocities were predominantly aimed at the annihilation of the Jews, thereby implementing the so-called "Final Solution to the Jewish Question," "Shoah" becomes an appropriate term to designate the genocide that involved the murder of six million Jews and a term justifiably preferred by the Jews themselves. The term "Holocaust," on the other hand, "is derived from the Greek for burnt offering and is generally defined as a vast destruction caused by fire or other non-human forces" ("What Is the Difference"). The term "Holocaust," which came to be widely employed following the popularity of the 1978 American TV series *Holocaust*, is used predominantly in the English-speaking world to describe the Nazi atrocities and, thus, loses the antisemitic specificity of Jewish victimhood caused by the Nazis. Therefore, the Holocaust, one could argue, is an inaccurate term. Nevertheless, there are a few reasons why this term is chosen in this volume.

The obvious reason is the common practice. Although the preference of "Holocaust" to "Shoah" may be debated, these two terms are frequently used in the English-speaking world to mean the same thing. Daniel H. Magilow and Lisa

Silverman, for example, define the Holocaust as "the State-sponsored genocide of European Jewry perpetrated by Nazi Germany and its collaborators" (3). The website of Yad Vashem mentions the following: "The Holocaust was unprecedented genocide, total and systematic, perpetrated by Nazi Germany and its collaborators, with the aim of *annihilating the Jewish people*" ("What Was the Holocaust?"; italics added). In some cases, it is considered important to capitalize "H" in Holocaust and use the article "the" before it to highlight the fact that the Holocaust was principally a Jewish genocide. But this is more or less an accepted convention now, for instance, Peter Hayes follow this. We have followed this too.

The preference of the term "Holocaust" over "Shoah" is also critically informed. The Nazi atrocities in question did not cost the lives of six million Jews only although they were undoubtedly the main persecuted community. Nazis killed an additional approximately 5.5 million victims, from among the Roma and Sinti people ("Gypsies"), Jehovah's Witnesses, Poles, Slavs, homosexuals, persons with disabilities, political prisoners including communists and socialists, and others. As one scholar argues, the fate of the Roma and Sinti people "is generally accepted as being nearest to that of the Jews in the Nazi vision of a future 'world without Jews' and Judaism" (Rosenbaum 2). One must talk about "Gypsy genocide" to include the sufferings of the Roma and Sinti people alongside talking about the Jewish sufferers. In fact, when we first published the "call for papers" for this volume on the internet, one of the initial emails we received was from a member of the "Families of Roma and Sinti Holocaust Victims." She wrote to us, "I am curious as to your reasoning for implicitly defining the Holocaust and the final solution as solely being directed against Jews. What is the historiographical basis for excluding the final solution to the 'Gypsy Question'?" (Gelbart) We argue that while the term "Holocaust" should be used to encompass all of the Jewish and non-Jewish victims, the use of the term "Shoah" might be narrower because it would demand that we focus on the Jewish victims only and that the Nazi atrocities were somehow exclusively targeted at the Jewish victims. The term "Holocaust," unlike "Shoah," can be used as a more inclusive word and suitable for a volume that debates the question of uniqueness of the Holocaust. Furthermore, this volume proposes the possibilities of reading the Nazi genocide in conjunction with other genocides. The term "Holocaust," given its inclusivity and fluidity, may enable such comparative and universalistic study. For instance, it can help us debate the "Black holocaust" or the "holocaust of Indian Partition." This would not necessarily reduce, we argue, the uniqueness of the Nazi Holocaust or the specificity of Jewish victimhood.

The term "Popular Culture" is used in this volume in an open-ended sense. Popular Culture is broadly understood in terms of certain media and artifacts: movies, sports, television programs, social media, cyberculture, advertisement, dance, comics and graphic novels, anime, videogames, popular music, popular literature, museums, linguistic conventions, and so on. This volume analyzes such forms of Popular Culture insofar as they represent the Holocaust. Whereas these are instances or products of Popular Culture, the notion of Popular Culture is understood in various ways by scholars in general and the contributors to this volume in particular. Some of the relevant definitions of Popular Culture have been provided by John Storey and have been supplemented by Holt N. Parker.

Storey has offered a comprehensive, albeit not altogether unproblematic, list of definitions of Popular Culture. He notes at the outset the great difficulty in defining Popular Culture because it is "in effect an empty conceptual category, one that can be filled in a wide variety of often conflicting ways, depending on the context of use" (1). Drawing on Raymond Williams, who defines "culture" as "particular way of life, whether of a people, a period or a group" and as "the works and practices of intellectual and especially artistic activity" (Williams quoted in Storey 2), Storey mentions "seaside holiday, the celebration of Christmas and youth subcultures" as examples of Popular Culture as per the first definition and "soap opera, pop music, and comics" as examples of Popular Culture as per the second definition (2). Storey, drawing on Williams, also refers to the various semantic possibilities of the term "popular" including "well-liked by many people," "inferior kinds of work," "work deliberately setting out to win favor with the people," and "culture actually made by the people for themselves" (5). Storey also reaffirms the idea that the advent of Popular Culture is mainly determined by "a capitalist market economy" (13) and is something that happened during the Industrial Revolution. Based on these implications, Storey formulates six definitions of Popular Culture. First, Popular Culture is to be defined in quantitative terms as something "widely favored and well-liked by many people" (6). Second, Popular Culture is an inferior form of culture compared to the so-called high culture. In this sense, Popular Culture becomes a culture of the numerical majority deserving only a "fleeting sociological inspection" as opposed to high culture, which is the culture of the few, is "the result of an individual act of creation," and "deserves only a moral and aesthetic response" (6). Such a binary is considered transhistorical, and for Storey, this is problematic because what is popular at one point (Shakespeare's works as late as the nineteenth century or Luciano Pavarotti's 1990s massively popular rendering of Giacomo Puccini's "Nessum Dorma" beyond the opera world) may become or may have been high culture at an earlier or later point in time (Shakespeare in twentieth century or Puccini in early twentieth century). Third, Popular Culture is defined as "mass culture" or "a hopelessly commercial culture" because it is "mass produced for mass consumption" or produced for consumption by "a mass of non-discriminating consumers . . . with brain numbed and brain-numbing passivity" (8). Fourth, Popular Culture is "culture that originates from 'the people'" as opposed to "something imposed on 'the people' from above." In this sense, Popular Culture would be described as folk culture or "a culture of the people for the people" (9). Fifth, informed by Antonio Gramsci's notion of hegemony, Popular Culture is neither an "imposed culture" nor the culture "from below," but it is "a terrain of exchange and negotiation between the two" or "a site of struggle between the 'resistance' of subordinate groups and the forces of 'incorporation' operating in the interests of dominant groups" (10). Sixth, Popular Culture, informed by postmodernism, is not a binary vis-à-vis high culture because such distinctions are blurred in the postmodern context. One could mention the films of Alfred Hitchcock as theorized by Slavoj Žižek, who indicates that Hitchcock's works are simultaneously high culture (exemplifies poststructural and psychoanalytic theories) as well as Popular Culture (movies having commercial success) ("Alfred Hitchcock" 1–3). The movies of Quentin Tarantino also mix the high and low as they incorporate references to Japanese B-grade films. Holt N. Parker, who finds Storey's definitions unsatisfactory, offers four more "tentative definitions." First, "Popular culture consists of the productions of those without cultural capital, of those without access to the approved means of symbolic and cultural production." Second, "Popular culture consists of products that require little cultural capital either to produce or else to consume." Third, " 'Popular art' is that which is not authorized by the artworld." And fourth, by extension, "Popular culture is unauthorized culture," that is, not approved of by the so-called elite world of high art (Parker 161–165).

These definitions of Popular Culture are mentioned here to situate the volume in the larger context of cultural studies and prepare the reader for exploring the interface between the Holocaust and Popular Culture. As the reader will see, some of these notions are variously used, extended, and debated by the contributors of the volume.

Structure of the Volume

This volume explores the possibilities of theorizing "Holocaust Popular Culture," without this being a contradiction in terms. It debates the "versus thesis" from diverse points of view and across a broad temporal spectrum wherein works of Popular Culture from the 1940s to 2021 are analyzed and/or referred to. The central thrust of deconstructing the "versus thesis" is elaborated through a cross-generic, cross-generational, cross-gender (including women writers of the Holocaust) and transnational engagements with the Holocaust in the field of Popular Culture. No existing book on the Holocaust addresses this subject from the perspective we have adopted and in relation to the range of Popular Cultural artifacts we have selected.

The volume is divided into three parts. Part I, titled "Explicating Incompatibility" and comprising four chapters, explains why Popular Culture and the Holocaust are incommensurable. In Chapter 1, titled "Popular Fiction, Literary Culture, and Artistic Truth: Thane Rosenbaum's *The Golems of Gotham* and Twenty-First Century Holocaust Representation," **Craig Smith** demonstrates how popular fiction and films have tried to create a mass market for the mass murder and have taken utmost care to (re)present the Holocaust in such a way that it becomes a commodity for mass consumption. Rosenbaum's novel includes Holocaust survivors as characters through whom such a critique of Popular Culture is articulated. Although this becomes somewhat paradoxical, because one form of literary representation is used to critique other (popular) forms of literary and cinematic representation, the crux of Rosenbaum's text is that it is rooted in the survivors' testimonies and is absolutely aware of the limits of representation. As Smith notes, "While the novel includes famous Holocaust survivors and writers as characters, it deliberately eschews representing their wartime experiences, rendering ambiguous its status *as* Holocaust literature." The novel, according to him, becomes a critical and metafictional reflection on "the difficulties of remembering and representing the Holocaust" in the late capitalist era of internalized and commodified "phrases and images of atrocity." Rosenbaum's text not only exposes the incompatibility between the Holocaust and Popular Culture, but it also points to the possibilities of correct and corrective way to represent the Holocaust outside the field of Popular Culture.

Chapter 2, written by **Iker Itoiz Ciáurriz**, is titled "Playing With the Unspeakable: The Holocaust and Videogames." Ciáurriz explains the controversial phenomenon of how Popular Culture in the form of videogames is increasingly drawn to Holocaust history and thematics. While a few videogames representing the Holocaust have been censored, Ciáurriz shows and analyzes how in the recent years the ludic engagement with Holocaust has, nonetheless, increased remarkably through indie games. While such videogames can be used for pedagogic purposes, Ciáurriz, nevertheless, reaches the following conclusion: "Whether videogames, as Popular Culture, can represent the Holocaust is not yet clear . . . even with the possibilities videogames open up, it is hard, almost impossible to reconcile the many tensions involving the representation of the Holocaust."

In Chapter 3, "Representation, Appropriation, and Popular Culture: Food and the Holocaust in Roman Polanski's *The Pianist*," **Ved Prakash** delves into the topic of food and starvation, which remain one of the primary, albeit underrepresented, aspects of the Holocaust. His study highlights the issues of food acquisition, food denial, eating behaviors, passing down of recipes, kitchen spaces, food bribery, and food smuggling—all of which had been intricately linked to the Judeocide. Through a critical engagement with Roman Polanski's *The Pianist*, Prakash attempts to answer whether films can do justice to the depiction of the pangs of hunger that the Jews had to face within ghettos and camps or if they end up dramatizing and exoticizing the pain for extracting maximum sympathy from the audience. While Polanski's identity as a victim of Nazism safeguards his artistic endeavor to be discarded entirely, his memory of the genocide as a 6-year-old remains questionable and, as Prakash argues, may have overlapped with the collective memory of the tragedy. Films like *The Pianist*, Prakash believes, though offering a glimpse to the world of the Holocaust, often fail to overcome market forces and, therefore, cannot be treated as authentic sources for analyzing the Holocaust.

Chapter 4 is titled "Nazi Linguistics and Mass Manipulation: An Analysis of Holocaust Primary Sources Vis-à-vis Popular Culture" and is authored by **Sarah Spinella**. In this chapter, Spinella, through her analysis of Victor Klemperer's and Nachman Blumental's works on Nazi manipulation of German language, goes to the root of the problem by showing how in order for the Holocaust to happen a new worldview had to be created, and this was done by redefining the spoken language of the people. By emphasizing the "popular" in Popular Culture, she shows the opposing relation between Nazism and humanity mediated through a deliberate inversion of popular conventions of linguistic communication and how the Nazi genocide, therefore, involved a form of "semanticide." In other words, Popular Culture, understood here as linguistic conventions and consciousness of the masses, was manipulated and used to normalize Nazism. Here, Popular Culture and the Holocaust are incompatible in the specific sense that Popular Culture

24   *Mahitosh Mandal and Priyanka Das*

cannot protect or do justice to the victims of the Holocaust but instead aids its perpetrators. Spinella, thus, tries to understand "the symbiotic relationship between totalitarian languages and Popular Culture" and how the Nazis "managed to narcotize the critical capacity of masses" through certain "linguistic strategies."

Part II, titled "Rethinking Universalization," extends the incompatibility argument and predominantly interrogates, but remains careful not to reject, the practice of transnational remembrance of the Holocaust in non-European context. Although scholars like Mintz have used the term universalization to basically mean Americanization of the Holocaust or Daniel Levy and Natan Sznaider have used terms like "globalization," we try to locate the Holocaust memory in Popular Cultures in Europe and America as well as in non-Western contexts like India and Japan. Some of the contributors interrogate the universalization of the Holocaust memory as politically risky and ethically undesirable whereas others contend that transnational practice of Holocaust remembrance can do justice to the victims and expose the Nazis and neo-Nazis. Part II comprises five chapters, as follows.

In Chapter 5, titled "Hitler's Popularity and the Trivialization of the Holocaust in India," **Navras J. Aafreedi** investigates the strange popularity of Hitler in India and analyzes some of the relevant instances of representation of Hitler in Popular Culture in this context. "Absence of the education of Jewish history and the Holocaust," Aafreedi argues, "compounded by the lack of credible sources of information on Jews in vernaculars has led to widespread ignorance of who the Jews are and how they suffered during the Holocaust." Such ignorance is responsible for the "domestication, normalization, popularization and commercialization of Hitler" in India. Such ignorance is also manipulated by the rightist ideologues of India, who both covertly and overtly follow Nazism and fascism, and makes the masses "susceptible to anti-minority propaganda," leading to the thriving of communalism, xenophobia, and antisemitism. The Holocaust, in Aafreedi's analysis, tends to be completely trivialized as Hitler's crimes and attributes are simplified as commonplace and even things to be proud of, and Nazism is safely reproduced in a transnational context. The Holocaust memory is, thus, maintained in a distorted and perverted way by the masses in such transnational locations. Aafreedi suggests a corrective to this situation as well as he notes, "We need to make efforts to raise historical awareness via education as well as popular culture to combat the rising popularity of Hitler." As mentioned earlier, alongside the popular and mass-scale distortion of the Holocaust, one could also consider the discourse of critical parallelism between the Holocaust and other Indian genocides such as the Partition and caste-based atrocities.

In Chapter 6, titled "Decoding Holocaust Narratives in Japanese Pop Culture: Through the Lens of *Anne no Nikki* (1995) and *Persona Non Grata* (2015)," **José Rodolfo Avilés Ernult** and **Astha Chadha** take us through the Japanese response in contextualizing and commemorating the Final Solution. Their central argument is to show how Japanese rendering of the Holocaust, particularly the two Popular Cultural narratives mentioned in the title, in their attempt to celebrate fallen national heroes and to achieve identification with the Holocaust victims, ultimately fails to depict the actual brutalities of the genocide as effectively as its

Western counterpart. Most Popular Cultural productions, they argue, strive to sanitize Japan's involvement as a member of the Axis Powers in World War II, situate both Japan and Jews as victims of the war, and meet the quintessential expectations of the nation when located within the Japanese war framework, thereby carefully dissociating Japan from "its imperialist past." They find two common tropes in Japanese cinematic representation of the Holocaust, one being the ritual of "sanitization, context omission and distancing the portrayed narratives from the Asia-Pacific war" and the other being "dilution of onscreen violence." Such deliberate attempts of sanitization and alienation result in the production of "heartwarming flicks" that celebrate the Gentile characters, discounting the antisemitic concerns and the wider Jewish experience of the Holocaust.

It may be noted that Asian response to the Holocaust through Popular Culture is more diverse and complex than it may appear. As an example, mention may be made of *Castlevania*, a Japanese action-adventure videogame series that has enjoyed a remarkable popularity since its debut in 1986. The third game in the series *Castlevania III: Dracula's Curse* teleports us to a medieval world that is threatened by Count Dracula and his minions. This game engages with the Holocaust in an intriguing way (Das). To begin with, the very name *Castlevania* is an allusion to the Romanian town of Transylvania which, in the twentieth century, became a site for political contestation and violence that informed the Jewish memory. Holocaust survivor and author Elie Wiesel, in *Night*, recounts the abuses, expulsion, deportation, and ultimate extermination experienced by the Jews of Sighet in Nazi-occupied Transylvania. Second, the figure of Count Dracula, as depicted in *Castlevania*, manifests racist hatred and unmistakably evokes Hitler. Count Dracula, like Hitler, shares the attributes of Nietzschean *Übermensch*. Count Dracula's indomitable desire to annihilate humanity, for personal vengeance and for the sake of upholding the vampiric race, parallels Hitler's antisemitic worldview to purify the Aryan race and make Germany *Judenfrei*, through extermination of the European Jewry. The videogame, thus, reduces the proto-Hitler figure to a monstrous vampire. Third, Count Dracula's War Council, alludes to the Hitler Cabinet comprising his henchmen, or as they are called, the Devil's disciples. The infamous Nazi official Heinrich Himmler is evoked in the figure of Hector or *Hekuta,* who is a promising general and Dracula's favorite. Hector, like Himmler the overseer of the Nazi genocidal programs, earns the title of Devil Forgemaster for mastering the arts of Devil alchemy that enable him to create demons using base materials. *Castlevania* makes utmost use of the lesser-known chapter of Himmler's betrayal of Hitler through secretly negotiating a peace treaty with the Allies after the latter demoted the former, by making Hector abandon and betray Dracula in the *Castlevania* saga. Godbrand or *Godduburando*, the Viking vampire who is obsessed with killing and lust for material wealth, becomes a Japanese counterpart of the politically successful Hermann Goring, who amassed capital by collecting Jewish property and artwork and was declared Hitler's successor. Furthermore, the bloodthirsty beasts of Hell, summoned and unleashed by Count Dracula to annihilate mankind, evoke the monstrous Nazi Waffen SS guards of the concentration camps. Fourth, the "internment camps" in *Castlevania,* where humans are treated as livestock for feeding

26 *Mahitosh Mandal and Priyanka Das*

the vampires, are an unmistakable allusion to the Nazi concentration camps. Like the Nazi Konzentrationslager, the Castlevanian internment camps were driven by destructive utopianism, aiming to create a perfect society by eliminating the "worthless" human beings. Last, the vocabulary used in *Castlevania* is uncannily informed by the Nazi rhetoric of Final Solution. The repeated reference to genocide and a godless world cannot be overlooked.

Thus, *Castlevania*, although it engages with the Holocaust only implicitly, does not dilute the violent events or the perpetrators. Unlike Japanese films, which have a tendency to sanitize Japan's involvement as an Axis Power, *Castlevania* makes an oblique yet powerful response to and criticism of the Holocaust and, by extension, contributes to the transnational discourse of Holocaust through the Popular Cultural medium of videogames.

In Chapter 7, titled "Holocaust Representations Through Popular Music: Ferramonti di Tarsia Amidst Documentation, Commemoration, and Mystification" **Silvia Del Zoppo** studies the neglected history of persecution in the fascist internment camps in Italy during the 1940s in comparison with the more frequently talked about Holocaust concentration camps. It is this comparativism that qualifies her chapter to be a part of the section on universalism. She differentiates between music composed and performed within the concentration camps ("Lagermusik") and the music composed in the aftermath of the Holocaust to commemorate the victims. While the first category of music has a testimony-like status and is a form of documentation, the latter (re)presents the Holocaust and runs the risk of oversimplifying and trivializing the Holocaust memory. Nevertheless, Silvia Del Zoppo feels that the latter category of representations of the Holocaust, particularly through collective performance of the popular music on the Holocaust, might contribute to the "processes of preserving individual and collective identities and values." According to the author,

> together with surviving musical testimonies from the Holocaust, they [popular music representing the Holocaust] act as self-representational, restlessly questioning response to statements of Holocaust iconoclasm, most noteworthily raising individual and public awareness of the threshold of understanding and the never-ending discourse on the nature of human being.

In Chapter 8, titled "Holocaust Museums: A Study of the Memory Policies of the USA and Poland," **Adriana Krawiec** renegotiates the idea of global memory of the Holocaust by studying the nexus of nationalist politics and memory policies of the United States Holocaust Memorial Museum (USHMM), an example of Americanization of the Holocaust, in conjunction with those of the Auschwitz-Birkenau Museum. The chapter theorizes and problematizes the Holocaust museums, which have become "fashionable destinations," as sites for Popular Culture structured by certain relations of power. Referring to the role politicians and ideologues, alongside Popular Culture, play, she argues how such museums simultaneously appropriate and promote the Holocaust memory. This is the case not only with USHMM but also with Auschwitz-Birkenau Museum. While pointing out that

Popular Culture, particularly film, trivializes and even "idealizes" the Holocaust, museums cannot always avoid strategies which are somewhat similar to those of Popular Culture. She argues, "Without an audience, museums lose their raison d'être, thus a museum has to do something to gain visitors." But ultimately, museums are more effective in imparting authentic Holocaust memory than Popular Culture. One has to choose between films sending out distorted views about the Holocaust and the Holocaust education imparted by museums. "Whereas the Polish museum documents the Nazi crimes," Krawiec writes, "the American museum creates a spectacle of suffering, all in order to prevent crimes in the future." But has such documentation or has the Popular Cultural representation been substantially effective? Have we learned the lessons from the Holocaust? Krawiec is not sure as she refers to the increase in crimes against humanity, for instance, the genocide against the Rohingyas in Myanmar.

In Chapter 9, titled "Trace and Trauma: Early Holocaust Remembrance in American and Canadian Popular Culture," **Roger Chapman** analyzes the vastness of the Holocaust "trace" in diverse instances of Popular Culture from the USA and Canada. Using John Stratton's concept of "cultural trauma," he studies a wide variety of works of Popular Culture including Marc Chagall's painting, Anno Sokolow's choreography, Leonard Cohen's lyrics, and Emanuel Bronner's soap labels. He describes such works as "popular culture offerings by Jews who did not directly experience the Holocaust" and points out how they have quite remarkably and successfully contributed to the universalization of the Holocaust.

Part III, titled "In Defense of Popular Culture" and posited in opposition to Part I and partly to Part II as well, discusses the possibilities opened up by Popular Culture in aiding and revitalizing the remembrance of the Holocaust. This final part of the book comprises eight chapters, as follows.

In Chapter 10, titled "Mothers, Daughters, and the Holocaust: A Study of Miriam Katin's Graphic Memoirs," **Sucharita Sarkar** draws attention to many graphic memoirs, other than Spiegelman's *Maus*, that have deployed the verbal-visual medium of comics to commemorate the Holocaust. Two such memoirs by Miriam Katin, a Holocaust survivor and self-taught artist, are analyzed in-depth. According to Sarkar, Katin's works constitute a "matricentic response" to the Holocaust by combining visual aesthetics and feminist politics and by intertwining memory and postmemory. Such response challenges the concept of Holocaust kitsch often used to condemn the works of Popular Culture. According to her, "The graphic medium—a 'seriality' of frame-gutter sequences which literalize the process of representation through presences (frames/panels) and absences (gutters)—is capable of engaging with the overt and covert details and depths of trauma." For her, "the genre of graphic narratives—and the medium of comics—does not need to be limited by the forms and stereotypes that dominate popular culture." Katin's graphic memoirs, therefore, are considered as "resistant memoirs" that "are an emerging and legitimate part of the ongoing project of Holocaust sense-making: the documenting of its trauma and the search for healing from this trauma."

In Chapter 11, titled, "Superheroes and the Holocaust in American Comics," **Michaela Weiss** adds to the discourse of Americanization of the Holocaust by closely inspecting the genre of American superhero comics and its educative role. As a medium that is usually discarded in the mainstream framework of Holocaust knowledge acquisition, the superhero comics go beyond being simply a form of entertainment for children to become a dynamic site of expression for Jewish artists. While moral dilemma in the choice of medium to depict the Holocaust in an ethical and authentic way, further amplified by Adorno and Wiesel's resistance to Holocaust representation, engulfed creators, American Jewish artists, while fighting antisemitic and anti-immigrant sentiments themselves, took recourse to superhero comics to represent the tragedy. The patriotic superheroes with their power to destroy Nazism also motivated the American army, besides spreading awareness of the genocide. Weiss highlights the flexibility of comics that allows it to address pressing social concerns and the liberty to employ fantastic elements that enable it to represent the unspeakable. Such comics not only enhance our collective understanding of the trauma but also empower Holocaust survivors by positioning them as superheroes, thereby rejecting the passivity usually attached to Jewish victims. Weiss emphasizes how comic series such as Batman, Superman, Captain Marvel, and X-Men, which we usually do not register as Holocaust narratives, are, in fact, replete with symbols and characters significant to the Nazi genocide. She argues that superhero comics manifest "the ominous presence of the Holocaust and its impact on the lives of the survivors, challenging the image of America as a safe space."

In Chapter 12, titled, "Unearthing the Real in the Magical: Holocaust Memory and Magic Realism in Select Post-Holocaust Fictions," **Tiasa Bal** studies magic realism as an alternative contextual form of Popular Culture that accommodates the Holocaust and challenges the dominant narrative modes that are otherwise accountable to diplomatic convenience. Magic realism, Bal argues, as a manifestation of popular consciousness, integrates magic and reality to compensate for historical silences and blank spaces. Echoing Stuart Hall and the Birmingham School, Bal upholds Popular Culture as a tool of resistance and subversion and endows magic realism with the capacity to portray the Holocaust trauma, particularly of those politically and culturally disempowered communities who are largely neglected in mainstream historiography. Her work concentrates on three post-Holocaust fictions that employ fantastic elements of magic realism to deal with death, intergenerational trauma, and Jewish folk beliefs. Written by second- and third-generation writers, Thane Rosenbaum, Joseph Skibell, and Anne Michael, these magic realist fictions encourage the project of ethical Holocaust representation in a post-testimonial world. A tool of conveying the unthinkable horror of the genocide, magic realism, as Bal argues, prevents the "difficult histories from erasure and reinforces the narrative agency of voices that are lost in the echo."

In Chapter 13, titled " 'Once-upon-a-very-real-time': Fairy Tales and Holocaust in Jane Yolen's Novels," **Anisha Sen** explores the complexities of fairy tales, usually considered tales for children, in terms of a study of the retellings of fairy tales in three of Jane Yolen's novels that are set against the backdrop of the Holocaust. The chapter explores the interface between fairy tales, Popular Culture, and the Holocaust. Sen demonstrates that even though "blending something as horrific as the Holocaust with something as dreamy as a fairy tale" might sound "incongruous," this is not always the case. She argues that a fairy tale, "with a simple change in the ending," can evoke horrors comparable to some of the experiences of the Holocaust. Sen also argues that "the Holocaust has in itself become a kind of dark fairy tale, to be handed down from one generation to the next in the form of stories." The possibilities of commensurability between fairy tales, Popular Culture, and the Holocaust are, thereby, explored.

In Chapter 14, titled, "Retelling the Holocaust With Children: A Pedagogic Study of Stephen King's *Apt Pupil* and Jane Yolen's *The Devil's Arithmetic*," **Diganta Ray** offers a pedagogic way to deal with the Holocaust as he stresses the importance of disseminating Holocaust narratives among children by not only conveying it to them but also engaging them with the difficult questions of violence and trauma. Focusing on Stephen King's *Apt Pupil* and Jane Yolen's *The Devil's Arithmetic*, Ray studies popular fiction as a site of power struggles and subversive resistance, which also invites the young reader to actively participate in culturally determined debates of race, class, and gender identities. He argues that both the texts subvert the established idea of Popular Culture's inherent association with mass media, whose repetitive and commercialized aspect deprives the popular literature of its due respectability. He also expresses concern that imparting Holocaust education through historical references alone runs the possible risk of maintaining a safe distance from a chronologically and temporally distant historical event. Ray enlists three crucial factors of Holocaust education that involve the instructor, the mode of instruction, and the learner, respectively. For Ray, "the pedagogical objective of teaching about the Holocaust . . . should therefore be to excite the moral imagination of the current generation to break the barrier between the Self and the Other."

In Chapter 15, titled "'Is it safe?': *Marathon Man* as Holocaust Drama" Douglas C. MacLeod, Jr. studies John Schlesinger's gritty masterpiece *Marathon Man* (1976) by analyzing several key scenes connected to the cinematic representation of the Holocaust. The author argues how the film is marked by "genre bending" since it is a thriller that at the same time tellingly represents the "savagery of the Holocaust." To establish his point, MacLeod reads the film in conjunction with multiple survivor testimonies and nonfiction writings. "Although theorists and historians feel that to represent the Holocaust as a Hollywood genre picture is tasteless, immoral, and unacceptable," he states, "we all must realize that without representation there can be no remembrance." The message of the film is that "the Holocaust must be represented for further study and remembrance." As such, instead of being an example of trivialization of the Holocaust, "it forces audience members to learn about what happened during the Holocaust."

In Chapter 16, titled, "Child's Play, Fantasy, and the Holocaust in *Jojo Rabbit* and *The Boy in the Striped Pajamas*," **Medha Bhadra Chowdhury** digs into the complex subject of Holocaust representation through a child's perspective that challenges the mainstream representation of Holocaust as a tragedy confined within adult recollection. Chowdhury closely investigates two popular films, *Jojo Rabbit* (2019) and *The Boy in the Striped Pajamas* (2008), which have child protagonists

30 *Mahitosh Mandal and Priyanka Das*

experiencing the Final Solution through their innate playful order of reality and capture the child's essence that is otherwise sidelined in adult fictions. The first film, she argues, treats fantasy and hallucination as tools of survival for psychologically confronted children like Jojo. The second one, she notes, employs child's play to carve out a space for mutual sympathy and shared realities. She argues that films focusing on child victims penetrate the collective amnesia of the larger audience, and the Holocaust becomes more unsettling when a child is depicted at the receiving end of such violence. Withstanding all the relevant criticisms against both the films, she insists that these films offer "a vicarious form of witnessing and an empathetic identification with Holocaust victims to transmit the traumatic memory of the genocide and ensure its circulation in cultures of waning historicity."

In Chapter 17, titled "*In*correctamundo?: Holocaust, Humor, and Anti-Hate Satire in the Works of Brooks and Waititi," **Kyle Barrett** studies Holocaust comedies which, according to him, "do not excuse the heinous actions of the Nazis" but instead "reveal the absurdity of far-right ideology." Both Brooks and Waititi, in his reading, use humor "not at the expense of the victims of the Holocaust, but as a tool to undermine fascism." Rather than condemning films about the Holocaust as mechanism of trivialization, it is, therefore, possible to look at cinema as "an empathy machine." Holocaust films analyzed by him become "an avenue to deconstruct and counter intolerance" and play "a substantial role in generating and perpetuating empathy." Thus, comedy, for Barrett, enables the speaking of the unspeakable, confirming a similar position taken by Žižek in "On Holocaust and Art," as mentioned earlier.

Conclusion

In the light of the debates for and against Popular Culture, as mentioned previously, it should be said that insofar as the Holocaust is concerned we experience an ongoing tension between history and memory and between testimony and fiction. We admit that opinions continue to stay divided. However, we feel that it would be too easy and simplistic to consider the (testimonial) history of the Holocaust and the artifacts of Popular Culture as epistemologically oppositional. This volume, however, goes beyond such superficial condemnation of Popular Culture and urges for a more nuanced approach to the interface. Rather than either condemning or glorifying Popular Culture, this book pragmatically proposes the inevitability and usability of Popular Culture in advancing the remembrance of the Holocaust and alerting us to potentially similar genocides. It contends that debating the accuracy of Popular Culture representations of the Holocaust is in itself a critical exercise that helps in the preservation of Holocaust memory, ensuring it does not fade into oblivion as time progresses and as new forms of genocide and mass suffering emerge. Since Holocaust remembrance ought to be an eternal requirement, any discourse, including that of Popular Culture, that can contribute to such remembrance, to whatever extent, should, perhaps, be welcomed. This volume encourages such a move but, of course, not without the required amount of criticality, that is, looking at Popular Culture, nevertheless, with a pinch of salt. In that spirit, it accommodates three diverse forms of reading that move from a critical interrogation of Popular Culture to a more balanced viewing of Popular Culture to, finally, looking at the potential of Popular Culture in contributing to the remembrance of the Holocaust. Such a tripartite interpretative gesture is articulated respectively through a) explicating the incompatibility between Holocaust and Popular Culture by explaining why the universalization of the Holocaust memory through Popular Culture is a commercially profitable but politically and ethically risky exercise; b) contending that the transnational practice of the Holocaust remembrance can do justice to the victims and expose the contours of Nazism and neo-Nazism; and c) establishing the potential of Popular Culture to become an empathetic medium of Holocaust remembrance. The readings in this volume are informed by an interdisciplinary, intergenerational, and international approach to the Holocaust by way of critiquing a wide variety of Popular Culture works including language, literature, films, television shows, soap operas, music, dance, social media, advertisements, comics, graphic novels, videogames, and museums. The volume would hopefully contribute to transcending the "versus thesis" (i.e., the binary between the Holocaust and Popular Culture) and offer the readers a way forward wherein the practitioners of Popular Culture as well as those committed to remembering the Holocaust would together contribute to alerting the world of future genocides.

Works Cited

Adorno, Theodor W. *Negative Dialectics* (Translated by E. B. Ashton). Routledge, 1973.
———. *Prisms* (Translated by Samuel Weber and Shierry Weber). MIT Press, 1997.
Agamben, Giorgio. *Remnants of Auschwitz: The Witness and the Archive.* Zone Books, 1999.
Ambedkar, Bhimrao Ramji. "Philosophy of Hinduism." In *Dr. Babasaheb Ambedkar: Writings and Speeches* (vol. 2, compiled by Vasant). Dr Ambedkar Foundation, 2014, pp. 3–92.
———. "Ranade, Gandhi and Jinnah." In *Dr. Babasaheb Ambedkar: Writings and Speeches* (vol. 1, compiled by Vasant Moon). Dr Ambedkar Foundation, 2014, pp. 205–240.
———. "Untouchability: Its source." In *Dr. Babasaheb Ambedkar: Writings and Speeches* (vol. 5, compiled by Vasant Moon). Dr Ambedkar Foundation, 2014, pp. 3–5.
———. "Why Indian labour is determined to win the war." In *Dr. Babasaheb Ambedkar: Writings and Speeches* (vol. 10, compiled by Vasant Moon). Dr Ambedkar Foundation, 2014, pp. 36–43.
Ben-Naftali, Michal. "Interview with Professor Jacques Derrida: Ecole des Hautes Etudes en sciences sociales, Paris." *Yad Vashem: The World Holocaust Remembrance Centre,* 8 Jan. 1998, www.yadvashem.org/articles/interviews/jacques-derrida.html. Accessed 21 Dec. 2021.
Berberich, Christine. "Introduction: The Holocaust in contemporary culture." *Holocaust Studies,* vol. 25, nos. 1–2, 2019, pp. 1–11. DOI: 10.1080/17504902.2018.1472871.
Bergen, Doris L. *War and Genocide: A Concise History of the Holocaust.* Rowman & Littlefield, 2009.
Bloxham, Donald. *Genocide on Trial: War Crimes Trials and the Formation of Holocaust History and Memory.* Oxford University Press, 2001.
Boswell, Matthew. *Holocaust Impiety: In Literature, Popular Music, and Film.* Palgrave Macmillan, 2012.

Brackney, Kathryn L. "An Alien world at the limits of modernity." *Representations*, 7 Feb. 2019, www.representations.org/an-alien-world-at-the-limits-of-modernity/. Accessed 1 Dec. 2021.

Brocklehurst, Steven. "Partition of India: 'They would have slaughtered us.'" *BBC News*, 12 Aug. 2017, www.bbc.com/news/uk-scotland-40874496. Accessed 21 Dec. 2021.

Cargas, Harry J. "An interview with Elie Wiesel." *Holocaust and Genocide Studies*, vol. 1, no. 1, 1986, pp. 5–10.

Castlevania. Konami, 1986.

Castlevania III: Dracula's Curse. Konami, 1989.

Chute, Hillary. *Disaster Drawn: Visual Witness, Comics, and Documentary Form.* The Belknap Press of Harvard University Press, 2016.

Crim, Brian E. *Planet Auschwitz: Holocaust Representation in Science Fiction and Horror Film and Television.* Rutgers University Press, 2020.

Das, Priyanka. "There are no innocents, not anymore: Holocaust and medievalism in Japanese videogame Castlevania." *Reshaping the Middle Ages in and through Asian Popular Culture, 36th Annual Conference on Medievalism*, 6 Nov. 2021, Delta College (Conference Presentation).

Demsky, Jeffrey. *Nazi Holocaust Representation in Anglo-American Popular Culture, 1945-2020: Irreverent Remembrance.* Palgrave Macmillan, 2021.

Felman, Shoshana and Dori Laub. *Testimony: Crises of Witnessing in Literature, Psychoanalysis, and History.* Routledge, 1992.

Felstiner, John. *Paul Celan: Poet, Jew, Survivor.* Yale University Press, 2001.

Forman, Sharon G. "Mindy Kaling's Netflix hit does a disservice to its Jewish characters." *STL Jewish Light*, 4 Aug. 2021, https://stljewishlight.org/arts-entertainment/mindy-kalings-netflix-hit-does-a-disservice-to-its-jewish-characters/. Accessed 1 Dec. 2021.

Fox, Mira. "Mindy Kaling's hit teen comedy has a serious Jewish problem." *Forward*, 8 May 2020, https://forward.com/culture/446044/mindy-kaling-never-have-i-ever-ben-gross-jewish-stereotype/. Accessed 1 Dec. 2021.

Gelbart, Petra. "Holocaust in popular culture." *Email received by Mahitosh Mandal and Priyanka Das*, 20 Feb. 2020.

Godbole, Madhav. *The Holocaust of Indian Partition.* Rupa, 2006.

GoNews Desk. "8 Dalit women get raped in India every day, UP has most victims." *GoNews India*, n.d., www.gonewsindia.com/latest-news/news-and-politics/8-dalit-women-get-raped-in-india-every-day-up-has-most-victims-19156. Accessed 21 Dec. 2021.

Hayes, Peter. *Why?: Explaining the Holocaust* (Kindle file). Norton, 2017.

Jyoti, Dhrubo. "Crimes against Dalits, tribals increased in Covid pandemic year: NCRB." *Hindusthan Times*, 16 Sep. 2021, www.hindustantimes.com/india-news/crimes-against-dalits-tribals-increased-in-covid-pandemic-year-ncrb-101631731260293.html. Accessed 21 Dec. 2021.

Kaźmierczak, Marek. "Broken images—'Auschwitz,' nostalgia and modernity: The reception of the Holocaust in popular culture." *Images*, vol. 8, nos. 15–16, 2011, pp. 101–120.

Kerner, Aaron. *Film and the Holocaust: New Perspectives on Dramas, Documentaries and Experimental Films.* Continuum, 2011.

Lanzmann, Claude. *Claude Lanzmann's Shoah: Key Essays* (edited by Stuart Liebman). Oxford University Press, 2007.

Levy, Daniel and Sznaider Natan. *The Holocaust and Memory in the Global Age* (Translated by Assenka Oksiloff). Temple University Press, 2005.

Lyotard, Jean-François. *The Differend: Phrases in Dispute* (Translated by Georges Van Den Abbeele). University of Minnesota Press, 1988.

Magilow, Daniel H. and Lisa Silverman. *Holocaust Representations in History: An Introduction*. Bloomsbury, 2015.

Mandal, Mahitosh. "'Holocaste?': Holocaust and the caste question." *Workshop on Actors of Transnational Memory at the 6th Bergen-Belsen International Summer School*, 9 Aug. 2019, Ludwig-Harms-Haus, Hermannsburg (Workshop presentation).

———. "Liars masquerading as communists: The curious case of CPIM in Bengal." *Round Table India: For an Informed Ambedkar Age*, 17 May 2020, https://roundtableindia.co.in/index.php?option=com_content&view=article&id=9910%3Aliars-masquerading-as-communists-the-curious-case-of-cpim-in-bengal&catid=119%3Afeature&Itemid=132. Accessed 21 Dec. 2021.

Marshmann, Sophia. "From the margins to the mainstream? Representations of the Holocaust in popular culture." *eSharp*, vol. 6, no. 1, 2005, pp. 1–20, www.gla.ac.uk/media/Media_41177_smxx.pdf. Accessed 21 Dec. 2021.

Mintz, Alan. *Popular Culture and Shaping of Holocaust Memory in America*. University of Washington Press, 2001.

Moses, Dirk A. *German Intellectuals and the Nazi Past*. Cambridge University Press, 2007.

"Muselmann." *Yad Vashem: The World Holocaust Remembrance Centre*, www.yadvashem.org/odot_pdf/Microsoft%20Word%20-%206474.pdf. Accessed 21 Dec. 2021.

Never Have I Ever (Created by Mindy Kaling and Lang Fisher, composed by Joseph Stephens). Netflix, 2020.

Novick, Peter. *Holocaust in American Life*. Houghton Mifflin, 1999.

Nuit et brouillard (Directed by Alain Resnais, written by Jean Cayrol, and narrated by Michel Bouquet). Argos Films, 1956.

Pandey, Geeta. "Indian MP Mahua Moitra's 'rising fascism' speech wins plaudits." *BBC News*, 26 Jun. 2019, www.bbc.com/news/world-asia-india-48755554. Accessed 21 Dec. 2021.

Pandey, Gyanendra. *Remembering Partition: Violence, Nationalism, and History in India*. Cambridge University Press, 2001.

Parker, Holt N. "Toward a definition of popular culture." *History and Theory*, vol. 50, no. 2, 2011, pp. 147–170, www.jstor.org/stable/41300075. Accessed 21 Dec. 2021.

Raja, Irfan. "Is India sleepwalking toward a Muslim holocaust?" *Daily Sabah*, 28 Feb. 2020, www.dailysabah.com/opinion/op-ed/is-india-sleepwalking-toward-a-muslim-holocaust. Accessed 21 Dec. 2021.

Rose, Gillian. *Mourning Becomes the Law: Philosophy and Representation*. Cambridge University Press, 1997.

Rothberg, Michael. *Multidirectional Memory: Remembering the Holocaust in the Age of Decolonization*. Stanford University Press, 2009.

Santayana, George. *The Life of Reason: Introduction and Reason in Common Sense. The Works of George Santayana* (vol. 7, book 1, edited by Marianne S. Wokeck et al). The MIT Press, 2011.

Sarukkai, Sundar. "The 'other' in anthropology and philosophy." *Economic and Political Weekly*, vol. 32, no. 24, 1997, pp. 1406–1409.

Shashkevich, Alex. "Stanford scholar explains the history of India's Partition, its ongoing effects today." *Stanford News*, 8 Mar. 2019, https://news.stanford.edu/2019/03/08/partition-1947-continues-haunt-india-pakistan-stanford-scholar-says/. Accessed 21 Dec. 2021.

Sierp, Aline and Jenny Wüstenberg. "Linking the local and the transnational: Rethinking memory politics in Europe." *Journal of Contemporary European Studies*, vol. 23, no. 3, 2015, pp. 321–329. DOI: 10.1080/14782804.2015.1058244.

34 *Mahitosh Mandal and Priyanka Das*

Storey, John. *Cultural Theory and Popular Culture: An Introduction* (5th ed.). Pearson Longman, 2009.

Teltumbde, Anand. *Persistence of Caste*. Zed Books, 2010.

The Big Bang Theory (Directed by Chuck Lorre and Bill Prady). CBS, 2007.

"The politics of defining: A roundtable discussion about the Jerusalem Declaration on Antisemitism." *Religion and Public Life*, 17 Mar. 2021, https://rpl.hds.harvard.edu/news/2021/05/17/video-politics-defining-roundtable-discussion-about-jerusalem-declaration-antisemitism. Accessed 12 Feb. 2023.

Venkataraman, Meena. "Never Have I Ever can do better" *Harvard Politics*, 16 May 2020, https://harvardpolitics.com/never-have-i-ever-can-do-better/. Accessed 1 Dec. 2021.

"What is the difference between 'Holocaust' and 'Shoah'?" *World Jewish Congress*, https://aboutholocaust.org/en/facts/what-is-the-difference-between-holocaust-and-shoah. Accessed 21 Dec. 2021.

"What was the Holocaust?" *Yad Vashem: The World Holocaust Remembrance Centre*, www.yadvashem.org/holocaust/about.html. Accessed 21 Dec. 2021.

Wiesel, Elie. *Night* (Translated by Marion Wiesel). Hill and Wang, 2006.

Wiesel, Elie, et al. *Dimensions of the Holocaust: Lectures at Northwestern University*. Northwestern University Press, 1990.

Žižek, Slavoj. "Alfred Hitchcock, or, the form and its historical mediation." In *Everything You Always Wanted to Know about Lacan (But Were Afraid to Ask Hitchcock)*, edited by Slavoj Žižek. Verso, 1992, pp. 1–14.

———. "Laugh yourself to death: The new wave of holocaust comedies!" *Lacan.com*, 15 Dec. 1999, www.lacan.com/zizekholocaust.htm. Accessed 22 Dec. 2021.

———. "On Holocaust and art." *Diaphanes*, n.d., www.diaphanes.net/titel/description-without-a-place-542. Accessed 21 Dec. 2021.

Part I
Explicating Incompatibility

1 Popular Fiction, Literary Culture, and Artistic Truth

Thane Rosenbaum's *The Golems of Gotham* and Twenty-First Century Holocaust Representation

Craig Smith

In America today, the Holocaust is everywhere and nowhere, simultaneously remembered and forgotten. On the one hand, "Discussions of the Holocaust have become—for better or worse—central in the American public and cultural spheres" (Tweraser 1), especially since the mid-'80s when a "new 'memory culture' was developed [within] a public and institutional context" (Assmann 23). The 1993 opening of the United States Holocaust Memorial and Museum (USHMM) arguably best exemplified this development, as it formally committed the nation to ongoing commemoration of the event. For a while, the USHMM even "rivaled the clearly populist Air and Space Museum at the Smithsonian in terms of public interest" (Metz 33), a marker of the Holocaust's "intensified presence in contemporary culture" (Rothberg 184). Of course, contributing to the Holocaust's omnipresence are the film and television industries, which return to the Nazis and their victims with such regularity that the world is "teeming with symbolic representations . . . of the Holocaust" (Assmann 35). Moreover, because "well-known images of Nazism and the Holocaust comprise a basic part of our cultural reservoir of representing atrocities" (Ebbrecht 90), an entire lexicon of evil drawn from the Holocaust has routinely been mobilized across a broad ideological spectrum, guaranteeing the event's persistence within American cultural life. On the other hand, the ubiquity of Holocaust museums, the "popularization and decontextualization" of "migrating images" (Ebbrecht 87), and the evocation of Nazi victims in varied political activisms have not resulted in the Holocaust being well remembered or understood. One of those rare events that become "a moral reference point" (Novick 13), the Holocaust's very ubiquity may contribute to its misremembrance, for "individuals from every point on the political compass can find the lessons they wish in the . . . moral and ideological Rorschach test" that is the Holocaust (Novick 12). It is, thus, unsurprising that Holocaust awareness in America reveals how "memory and forgetfulness are facets of the same phenomenon of understanding" (Bernard-Donals 3).

This paradox surrounding the Holocaust may be especially prevalent in America, but a similar phenomenon exists internationally. In a recent poll, "a third of Europeans said they knew just a little or nothing at all about the Holocaust," including 1 in 20 Europeans who claim, incredibly, never to have heard of it (Greene). As in America, then, popular interest in the Holocaust and official commemorations have not led to its universal remembrance.[1] The same CNN poll chillingly

DOI: 10.4324/9781003251224-3

38   *Craig Smith*

revealed that almost a quarter of those asked believe "Jews have too much influence in conflict and wars across the world," and about 20 percent think Jewish people are too influential in the media and/or politics (Greene). This confluence of increased Holocaust forgetfulness and the revitalization of old antisemitic tropes is particularly problematic as we move from the "embodied memory of survivors to an exclusively mediated memory" (Assmann 23). Such a prospect raises increasingly urgent questions about how the Holocaust might best be represented and remembered in the years ahead.

Though published almost two decades ago, Thane Rosenbaum's *The Golems of Gotham* remains a timely novel capable of addressing the problems of twenty-first-century Holocaust remembrance. Taking on urgent questions of remembrance, the text inscribes its own idiosyncratic act of remembering in an era characterized by the paradox of forgetful memory. Written by a child of survivors, *The Golems of Gotham* also mourns the passing of witnesses to atrocity, testifies to the generational trauma of genocide, and highlights the imbrication of Holocaust memory with ongoing political issues and aesthetic debates. Much like Rothberg says of Art Spiegelman's work, "the terrain" of Rosenbaum's "postmemory" novel "is much more the present than the past" (189), which manifests in its insistence on the continuing cruciality of Holocaust remembrance. As early as 1987, Rosenbaum writes:

> [Something] had obscenely, and unconscionably, returned. Neo-Nazis were marching all over Europe. Their numbers were small, but so had Hitler's storm troopers been fifty years earlier. There is no comfort in knowing that fascism begins at the margins . . . such ideas often have a tendency to creep their way into the center of human life—when the conditions are right, when morality is on hiatus, when the conscience is forever clear, when guilt loses its meaning, and when all that matters is the deaf drum of indifference. The Nazis had come back. They were once again young, towering, blond, and monstrous, and at the same time in denial of what their forebears had done.
>
> (58–59)

For Rosenbaum, the stakes of Holocaust remembrance could not be clearer: To remember is to keep fascism from claiming even the margins of political discourse, to keep alive the political and moral meaning of guilt, and, echoing Elie Wiesel, to forestall the onset of indifference.

This is not to say that *The Golems of Gotham* is straightforwardly a work of Holocaust representation. Rosenbaum "generally recoil[s] at . . . being thought of as a Holocaust writer" (Royal, "Interview" 3), and while the novel includes famous Holocaust survivors and writers as characters, it deliberately eschews representing their wartime experiences, rendering ambiguous its status *as* Holocaust literature. This is unsurprising coming from an author who makes "no claims to the Holocaust as an event, only its generational consequences" (Royal, "Interview" 3), a point echoed in *Golems*: "Children of Holocaust survivors are not survivors of the Holocaust. They may have survived something, but not that" (333). *Golems* might be seen, then, as engaging in a form of secondary witnessing, which, for

Popular Fiction, Literary Culture, and Artistic Truth 39

Geoffrey Hartman, constitutes "an important [element] in the long-term guardianship of Holocaust memory" (Assmann 36), for it "deals with the Holocaust not as an event in *history* that is receding into a more and more distant past, but as an event in *memory* that retains its charge in the present and into the future" (Assmann 37, italics in original).

Refraining from trespassing on unshared experiences, Rosenbaum's novel takes New York City in 1999 as its setting and concerns itself more with Holocaust representation and commodification than with the event as such. Indeed, if, for Rothberg, "issues of publicity and the marketplace [are] often overlooked in discussions of Holocaust representation" (14), Rosenbaum's novel addresses this very aporia. Wide-ranging, wildly varied in tone, and highly self-referential, *Golems* partakes of the postmodern milieu that gave birth to it, allowing Rosenbaum to speak to the difficulties of remembering and representing the Holocaust, particularly in a late capitalist era that has "internalized the phrases and images of atrocity" (190) and transformed the Holocaust into a "legitimate, moneymaking commodity" (294).

In the novel, six Holocaust survivor-writers who had committed suicide, return to life as golems. The golems—Primo Levi, Paul Celan, Tadeusz Borowski, Jerzy Kosinski, Jean Amery, and Piotr Rawicz[2]—are accidentally called back by teenage klezmer prodigy Ariel Levin, whose dabbling in kabbalah is meant to reanimate only her Holocaust-surviving grandparents, Rose and Lothar Levin, whose suicides open the novel. Ariel ostensibly aims to alleviate the writer's block afflicting her father, Oliver, a New York–based child of Holocaust survivors. However, it soon becomes clear that Oliver's personal problem is connected to a wider end-of-the-century cultural malaise. Though the golems haunt New York, committing acts ranging from playful mischief to vengeful vandalism that force the "cruel" and "ungrateful" (323) world to acknowledge those it has forgotten, it is what they have returned to that truly haunts: a frenetic postmodern America in which Holocaust curricula, blockbuster films, and well-funded memorials coexist alongside Holocaust denial, globally resurgent neo-Nazism, and the reduction of Holocaust memorialization to "some sound bite" (268). As such, *The Golems of Gotham* foregrounds the paradoxically forgetful nature of Holocaust omnipresence at the same time that it seeks to memorialize Holocaust victims within a cultural economy where "mass murder is not for mass markets" (264). Looking self-consciously to the cultural marketplace as the arena where different types of narratives compete, Rosenbaum highlights a tension between the mass appeal of the consolatory aesthetics of popular, award-winning works and the more truthful but less appealing accounts of mass death. I argue, then, that *The Golems of Gotham*'s self-consciousness and carefully wrought formal features—particularly its relentless mixing of popular and literary fiction practices—can best be understood as its attempt to forge an aesthetic form capable of conveying those stories that are "morally entitled to be told in a certain way or not at all" (292).

Rosenbaum's writing consistently pays attention to form as a crucial conveyer of meaning. In his first book, *Elijah Visible*, "the very medium of the [short story] cycle genre determines the message, with the narrative structure becoming the metaphor for the ruptures the Holocaust has wrought" (Royal, "Fragmenting" 78).

40   *Craig Smith*

Given Rosenbaum's awareness of form's semantic power, genre's early surfacing as a subject in *The Golems of Gotham* is unsurprising. In the first chapter Oliver narrates,[3] he states "I *am* a writer," only to concede "but I'm no artist" (30, italics in original). Oliver's defensiveness reveals his writerly self-perception. He explains:

> I write gothic mysteries; courtroom legal thrillers. My aesthetic never qualifies as emotionally complex or intellectually challenging. I provide no insight into life, no glimpse of the human condition, no window into the inner workings of a troubled soul. My work is all a mindless, connect-the-dots formula—pablum that leaves you hungry.
>
> (30)

Oliver's self-loathing description of his craft locates his work in the field of popular fiction, which "is so often cast not just as escapist, but as ephemeral, transient, destined for almost immediate obscurity" (Gelder 7), making it the "literary equivalent of high-calorie, low-quality fast food" (Murphy 4). Oliver's writing, then, is the unvalued half of an artistic binary, distinct from literary writing that "deploys a set of logics and practices that are different in kind" (Gelder 13) from what Oliver produces. Oliver himself voices such a binary view:

> a real artist doesn't care about facts, details, adventure, intrigue, or even plot—just truth. When art is pumping on all emotional cylinders, when it shakes itself loose from what the mind will believe, when it aspires not to copy but to reinvent, not to please but to disturb—to rub everyone the wrong way—the result can split your veins, crush your heart like a piece of fruit, make you gasp and breathe backwards.
>
> (31)

Literary fiction holds value for Oliver precisely because it conveys profound truths that formulaic popular fiction cannot. However, if Oliver's words reflect a standard dismissive view of popular fiction, *The Golems of Gotham* offers more overall balance. When Evelyn, Oliver's agent, discusses his writer's block with him, she initially reinforces popular fiction's devaluation by noting that she's "never had a bestselling author with writer's block before" as it is "usually the serious, literary types . . . [her] better writers" who are afflicted (52). However, to appease Oliver, she reminds him, "We both know who pays the bills around here" (52). After all, if "from the point of view of popular fiction, it is [literary fiction] that would seem to be lacking" (Gelder 20), then that is because the latter "lacks the thing popular fiction values most of all: a large number of readers" (Gelder 20). Though Evelyn maintains a conventional distinction between higher-selling entertainment and higher-quality writing, Rosenbaum suggests that, regarding Holocaust remembrance, the consequences of this distinction exceed commercial considerations.

In response to Oliver's latest book, his first foray into Holocaust writing, Evelyn receives a rejection letter that baldly states, "Holocaust novels don't sell" (264).

Popular Fiction, Literary Culture, and Artistic Truth 41

She informs Oliver that "nobody wants to read this stuff" because the "whole subject is too dark and depressing" (264–265). Even the fact that Oliver's novel is "ambitious and worthy" (263) is insufficient to make the publisher "willing to risk" (264) publishing it. Therein, for Rosenbaum, lies the problem of Holocaust representation: The glut of Holocaust materials available belies a lack of genuine, sustained consumer interest, at least in the ambitiously worthy texts. The golems realize this when they visit the New York Public Library and discover that although "they wanted to be read . . . [and] while their books were on the shelves, they looked as though they had rarely if ever left them. Their bound words appeared new, without stamped due dates or dog-eared pages" (171). The golems' discovery, poignantly painful as it is, allows Rosenbaum to underscore the irony of a situation in which a "set of institutions dedicated to Holocaust memory and a substantial cadre of Holocaust-memory professionals" (Novick 6) exist alongside widespread Holocaust ignorance.

That the Holocaust can be both central to *official* American consciousness yet unknown to so many Americans is an inescapable troubling feature of contemporary life as Rosenbaum represents it. Hoping to enhance a photo of her grandparents so she can include their prisoner numbers in her reanimating ritual, Ariel seeks assistance from a shop employee. He initially cannot see them, but when he finally notices the tattoos, he asks, "Why would these people have numbers on their arms? Were they in some kind of college fraternity or something?" (46). The employee's ignorance of one of the Holocaust's most iconic images is especially striking in context, as it was precisely during the 1990s that "the Holocaust ha[d] come to loom so large in [American] culture" (Novick 1): After all, it was 1993, six years earlier than *Golems'* setting, that the TV show *Nightline* declared the "Year of the Holocaust" (Rothberg 181). The Holocaust's emergence in this period as arguably *the* defining story of the twentieth century should probably have entailed near universal recognition of its most familiar signifiers, but in the late '90s America of Rosenbaum's novel, too many resemble the photo-shop employee: kind and well-meaning enough but hopelessly unaware. It is little wonder that the employee leaves Ariel feeling "sad for all of us" (46).

The novel validates Ariel's response, as the employee's ahistoricism is part of a broader cultural openness to a historical revisionism that ultimately culminates in Holocaust denial. Rosenbaum's performance of Holocaust denial lays bare both its fundamental disingenuousness and the antisemitic dangers enabled by Holocaust forgetfulness:

> The genocide of six million Jews continued to be a debatable bone of contention. Surely no one doubted that the Armenians, Cambodians, Rwandans, Bosnians, and Kosovars all were casualties of genocide in this century, but the Jews . . . well . . . they made it all up. It didn't happen to them. And if it did happen, then it wasn't as bad as they say. And if it was as bad as they say, then they must have deserved it somehow, otherwise why would anyone have unleashed such savage fury against innocent people?
>
> (290, ellipses in original)

42   *Craig Smith*

In light of such bad-faith arguments, Rosenbaum's repeated references to the unmarketability and peripherality of serious, literary representations of the Holocaust become especially meaningful. The issue, for Rosenbaum, is not only that knowledge of the Holocaust remains vital in a world where forgetfulness and antisemitic malice combine to obscure and misrepresent the genocide but also that Holocaust representations incapable of generating widespread, continued interest are implicated in its simultaneous remembrance and forgetting.

That Rosenbaum might find fault with the Holocaust writers populating his novel may surprise, given that *Golems* generally pays homage to survivors who had made "the aesthetics of death . . . their domain" (181). Rosenbaum's comprehensive knowledge of their post-Holocaust lives and writings is frequently on display. Direct quotations from their works—including Borowski's "This Way for the Gas, Ladies and Gentlemen" (62), Celan's "Death Fugue" (63), and Amery's *At the Mind's Limits* (64)—are woven into the novel, reminding readers of key passages and ideas. More subtly, skillful paraphrasing evokes the spirit of their writings. Primo's claim that "we used words, inadequate ones, to describe what we had seen" (126) parallels the lament that Primo Levi voices in *Survival in Auschwitz* when he claims that "our language lacks words to express this offence, the demolition of a man" (26). Similarly, when Jean angrily asserts that "there are no lessons! . . . The Holocaust taught us nothing other than that human beings are quite capable of mass murder" (Rosenbaum 126), his contrarian refusal to find reassuring meaning in the Holocaust remains faithful to the Améry who rejected sympathetic but simplistic (mis)understandings of torture victims' experiences, writing, "I don't know if the person who is beaten by the police loses human dignity. Yet I am certain that with the very first blow that descends on him he loses . . . 'trust in the world'" (28).

Golems' respectful affection for its survivor-artist characters is evident, yet a refrain of failure strikes a persistent note. Jerzy bluntly states, "We were failures as artists. . . . We couldn't make any sense of that lost world" (126). Even if the writerly failure Jerzy refers to is mitigated by fact that they "weren't born artists" and "would have likely settled on more earthly, practical pursuits" if not for the Holocaust (181), the novel's harsh assessment of the golems does not cease with their writings. Granting that "not all trauma can end in recovery" and that "the best one can hope for is not a cure, but an accommodation, a determination to go on even when there is no reason to do so" (180), Rosenbaum still asserts that the golems "had been failures in this regard" (181). Oliver later notes that despite being "men of such literary virtue and accomplishment," the golems "completely failed" in "their own most crucial tests as writers" (331): "These men who had survived one of the world's greatest mysteries decided to leave behind an even greater one" (332) in not explaining their final actions. Particularly given their roles as Holocaust memorialists, Oliver feels that more might have been asked of writers who "exited without saying even the bare minimum, checking out without so much as a chicken-scratched farewell, scribblings on a napkin, codewords smeared on toilet paper" (332).

In suggesting the golems failed to meet their obligations, the novel risks making unreasonable demands of suicides—writers or not—and being insufficiently

Popular Fiction, Literary Culture, and Artistic Truth   43

respectful toward its Holocaust survivor characters. With the golems' writings in mind, however, Rosenbaum's refusal to write hagiographies aligns more with their practices than it transgresses against their memories. If survivor-writers felt any temptation to balance the cosmic scales of justice—even if in only the smallest of ways—by representing Nazi victims in the most favorable light, the writers who become Rosenbaum's golems resisted that understandable impulse, committing themselves to discomforting truths in place of consolatory fictions. Levi's late essay "The Gray Zone" exemplifies this, declaring, "It is naïve, absurd, and historically false to believe that an infernal system such as National Socialism sanctifies its victims: on the contrary, it degrades them, it makes them resemble itself, and this all the more when they are available, blank, and lacking a political or moral armature" (40). Years earlier, Borowski had represented this process in a memorably brutal scene. After a new arrival disavows a child who follows her and calls her "Mama,"[4] a prisoner from Sevastopol named Andrei, his eyes "glassy from vodka and the heat" and lacking the armature Levi speaks of, responds with physical violence before calling her a "bloody Jewess" and throwing her and the child on a truck headed directly to the gas chambers. This gains the approval of a nearby SS officer, who says "*Gut gemacht*, good work. That's the way to deal with degenerate mothers. . . . *Gut, gut, Russki*" (43). Regarding his experience of being tortured, Améry admits, "What they wanted to hear from me in Breendonk, I simply did not know myself. If instead of the aliases I had been able to name the real names, perhaps, or probably, a calamity would have occurred, and I would be standing here now as the weakling I most likely am, and as the traitor I potentially already was" (36). In different contexts, writing in different genres, the golems agree: There was room for neither saintliness nor exceptional heroism in the moral abyss of Auschwitz. It is for this reason that I see *The Golems of Gotham* as using rather than abusing the memory of the golems who haunt its pages. It is in his role as a secondary witness that Rosenbaum guards the memory of his subjects, even and especially when that entails brutal honesty about the golems themselves.

Rosenbaum does not speak over the golems by (re)presenting their experiences of the Holocaust, but he certainly carries on in their tradition of writing in a literary mode, one "intimately connected to life" (Gelder 19), albeit in his own metarepresentational style. Indeed, the metafictional elements of Rosenbaum's aesthetic practice are key to the author's aims in *The Golems of Gotham*. Although Rosenbaum does not make it clear until the fourth chapter, the sustained conceit governing *The Golems of Gotham* is that its authorship belongs to Oliver. He states, "This book in your hands, the words inverted in your eyes, is a new beginning for me" (31). Later, he again addresses his audience directly, referring to "you, the readers of *Salt and Stone*" (331). In a recognizably postmodern sleight of hand, then, *Salt and Stone* is both a text rejected for publication within *The Golems of Gotham* and that which comprises Rosenbaum's published novel. If *Golems*, like *Salt and Stone*, is "a novel essentially about pondering" (263), its own published existence raises questions about what separates the two books.

The answer, I think, is that *Golems* embraces what Oliver would reject. Seeing himself as having previously been the writer "of crass, tawdry, cheap thrillers"

44   Craig Smith

(332), Oliver is committed to newfound literary seriousness, suitable for writing about a topic that he describes as "encyclopedic in its vastness and complexity" (265). This makes his book "too ambitious" (263) for the publishing world and leaves the publisher looking hopefully to the future, "should Oliver Levin decide to one day return to the genre that made him famous" (264). In short, the publisher who rejects *Salt and Stone* knows that popular fiction "is, essentially, genre fiction" (Gelder 1) and that, because popular writers are "imprinted over their works like brands or logos" (Gelder 29), Oliver is divesting himself of his popular brand by writing *Salt and Stone*. Yet, for all Oliver's reticence about popular fiction practices, *Golems* is replete with elements that would sit comfortably within the field. The first chapter invites easy generic identification, beginning with a literal bang: "[Lothar Levin] was called to the Torah, and before reciting the blessing he reached into the *tallis* bag, removed the silencer, aimed it at his temple, and pulled the trigger. A Jewish brain shot out from his head and splattered all over the sheepskin" (1). Aside from the overtly Jewish referents, the opening paragraph could be part of any popular thriller. The sudden violence promising future action, the blasé tone of hardboiled crime fiction, and a direct and choppy style designed for quick reading are all hallmarks of popular fiction. The same can be said of the formulaic dialogue—"Who's got the piece?" (2)—employed by the officer investigating Lothar's suicide, while the mystery hinted at by Lothar's having "left no note" (1) of explanation and the intrigue of "murder in a synagogue" (2) are well-suited to "gothic mysteries" (30) like the ones Oliver typically writes.

However, if the overt generic markers that begin the novel prepare readers for a recognizable popular fiction romp, things change quickly; within a few pages, Rosenbaum turns to the theological implications of nobody taking sin "seriously anymore" on account of God "arriving late at Auschwitz" (3). If this is an issue more profound than is typical for popular fiction, the individual, character-driven mystery promised by the mutual suicides of Lothar and his wife Rose (who quietly poisons herself) is similarly replaced by a more complicated mystery: how to account for their suicides when "statistically, Holocaust survivors, as a group, didn't kill themselves" (5)? The first chapter, thus, establishes the novel's pattern of oscillating between the practices of literary and popular fiction. If it "has often been asserted that popular fiction's primary purpose is to *entertain*" (Murphy 4), the signs of that purpose are evident in the semi-comic antics of the golems as they hide in Oliver's shower (72), limit the number of travelers in subway cars, close the "entire industry" of tattooists in all five boroughs (98), and infuse cosmopolitan Manhattan with the "scent of the shtetl" (103). Similarly, while literary fiction "doesn't need a story or a plot," popular fiction "couldn't function without one" (Gelder 19), even, sometimes especially, if it is contrived or convoluted. The climactic scene in Rosenbaum's novel involves Oliver's plan to kill himself with a "German made" gun that once "belonged to a young SS officer in the ghetto of Radom" (343). Only after Lothar reveals that the gun in Oliver's hand, "the one I turned on myself . . . is the same gun that killed my parents and two of my sisters" (343) and is also the same gun Lothar had used to exact vengeance on its original owner (344) does

Popular Fiction, Literary Culture, and Artistic Truth   45

Oliver accept that enough blood has been shed—a highly (melo)dramatic moment, perfectly suited to a generic thriller.

Yet such staples of popular fiction do not seem out of place in a novel that also indulges in the serious reflections that are often restricted to the domain of literary fiction: Primo tells his fellow golems that "the bloodiest century is ending. . . . The world must learn to live with the Holocaust as it steps into the future, otherwise there will be no future" (81). Later, Jean weighs in against prevailing psychotherapeutic languages of healing, claiming, "Anger is a far more honest emotion than all your words of healing" (124). In the novel's penultimate chapter, Rabbi Vered—another survivor who committed suicide mistakenly reanimated by Ariel's magic—asks a seemingly unanswerable question: "How do you sell God to a world that has heard of Auschwitz?" (356). The novel's forays into politics, psychoanalysis, and theology stand alongside its tabloid-like references to contemporary events like "the O.J. trial" or the scandal surrounding "that Jewish girl who gave the president a blow job" (81). If the novel's indulgence of contemporaneous fascinations with murder and scandal lowers its tone, the loftier intellectual and artistic pursuits animating the text put a more respectable finish on its appeals to an audience that it knows only shows up for "The voltage. The wattage. The juice. The incandescent, swaggering, primitive allure of fire" and "the flying-chair circus of professional wrestling" (214). *Golems,* thus, can be understood alongside the trend toward genrification, a twenty-first century phenomenon in which "boundaries between popular fiction and literary fiction are being eroded by the increasing use of genre conventions and tropes by younger writers who are as influenced by popular fiction and popular culture as they are by the traditional canon" (Murphy 46–47). Populating itself with the familiar patterns of generic writing, Rosenbaum's novel parallels this trend; however, its *deliberate* playing with generic boundaries shows more than the influence of popular fiction and culture.

Indeed, if the novel's popular fiction elements add narrative excitement and stylistic accessibility to render its pondering of the complexities of Holocaust representation more readable, the text's literary aspects exhibit the valued influence of a traditional Holocaust canon and play a vital counterbalancing role. Rosenbaum observes that Americans' classroom exposure to Wiesel's *Night* and Levi's *Survival in Auschwitz* was succeeded by the "required viewing" of *Schindler's List,* "with all its good-guy-triumphs-over-bad-guy sanctimony, its ultimate feel-good imperatives, its insulting inversion of contrasting truths" (292). The film's "mass appeal" (292), Rosenbaum suggests, is inseparable from its simplifying falsehoods, its "low-cal substitute" (292) for the more intellectually nourishing harsh truths found in the golems' writings. Spielberg's film comes in for harsh treatment, but it pales compared to the scorn heaped on the "movie made by an Italian clown in which Auschwitz [is] depicted as no more threatening than a circus" (293). That Rosenbaum withholds even the name of the film—*Life Is Beautiful*—until he lists it alongside *Arbeit Macht Frei* as "the two greatest false advertisements about the Holocaust" (294) indicates his attempt to separate *Golems,* which contains some of the same "sentimentality" and "comedic sight gags" (294) as *Life Is Beautiful,* from the film his novel excoriates. Rosenbaum's novel is not without its own

46 *Craig Smith*

consolations as Oliver gets to rectify "never [having] said Kaddish" at his parents' gravesites (364). However, as Ariel metafictionally concludes, the book's ending "still wasn't a happy one" (367), and, to the end, Rosenbaum resists the easy sentiment and false consolation that his use of the patterns of popular writing might encourage readers to expect.

Popular Culture and popular literature hold some value in *The Golems of Gotham*. How could they not in a novel replete with references to "Backstreet Boys backpack[s]" (25), the bands Sugar Ray and Smash Mouth (41), and staples of 1990s daytime television Jerry Springer and Sally Jesse Raphael (293)? Their recognizability is indicative of Popular Culture's capacity to imbue names and images with cultural meaning, and such references in Rosenbaum underscore how "there are possibilities for knowledge even in the most commodified zones of culture" (Rothberg 184). Indeed, for some younger scholars studying the interface of popular media and the Holocaust, it is "thanks to the transmission of Holocaust memory through the channels of popular culture . . . [that] it has acquired the status of a global, universal or cosmopolitan memory" (Assmann 36). However, a crucial question remains: "What will be the quality of this memory in the future?" (Assmann 36).

Whatever the capacity for its artifacts to entertain and inform, popular forms of memory might falsely permit one to say, as one museumgoer in the novel does, "I think I understand the Holocaust now" (294). When that understanding comes from *strictly* popular representational forms that do the remembering for their audience, the danger is clear, for a popular form "gratifies in part because it provides us with what we want, or . . . with what we have been conditioned to *think* we want" (Murphy 5–6, italics in original). What *The Golems of Gotham* suggests we want when it comes to mysteries big and small is answers, finality, closure, for "the human impulse to claim that all mysteries have been solved is quite strong" (Rosenbaum 294).

Popular fiction, which may gratify that impulse, has broad reach while literary fiction, perhaps more capable of registering the unassimilable mystery of the "black death" (342) the golems witnessed, may not bring the Holocaust's essential mystery to enough readers to ensure remembrance. Operating within both popular and literary fields, *The Golems of Gotham* finds in each a necessary corrective to the other's shortcomings and points to a way in which we might remember the Holocaust properly, when "moving on is the enemy of remembering" and "not moving on is the enemy of life" (366).

Notes

1 The Holocaust "became a compulsory topic in the English history curriculum" (Rauch 160), while in Germany "the Jewish Museum Berlin is the most popular museum in Berlin, flooded each day not only with tourists but also huge numbers of public school children" (Metz 32).
2 Within the novel, the golems are referred to by their first names. To be consistent with Rosenbaum's practice, and to avoid confusing the fictional characters with the Holocaust authors, I shall maintain this practice.

3 *Golems* alternates between a third-person narrator and two first-person narrators in Ariel and Oliver.
4 Rosenbaum quotes this scene while introducing Borowski (62).

Works Cited

Améry, Jean. *At the Mind's Limits: Contemplations by a Survivor on Auschwitz and Its Realities* (Translated by Sidney Rosenfeld and Stella P. Rosenfeld). Indiana University Press, 1980.

Assmann, Aleida. "Transformations of Holocaust memory: Frames of transmission and mediation." In *Holocaust Cinema in the Twenty-First Century: Memory, Images, and the Ethics of Representation*, edited by Oleksandr Kobrynskyy and Gerd Bayer. Wallflower Press, 2015, pp. 23–40.

Bernard-Donals, Michael. *Forgetful Memory: Representation and Remembrance in the Wake of the Holocaust*. SUNY Press, 2009.

Borowski, Tadeusz. "This way for the gas, ladies and gentlemen." In *This Way for the Gas, Ladies and Gentlemen* (Translated by Barbara Vedder). Penguin, 1976, pp. 29–49.

Ebbrecht, Tobias. "Migrating images: Iconic images of the Holocaust and the representation of war in popular film." *Shofar: An Interdisciplinary Journal of Jewish Studies*, vol. 28, no. 4, 2010, pp. 86–103.

Gelder, Ken. *Popular Fiction: The Logics and Practices of a Literary Field*. Routledge, 2004.

Greene, Richard Allen. "A shadow over Europe: CNN poll reveals depth of anti-semitism in Europe." *CNN*, Nov. 2018, www.cnn.com/interactive/2018/11/europe/antisemitism-poll-2018-intl/

Levi, Primo. *Survival in Auschwitz: The Nazi Assault on Humanity* (Translated by Stuart Woolf). Touchstone, 1996.

———. "The Gray Zone." In *The Drowned and the Saved* (Translated by Raymond Rosenthal). Vintage, 1989, pp. 36–69.

Metz, Walter C. "Show me the Shoah: Generic experience and spectatorship in popular representations of the Holocaust." *Shofar: An Interdisciplinary Journal of Jewish Studies*, vol. 27, no. 1, 2008, pp. 16–35.

Murphy, Bernice. *Key Concepts in Contemporary Popular Fiction*. Edinburgh University Press, 2017.

Novick, Peter. *The Holocaust in American Life*. Mariner, 2000.

Rauch, Stefanie. "Understanding the Holocaust through film: Audience reception between preconceptions and media effects." *History & Memory*, vol. 30, no. 1, 2018, pp. 151–188.

Rosenbaum, Thane. *The Golems of Gotham*. Harper Perennial, 2003.

Rothberg, Michael. *Traumatic Realism: The Demands of Holocaust Representation*. University of Minnesota Press, 2000.

Royal, Derek Parker. "An interview with Thane Rosenbaum." *Contemporary Literature*, vol. 48, no. 1, 2007, pp. 1–28.

———. "Fragmenting the post-Holocaust subject: Uses of the short story cycle in Thane Rosenbaum's Elijah Visible." *Modern Jewish Studies*, vol. 14, no. 4, 2006, pp. 72–89.

Tweraser, Felix. "Imagining the Holocaust: The problems and promise of representation." *Rendezvous: Journal of Arts and Letters*, vol. 34, no. 1, 2000, pp. 1–9.

2 Playing With the Unspeakable

The Holocaust and Videogames

Iker Itoiz Ciáurriz

In 2018 a scandal arose around the videogame *The Cost of Freedom*. Developed by a Ukrainian company, the game allowed you to play as SS guards at an Auschwitz-like Nazi death camp, where you could torture and send prisoners to the gas chamber. Part of the scandal focused on the fact of "interactivity" the game allowed, as the players could decide who lived or died in the camp. It was widely condemned as outrageous by critics including the Auschwitz-Birkenau Memorial and Museum in Poland, for making entertainment out of human suffering. Polish journalist Wojciech Wybranowski reportedly thought it might be an elaborate Russian attempt to put a strain on Polish-Ukrainian relations.[1] The game was put on hold and the location was changed to Antarctica to avoid any historical reference (Bridge).

The prior example shows the role that videogames can play to shape Popular Culture. In response to the scandal, the Polish government opened an investigation to see whether the videogame was insulting the Polish nation and encouraging fascist regimes. The outrage was not only due to the representation of an Auschwitz-like Nazi death camp but owed to the fact that you could "play" as one of the guards. While videogames today represent an important aspect of Popular Culture, especially for young people, they are underexplored as creators of historical narratives and depositors of collective memory.[2] While World War II is a frequent theme for videogames, such as bestseller *Call of Duty* or *Medal of Honor*, the Holocaust is almost never mentioned, and elements associated with it (Nazi ideology, organizations, symbols, leaders, and particularly military units) are frequently excluded. The few videogames that represent it (e.g., *Prisoners of War, The Great Evasion, Call of Duty: WWII, The Cost of Freedom*) tend to obscure or misrepresent many elements of the Holocaust. It is relatively uncontroversial to argue that, for most people, imagery and understandings drawn from popular media probably construct the past as much as, if not more than, the books of professional historians.[3] Therefore, I believe, we need to consider videogames, as we regard other cultural productions like films, literature, and television shows, as constructers of historical memories. I argue that videogames also shape how we interact with the past. They create images, memories, and narratives, and, as such, it is important to understand how recent videogames have portrayed the Holocaust.

Popular Culture is not as easy to define as it looks at first sight. Conventionally, culture has been defined as:

DOI: 10.4324/9781003251224-4

a means of organizing and stabilizing communal life and everyday activities through specific beliefs, rituals, rites, performance, art forms, symbols, language, clothing, food, music, dance, and other human expressive, intellectual, and communicative pursuits and faculties that are associated with a group of people at a particular period of time.

(Danesi 15)

From this definition of culture, historian Peter Burke distinguished between "High Culture," for the privileged, and "Popular Culture," for the majority (23–65). Such a perspective has led to the classic definition of Popular Culture as "the set of practices, beliefs, and objects that embody the most broadly shared meanings of a social system. It includes media objects, entertainment and leisure, fashion and trends, and linguistic connections, among other things" (Kidd). Videogames constitute the most recent example of Popular Culture as millions around the world play them. They represent a "virtual" reality. This characteristic has drawn attention when they represent historical events such as the Holocaust. Understandably, through a historiographical lens, there have been frequent debates on whether the Holocaust can be represented historically (e.g., Magilow & Silverman, Friedländer). Since the boom in Holocaust representation in the '60s and '70s, there is a growing interest in knowing about the Holocaust at the cost of what Anne Rothe calls "selling the pain." The Holocaust experience represents "a very condensed version of most of what life is about: it contains a great many existential questions that we manage to avoid in our daily living, often through preoccupations with trivia" (Laub 72). In this chapter, what I expect to show is how the Holocaust has been portrayed in recent videogames. While the Holocaust had not earlier been sufficiently represented in videogames, there has been an increase in recent years with the rise of indie games. Indie (independent videogame development) games are videogames commonly created by individuals or small teams of developers and usually without significant financial support from videogame publishers or any other source. These games may take years to build from the ground up or can be completed in a matter of days or even hours depending on complexity, participants, and design goal. From 2008, the success of *The Dark Ascent, Limbo,* and *Little Nightmares* have popularized these kinds of videogames. Contrary to high-cost productions, their low-budget has helped them to explore themes that are not usually portrayed in videogames such as *Call of Duty* as their market target is relatively small.

By reflecting on the theoretical perspectives on how videogames and players interact with the past and by focusing on particular examples, I aim to show how recent videogames have attempted to represent the Holocaust. Due to the word limit of the chapter, I will not focus on every game that has engaged with the Holocaust. On the contrary, I have decided to choose some recent examples that highlight the representation of the Holocaust in videogames. First, I will focus on the bestseller *Call of Duty*, a mass-production, and one of its last installment *Call of Duty WWII* that, for the first time, tried to represent the Holocaust and failed. Second, I will focus on some indie productions in the Czech Republic and Poland by focusing on *Attentat 1942* and *My Memory of Us* respectively. These games adopt opposite

50 *Iker Itoiz Ciáurriz*

approaches to the representation of the Holocaust.[4] While the first looks for accuracy and appeals to the conscience of the third-generation of survivors, that is, the grandchildren of survivors, on the occupation of Czechoslovakia and the Holocaust, the second fails in its use of metaphors to represent the Holocaust. In fact, one can argue that it vindicates the Poles who fought the Nazis during Poland's occupation, but not the Jews. To sum up, I hope to encourage further reflections on the role of videogames not only in the way they represent the Holocaust but also the past in general.

Representing the Unspeakable?

Call of Duty WWII *and the Concentration Camps*

Call of Duty is one of the most famous shoot-game videogames from the past two decades. Usually, the common background is World War II—only in the last decade have they experimented with other scenarios. However, until *Call of Duty* in 2017, the Holocaust was not only never represented, but it was not even mentioned. In the last installment of the series, *Call of Duty WWII*, a prisoner camp was represented in the epilogue of the game.

To summarize briefly, the game's campaign is set in the European theater and is centered around a squad in the First Infantry Division following its battles on the Western Front and set mainly in the historical events of Operation Overlord. The player controls Ronald "Red" Daniels alongside his squad mates, showing powerful resemblance to the HBO television show *Bands of Brothers* Close to the end of the game, American soldier Zussman is captured and taken to a German prisoner of war camp, Stalag IX-B. There, he is interrogated on his Jewish heritage by SS officer Metz and then beaten and sent to a concentration camp. In the epilogue of the game, the main characters and the squad head into Germany, liberating concentration camps in search of Zussman, eventually reaching the Berga concentration camp, which they find abandoned; the camp's survivors had been sent on a death march. Daniels finds and saves Zussman by killing Metz before he can execute him.

From the beginning, the game sparked a lot of controversy on how the concentration camp, in fact, a prisoner camp, was represented. Just before the game was published, its senior creative director, Bret Robbins, had said in an interview that "some very, very dark things happened during this conflict [World War II] and it felt wrong for us to ignore that," indicating the Holocaust, though he did not mention it. He continued, "It's an unfortunate part of the history, but . . . you can't tell an authentic, truthful story without going there. So we went there" (Pink). When the American troops arrived at the camp and they walked slowly through the abandoned hut, one of the soldiers said, "These were our guys." "Take out your camera," another responded, "The world's got to know." "They were beaten, starved, and worked to the bone," we are told in voice-over, but it soon becomes clear that the subject of lament is not the Jews or other civilians but fellow American soldiers. We see two of them, tied to wooden posts and shot. It is the only evidence of Nazi barbarism in the game, and its victims are not Jews, women, or children, but men in uniform. Here lies the biggest controversy; the American soldiers are shocked because it was their soldiers who had been murdered, and it did not involve the Holocaust per se. Moreover, there is no mention of the Jews as victims. Even though Zussman is implied to be Jewish, he is sent to the camp because he had been captured as a solider. This shows the problems of representing the Jewish and non-Jewish victims of the Holocaust as have been theorized by Peter Hayes (3–36).

The representation of the camps has always been complicated in videogames. The example of *Call of Duty WWII* reflects one problem related to design: Can the present technology faithfully represent the camps as they were? Analyzing instances where videogames generated controversy by including content perceived as inappropriate, previous research found that games are often seen as an unsuitable medium for exploring contentious and/or serious themes. Controversies seem to revolve around two particular issues. First, the fear that placing serious themes into a ludic frame in which they inevitably gain a double meaning (as both representational and gameplay elements) means these themes risk becoming trivialized because players might only attend to their gameplay meaning, thus treating them less respectfully than they deserve. The second, related fear revolves around the appropriateness of particular playable positions, that is, instances where a game "casts at least some of the players in the role of the generally perceived historical antagonist and thus allows the players to re-enact historical episodes of exploitation, cruelty, and abuse through their in-game actions" (Chapman and Linderoth 140). A second problem relates to how prisoner camps are preferred to the concentration camps, the main symbol of the Holocaust.

Attentat 1942 *and the Accuracy of the Occupation*

If *Call of Duty WWII* had been a failed attempt of mass production to represent the Holocaust, *Attentat 1942* (2017) became an example of how videogames could represent the traumatic past. *Attentat 1942* is a Czech point-and-click adventure game, in which players assume the role of Jindřich Jelínek's grandchild. Jelínek was arrested by the Gestapo shortly after the assassination of Reinhard Heydrich, who was in charge of the Nazi-occupied Czech lands and the leading architect of the Holocaust. The objective of the game is to establish what role Jelínek played in the attack as well as the reasons for his arrest. Throughout the investigation, players interview eyewitnesses, discover the family's back story, and learn more about life in the Protectorate of Bohemia and Moravia. Contrary to the creation of *Call of Duty*, this game was developed by Charles University and the Czech Academy of Sciences inside the project "Czechoslovakia 38–89," which seeks to cover different events in the contemporary history of the country.

By following the story of Jelínek's grandchild, the game looks at the Nazi occupation of Czechoslovakia by weaving together archival footage, testimonies from civilians who lived under German occupation, interactive comics, and other innovative forms that make gameplay not only entertaining but edifying. Beyond how

52 *Iker Itoiz Ciáurriz*

the past is represented, *Attentat 1942* tries to explore the trauma and hidden family histories through a combination of full motion video-style interviews with actors, encyclopedia articles, historical footage, and animated segments. Almost every family in Eastern Europe and not just in Czechoslovakia had been affected by the war and the Holocaust. However, due to different reasons, they tend not to speak about it. This has been studied by historians such as Annette Wieviorka, Victoria Aarons, and Alan L. Berger. By following the story of Jelínek's grandchild, the game explores how the third generation looks at the past, in particular their familial past. Because the third generation has not been directly implicated in the aftereffects of the trauma and the restitution for loss, the generation of grandchildren takes their place on the stage of history and enters the landscape of memory in pursuit of the tapestry of familial connections and continuity, of "unlocking family history and reactivating family roots" (Fossion et al 523). The game uses the resource of past objects such as radios, leaflets, passports, and diaries to trigger memories of the first generation. For instance, at the beginning of the game, the grandchild complains why his grandmother does not "throw away" the old radio. This triggers a memory of the grandmother about the day Reinhard Heydrich was assassinated and the grandfather was arrested, when they were both listening to the same radio.

One of the challenges of the developers was to translate these stories into the format of a game while remaining sensitive to the grave realities of history.[5] One of their solutions to avoid misrepresentation was to present the scenes that take place in the past as a fixed event for players to experience, with players making only microscopic decisions—such as where to hide an anti-Nazi leaflet before your grandfather's arrest—that have no impact on the overall outcome. These moments accompany most of the interviews. However, in this attempt to avoid misrepresentation, the developers fell into the paradox presented by Aarons and Berger that the third generation "arises from the tension between knowing and not knowing, direct and indirect witnessing, in the tenuous transfer of memory and trauma. . . . [T]he third generation, the generation of grand children of survivors, comes to the past through a far more circuitous passage" (Aarons and Berger 63). The player—and the third generation—must navigate with an inexact, approximate map, a broken narrative. Theirs is a "re-created past," a matter of "filling in gaps, of putting scraps together" (64). This highlights the question raised by Saul Friendländer back in 1992 that we cannot "represent" the Holocaust due to an inability to comprehend it fully (2).

The game has also suffered from censorship by other countries such as Germany, France, Russia, and Austria because of its search for accuracy. In particular, one of the problems faced by the game is that it shows Nazis and Nazi symbology. Google has rejected the game several times because it argues it could foster hate (McAloon). As the developers tweeted, "How we're supposed to make an historically-accurate game about WW2 horrors without Nazis? We don't know" (McAloon). The censorship shows the problems when developers try to represent traumatic moments such as the Holocaust. One common criticism against videogames that are set in World War II is how they tend to obscure the realities of the Holocaust, as they present a narrative of good and evil that avoid clear representation of the

Playing With the Unspeakable 53

Holocaust (in any form) and its victims (the Jews mainly, but also other persecuted groups). Nonetheless, this example with Google proved that if showing clear representations lead to your game being banned, why would you engage in such representations at all?

Polish Videogames and the Memory of the Holocaust

If *Call of Duty WWII* was a failed attempt of representation and *Attentat 1942* was a Czech production that tried to represent the past as it was, looking for accuracy, the approach of some Polish videogames to World War II and occupation is much more complicated. At the beginning of 2018, matters of Polish historical memory became the topic of international news when the Polish government found itself in the midst of a diplomatic row over an amendment to the law pertaining to the Institute of National Remembrance (often referred to by foreign news media as the "Holocaust Memory Law" or "Polish Memory Law"). The amendment sought to impose sanctions of up to three years of imprisonment to anyone who attributes "responsibility or co-responsibility to the Polish nation or state for crimes committed by the German Third Reich" (Belavusau and Wójcik). This was widely interpreted internationally as an attempt to whitewash Polish history of World War II and, especially, to hide or downplay antisemitic acts committed by regular Polish people without coercion from Nazi Germany (Zubrzycki). As Jannie Hole has shown, much of the public memory of the Polish during World War II is conflicted as to what degree non-Jewish Poles were implicated in anti-Jewish violence. Examples of research referring to the implication of the non-Jewish Poles in this context include Jan Grabowski's *Hunt for the Jews,* which mentions the practices by Poles of seeking out Jews in hiding during the war to turn them over to the Nazis, and Jan Gross's *Neighbours,* which documented the roundup and mass killing of the Jewish members of a small town by their non-Jewish neighbors (1–20).

Piotr Sterczewski has studied the role of games, including videogames, in the shaping of historical memory. As he has established, Polish historical board games often "serve as 'machines of narrative security,' repeating and reinforcing mainstream, government-backed views of Poland's past and present, painting a picture of a brave, heroic, defiant and united nation" (130). Sterczewski does not deny that they can also create alternative memories to the hegemonic discourses; however, he argues that, in the case of Poland, the role of the PiS (Law and Justice, Prawo i Sprawiedliwość) and its defense of the national identity made it difficult to have alternative games. While Poland has many games, including videogames, dealing with World War II, many do not mention the Holocaust. In fact, the majority focus on the Rising of Warsaw in 1944—a "proud national moment" in historical memory in Poland (Sterczewski, par. 4). Due to paucity of space, Sterczewski, having already focused on many games, does not mention one of the latest games published: *My Memory of Us.* This videogame does not mention the Holocaust directly, but its plot centers on two young friends, one of whom, as a "red person," is hunted by an extremely Nazi-looking robot army.[6]

54   *Iker Itoiz Ciáurriz*

My Memory of Us (2018), a game by Polish developer Juggler Games that focuses on the plight of two Polish children during a robot uprising, serves as an allegory for World War II. This puzzle platformer aims to pay tribute to the Polish citizens who lost their lives during the Nazi occupation, especially those who provided shelter and help to the people around them. The game feels like it intends to be respectful, especially in the collectible "memories" that tell you more about the real-world people who inspired the game.

A bigger problem is the concept of dressing up a Nazi invasion as a robot invasion. The plot's framing device—that the boy, now an old man voiced by Patrick Stewart, is telling a story to a young girl who visits his bookshop—can only justify the game's euphemisms so far. The conceit is that the story is being changed to make it child-appropriate and more exciting; in practice, though, obscuring the truth of the story just makes things weird. Stewart delivers his lines, set against static cutscenes between missions, with his trademark timbre, but it is hard to get past the fact that the game has taken something horrific and made it cute. Partway through the game, the girl is marked as "red" by the robot army. The game's "red" people wear red clothing, painted on by the robots' machines, and suddenly find themselves treated like lesser beings by everyone. It is a tribute to the girl in the red coat from *Schindler's List*, but as a metaphor for how the Polish Jews were treated, it feels too clumsy and far from the horror of what it is meant to fill in for, especially when it seems like the citizens being painted are being chosen, essentially, at random.

The Concentration Camp in Videogames

As I have been showing in this chapter, the Holocaust is generally eluded to in videogame representation. It is neither mentioned nor critically portrayed. However, there have been moments when videogames have tried to portray the concentration camp. In the earlier 2000s, there was an important attempt with videogames *Prisoner of War* (2002) and *The Great Evasion* (2003) that did not represent concentration camps but prisoner camps during World War II.

In *Prisoner of War* (POW), we play as an American pilot who has been kidnapped by the Nazi armies. The game never mentions that they were Nazis or that it was World War II. However, not only are the characters portrayed in World War II uniforms, but the soldiers also speak English in a strong German accent and there are constant mentions of the complications in the Russian front. POW is quite different from other stealth games in that, although other stealth games utilize some small form of violence for the players to achieve its objectives, this game portrays little to no violence. For example, if the Nazi guards on duty spot the player acting suspiciously, they will not shoot on sight. Instead, they will call on the player to cease his activity. If the player continues to disobey the guard, the guards will shoot him. It would never kill the player, just send him to the infirmary. The everyday life in the camp includes the morning and evening calls, two meals, time for physical exercise in the morning, and break time in the afternoon, something unlikely in the context of concentration camps and, to some extent, in the prisoner camps.

Playing With the Unspeakable   55

This "positive" representation of the prisoner camps happened as the game was developed by a US company. During the game, players visit Stalag Luft and Colditz, two famous prisoner camps for US and UK prisoners of war. As Simon Mackenzie has shown, Colditz played a major role in shaping perception of the POW experience in Nazi Germany, an experience in which escaping is assumed to be paramount. However, the reality of Colditz was far more complicated than the myth and representations created after World War II in British culture (1–35).[7] A closer reference to the Holocaust is Private Michael Kapowski, a Polish Jew prisoner in Colditz, who disappears in the last mission of the game, set in the spring of 1945, presumably taken to a Jewish concentration camp. However, this is never explicitly mentioned; it is the player who assumes that is what happened to Kapowski.

Perhaps, one of the most interesting attempts to represent the Holocaust in videogames is *Witness Auschwitz* by the Italian company Studio 101%. A VR (virtual reality) game, *Witness Auschwitz* is not a game per se but an education tool currently in development that will allow users to explore the most infamous of the Nazi camps. Presented in 2017, it has only shown the opening sequence, at the entrance to Birkenau, which, even without any faces visible, the camp slowly moving closer, with the barking of dogs interspersed with the howling of sirens, was disturbing.

What is interesting is the attempt to use technology and videogames to teach about the Holocaust. However, since the beginning, controversy erupted on whether it was possible to represent the Holocaust in a videogame. According to creative director Daniele Azara, "*Witness: Auschwitz* is a completely immersive experience that allows users to interact with the world that surrounds them, with the people, with themselves, and become 'witnesses' to one of the most tragic events in the history of humanity." In herview:

> The project is a new approach to teaching about the Shoah [the Hebrew word for the Holocaust]. The context, generated in VR, increases the emotional engagement and the experience is imprinted in the mind in a completely innovative way compared to traditional media.
>
> (McKeand)

Based on testimonials of the people who stayed there and supported by the Union of Italian Jewish Communities (UCEI), the game tries to represent everyday life in the camps and avoid the most known violent representation of the Holocaust.

Witness: Auschwitz raises important questions about the uses, ethics, and purpose of virtual-reality technology. VR is an incredible tool, but the question remains: Should its immersive nature be used to portray such weighty experiences? Concerns have been raised about the ability of VR to desensitize the user to graphic imagery, but the reverse could also be true. While the team in this instance is avoiding the more violent imagery of the time, similar projects will have to weigh the potential for viewers to be traumatized, especially when dealing with highly accurate representations of real-life events. This is what happened with *The Cost of Freedom*, the videogame that started this article. The possibility to play as a SS guard

56   *Iker Itoiz Ciáurriz*

and to send prisoner to the gas chamber sparked a strong controversy. These two cases show different possibilities on the way videogames can shape representations of the Holocaust. In his classic study of videogames, James Paul Gee argued that videogames can be powerful tools to teach kids; however, *The Cost of Freedom* also shows the potentialities for the opposite. Making the Holocaust an episode "to play" and "enjoy," rather than an educational tool, complicates the possibilities to represent the Holocaust in Popular Culture (1–12, and 207–212).

Conclusion

Are the Holocaust and videogames compatible? Can videogames represent the Holocaust? From mass productions to indie games, there is an inner tension between the representation of the Holocaust, looking for "authenticity," if this is possible, and the fact that videogames are interactive. You do not simply watch or read a videogame, but on the contrary, you play an active role in it. Based on the analysis presented in this chapter, one could mention three main problems/findings:

First, it is the problem of representation, mainly, how the Holocaust is shown with the help of current technology. The graphics and design play a huge role in developers' decision. Any representation of the Holocaust is a creative decision taken by the developers. It undermines the possibilities of "representation" or "authenticity." What is seen on the screen is a decision taken by the developers, and the people who play will absorb this vision. It does not mean they accept it uncritically, but their "image" of the Holocaust would be biased by what they are showed while playing.

Second, it is the problem of the Holocaust per se, the murder of millions of Jews and non-Jews. One common element among these videogames is how they tend to obscure the realities of the Holocaust, as they present a narrative of good and evil that avoids clear representations of the actuality of the Holocaust (in any of their forms) and its victims (the Jews mainly, but also other persecuted groups). This whitewashing of the Holocaust has far-reaching consequences. Millions of players play a mass production like *Call of Duty WWII*, but no mention of the Holocaust is made.

A third problem, envisaged with *Witness: Auschwitz* and exacerbated with *The Cost of Freedom*, is the role of interaction and interactivity in videogames. *Attentat 1942* avoided misrepresentations by showing the past as a fixed event for players to experience, with players only making microscopic decisions. Yet, as Barbie Zelizer highlights, "We know that the visualization works best when it plays to the schematic, iconic, and simplistic features of a representation, we have not yet figured out the ways in which those dimensions facilitate our understanding of real-life events in certain ways and not others" (1). *The Cost of Freedom* was supposed to allow you to play as a SS guard at an Auschwitz-like Nazi death camp, where you could torture and send prisoners to the gas chamber. In her classic study about "Dark Tourism," Kathryn N. McDaniel argues the possibility of dark tourism for teaching about the past. As she mentions:

Playing With the Unspeakable   57

These simulated journeys [like videogames] bring the past into the present, encourage empathy for past peoples, provide opportunities for public grieving and spiritual questioning, produce vicarious thrills and chills, offer solace for tragic losses, and invite reflections on the possibility of catastrophe in the here-and-now.

(McDaniel 2)

In sum, videogames can be important tools for teaching about the past and, in particular, the Holocaust for future generations, as James Paul Gee argues. They create images, memories, and narratives, and, as such, it is important to understand how recent videogames have portrayed the Holocaust. We must understand the role they play, and we must use them to teach about the "dark" moments of our history. Whether videogames, as Popular Culture, can represent the Holocaust is not yet clear. As we have seen, even with the possibilities videogames open up, it is hard, almost impossible, to reconcile the many tensions involving the representation of the Holocaust.

Notes

1 Since the elections of PiS (Law and Justice), the foreign relations between Germany and Ukraine have been tense (Jasiewicz 1573–1590).
2 It is calculated that at the moment there are more than 2.5 billion video-gamers and it is expected a profit in videogames market to be worth over 90 billion U.S. dollars. Data collected from "2000 Video Game Industry Statistic, Trends & Data" in www.wepc.com/news/video-game-statistics/ (visited 8–7–2020).
3 An attempt to study the role of videogames in shaping historical memory is Adam Chapman's work (2016).
4 As noted by Andrew B.R. Elliot and Matthew Wilhelm Kapell, besides whether videogames search for historical accuracy or not, they also show how the past is seen by the developers and what effect this might have in the players (8).
5 For an account of the difficulties carried by the developers in representing the past in *The Washington Post* (2020).
6 The metaphor of Nazis like robots or zombies happened frequently in videogames such as *Return to Castle Wolfenstein* or *Call of Duty* as a sub-mode of the videogames (Gee, 123 and Chapman 91–111).
7 See: Simon P. Mackenzie, *The Colditz Myth: British and Commonwealth Prisoners of War in Nazi Germany* (Oxford: Oxford University Press, 2006), especially the introduction.

Works Cited

Aarons, Victoria and Alan L. Berger. *Third Generation Holocaust Representation: Trauma, History, and Memory*. Northeastern University Press, 2017.
Belavusau, Uladzislau and Anna Wójick. "Polish memory law: When history becomes a source of mistrust." *New Eastern Europe*, 19 Feb. 2018, https://neweasterneurope.eu/2018/02/19/polish-memory-law-history-becomes-source-mistrust/. Accessed 28 Nov. 2021.
Bridge, Mark. "Fury over death camp video game Cost of Freedom that offers players Nazi guard role." *The Times*, 2 Nov. 2018, www.thetimes.co.uk/article/fury-over-death-camp-video-game-cost-of-freedom-that-offers-players-nazi-guard-role-56g633d0j. Accessed 8 Jul. 2020.

58   Iker Itoiz Ciáurriz

Chapman, Adam. *Digital Games as History: How Videogames Represent the Past and Offer Access to Historical Practice.* Routledge, 2016.

———. "Playing the historical fantastic: Zombies, mecha-nazis and making meaning about the past through metaphor." In *War Games: Memory, Militarism and the Subject of Play*, edited by Holger Pòtzsch. Bloomsbury Academic, 2019, pp. 91–111.

Chapman, Adam and Jonas Linderoth. "Exploring the limits of play: A case study of representations of Nazism in games." In *The Dark Side of Game Play: Controversial Issues in Playful Environments*, edited by Torill Elvira Mortensen, Jonas Linderoth and Ashely M. L. Brown. Routledge, 2015, pp. 137–154.

Elliot, Andrew and Wilhelm Kapell. "Introduction: To build a past that will 'stand the test of time'—Discovering historical facts, assembling historical narratives." In *Playing with the Past: Digital Games and the Simulation of History*, edited by Andrew B. R. Elliot and Matthew Wilhelm Kapell. Bloomsbury Academic, 2013, pp. 1–30.

Fossion, Pierre, Laurent Servais, Mari-Carmen Rejas, Isy Pelc and Hirsch Siegi. "Family approach with grandchildren of Holocaust survivors." *American Journal of Psychotherapy*, vo. 57, no. 4, 2003, pp. 519–527.

Friendländer, Saul. "Introduction." In *Probing the Limits of Representation: Nazism and the 'Final Solution'*, edited by Saul Friendländer. Harvard University Press, 1992, pp. 1–21.

———, editor. *Probing the Limits of Representation: Nazism and the 'Final Solution.'* Harvard University Press, 1992.

Gardner, Elliot. "Does a VR Auschwitz simulation cross an ethical line." *ALPHR*, 4 Oct. 2017, www.alphr.com/life-culture/1007241/does-a-vr-auschwitz-simulation-cross-an-ethical-line/. Accessed 28 Nov. 2021.

Hayes, Peter. *Why?: Explaining the Holocaust.* Norton, 2017.

Hole, Jannie. *The Politics of Trauma and Memory Activism. Polish-Jewish Relations Today.* Palgrave Macmillan, 2018.

Hugo Jarausch, Konrad. *After Hitler: Recivilizing Germans, 1945–1995.* Oxford University Press, 2016.

Jasiewicz, Joanna. "When the past matters: Memory politics and ethnic relations in Poland." *Ethnic and Racial Studies*, vol. 38, no. 9, pp. 1573–1590.

Kidd, Dustin. "Popular culture." *Oxford Bibliographies*, www.oxfordbibliographies.com/view/document/obo-9780199756384/obo-9780199756384-0193.xml. Accessed 28 Nov. 2021.

Laub, Dori. "Bearing witness, or the vicissitudes of listening." In *Testimony: Crises of Witnessing in Literature, Psychoanalysis, and History*, edited by Soshana Felman and Dori Laub. Routledge, 1992, pp. 57–74.

Limmund Discussion: Can It Ever Be Appropriate for a Videogame to Depict Elements of the Holocaust? www.thejc.com/news/uk-news/far-more-than-a-game-a-discussion-of-the-depiction-of-the-holocaust-in-video-games-1.474328. Accessed 8 Jul. 2020.

Mackenzie, Simon. *The Colditz Myth: British and Commonwealth Prisoners of War in Nazi Germany.* Oxford University Press, 2006.

Magilow, Daniel H. and Lisa Silverman. *Holocaust Representations in History. An Introduction.* Bloomsbury, 2015.

McAloon, Alissa. *Despite Gov't Approval, Google Rejects Attentat 1942 from Google Play Store in Germany*, www.gamasutra.com/view/news/366724/Despite_govt_approval_Google_rejects_Attentat_1942_from_Google_Play_Store_in_Germany.php. Accessed 28 Jul. 2020.

McDaniel, Kathryn N. "Introduction to virtual dark tourism: Disaster in the space of the imagination." In *Virtual Dark Tourism. Ghost Roads*, edited by Kathryn N. McDaniel. Palgrave Macmillan, 2018, pp. 1–18.

McKeand, Kirk. "Videogames' portrayal of the Holocaust does disservice to both players and victims." *PC Games*, 18 Jan. 2018, www.pcgamesn.com/jewish-opinions-on-nazis-in-videogames. Accessed 28 Nov. 2021.

Parker, Laura A. "Inside controversial game that's tackling the Holocaust." *Rolling Stone*, 31 Aug. 2016, www.rollingstone.com/culture/culture-news/inside-controversial-game-thats-tackling-the-holocaust-251102/. Accessed 22 Jul. 2020.

Paul Gee, James. *What Video Games Have to Teach Us about Learning and Literacy*. Palgrave Macmillan, 2003.

Pink, Aiden. "New World War II 'Call of Duty' video game will depict the Holocaust." *Forward*, 3 May 2017, https://forward.com/fast-forward/370790/new-world-war-ii-call-of-duty-video-game-will-depict-the-holocaust/. Accessed 28 Nov. 2021.

Rothe, Anne. *Popular Trauma Culture. Selling the Pain of Others in the Mass Media*. Rutgers University Press, 2011.

Sterczewski, Piotr. "Machine(s) of narrative security: Mnemonic hegemony and Polish games about violence conflicts." In *War Games: Memory, Militarism and the Subject of Play*, edited by Holger Pèotzsch. Bloomsbury Academic, 2019, pp. 111–135.

———. "This uprising of mine: Game conventions, cultural memory and civilian experience of war in Polish games." *Game Studies*, vol. 16, no. 2, gamestudies.org/1602/articles/sterczewski. Accessed 12 Jul. 2020.

WEPC, *Video Game Industry Statistic, Trends & Data*, 2000, www.wepc.com/news/video-game-statistics/. Accessed 8 Jul. 2020.

Wieviorka, Annette. *The Era of the Witness*. Cornell University Press, 2006.

Yarwood, Jack. "Can videogames tactfully handle Nazism and its aftermath? These Czech historians say yes." *The Washington Post*, 6 Jul. 2020, www.washingtonpost.com/video-games/2020/07/06/can-video-games-tactfully-handle-nazism-its-aftermath-these-czech-historians-say-yes/. Accessed 28 Nov. 2021.

Zelizer, Barbie. "Introduction: On visualizing the Holocaust." In *Visual Culture and the Holocaust*, edited by Barbie Zelizer. The Athlone Press, 2001, pp. 1–12.

Zubrzycki, Geneviève. "New 'Holocaust law' highlights crisis in Polish identity." *The Conversation*, 12 Feb. 2018, theconversation.com/new-holocaust-law-highlights-crisis-in-polish-identity-91283. Accessed 14 Jul. 2020.

3 Representation, Appropriation, and Popular Culture

Food and the Holocaust in Roman Polanski's *The Pianist*

Ved Prakash

The Holocaust was a state-sponsored pogrom in which millions of Jews and other so-called invalid individuals were persecuted in the name of maintaining the purity of race. The incarceration of Jews and other unaccepted subjects was primarily based upon the policy and politics of abhorrence. One of the ways to segregate the Jews or kill the Jews was the tool of starvation. All those who were confined within the borders of the concentration camps or ghettos were given basic meals that would just be enough to keep the Jews alive. The Wiener Holocaust Library, one of world's leading and extensive archives on the Holocaust, formed in 1933, mentions, on the home page of its website, that food was never enough inside the camps for prisoners and the situation deteriorated with the arrival of the Second World War. Before the war, porridge or bread along with tea or low-cost coffee would be served for breakfast, vegetable soup with bread at lunch, and some more soup for dinner. With the outbreak of war in January 1940, food became insufficient; it got reduced to soup for lunch as well as dinner with just one piece of bread (The Wiener Holocaust Library).

The present chapter looks at the issue of survival and death concerning food. The chapter examines the treatment and representation of food through *The Pianist*. The chapter will further attempt to analyze whether Polanski's *The Pianist*, being a popular text, does justice to the Holocaust memory? It also aims to understand whether the genre of film simplifies the Holocaust for the consumption of the mass. Therefore, the question that becomes relevant is how much can one rely on cinema to understand the Holocaust and the struggle, suffering, and hunger that people had to face within the border of ghettos. Within Popular Culture, there have been multiple narratives representing the Holocaust with very little regard whether the narratives and their representation are authentic. Moreover, historians fear that Popular Culture and the pattern of mass production and consumption of images may replace the historical details and accounts of Holocaust survivors and may further complicate the public memory of the Holocaust. The chapter addresses some of these issues while critically engaging with Roman Polanski's film *The Pianist* (2002). The film is based on the memoir (1946) of the same name by Wladyslaw Szpilman. The memoir is a first-person narrative recounting the horrors of Nazi rule faced by Szpilman. The film essentially looks at the Warsaw ghetto located in Poland and attempts to foreground the methodology of exploitation and suffering

DOI: 10.4324/9781003251224-5

that was inflicted upon the Jews and the Poles. Szpilman writes that people in the ghetto had to live in deplorable conditions with no money or secret savings and had to earn their bread by trading (67). In this context, the chapter explores whether Popular Culture mediums, such as cinema, are adequate enough to document the suffering of the Jews with reference to food and what food meant during the Holocaust. While the discipline of film studies often addresses the issues of authenticity and representation when it comes to moving images, one cannot ignore the fact that imagination is an essential part of storytelling when it comes to cinema. How do we address the question of imagination and fiction with reference to the representation of an event like the Holocaust? French film theorist André Bazin writes that when a filmmaker is to adapt a literary text into a film, then s/he or they must possess enough visual imagination (42). If one is to agree with Bazin, then one can deduce that the film *The Pianist* based on the memoir titled *The Pianist: The Extraordinary True Story of One Man's Survival in Warsaw, 1939–1945* (1946), too, is a creation of various elements, some perhaps imaginary in nature. Can imagination be termed as authentic in nature? One argument that often comes up is that *The Pianist* by Polanski deals with the Holocaust with sincerity as Polanski himself has been the victim of the Holocaust. It should also be pointed out that Polanski was 6 years old when the Holocaust took place. While the trauma of what the Nazis did may have continued for years for Polanski, it should be noted that often personal memory tends to overlap with the collective memory in case of a tragic event. If such is the case, then the question of both remembering and forgetting becomes intriguing. The discipline of "life writing" argues that often the memory of a person also gets shaped by the memories of others and the circulation of dominant narratives within a society. Polanski's *The Pianist* is certainly not as dramatic as other Holocaust films; however, it still qualifies as a cinematic document based on a memoir and not a historical document.

Food and Culture

Food is a marker of culture and identity as well as individuals and occasions. While a lot has been written about the presence of food in communities and how food defines one's past as well as present, the pertinent question in the context of the Holocaust is the absence of food. What happens when the basic need of an individual is seen as an act of luxury? What happens when food, which determines one's survival, becomes the signifier of death and fretfulness? Linda Civitello writes that the ambit of food is quite vast. There are regulations about how a certain recipe is prepared. The act of passing food-related guidelines to generation after generation holds great significance as it defines the historicity of both food and communities. According to Civitello, how a particular food is cooked, the kind of utensils that are used for cooking, how food is served, and what time food is eaten, etc., have meaning (Civitello xiv).

Viktor E. Frankl talks about the everyday struggle that the Jews had to go through in the concentration camps. Several references to food come up while Frankl narrates the senselessness and futility of the Nazi's exercise regarding the

62   Ved Prakash

extermination of the Jews. The small piece of bread and thin soup which would be given to the Jewish people in the camp did not have enough nutritional value. Moreover, the constant anxiety about the well-being of acquaintances and family made things even more difficult (Frankl 40). It is important to highlight that the capos in camps would agree to work for the SS guards as this would ensure extra food, cigarettes, alcohol, and other privileges. Frankl writes, "While the ordinary prisoners had little or nothing to eat the Capos were never hungry" (16–17). Wolfgang Benz writes about the economic and social exclusion of the Jewish community by the National Socialist Party, which further led to the dispossession of individual and political rights (Benz 40). The complete isolation of the Jewish community forced many into a state of starvation, and the dispossession of labor was another tool to push the entire community toward hunger. This reflects the hierarchy in consumption and circulation of food. The ones who chose to stand with the oppressive system of Nazi control had ample access to food. The policy of segregation in the name of food represents the sinister nature of the Nazi party.

Hate, the Holocaust, and the Market

Cinema has been a capital-centric industry to a large extent. The progression concerning technology with reference to cinema has been a quest to bring people to the movie theatre and make them experience a spectacle in exchange for money. It is also a fact that within Popular Culture any subject can become the object of consumption and commodification depending upon how the mass responds to it. Sophia Marshman argues that the Holocaust has been popularized through narratives that affirm life over death, survival over destruction, marginalizing the testimony of a survivor and how the Holocaust gets appropriated through Popular Culture (1). Marshman further points out that it may take years for a person to articulate his or her violent past; however, testimonies and accounts of the Holocaust get marginalized and ignored by society (7). The rejection may also have to do with the preoccupation of the mass with the visual representation of pain, sorrow, misery, and suffering. Even though *The Pianist* is based on a memoir, the question of market while adapting a text into a film cannot be overlooked. Marshman argues that "a sanitised, popular image of the Holocaust has come to dominate the public imagination" (4). The film *The Pianist* certainly dominates the public imagination when it comes to the Holocaust, however, an adaptation cannot be termed as the absolute account of authenticity.

Alan Mintz theorizes the "constructivist" approach as one of the methods to engage with the Holocaust. This method has to do with the various cultural lens through which the Holocaust is portrayed. Mintz argues that Holocaust memory is shaped differently in different societies depending upon the availability of cultural tools of representation (xi). Mintz remarks that America's overidentification with the Holocaust has to do with it being the subject of profit in the public domain (3–4). Many believe that America played an important role in selling grief with reference to the Holocaust as a commodity. Anne Rothe, for instance, attempts to understand the Holocaust as an industry. While one may be apprehensive about the veracity of Holocaust accounts in relation to food narratives represented through film, one may rely on testimonies or life accounts to get a more genuine representation of food and hunger.

Frankl takes up the discussion around food among the Jews in the camps in his memoir. The prisoners would talk about Jewish dishes and recipes while working next to each other (41). This imagination of food would become an effective device to deal with the reality of the present. Films such as *Playing for Time* (1980), written by Arthur Miller and based on the famous musician Fania Fénelon's autobiography *The Musicians of Auschwitz* (1976), and *The Boy in the Striped Pajamas* (2008) by Mark Herman based on the novel (2006) of the same title by John Boyne, engage with the issue of food; however, the questions of appropriation and oversimplification of food narratives in films concerning the Holocaust cannot be ignored. *Playing for Time* gives the message that sharing food in the camps is important to retain some semblance of humanity. On the other hand, *The Boy in the Striped Pajamas* represents how food becomes one of the tropes of friendship between Shmuel, a Jew child prisoner in the camp, and Bruno, whose father works for the Nazi party. Food, indeed, played a significant role in saving lives during the Holocaust; however, films often pass off a simplified narrative of food history. This oversimplification may have to do with cinema supplying narratives that are appropriate for mass consumption.

The Pianist and the Question of Food

As it has been argued already, with the collapse of German democracy, the whole process of isolating the Jews started. The Nazi party through its fascist propaganda destabilized the whole of Europe. Jews were legally and socially segregated. There was a circulation of a notion that Jews were vile, clever, and harmful, and that they could deceive anyone for their gain. Erich S. Gruen writes about how the Jews were attacked for the practice of Sabbath[1] and how the fact that Jews did not consume pork was also frowned upon by the Christians. Casual observations such as Jews must worship the pig god and that is why they do not eat pork were an addition to the bizarre discourse around the behavior of worship by the Jews (267).

Adolf Hitler, in his autobiography *Mein Kampf*, claims that Jews do not have a culture of their own. Jews possess the property of other people, and whatever the Jews touch gets polluted. The observation that Jews are mere imitators, imitating other cultures (416–417) was an attempt to de-historicize the Jewish past. The idea of excluding, demonizing, and alienating a particular culture may have a discursive impact on how it is perceived in the public domain. The otherization of the Jewish community through narratives of falsity and propaganda resulted in the complete disregard of Jewish lives. In addition, the denial of food became one of the tools of isolation and segregation. Food was seldom a luxury; one had to ration food, keeping in mind the hostile conditions of existence. Many would save a tiny piece of bread in their pockets to sustain themselves. When the Jews had lost everything during the Holocaust, it was food that became the prized possession.

64   *Ved Prakash*

During the Holocaust, lives and labels changed overnight. The element of peripeteia can be found across narratives. Roman Polanski's *The Pianist* looks at the plight of the Polish Jews. The film revolves around Wladyslaw Szpilman, who was a famous pianist at the Polish Radio station in Warsaw; however, the occupation of Poland by the Germans during the war brings massive destruction in all spheres. The film begins with a radio announcement that Britain and France have declared war on the Nazi party and Poland is no longer alone. Many events take place before Poland, with the help of Russians, manages to overcome the brutality practiced by the Nazi party. It is important to mention that occupied Poland was one of the most significant sites of the massacre of Jews by the Nazis. After invading Poland in 1939, Germany used Auschwitz to keep Polish political prisoners. It is also a fact that Auschwitz was used to kill Jews by starving them or by simply sending them to the gas chambers.

The Pianist looks at the Holocaust from the point of view of Szpilman, who is constantly on a run as his Jewish identity may become the reason for his execution; therefore, he decides to hide in abandoned buildings. The film highlights how Jews were confined to the ghettos, where food was not easily available. In the ghetto, potatoes became the most consumed commodity as there was hardly any money to buy anything else. Szpilman's mother states how she is sick of cooking potatoes. While Szpilman's family embarks upon a journey of uncertainty, he decides to sell his piano to get money for food. The Jewish community was not prepared to process the sudden change of events. The culture of hate and killing the non-Aryan race was absurd. Needless to say, the ghettos that were assigned to the Jews were not spacious enough, so many decided to use the kitchen space not only for cooking but for sleeping, too, and the reference of the same appears in *The Pianist*. Leonard Quart writes that *The Pianist* highlights the systemic dehumanization of the Jews. The act of forcing them to wear the Star of David on their arms in public led to creating a binary between the Jewish and the non-Jewish community. The policy of identification and separation was directly linked with the atrocities that the Jews had to witness on a daily basis (43). The film also depicts the plight of the young boys who would supply food in and out of the holes made in the ghetto walls, risking their lives. *The Pianist* peeps into the struggle of Szpilman, who finds a place, close to the ghetto, to hide. Wladyslaw Szpilman witnesses the horrific developments in Warsaw and the constant conflict between the Polish army and the German troops. While Szpilman has taken a shelter in a flat all alone, his food is arranged by a Polish underground member who pays him a visit whenever it is safe. The film invests significantly in projecting the efforts Szpilman had to make in arranging food for himself when he constantly changes places to hide. While *The Pianist* shows the misery and murder of Jews, it also accommodates exoticized portrayals of atrocities toward the Jewish community to invoke sympathy and shock from the viewers. For example, in the film, a Jewish family sitting around the dining table is vandalized by the Nazi soldiers; at that moment of invasion, everyone gets up except a disabled wheelchair-bound old man. The Nazi soldiers, without wasting a moment, pick up the man along with his wheelchair and throw him off the balcony. The disabled man hits the concrete road and bleeds to death. The rest of the family members are taken outside on the street and shot brutally thereafter. *The Pianist* also has a reference to an old Jewish man who attempts to snatch the food away from a helpless woman. In the process, the food falls on the ground, and he starts to consume the food hastily off the ground. This visual image conveys the despair of an old hungry man, but it also dramatizes hunger for the viewers. The image of eating spilled food invokes both pity and horror. The element of shock has been at the forefront of Holocaust cinema, and this may also have to do with how spectators view and imagine the Holocaust in general, hence, reducing a work of art to a certain cinematic framework controlled by a flawed imagination of the Holocaust.

Within film studies, the question of representation is often raised including whether films can represent historical events in a non-problematic way. When it comes to the question of authentic representation, the genre of "documentary cinema" is often considered to be one that is closer to facts and reality. Daniel H. Magilow and Lisa Silverman mention that (let alone mainstream popular films) the documentary film *Nazi Concentration Camps* accommodates images taken from the camps; however, when arranged, the images are woven around a constructed framework. For example, the declaration made by George C. Stevens of the United States Army in August 1945 about the documentary being an honest representation of the events creates a sense of doubt about the authenticity of the film (27). There is indeed a difference between the "mainstream popular cinema" and "documentary cinema;" however, the two genres of visual representation may overlap. Quart goes on to mention that some of the imagery in *The Pianist* is influenced by Nazi documentaries depicting life in the Warsaw ghetto (43). Cinema, irrespective of the genre it belongs to, may act as a medium to convey a constructed reality. A film, as a text, always remains a representation of events. If such is the case, then, where can one place *The Pianist*? Should one see the film as an adaptation alone? Or is it a mere visual representation that incorporates elements both literal and fictional? What about the role of the auteur? The auteur theory looks at the film as the sole product and imagination of the film director—the director controls the name and nature of the film narrative. Can one propose that Polanski's personal trauma of the Holocaust may have influenced the film narrative and how he reads and documents images of food and hunger in the film? Polanski, along with his photographer friend Ryszard Horowitz, revisit the days of survival during the Holocaust in the documentary *Polanski, Horowitz, Hometown* (2021). In the film, both the artists revisit the streets of Kazimierz, a place where the Polish and Jewish culture came together. Kazimierz is Kraków's historic Jewish quarter, and during the Holocaust, it saw significant violence toward the Jewish community. The film mentions the Polish couple Stefania and Jan Buchala, who provided shelter as well as food to Polanski during the Holocaust. Polanski states that Stefania didn't hesitate in helping him: "Despite poverty and scant food, she made sure that I was safe and fed" (Scislowska). Polanski own's experience with hunger and food may have shaped the portrayal of Szpilman's struggle for food in *The Pianist*. However, one cannot deny the possibility of dramatization when it comes to translating experiences of the past through a visual medium.

66   Ved Prakash

The issue of hunger and survival is highlighted several times in the film by Polanski. Bread and potatoes are represented as the most common food items during this period. Soup along with a piece of bread was the most usual food that was given in the camps. One perhaps needs to look into the complexities of food distribution among people in the camps. One may also need to explore whether lack of food led to crisis and conflicts? Did Jews across class get the same food? Could one with contacts and power procure more food? While these questions are yet to be addressed within Popular Culture, an alternative history of resistance with relation to food could act as a worthy digression. Samuel D. Kassow mentions how the Oyneg Shabes (OS) archive led by the historian Emanuel Ringelblum created a history of resistance. OS was a secret society documenting the lived experiences of the Jews under the Nazi occupation. The members of the society would secretly write about their lives and hide the documents in tin boxes or milk cans. One of the notes that were found in a milk can by Gustawa Jarecka, a writer, reads, "We despise them (words) for they pale in comparison with the emotion tormenting us" (6). A group of Jewish people used food containers to document history. It is interesting to observe that food containers and boxes played a significant role in the protest of the underground secret groups. There were underground Jewish groups in the ghettos, which were active in their struggle against the Germans. Ammunition hidden in food sacks would be smuggled into the ghettos with the assistance of people who would go to the city to bring potatoes and other grains for the Jews. While suffering, hunger, and death are indeed imperative issues concerning the Holocaust, it is important to mention that food packets and sacks played an essential role in hiding guns and grenades to start a revolution against the Nazi regime. This history often gets ignored by films that deal with the Holocaust.

Conclusion

Popular cinema represents Jews as emaciated beings to fit the common perception that the mass and the market hold about the victims of the Holocaust, and this may have to do with the perverse pleasure that people get while consuming images of a select nature. While *The Pianist* engages with the issue of hunger, it may not act as a valid source of reference when it comes to the historicity of food and its consumption within the ghettos. One certainly needs to revisit the Holocaust time and again so that one can understand the past better. However, what is equally important is to critically engage with the dominant representation and treatment of the Holocaust within Popular Culture. One needs to read the Holocaust while being aware of the forces of capitalism. Barbie Zelizer raises the question regarding how the Holocaust needs to be visualized. Who decides what aspects of the Holocaust need to be highlighted and whether the Holocaust lies beyond the limits of representation? Zelizer remarks that the visuals of the Holocaust have been reclaimed within the conventions and limitations of the mode of visual representation (2–3). Therefore, the documentation of the Holocaust remains inadequate. As far as Popular Culture is concerned, one may opine that the Holocaust certainly remains one of the most explored chapters of history, and yet, it remains confined to the dominant visual lexicon concerning the Holocaust and the Jews. As far as the representation of the Holocaust through food imagery in popular cinema is concerned, one could argue that such a representation remains peripheral. The genre of Holocaust cinema primarily discusses the mass killings of the Jews and the criminal nature of the Nazi party. This chapter, while looking at the Holocaust, finds that there is not enough work done on understanding the Holocaust through food. In this regard, kitchen space, food recipes, food ingredients, tiffin boxes, cooking pots, food habits, cuisines, eating routine, etc., may provide an alternative way to engage with the Holocaust. The chapter further discovers that as far as the treatment of food in Holocaust cinema is concerned, often, oversimplified images of food history are produced for the consumption of the masses. This oversimplification may have to do with the idea of the market and profit. Moreover, the chapter highlights how Holocaust cinema portrays the exotic representation of hunger and suffering for the perverse pleasure of the viewers. It is important to mention that post-1950s, cinema developed a well-crafted language of representation of the Holocaust confined to the popular signifiers such as naked bodies of the Jews, pictures through the barbed wires, Jews in striped uniforms, photographs of emaciated bodies, shaved heads, etc. Such documentation and representation, more than helping the scholars of the Holocaust studies, may create further stereotypes, gaps, and binaries around the Holocaust that are already present.

Note

1 Sabbath is considered to be a day of rest and worship; it is observed from Friday evening to Saturday evening. However, Christians consider Sunday to be the day of worship. This difference in praying, too, became a reason why the Jews were incarcerated.

Works Cited

Bazin, André. *Bazin at Work: Major Essays and Reviews from the Forties and Fifties*. Routledge, 1997.
Benz, Wolfgang. "Exclusion as a stage in persecution: The Jewish situation in Germany 1933–1941." In *Nazi Europe and the Final Solution*, edited by David Bankier and Israel Gutman. Yad Vashem and Berghahn, 2009, pp. 40–52.
Civitello, Linda. *Cuisine and Culture: A History of Food and People*. John Wiley & Sons, 2008.
Frankl, Viktor E. *Man's Search for Meaning*. Rider, 2008.
Gruen, Erich S. *The Construct of Identity in Hellenistic Judaism: Essays on Early Jewish Literature and History*. Walter de Gruyter GmbH & Co KG, 2016.
Hitler, Adolf. *Mein Kampf*. Houghton Mifflin Company, 1939.
Hometown (Polanski, Horowitz Hometown) (Directed by Mateusza Kudla and Anna Kokoszka-Romer, performances by Roman Polanski, Ryszard Horowitz, and Bronislawa Horowitz-Karakulska). KRK FILM, 2021.
Kassow, Samuel D. *Who Will Write Our History? Emanuel Ringelblum, the Warsaw Ghetto, and the Oyneg Shabes Archive*. Indian University Press, 2007.
Magilow, Daniel H. and Lisa Silverman. *Holocaust Representations in History: An Introduction*. Bloomsbury, 2015.

68 *Ved Prakash*

Marshman, Sophia. "From the margins to the mainstream? Representations of the Holocaust in popular culture." *eSharp*, vol. 6, no. 1, 2005, pp. 1–20.

Mintz, Alan. *Popular Culture and the Shaping of Holocaust Memory in America*. University of Washington Press, 2001.

Playing for Time (Based on *The Musicians of Auschwitz* by Fania Fenelon, directed by Vanessa Redgrave and Jane Alexander, performances by Vanessa Redgrave and Jane Alexander, screenplay by Arthur Miller). Szygzy Productions, 1980.

Quart, Leonard. "The pianist by Roman Polanski, Robert Benmussa, Alain Sarde and Ronald Harwood." *Cineaste*, vol. 28, no. 3, 2003, pp. 42–44.

Rothe, Anne. *Popular Trauma Culture: Selling the Pain of Others in the Mass Media*. Rutgers University Press, 2011.

Scislowska, Monika. "Roman Polanski honors Poles who saved him from the Holocaust." *AP News*, 16 Oct. 2020, apnews.com/article/poland-europe-roman-polanski-the-holocaust-92d5a9b7c4970efc934991bede2e01fd. Accessed 18 Dec. 2021.

Szpilman, Wladyslaw. *The Pianist: The Extraordinary True Story of One Man's Survival in Warsaw, 1939–1945*. Orion Publishing Group, 2000.

———. *The Pianist: The Extraordinary True Story of One Man's Survival in Warsaw, 1939–1945*. Picador, 2003.

The Boy in the Striped Pajamas (Based on *The Boy in the Striped Pajamas* by John Boyne, directed by Mark Herman, performances by Asa Butterfield and Jack Scanlon). BBC Films, Heyday Films, Miramax Films, 2008.

The Pianist (Based on *The Pianist* by Wlayslaw Szpilman, directed by Roman Polanski, performance by Adrian Brody, Studio Canal+). Studio Babelsberg, 2002.

The Wiener Holocaust Library. *Meals*, www.theholocaustexplained.org/the-camps/ss-concentration-camp-system/meals/. Accessed 26 Feb. 2020.

Wiesel, Elie. *Night*. Hill and Wang, 2006.

Zelizer, Barbie. *Visual Culture and the Holocaust*. The Athlone Press, 2001.

4 Nazi Linguistics and Mass Manipulation

An Analysis of Holocaust Primary Sources Vis-à-vis Popular Culture

Sarah Spinella

Holocaust Memory and Popular Culture

Since the very aftermath of World War II, the urgency of bearing witness of the Holocaust permeated almost all fields of culture, from academics to Popular Culture (hereinafter POPULAR CULTURE), here understood in its broader forms, from novels to cinema, to television series, to artistic performances and music. It is often argued that POPULAR CULTURE has the tendency to trivialize the Holocaust, minimizing or even sparking outrage when approaching the tragedy of Holocaust. Despite the accusation of offering a merely superficial vision of the Holocaust, and with the aim of spreading awareness of the persecution and the genocide of the European Jewish community, the representation of Shoah through the different means used by POPULAR CULTURE has become a commonly accepted practice, even though with some caveats. Indeed, it would not be unacceptable to say that POPULAR CULTURE has vastly, and perhaps decisively, contributed to the Holocaust memory and that it would be fruitful and illuminating to investigate this relationship. Although it may seem somehow inappropriate, POPULAR CULTURE may be considered a privileged point from which to span ideas, knowledge, and awareness of the Holocaust. Lamentably, even if the interest among scholars is a growing trend, there are very few studies on the relationship between POPULAR CULTURE and the Holocaust. Too many conflicting, contradictory, and incomplete definitions may be applied to POPULAR CULTURE, and this chapter is not aimed at making a sterile résumé of the different theories. Nevertheless, it could be useful to shortly remind the major insights that reflect the impact and the essential lines of the different ideas behind Holocaust Popular Culture.

It can be said the *querelle* about the incompatibility of POPULAR CULTURE and the Holocaust started with the maxim of Adorno: "Nach Auschwitz ein Gedicht zu schreiben ist barbarisch" ("To write poetry after Auschwitz is barbaric") (Adorno 26), which defined the Holocaust as the epitome of human evil. In the same vein, the aporetic and the unspeakable nature of the Holocaust was reminded by thinkers like Berel Lang and George Steiner, who stated that it should be represented in factual form, without any romanced narration. On the other side, some schools of thought, mainly based on the works of Emmanuel Levinas and Jacques Derrida, followed another path, promoting POPULAR CULTURE as a powerful

DOI: 10.4324/9781003251224-6

70 *Sarah Spinella*

response to the Holocaust. From canonical and individual experience to collective and politicized tragedy, from trauma to drama, from purists to postmodernists, the debate does not end on a neat conclusion. It is true that different perspectives may create prolific fieldwork for future research. In this context, a crucial but less highlighted point of view is expressed by Holocaust survivors such as Victor Klemperer and Nachman Blumental. Focusing on the linguistic aspects that constitute their key concerns, the following analysis is intended to create new stimulating perspectives in the debate on the Holocaust and POPULAR CULTURE.

The Holocaust's Hedgehogs

In 1947, Viktor Klemperer, a German linguist, published *Lingua Tertii Imperii: Notizbuch eines Philologen* (The Language of the Third Reich: A Philologist's Notebook), a diary on Nazi usage and misusage of the German language. That same year, another intellectual, Nachman Blumental published *Slowa niewinne* (Innocent Words) the first volume of a dictionary of Nazi language. These two similar papers relate to the Holocaust showing how Nazis distorted and contaminated the German language. Nazis changed the meaning of words, corroding and corrupting in whole the critical thinking of the Germans. For this reason, Klemperer creates a coded formula, *LTI* (Lingua Tertii Imperii), for naming the enemy and keeping the distance from the language of totalitarianism.

The two authors carried on accurate, methodic, and brilliant research on the use of language in a coercive context. They relate the tragedy of all German Jews, accused, threatened, and insulted in their language. They show the genocide of a language system and, as a consequence, of a thought system. Besides the intimate grief, the most difficult aspect of their work has been writing about language without being trapped in language. And it was resistance, *tout court*.

Among the controversies that have shaped Holocaust studies, the linguistic aspect is a unique reference point for understanding the symbiotic relationship between totalitarian languages and POPULAR CULTURE, focusing on how the project of the Holocaust was accomplished by reshaping popular consciousness through the misuse of the German language and its structures of signification. Far from being a *Blitzkrieg*, the semantic strategy of the Third Reich was most nearly akin to a slow, methodic, punctilious process of distrust of German intellectual ideas and models of *Aufklärung*. Faced with the extreme historical period of the short twentieth century, both Klemperer and Blumental developed investigations of the Nazi language with different approaches. In reconstructing Jewish experience during the 12 years of the Third Reich, the two researchers chose German language as the starting point from which they structured their struggle. Both developed a linguistic methodology with the aim of deconstructing phonology, grammar, vocabulary, and semantics of Nazi German by creating a sort of *Gegensprache*, to be intended in a figurative sense as *language of Resistance*. In diaries[1] Victor Klemperer kept during the Nazi regime, he mostly concentrated on the sphere of the action, on the frame of the intentionality, on the field of perception, and on the domain of the relationship between personal freedom and its external determinations. He worked on the analysis of

Nazi Linguistics and Mass Manipulation   71

single sentences and examined isolated speech acts. The German philologist made a meticulous study of the statements and sentences of the Third Reich. Indeed, Klemperer made a rigorous sociolinguistic analysis of the language. His diary contains stimulating information about the misuses of the German language and the description of symbols, slogans, and ceremonies of the regime and testifies to the attack of the Nazis against the language, the soul, and the culture.

At the same time, Nachman Blumental worked on a glossary of the terminology used by the Nazis and sought to document the experience of as many survivors as possible in the very aftermath of World War II. He used language to explain the Nazi horror and also to make sense of his personal grief, moving forward in the wake of the postwar devastation. *Slowa niewinne*[2] was the first volume—containing the letters A through I, the first word being *Abbruch* (termination), the last *Israel*—of a larger and more structured project, *Verter un Vertlech fun der Khurbn-Tkufe* (Words and Idioms of the Khurbn Period), written in Yiddish and published in 1981.

The two authors do share several characteristics that make them worthy of close comparative reading. The following is, thus, an analysis that seeks to understand, mostly on the linguistic plane, the mystification process that affected the German language in the Nazi period through the inquiries the two authors carried out.

Klemperer the Writer, Klemperer the Witness

Victor Klemperer was a German. Son of a rabbi who converted to Lutheranism, he studied literature in Munich and in Berlin. He was a decorated military veteran in World War I, volunteering for his country: Germany. Then, he became a professor of Romance languages at the Technical University of Dresden. He was one of those completely assimilated Jews in Weimar Germany. Nevertheless, he escaped deportation only because he was married to an Aryan woman, Eva Schlemmer. Under assumed names, Klemperer and his wife survived moving from one *Judenhaus* to another. In his diaries, with a multidisciplinary approach, from linguistics to rhetoric to psychoanalysis, Klemperer inquired about links between totalitarianism and language. When did a particular word change its meaning or when did the semantic shift occur? Is it possible to manipulate, modify, or destroy the language? His diary is an acute study of micro linguistic phenomena of Nazi terminology.

The exercise of the right to freedom of speech is the true sense of Viktor Klemperer's work. This is his partisan battle against Nazi occupation of the German language, his personal resistance against the totalitarian language of the Third Reich. On 13 June 1942, Klemperer, filled with grim determination, wrote in his diary: *Ich will Zeugnis ablegen bis zum letzten* (I want to bear witness until the very end).[3]

The Language and the Blood

In 1934, Emmanuel Levinas wrote a critical essay on Hitlerism: *Quelques réflexions sur la philosophie de l'hitlérisme*. Within the phenomenological tradition, the French author proposed a critical interpretation of the Third Reich. A Cassandra of

72 Sarah Spinella

history, Levinas prudently used the terms *philosophy, idea,* and *thinking* for referring to Hitlerism. Still, this is the only way of giving a correct interpretation of this phenomenon. In the essay, he explains the most barbaric and dangerous concepts of Nazi ideology, without underestimating or reducing National Socialism to a contingent anomaly of human reason or to an accidental ideological misunderstanding. As 1934 was the *annus mirabilis* of Hitlerism, the publication of the article of Levinas can be read as a denunciation *in actu* of Nazism.

By 1934, Victor Klemperer had already started his diaristic analysis of the Third Reich, and needless to say, one of the most challenging and controversial topics he approached was Jewishness. The anthropology of Nazi official texts is based on numerous taboos, the strongest of which is "the Jew." Concerning this aspect, Klemperer noted:

> The Jew is the most important person in Hitler's state: he is the best known Turk's head of folk history and the popular scapegoat, the most plausible adversary, the most obvious denominator, the most likely brackets around diverse of factors. Had the Führer achieved his aim of exterminating all the Jews, he would have to invent new ones, because without the Jewish devil—anyone who doesn't know the Jew doesn't know the devil—without the swarthy Jew, there would never have been/never be the radiant figure of the Nordic Teuton.
>
> (Klemperer, LTI 164)

As Klemperer shows in detail, Jews were represented as allegoric figures of evilness with the specific intent of manipulating mass thinking and subordinating rational thought to the emotional sphere.

Nonetheless, it should not be forgotten that Klemperer considered himself to be a German even after Hitler's rise to power in 1933 and almost to the bitter end. In his diaries, he referred often to his *Deutschtum*, Germanness. Furthermore, he regarded the Nazis as non-German; moreover, he considered Nazis as a-German, with a privative alpha, that expresses the negation of the beloved culture of Germany: "I am German forever, a German nationalist. The Nazis are un-German" (Klemperer, Notebook I 210). Klemperer repeatedly uttered his Germanness throughout his diary: "11 May 1942. . . . I am fighting the hardest battle for my Germanness now. I must hold on to this: I am German, the others are un-German. I must hold on to this. The spirit is decisive, not blood. I must hold on to this" (Klemperer, Notebook II, 83–84). Although living the horror of the illegal Nazi regime, Klemperer's feeling of German identity never vacillated. Consequently, it is easy to understand why he inscribed his book with an epigraph, a splendid phrase of Franz Rosenzweig: "Language is more than blood." In this sentence, readers feel the tragedy of German Jews that lived the genocide of their language and their thought system and that suffered accusations, insults, and threats in a language that was also theirs. Written in German, as we have seen itself a source of personal tension, Klemperer's *LTI* represents one of the authentic and most vivid records of daily life in the Third Reich, not only from the standpoint of a Jew, but also from the perspective of a German.

The Flowers of Blumental

Nachman Blumental can be considered as one of the key figures among Holocaust literary sources. In 1944, when he began the challenging assignment of recording the then recent traces of evil, the doublespeak of the Nazi mass murder, the Polish historian was a widower, a stateless loner. But 1944 was not *Stunde Null* for Blumental. Instead, he focused on observing, collecting, selecting, and describing the evil. The result is a gold mine of information for both linguistic and historical research on the Holocaust. He created a huge corpus of linguistic evidence against war criminals, examining thousands of words and word combinations in the German language, including neologisms, references, and words with elusive, conjectural, hidden meaning. He provided a unique historical insight into how German language was manipulated during the Third Reich and how Nazis changed words and tried to control the speakers.

Born in Borszczów, Poland in 1902, Blumental was raised in a German-speaking Jewish family. He studied literature in Warsaw before the outbreak of World War II, but, by the time the war began, Blumental escaped into the Soviet Union. In 1939, he was back in his native Poland to find his family, but they had already been killed by the Nazis. The execution of his first wife, Miriam Taibel, and his son, Ariel, haunted him all along his life. In response to horror and trauma, Blumental started collecting evidence of the Jewish genocide. He searched for (and found) any kind of Nazi documents—from private correspondence to official reports—and analyzed the Holocaust euphemisms and the Nazi bureaucratese. In official Nazi documents, words were silent and acquiescent. Words seemed innocent enough. But Blumental, skeptical and obstinate, circled, gridded, underlined, and collected Nazi documents and certificates and written and oral testimonies of the survivors. And he worked on the etymology of innocuous, *innocent words*, like the sadly well-known *Abgang* (exit). He collected proofs of the contamination of the German language; he gathered evidence of the genocide for the postwar trials. Blumental deconstructed the German language to reveal the Nazi code. He eradicated the flowers of evil, the bad seeds Nazis spread into the German language. *Nomen omen.*

The First Holocaust Dictionary

Editing the first edition of a dictionary of Nazi language in the aftermath of World War II was a project of unprecedented historical and cultural importance. One could think, in the postwar scenario, lexicography was not essential. Instead, Blumental was an accomplished polyglot (in addition to German and Polish, he also knew Yiddish, Hebrew, and French, among many other Slavic languages) and he was moved and saved by his love for language. He searched among the words of the enemy, facing the complex relationship he had with the German language and claiming his status of *Außenseiter* (outsider). His variegate linguistic humus represents the basis of his language. His work is a *khurbn-forshung* (destruction research), and for its lucid power of observation, Blumental's glossary has been hailed as a document of rare and great value.

74 *Sarah Spinella*

The Polish historian became an expert and fervent Holocaust scholar throughout his life. He was a founding member of the Centralna Żydowska Komisja Historyczna (The Central Jewish Historical Commission) and later formed part of Yad Vashem. In 1947, he published the dictionary *Słowa niewinne* written in Polish. After this, Blumental wrote a series of essays for a Yiddish review under the heading *Verter un Vertlech fun der Khurbn-Tkufe*, which were collected in 1981 with the same title in a book, his *magnum opus*, that is the most exhaustive work within the lexicographical corpus of Nazi German glossary. Furthermore, Blumental's 1981 work synthesizes his outcomes and efforts from the rigid and complex lexicographical fieldwork started in 1944. Additionally, it includes a compilation of textual lexica of several *khurbn-shprakh*[4] spoken in ghettos and camps. This glossary of *khurbn-shprakh* contains linguistic neologisms, antiphrasis, and borrowings from German, Slavic languages, and Yiddish and confirms, once again, Blumental's multilingualism.

His lexicographical design was ambitious and meticulous but, despite its objectivity and punctiliously, the personal grief of the author comes and goes between its pages. Both the philologist and the man have to be taken into account if we want to understand the complex project of the Polish linguist. With this understanding in mind, it is significant to read the following words Blumental wrote in his notebook (for the two following quotes see Haimovich) for documenting the death of his family:

> My wife claimed to be Polish and asked to be brought to her by a priest. They did not let the priest come. She refused to undress. Her clothes were torn off her. She asked to be shot first. She doesn't want to watch the child die. With her last breath, and to save Ariel, she tried to prove that she was Polish. She exclaimed: 'Hello, Mary, the Most Merciful.' One shot was fired at her.
>
> (Haimovich)

And in another passage he added: "The boy cried: 'Mom, Mom, where's Mom?' They shot him once and he rose in the air, they shot him again and he fell breathless into the grave dug beforehand. It was 11:20 a.m. June 7, 1943."

Language Is Alive

As previously argued, the criminal experience of Nazism was also a crime against the German language. Victor Klemperer understood that the language had been abused by the Nazis who manhandled, mystified, and murdered the beauty of the German language. His reaction to Nazi semanticide was to act as a pure philologist, and in order to better understand the manipulation of language, he chose to write in German. The German language shared with the murderers, annihilated in the concentration camps, raped during Nazi's harangues, had survived. Indeed, filtered in through pain, language gets richer. Although anchored in present, language carries out a search for origins, almost a topologic search that during the catastrophe of the Holocaust could be done only in a specific context, such as personal diaries.

Nazi Linguistics and Mass Manipulation   75

While many diarists of the Holocaust period chose languages other than German in their writings, Klemperer purposely chose to write in German. In another vein, Blumental needed new and different linguistic strategies to express what he had lost and his status as a Holocaust survivor, and he chose Polish for his *Slowa niewienne*. In this respect, it is worth mentioning Blumental wrote his other works in Yiddish. For Blumental, the use of Polish and Yiddish is also a way of distancing himself from the enemy, a subconscious choice to desensitize his suffering. It also seems plausible to think that Klemperer had a more trained philologist's approach to language analysis. As an accomplished linguist, he was tuned to every changing inflection others might not notice in the corrupted Nazi version of the German language. Klemperer also knew that semantic structures predetermine one's perception of the world:

> But language does not simply write and think for me, it also increasingly dictates my feelings and governs my entire spiritual being the more unquestioningly I abandon myself to it. And what happens if the cultivated language is made up of poisonous elements or has been made the bearer of poisons? Words can be like tiny doses of arsenic: they are swallowed unnoticed, appear to have no effect and then after a little time the toxic reaction sets in after all.
>
> (Klemperer, LTI 14)

Victor Klemperer's diary is philological antidotism and a manifesto that testifies how impossible it is "to break a man's spirit permanently" (Steinbeck *The Moon is Down* 44).

Klemperer analyzed the strategies of the language and the specific linguistic phenomena of the Third Reich jargon as a consequence of the extreme historical period of World War II, when politics and ideologies not only intruded upon spheres of cultural and social life but also invaded the linguistic field. The German linguist of Dresden proposed an analysis of language as a factor that determines the comprehension of history and its institutions. His extensive inquiry of the *langue de bois*, made of conceptual banalities, suggests that the use of some linguistic strategies was managed to narcotize the critical capacity of masses.

The elegance of the German of the Dresden professor cares about precision, rigor, lucidity. Instead, the charm of the language of Blumental does not lie in its purity, rather in the immense richness of the contaminations that go through his language, made of lost words and memories of a linguistic past that resisted to the barbarity of the war. He created a "shibboleth" language. Blumental wrote for a biological need. He explored language as a corpse, even more behind the limits of the language. The great potential of his work lies in the originality of lexical research that gleans from several languages, explores the whole spectrum of the semantic possibilities of the words, and invents a new language of grief. Blumental expressed himself in a direct, genuine style that testifies his refusal to abandon himself to any language hoax.

The Hidden Words

Besides the most sadly known euphemisms of Nazi language, such as *Sonderbe-handlung* (special treatment) and the term *Endlösung* (final solution) to refer to the extermination of Jews, other words were manipulated by Nazis, such as *Volk* (people):

> The obligatory, universal and interminable emphasis on the link between any object, relationship or person and das Volk [the nation, the people]—you are either a Volksgenosse [national comrade], Volkskanzler [national chancellor], Volksschädling [national pest], volksnah [close to the people], volksfremd [an enemy of the people], volksbewußt [responsive to the people] etc., ad infinitum—this alone makes for an abiding emotional intensity which to some extent always sounds hypocritical and shameless.
>
> (Klemperer, LTI 224)

Another frequently misused word was *Fanatismus/fanatische* (fanaticism, fanatical). Klemperer also noticed how the term, although used incorrectly, nevertheless became part of the official language of the Nazi language.

> I refer to this sort of things as a comic relapse, the reason being that since National Socialism is founded on fanaticism, and trains people to be fanatical by all possible means, the word "fanatical" was, throughout the entire era of the Third Reich, an inordinately complimentary epithet. It represents an inflation of the term "courageous," "devoted" and "persistent"; to be more precise it is a gloriously eloquent fusion of all of these virtues, and even the most innocuous pejorative connotation of the word was dropped from general LTI usage.
>
> (Klemperer, LTI 55)

Only with an expert lens is it possible to read properly the specificities of the perverse Hitlerian jargon. Receipts, official documents, and numbers were annotated by Nazis with extreme pedantry, as the same Blumental transcribed with punctilious fidelity. To give an example, after the arrival at the concentration camp, the personal data (full names, date of birth, address, occupation, etc.) of the prisoners were recorded and their property was described in detail:

> trunk, briefcase, bundle, cap, wooden shoes, shoes, hairpins, lighter, military book, overcoat, pairs of stockings, tie, tobacco, pipe, ID card, jacket, boots, cloth, leather, handkerchiefs, cigarettes, cigars, proof of work, waistcoat, collars, pairs of gloves, tissue paper, disability card, trousers, outer shirt, wallet, pullover, etc.
>
> (Blumental 139)

To give another example of Blumental's scrupulous exactness, one can mention the rigorous compilation of the letter A of his lexicon, full of infinitive forms

Nazi Linguistics and Mass Manipulation 77

such as *abdirigieren* (to detach), *abtransportieren* (to transport), *abschieben* (to remove) and of a great number of verbal nouns transcribed from the official scripts of Nazi functionaries as *Auflösung* (dissolution), *Aufliebung* (abolition), and the already cited *Abgang* (exit). Apparently, all these words have neuter meanings, but Nachman Blumental's linguist eye detected their true significance. Also "death" is defined in many ways: *entlassen* (to dismiss) (Blumental 79), *nicht befinden* (it is not located) (Blumental 93), or *besteht nicht mehr* (it does not exist anymore) (Blumental 112). The official name of the gas chamber in the Auschwitz documents was *Bauernhaeuser* (rural cottages) (Blumental 92), but Blumental also registered the locution *Bade und Inhalation sraeume* (bath and inhalation rooms) (89).

Besides the manipulated speeches and the imposed meaning, in the language of the Third Reich, it is also possible to find forbidden words. Generally, the communicative frame of all totalitarian regimes is subjected to censorship. The strict control of the lexical heritage and of the freedom of speech is a consequence of the fear of regimes. This linguistic policy is semi-formalized: the censorship creates proscription lists of words and expressions that never have to be used: forbidden words, imposed synonyms, indirect positioning. This secret aspect of the Holocaust was unveiled by Blumental's inquiry. Between his recordings, he reported a written communication addressed to the Lodz ghettos council:

The solution of the Jewish question is a highly political matter that will be settled exclusively and only by the people appointed to it by the Chief. . . . It is the highest duty of everyone employed here to ensure that everything related to the treatment of the Jewish question is kept in the strictest secrecy for general political reasons.

(Blumental 45–46)

Every member of SS also made a sort of secret oath, as Blumental documented:

Auschwitz concentration camp. Command. A statement in lieu of an oath. I am aware that after the camp guards have left the Waffen SS, I am not allowed to talk about the formation, service and concentration camps. Violation is tantamount to treason and causes the most severe punishment.

(Blumental 174)

In regard to this, it is worthy to remember the Posen speeches made by Himmler that are the only known public declaration of a high officer of the Nazi apparatus in which the Holocaust is directly mentioned.

In general, the key to the whole linguistic operation was never to name what was happening. Say nothing. Ask nothing. It is the prohibition of knowing what one participated in. Blumental's dictionary of Nazi language and its specialized terminology was the very first attempt to detect and illustrate the secret doublespeak of the Third Reich.

Conclusion

In 1947, when Blumental published *Słowa niewinne*, he was not aware of Victor Klemperer's work, published almost at the same time as his dictionary. For a long time, the work of the Polish polyglot remained in the shadow of Klemperer's diary, which indeed in a short time, reached sales of 100,000 copies and transformed its author into one of the most known Holocaust writers, so that German television even produced a drama series based on his diaries. Discussing the Holocaust during the war and in its immediate aftermath was the utmost defiance for Blumental and Klemperer. Far from silence, as they were instilled with a mighty sense of duty, their response to the Shoah was to witness through writing. The Nazi period was a prolific moment of autobiographical writings and memoirs. For Klemperer, diary use is first and foremost an intimate choice. The flow of consciousness, intended both as literary choice and psychoanalytic concept, is a radical act. Living in immediacy, utterly caught up in the time of horror, he channeled his feelings into memoir writing using the narrative method of stream of consciousness combined with a rigorous linguistic analysis. One crucial element of memoir being the use of the first-person, writing autobiographical texts is an intimate choice, but Klemperer's diary is also a documentary text: The author is the witness of the Nazi period and he represents a fundamental part of the context. Hence, even if Klemperer uses the first-person as most diary writers, the language is the real protagonist of his work so that his writing is perceived not only as intimate but also as documenting.

As mentioned earlier, one characteristic common to both authors is the awareness of the act of writing itself. Both works constitute thoughtful Holocaust documents in which Blumental and Klemperer describe the reality they experienced. In this regard, which is at the core of this chapter, the analysis of these two works can teach us a great deal about the structures that permeate the totalitarian culture, with particular attention paid to language. Although this analysis cannot include all forms of language misuse perpetrated by Nazis, the considerations and findings of the two writers offer impressive insights into the relationship between language and power.

As argued previously, Klemperer's diary focuses on the writer's personal experience with annotations on Nazi infiltrations in the German language, while the dictionary of Blumental concentrates on the murderer's language in all its strata and creates the basis for later lexicographical literature. Lexicography is generally seen as the simple writing or compiling of dictionaries. But this is just one aspect of this discipline and quite a *locus communis*. The other facet of lexicography is the awareness about what a dictionary is, how it is made, and why it is needed. For Blumental, writing a dictionary of Nazism was a personal, lucid, ultimate revenge.

The decision to use a dictionary as source of study in this chapter is intended to address its central role as a reference and to raise new questions. Are the dynamics of listing words, of transcribing expressions, of collecting information in themselves objective in nature? Is lexicography an objective lens to observe language changes and their impact on thought and identity? Is it possible to retrace a

Nazi Linguistics and Mass Manipulation 79

personal perspective in lexicographic work and similar documents? This chapter has been a brief *excursus* into studying how language can impart a crucial facet to analyze how identity is created, affirmed, and maintained in totalitarian contexts. The analysis of singular writings such as dictionaries could make a significant contribution to our understanding of how the language phenomena work in relation to power. Finally, this study has aimed to humbly contribute to providing a background for further discussions on nonhistorical Holocaust works as indispensable sources that connote totalitarian language as an insidious and proteiform system.

The central question this chapter has addressed pertains to the linguistic implications of the relationship between POPULAR CULTURE and Holocaust. Semantics being one of the components of semiotics of culture, it is easy to understand how the mass manipulation is generated through the use of language as persuasive instrument. Language is the *trait d'union* in this problematic relationship, and it makes sense to study the linguistic aspects of Nazi German in relation with POPULAR CULTURE in order to further analyze the question of language manipulation and mass persuasion.

Notes

1 Klemperer, Victor. *The Language of the Third Reich LTI—Lingua Tertii Imperii; a Philologist's Notebook.* Continuum, 2006 (hereinafter Klemperer, LTI).
2 Blumental, Nachman. *Słowa niewinne,* ed. Central Jewish Historical Commission. Kraków-Łódź-Warsaw 1947 (hereinafter Blumental). All translations are mine unless otherwise stated. For quotes, I have retained the original Polish source whereas, when quoting from secondary sources, full references are given at end of chapter.
3 Klemperer, Victor. *Ich will Zeugnis ablegen bis zum letzten, 1933-1945.* Aufbau Verlag, 1995, vol. 2, p. 124. See also Klemperer, Victor. *Ich will Zeugnis ablegen bis zum letzten. Tagebücher 1933–1941.* Aufbau-Verlag, 1996 (hereinafter Klemperer, Notebook I); Klemperer, Victor. *Ich will Zeugnis ablegen bis zum letzten. Tagebücher 1942–1945.* Aufbau-Verlag, 1996 (hereinafter Klemperer, Notebook II).
4 Khurbn-shprakh is a term used for referring to Yiddish speech or writing used in ghettos, hiding, concentration or death camps in German-occupied Eastern Europe. In this specific context, Yiddish language was influenced from other languages such as German, Polish, Ukrainian, Lithuanian, or Latvian.

Works Cited

Adorno, Theodor W. "Kulturkritik und Gesellschaft." In *Prismen, Kulturkritik und Gesellschaft.* Suhrkamp, 1963, pp. 7–26.
Beckerman, Gal. "The Holocaust survivor who deciphered Nazi doublespeak." *The New York Times,* 24 Jun. 2019, www.nytimes.com/2019/06/24/books/holocaust-nazi-archive. html. Accessed 22 Nov. 2021.
Blumental, Nachman. *Słowa niewinne.* Central Jewish Historical Commission, 1947.
Fischer-Hupe, Kristine. *Victor Klemperer's "LTI, Notizbuch eines Philologen": Ein Kommentar.* Olms, 2001.
Friedlander, Henry. "The manipulation of language." In *The Holocaust: Ideology, Bureaucracy, and Genocide,* edited by Henry Friedlander and Sybil Milton. Kraus International, 1980, pp. 103–113.

80   *Sarah Spinella*

Haimovich, Mordechai. "The Archive that Reveals the Polite Language behind the Nazi Death Machine." *Maariv*, 9 Sept. 2019, www.yivo.org/cimages/maariv_-_nachman_blumental.pdf. Accessed 27 Nov. 2021.

Himmler, Heinrich. "Heinrich Himmler's Speech at Poznan (Posen)." *The Holocaust History Project*, https://phdn.org/archives/holocaust-history.org/himmler-poznan/. Accessed 27 Nov. 2021.

Klemperer, Victor. *I Shall Bear Witness: The Diaries of Victor Klemperer 1933–41* (Translated by Martin Chalmers). Weidenfeld & Nicolson, 1998.

———. *I Will Bear Witness: A Diary of the Nazi Years 1942–1945* (Translated by Martin Chalmers). Random House, 2001.

———. *Ich will Zeugnis ablegen bis zum letzten, 1933–1945*. Aufbau Verlag, 1995.

———. *Ich will Zeugnis ablegen bis zum letzten. Tagebücher 1933–1941*. Aufbau-Verlag, 1996.

———. *Ich will Zeugnis ablegen bis zum letzten. Tagebücher 1942–1945*. Aufbau-Verlag, 1996.

———. *The Language of the Third Reich: LTI—Lingua Tertii Imperii: A Philologist's Notebook*. Continuum, 2006.

———. *The Lesser Evil: The Diaries of Victor Klemperer 1945–59*. Weidenfeld & Nicolson, 2003.

Lachmann Mosse, George. *Le origini culturali del Terzo Reich*. Il Saggiatore, 2008.

Levinas, Emmanuel. *Quelques réflecions sur la philosophie de l'hitlérisme*. Éditions Payot et Rivages, 2018.

Rademacher, Michael. *Abkürzungen des Dritten Reiches: ein Handbuch für deutsche und englische Historiker*. Anne Rademacher, 2000.

Saussure, Louis de and Peter Schulz. *Manipulation and Ideologies in the Twentieth Century: Discourse, Language, Mind*. John Benjamins Publishing Company, 2005.

Schmitz-Berning, Cornelia. *Vokabular des Nationalsozialismus*. Walter de Gruyte, 1998.

Steinbeck, John. *The Moon is Down,* 1942. Penguin Classics, 1995.

Vygotskij, Lev Semĕnovič. *Pensiero e linguaggio. Ricerche psicologiche* (edited by L. Mecacci). Laterza, 2021.

Young, John Wesley. Totalitarian Language: Orwell's Newspeak and its Nazi and Communist Antecedents. University Press of Virginia, 1991.

Part II
Rethinking Universalization

5 Hitler's Popularity and the Trivialization of the Holocaust in India

Navras J. Aafreedi

Introduction

Adolf Hitler is becoming increasingly popular in India. The rise in Hitler's popularity is inversely proportional to the decline in M. K. Gandhi's popularity[1] and directly proportional to the rise of majoritarianism and intolerance in India. The Holocaust did not have any direct fallout for India, but it is its ignorance in India that is responsible for Hitler's popularity there more than anything else. There are many other factors, too, but Nazism is not one of those. However, the strange phenomenon cannot be dismissed simply as an obsession with and a craving for strong leadership (Gramlich). We should all be alarmed if the world's most populous democracy, home to one-sixth of humankind, with the largest diaspora in the world, comes to admire Hitler more than any other non-Indian leader and is hardly aware of the Holocaust. The few who are not ignorant of the Holocaust often condone it for they consider it a necessary collateral damage for the greater good of the German nation or the only wrongdoing by Hitler. The fact that Hitler is gaining popularity in a country where antisemitism[2] remains largely unknown even today, except for certain sections of its Muslims and Christians, is paradoxical. It is symptomatic of a lot that is wrong with our society today, and if we ignore it, we do so at our own peril. Indians are at once obsessed and uncomfortable with history. History continues to figure large in their political debates, but they refuse to draw any lessons from it. The only museum dedicated to the Partition of India in 1947 is in Amritsar (established in 2016), if we do not count the virtual museum titled Kolkata Partition Museum, established in 2018. It is estimated that around one to two million people were killed and about ten million became homeless during the Partition of India in 1947, yet we do not have a single memorial dedicated to it, neither in India, nor in the other two countries, Bangladesh and Pakistan, that emerged out of undivided British India. We have no example of a people persecuted and discriminated against by their own coreligionists for centuries other than the Dalits in India, yet there is no museum to document their plight such as the National Museum of African American History and Culture in Washington, D.C.

The sales of *Mein Kampf* in India have increased to the tune of 15 percent in just a decade. Free of copyright in India, *Mein Kampf* is printed by half a dozen publishers. Hundreds of thousands of its copies have been sold in the last two decades, and

DOI: 10.4324/9781003251224-8

84 *Navras J. Aafreedi*

a steady rise in its demand has been registered. "The popularity in India of *Mein Kampf*, that bible of social and political intolerance, is not a new phenomenon," writes Satya Sivaraman. "From the time Hitler rose to power in Germany in the 1930s there have been strong currents in the Indian mainstream that admired the Fuhrer for all he stood for and indeed even sought transplantation of his perverted philosophy to Indian soil" (Sivaraman). According to historian Benjamin Zachariah, "The Nazi model of all organisations under the control of one party and one leader is an appealing one" to the Hindu nationalists, and "the depiction of Hitler as a German patriot serves that purpose" (qtd. in Sharma). The Nazis have always been admired by the Hindu right-wing, "whose discussion of Nazi policies towards the Jews was mediated by their general stand on the religious minorities of India, particularly on the Muslim community" (Egorova, *Jews and India* 39). This explains the growing popularity of Hitler among the Indian youth.

Hitler's popularity is not confined to his autobiography. All of his memorabilia sell like hot cakes. There have also been a number of films named after Hitler in India's various languages. The films, except *Gandhi to Hitler* (2011), neither are biopics on Hitler nor depict Hitler as a character. It is just that in all of these films the lovable protagonist, because of his authoritarian nature, is called Hitler (Siddiqui). Given how ignorant Indians generally are of the Holocaust, it seems appropriate to them to call anyone who comes across as too bossy, Hitler! An important example is the popular Hindi daily soap opera *Hitler Didi* ("*didi*" in Hindi is a respectful form of address for an elder sister), which had 448 episodes broadcast from 2011 to 2013 on the Hindi satellite television channel Zee TV and which is currently available on the OTT platform Zee5. It is the protagonist, a girl in Delhi burdened with the responsibility of providing for her family as the sole breadwinner, who has been called "Hitler" just because of her being a strict disciplinarian. According to the TRP television ratings, it was the fourth most popular show in India. It was later broadcast also in Pakistan, the fountainhead of Urdu antisemitic rhetoric, and its dubbed Farsi version, in Iran, notorious for holding Holocaust cartoon contests and Holocaust denial conferences. In North America and Europe, it was aired with the title *General Didi*, instead of the original title because of the Anti-Defamation League's objection to the use of Hitler in the title. However, the objection was overlooked by Zee Entertainment Enterprises when its Arabic version was broadcast to the Arab world on Zee Alwan, a Dubai-based satellite television channel, from 7 December 2014, under the title *Aukhti Hitler*. The Anti-Defamation League expressed its disappointment "with the return of Adolf Hitler's name in the title" in a statement it posted on its website within a fortnight of that (ADL). Wayne Anderson aptly demonstrated the key role television plays in shaping our perceptions when he reported in an op-ed he published in the *New York Times* in 1996 that half of his astronomy students at Sacramento City College believed that there was "a government conspiracy to conceal UFOs, and cited television programs as evidence" (Rothe 51). Holocaust scholar Alvin H. Rosenfeld rightly points out that:

> Hitler has become an allegorical as well as an historical figure . . . a presence
> that summons the attention of this generation and undoubtedly will continue

to be a compelling presence for years to come. While he remains a threatening figure on one level, on another he is undergoing a figurative process of domestication and normalization, which has the effect of disconnecting him from the criminal regime he established and the catastrophes he wrought.

(Rosenfeld 27)

He adds that "the historian's role is and will remain crucial to uncovering the past, yet historical memory broadly conceived may depend less on the record of events drawn up by scholars than on the projection of these events by writers, filmmakers, artists, and others." Considering this, *Gandhi to Hitler* (2011) becomes significant despite its commercial failure. It is a film based on a couple of letters M. K. Gandhi wrote to Adolf Hitler, driven by his profound belief in nonviolence and the principles of *Satyagraha*, according to which one must make every effort to be considerate of one's enemy and must genuinely try to understand him in situations of conflict (Suhrud). The first one, dated 23 July 1939, was concealed by the British censorship. In it, he appealed to Hitler not to wage war and signed it with the words, "I remain, your sincere friend" (Gandhi, Complete Works of Mahatma Gandhi). Gandhi's second letter to Hitler, a public one, was published in 1940, when the German forces were at the pinnacle of their success. Gandhi adds a disclaimer to it explaining why he calls him "Dear friend," despite his disapproval of his deeds:

Dear Friend,

That I address you as a friend is no formality. I own no foes. My business in life has been for the past 33 years to enlist the friendship of the whole of humanity by befriending mankind, irrespective of race, colour or creed. We have no doubt about your bravery or devotion to your fatherland, nor do we believe that you are the monster described by your opponents.

(Gandhi, "Letter to Adolf Hitler")

Gandhi told the then viceroy, Lord Linlithgow, that "Hitler is not a bad man" (Purandare 132). He wrote in *Harijan* that the future generations of Germans would "honour Herr Hitler as a genius, as a brave man, as a matchless organizer and much more" (Gandhi, *Harijan*). *Gandhi to Hitler*, released outside of India as *Dear Friend Hitler*, attempts to humanize Hitler. In a scene, Hitler dictates to his secretary while she types:

I know that after my death historians will portray me as a devil. However, I never wanted a war. It was imposed on us. I hold the Jews responsible for the ongoing sale and purchase of European countries like shares. I had said that if war breaks out millions of men, women and children of Europe will be killed and the guilty will not even be punished and that Germany will be split into two parts so that it is never able to raise its head again. I appoint Dr. Goebbels as the chancellor of the Third Reich after my death. For the sake of my country, I will prefer to get my head chopped off rather than bow it before the enemy.[3]

(Kumar)

86   Navras J. Aafreedi

The scene aims at projecting Hitler as a patriot. The daily newspaper *DNA* described the film as an "assault on senses and cinema" (Chettiar). Hitler has been used in Indian cinema also for the sake of humour. One of the most popular comic characters of Hindi cinema's history is a caricature of Hitler as a jailer [inspired by Charlie Chaplin's *The Great Dictator* (1940)], played by Asrani in the super hit thriller *Sholay* (1975). A politician from Meghalaya, who has also been a minister, is Adolf Lu Hitler R. Marak. He says, "Maybe my parents liked the name and hence christened me Hitler . . . I am happy with my name, although I don't have any dictatorial tendencies" (Arjunpuri). An undersecretary in the Ministry of Home Affairs, Government of India is a person called Hitler Singh. Muslims, from both India and Pakistan, and Hindus with the first name Hitler have a strong presence on the social networking site Facebook.[4] They come disproportionately more from those groups that fancy themselves as martial, such as Gujars, Jats, and Rajputs among Hindus and Pathans/Pashtuns among Muslims, as indicated by the surnames they use. They are generally those who associate aggression with masculinity and perceive it as a virtue. Their Facebook posts generally betray their right-wing leanings. Some of them cannot even spell the name Hitler correctly, but it is not enough to keep them from using it for themselves on social media, so strong is their admiration for him. A member of parliament in India, Naramalli Sivaprasad attended the parliament in 2018 dressed as Hitler and sporting a moustache identical to Hitler's ("Indian MP Shocks with Hitler Costume Protest in Parliament"). "Aryan" has recently become quite trendy as a first name among Indians (Aafreedi, "India's Response to the Holocaust"). The best known of those who bear the first name Aryan is Hindi cinema's popular lead actor Shah Rukh Khan's elder son Aryan Khan. Rosenfeld explains the strange phenomenon of Hitler's popularity in the following words:

> Such a figure—who seems to be able to satisfy at one and the same time our fantasies for power, madness, money, sex, murder, politics, pageantry, ambition, and art—obviously has appeal. It is not an appeal that will help us better understand the Nazi persecution and slaughter of the Jews, but then it is not meant to. Rather, it is meant to fascinate us with the Holocaust, to some degree even to entertain us with it, and ultimately to distract us from it by turning it into something else—a source of vicarious danger and excitement, a new mythology of sometimes pleasurable, sometimes violent sensations.
>
> (30)

Nazi Propaganda in South Asia

Perhaps the genesis of Hitler's popularity in South Asia can be traced to the Nazi propaganda there. Nazi propagandists were active in India from 1933 to 1939. Newspapers such as *Spirit of the Times, Sālār-é-Hind, Princely India, Karnataka Bandhu, Lokhandi Morchā, and Trikāl* carried direct Nazi propaganda. The propagandists tried to influence both the Hindus and the Muslims. They raised the issue of Palestine to win Muslim support. To win Hindu support, they highlighted the Nazi symbol of the swastika and the Aryan race theory because they were aware that the swastika is an ancient Hindu symbol and the North Indians consider themselves Aryan. They also tried to impress upon them that India belonged to them alone and not to the Muslims and other communities like Germany belonged only to Germans and not to the Jews, who were outsiders. The Nazis operated in India through various cultural and business organizations, both Indian and European, which included International Railway Information Bureau of Madras, Bombay Press Service, Indo-German News Exchange of New Delhi, Aligarh University German Society, Bhatachar Movement in Bengal (Bhattachari), German Institute of Bombay, and certain branches of Hindu Mahasabha in Maharashtra (Casolari). "One has to look at this issue as more than just transient fad," stresses Robin David. He cites a couple of examples from secondary education in Gujarat to illustrate the extent of ignorance about Hitler in India, which, according to some, Robin points out, is willful in nature. As part of class XII final examinations students were given an English grammar test on 22 April 2002 in which they were asked to remove "if" and paraphrase the sentence, "If you don't like people, kill them." They were instructed in the same examination to rewrite a short passage as a single sentence. The passage read: "There are two solutions. One of them is the Nazi solution. If you don't like people, kill them, segregate them. Then strut up and down. Proclaim that you are the salt of the earth." After giving these two examples, David tells us how he wished "many students failed this exam" (David).

When the Israeli government protested against the lack of mention of the Holocaust in the chapter on Hitler in the standard X History textbook in use in Gujarat, it was revised, but to only vaguely mention that many Jews were killed during the war, again without mentioning the Holocaust, the gas chambers, and the death camps.

India's Response to the Holocaust

While the plight of the Arabs in mandate Palestine emerged as a matter of concern in India, which was then home to the world's largest Muslim population, though still less than a quarter of its total population, the misery of the Jews was largely met with indifference. There were several reasons for it. Jews were numerically and politically insignificant in India, unlike the Muslims. While the Zionists were reluctant to display support for India's struggle for freedom from British colonial rule, the Arab nationalists had no qualms in doing so. The Indian Muslims and the Muslim League actively lobbied for their coreligionists in Palestine, but there was no Jewish constituency in India that could influence the Congress Party to adopt a more vocal stand with regard to the Holocaust. Since early 1920, the Indian National Congress adopted as many as six resolutions on Palestine expressing its sympathy and support for the Arabs there but remained silent on the Nazi gas chambers (Kumaraswamy).

M. K. Gandhi advised the Jews to adopt the method of *Satyagraha* (nonviolent civil resistance) in the belief that it would eventually soften even Hitler's "heart of stone." He called Hitler's deeds "the actions of a crazy but brave young man" and felt that:

88 *Navras J. Aafreedi*

The calculated violence of Hitler may even result in a general massacre of the Jews by way of his first answer to the declaration of such hostilities. But if the Jewish mind could be prepared for voluntary suffering, even the massacre I have imagined could be turned into a day of thanksgiving and joy that Jehovah had wrought deliverance of the race even at the hands of the tyrant.

> (Gandhi, M. K., *Harijan*, November 26, 1938, cited in Shimon,
> " 'Can the Jews resist this organised and shameless persecution?' "
> 347–373 & Shimon, "Melting Hitler's Heart of Stone")

Gandhi's lack of understanding of the Nazi evil and that of political realism were revealed in his proclamations on the eve of World War II, which evoked great resentment in the Jewish world.[5]

Muslim opinion strongly influenced India's response to the Holocaust. Conscious of the Muslim opposition to the grant of refuge to Jews from Nazi Europe, the British government of India made it mandatory for Jews seeking asylum to produce proof of guaranteed employment in India before being allowed entry, resulting in a sharp decrease in the number of people able to enter (Sareen 55–63). However, according to Weil's estimate, around 2,000 Jews found refuge in British India (Weil 64–84). Besides these Jews, there were several hundreds, including non-Jewish Poles, who found asylum in the princely states of India. The most prominent examples being Nawanagar and Kohlapur.[6]

Despite this, Jawaharlal Nehru sponsored a resolution in support of the Jewish refugees. However, the then-Congress president, Subhas Chandra Bose, rejected the resolution. Although by then Bose had left the Congress, he continued to command a strong influence in the party (Kumaraswamy 122–123). The Hindu Right, too, opposed Nehru's proposal. V. D. Savarkar labeled Nehru's proposal and the Diwan of Cochin's contemplation about granting refuge to Jews fleeing Nazi Europe as "the suicidal generosity [Indian] forefathers had been guilty of in other cases of inviting colonies of non-Hindus to India" (Savarkar, *Hindu Rashtra Darshan* [1949] cited in Egorova, "Memory of the Holocaust in India" 69f.). Although Savarkar had described the Indian Jews as harmless due to their small numbers and absence of proselytizing tendencies, yet he did not shy from making these statements. The fact that Bose met Hitler and tried to win his support in raising an army against the British in India often deludes the Indians into believing that Hitler actually made a significant contribution to India's struggle for freedom (Aafreedi, "The Paradox of the Popularity of Hitler in India" 14–16). Four years later, in 1942, the *Jewish Chronicle* of London reported that Bose had published an article in *Angriff*, a journal of Goebbels, saying that "anti-Semitism should become part of the Indian liberation movement since the Jews—he alleged—had helped the British to exploit and suppress the Indians (21 August 1942)" ("Report in the *Jewish Chronicle*," cited in Kumaraswamy 282). Interestingly that article by Bose has never been found. Bose is the same person who was convinced that "the next phase in world history will produce a synthesis between Communism and fascism" and that "it will be India's task to work out this synthesis." He called this synthesis *sāmyavāda* or "the doctrine or synthesis of equality" (Purandare 128).

Ignorance of the Holocaust Among Indians

There is little proper awareness of the Holocaust in South Asia. The word "Holocaust" is often used loosely to refer to just any episode of mob violence without taking into account its magnitude and scale and whether or not the violence was targeted against a particular group of people with the intention of completely or partially annihilating them. The term "Holocaust" was originally used exclusively for the Nazi genocide of the Jews, but later when it came to be used for other genocides as well, some people, including Elie Wiesel, advocated the use of an alternative term for it, *Shoah*. However, in India, the term "Holocaust" is often used even for episodes of mass violence that cannot qualify as genocides should we adopt its United Nations' definition. Given the lack of proper knowledge of the Holocaust, terms associated with the Holocaust are used loosely more often than not. An example is that whenever the pollution levels in any Indian city cross a certain level, the press starts reporting that the city has turned into a virtual gas chamber. So much so, even the Supreme Court of India made the same analogy in January 2019 (PTI).

It was primarily from the 2,000 European Jews who found refuge in India that Indians, including the Jews among them, learned about the Holocaust, and not from the press in India, which was at that time focused on reporting the struggle for national independence from the British and gave little space to news of the then ongoing Holocaust (Weil 64–84).

It is hard to find a book on the Holocaust in any Indian language, while the autobiography of Hitler and his biographies are omnipresent in almost every major Indian language for as little as less than a dollar. The Holocaust is seldom more than a mere passing reference if it figures at all in the history syllabus at the secondary level of education in India.

Eminent Holocaust scholar Dina Porat underscores the need for the education of Jewish history in general and not just Holocaust education to make the students completely understand why the colossal tragedy took place and not just how:

> Holocaust education has also not yet proved itself to be barrier against antisemitism, for youngsters, whose ignorance is coupled by naivete, often raise questions such as these: Why the Jews? Why all the Jews? What's wrong with them? Was their murder really initiated without any logical reason, or other good motive? Six million—how indeed did so many Jews, who do not seem to be helpless today, allow this to be done to them.
>
> (Porat 472)

Only education in Jewish history can answer such questions. Hence, so badly needed. Robert Wistrich cautioned us that "the ignorance about Judaism and Jewish history is, of course, a particularly fertile breeding-ground for antisemitism" (166). And in 2004, the United Nations Secretary General Kofi Annan rightly said that "the rise of antisemitism anywhere is a threat to people everywhere. Thus, in fighting antisemitism we fight for the future of all humanity" (Schweitzer 268). Widespread

90 *Navras J. Aafreedi*

ignorance of the Holocaust and Jewish history makes people susceptible to antisemitic propaganda aimed at denying or minimizing or trivializing the Holocaust.

Holocaust Education in India

National Socialism or Nazism finds mention in the Indian National Curricula for School Education (Banerjee and Stober 43–73) and in the syllabus for the National Eligibility Test (NET) for lectureships in history conducted by the University Grants Commission (UGC), but the mention of Holocaust is absent in both. Not all books mention Jews as the victims of Nazi rule. Even if the Holocaust finds a passing reference in a discussion of National Socialists (Nazis) it is often de-Judaized, lest it be perceived as an unwarranted and unfair focus on the plight of just one particular section of victims which included Blacks, Gypsies, homosexuals, Slavs, etc. "Transforming empirical Holocaust victims into a rhetorical figure is moreover unethical because it effaces the actual victimization experiences of real, non-metaphoric Jews," as Anne Rothe puts it (16). According to the NCERT (National Council of Educational Research and Training) textbook for year nine from 2006, Hitler's success indicates that he possessed specific personal qualities, even if used in a manipulative manner. These traits are presented by other books not merely as capabilities but as positive qualities. A 2005 textbook for year twelve, published by a private publishing house Saraswati House, even strikes a tone of admiration. While the Nazi rule is validated in general, when it comes to the characterization of Hitler, the tone of the text varies from profound condemnation to appreciation and admiration (Banerjee and Stober 58).

It has been indicated by scholars that the roots of Indian perceptions of Hitler and Nazism are to be found in certain features of twentieth-century Indian history. The Hindu nationalists tried to establish direct ties with Nazi Germany. For them, it was an alternative model for fulfilling their ambitions and achieving their goals. Hence, they tried to model their organization the Rashtriya Swayamsevak Sangh (RSS) on the pattern of the National Socialists and the Fascists. Subhas Chandra Bose sought Nazi Germany's help against British rule in India. Banerjee and Stober draw our attention to India's neutrality as a member of the Non-Aligned Movement after the foundation of the State of Israel on questions regarding the Jews and the Holocaust. However, they are quick to add that this posture later changed as the Muslim vote bank became increasingly important to mainstream politics. India's neutrality made her reluctant to accept the version of history allegedly written by the victors and imposed on the losers of the war. They write that "in this context, antisemitic Nazi arguments were reproduced as historical facts and Jews were presented as culprits" (Banerjee and Stober 61).

Hindu Nationalist Admiration for Nazism

Whenever Indian Jews have been attacked in India, the perpetrators have been Hindus who mistook them for Muslims because in their perception, according to Egorova, they were different enough from the expected mainstream. She finds

Hitler's Popularity and Trivialization of Holocaust in India   91

the genealogy of the very blueprints of anti-Muslim discrimination in India in European antisemitism. Hindu nationalists mask their "anti-Semitic presuppositions about the alleged intolerability of the Jews" by laying great stress in their discourse on the Hindu tolerance toward them in India (Egorova *Jews and Muslims in South Asia* 158). Official narratives display the alleged Indian/Hindu tolerance by particularly mentioning the history of Indian Jews. While Hindu nationalists construct the Indian Jews as the perfect other, they inscribe "India and Hinduism as a site of tolerance which succeeded in accommodating a community" that had been persecuted for centuries in Europe. "This professed positive interest in Jewishness masks anti-Semitic presuppositions about the alleged intolerability of the Jews and is intricately connected to anti-Muslim sentiments of the Hindu right," Egorova suggests (*Jews and Muslims in South Asia* 157–158). Their numerical insignificance and undemanding nature get them the status of a model minority.

In India, we find a situation where antisemitism of the past disguises itself as Islamophobia. Nazi discourse was used uninhibitedly by Hindu nationalist leaders such as Madhav Sadashivrao Golwalkar, Vinayak Damodar Savarkar, Keshav Baliram Hedgewar, and Bal Thackeray to promote discrimination against Muslims and other minorities in India. M. S. Golwalkar, one of the leaders of the Hindu nationalist organization Rashtriya Swayamsevak Sangh (National Volunteer Organization), expressed his approval of Nazi policy toward the Jews:

> To keep up the purity of the Race and its culture, Germany shocked the world by her purging the country of the Semitic Race—the Jews. Race pride at its highest has been manifested here. Germany has also shown how well-nigh impossible it is for races and cultures, having differences going to the root, to be assimilated into one united whole, a good lesson for us in Hindustan to learn and profit by.
>
> (Golwalkar 87–88)

Savarkar, a prominent figure in the Hindu Mahasabha, compared the Muslims to the Jews of Germany while accusing them of extraterritorial loyalties:

> Today we the Hindus from Kashmere to Madras and Sindh to Assam will be a Nation by ourselves—while the Indian Moslems are on the whole more inclined to identify themselves and their interests with Moslems outside India than Hindus who live next door, like the Jews in Germany.
>
> (Savarkar cited in Egorova, "Memory of the Holocaust in India: A Case Study for Holocaust Education" 217)

Their admiration for the Nazis brought the Hindu nationalists into direct contact with the Nazis. The first Hindu nationalist to get in touch with the fascists was B. S. Moonje, who, between February and March 1931, while returning from the Round Table Conference, made a tour of Europe with a long stopover in Italy, where he met Mussolini. The Nehru Memorial Museum and Library in New Delhi has his

92　*Navras J. Aafreedi*

13-page account of the trip and the meeting. The high points of his tour were visits to the Balilla and Avangardisti organizations, the keystones of the fascist system of indoctrination of the youth, strikingly similar to the RSS. Although it was the vision and work of Hedgewar, the founding supreme leader of the RSS, behind its structure, one cannot overlook the important role played by Moonje, seen as his mentor, in molding the RSS along Italian (fascist) lines. Fascinated by fascism, Hindu nationalists held a conference on it on 31 January 1934, which was presided over by Hedgewar. A year before the conference, the British intelligence in its report assessed that the RSS hoped to be in future India what the "Fascisti" were to Italy and the "Nazis" to Germany (NAI). Savarkar openly spoke in defense of the Nazis and the Fascists. After becoming the president of the RSS, Savarkar's rhetoric against Muslims turned increasingly radical and distinctly unpleasant. In a speech he made on 14 October 1938, he suggested to draw inspiration from the Nazi treatment of Jews in Germany in finding a solution to the Muslim problem in India: "A nation is formed by a majority living therein. What did the Jews do in Germany? They being in minority were driven out from Germany" (MSA, Home Special Department, 60 D(g) Pt. III, 1938, cited in Casolari 218–228).

Holocaust as a Trope in the Hindu Nationalist Anti-Muslim Critique and the Trivialization of the Holocaust

The Hindu right is certainly guilty of Holocaust trivialization, a covert form of denial even if not explicit denial. An Anti-Defamation League survey conducted among the Hindus who had heard of the Holocaust found them to be extremely ignorant. Forty-eight percent considered the number of Jewish victims to be highly exaggerated, and 11 percent thought of the Holocaust as a myth. Hindus make up 80 percent of India's total population and about 14 percent of the entire world's population (Uniyal). For the advancement of their communalist agenda, Hindu nationalists in their anti-Muslim critique use the Holocaust as a trope. Their deep-seated sense of majority victimhood leads them to indulge in competitive victim-hood amounting to Holocaust obfuscation and trivialization. Francois Gautier, a Delhi-based French journalist and a Hindu nationalist, even if not Hindu by faith, uses Holocaust imagery to depict the Indic religious communities "not only as the victims of Muslims but also as the ultimate victims in human history whose suffering was just as superior to that of the Jewish people as it was overlooked," resulting in the trivialization of the Holocaust (Egorova, *Jews and Muslims in South Asia* 60). In a speech he gave at a seminar titled "The Continuing Genocides in the Indian Sub-Continent," organized by Jammu Kashmir Unity Foundation in commemoration of the United Nations International Holocaust Remembrance Day on 27 January 2021, he said that "the genocide of the Hindus is the greatest genocide ever in the entire history of humanity. There is no doubt about that. Absolutely no doubt." He adds, "People have said 100 million died from Hindu Kush to Mumbai, 2011. Most probably true!" (Gautier). Rosenfeld rightly points out that "anyone with even a modicum of historical memory" would realize that "these analogies are not only in bad taste: they are subversive of good sense, sober judgement, and

Hitler's Popularity and Trivialization of Holocaust in India 93

reason itself" (37). Michael Bernstein helps us understand the incentives for this abuse of Holocaust memory. He writes, "Once victimhood is understood to endow one with special claims and rights, the scramble to attain that designation for one's own interest group is as heated as any other race for legitimacy and power" (Rothe 20). Tzvetan Todorov provides us further insight into this competitive victimhood:

> What pleasure is to be found in being a victim? None; but if no one wants to be a victim, everyone wants to have been one. . . . Having been a victim gives you the right to complain, protest, and make demands. . . . Your privileges are permanent.
>
> (Todorov qtd. in Rosenfeld 49)

Denial and Minimization of the Holocaust in Certain Sections of Indian Muslims

Holocaust denial and minimization is particularly common in the Urdu press in India and Pakistan (Aafreedi, "Muslim Antisemitism"). Urdu is the *lingua franca*, even if not the first language, of all Indian and Pakistani Muslims. Hence, its press is particularly influential in shaping the Muslim perceptions of Jews, Israel, and Zionism. The Muslims who deny the Holocaust do so because they believe, according to Meir Litvak, "that the memory of the Holocaust was the foundation of Western support for the establishment of the State of Israel. Therefore, refuting it would severely undermine Israel's legitimacy in the West and help in its eradication" (Livak 251). For them, "it never happened or else was hugely exaggerated" (Wistrich, "Anti-Zionist connections: Communism, Radical Islam, and the left" 407). As the eminent scholar of antisemitism, the late Robert Wistrich pointed out: "The denial of the Holocaust— whether in Britain, France (where it first originated), America or other Western countries—has become an integral part of the revamped antisemitic mythology of a world Jewish conspiracy" (Wistrich *Antisemitism* 112).

The fact is, had there not been a thriving self-governing community of 600,000-strong-*Yishuv* (the Zionist Jewish entity residing in pre-State Israel) built over years since the first settlement in 1860, the 360,000 survivors would not have found a shelter leading to the establishment of the State of Israel. As Dina Porat points out:

> And the UN November 1947 partition resolution, voting for the establishment of a Jewish State, came indeed after the Holocaust but not as its direct result. Political considerations, such as the Soviet interest in replacing Britain in the Middle East and in preventing American future influence in the area, were much more instrumental than belated empathy.
>
> (477)

Considering the widespread rhetoric among the anti-Zionists aimed at denying the Holocaust or minimizing its scale with the objective of delegitimizing the State of Israel, it must be pointed out that according to a working definition of antisemitism,

94   Navras J. Aafreedi

agreed upon by 27 EU countries, "denying the fact, scope, mechanisms (e.g., gas chambers) or intentionality of the genocide of the Jewish people at the hands of National Socialist Germany and its supporters and accomplices during WW-II (the Holocaust)," and accusing the Jewish people or the State of Israel of inventing or exaggerating the Holocaust are understood to be antisemitic acts (Porat 473). Porat draws our attention to the fact that "a more recent working definition of Holocaust denial, reached by the ITF member states in 2010, which draws on the EU decision, also defines denial as a form of antisemitism. Antisemitism is by now punishable by laws and other forms of regulations in some twenty countries" (Porat 473).

Holocaust Inversion in the English Language Press in India

India, the second most populous country, home to one-sixth of the global population, has 82,237 newspapers and news-magazines, out of which 12,000 are daily newspapers, with 1,406 out of these in the English language, and 462 million internet users (Pattanaik and Behuria 28–30). India is the third largest internet user after America and China ("India is now world's third largest internet user after U.S., China"). Thirty-nine percent of 1.2 billion Indians read newspapers (Sarma). Newspapers sell 125 million copies every day in India (Mishra). According to the World Association of Newspapers, one in every five daily newspapers in the world is published in India (Vaidyanathan). India is the world's second largest English-speaking country. It is estimated that around 10 percent of its population or 125 million people speak English, which is second only to the United States. The number is expected to quadruple in the next decade (Masani). There are altogether 12 major media houses in India, which control most of its print and online publications and radio and television channels (Bhattacharjee and Agarwal). Their owners generally have some political affiliation or the other at any given point of time (Thakurta). Cases of Holocaust inversion have generally been found only in the leftist or the left-liberal press.

"Holocaust inversion" or "Holocaust reversal" is what we call the point of view that "the Israelis not only have forgotten the lesson of the Nazis but also have even become the new Nazis, doing to others what was done to them" (Wald 8). Alan Johnson has identified four forms of Holocaust inversion that emanate out of "the unhinged portrayal of Israel as a genocidist state":

> First, the depiction of Israelis as the new Nazis and the Palestinians as the new Jews; an inversion of reality. . ... Second, the Zionist ideology and movement is made to appear in the Anti-Zionist Ideology as akin to Nazism, or is considered alongside of, or in comparison to, or even collaborating with Nazism. . . . . Third, the Holocaust is turned into "moral lesson" for, or a "moral indictment" of the Jews—an inversion of morality. . . .. Fourth, Holocaust memory appears within the Anti-Zionist ideology only as a politicized and manipulated thing, a club wielded instrumentally, with malice aforethought, by bullying Jews, for Jewish ends.
>
> (Johnson 267–268)

Hitler's Popularity and Trivialization of Holocaust in India 95

There are several examples of Holocaust inversion in the Indian press, but the one that particularly stands out is the one whose author is aware of his Jewish lineage and feels that his admission of it makes his argument(s) more compelling. It is not rare for anti-Zionist Jews to mobilize their Jewish identities in their rhetoric with the objective of creating an air of legitimacy to hostility to Israel. David Hirsh has identified this phenomenon as influential in the rise of anti-Zionism and antisemitism (Hirsch 9). One of India's best known novelists, playwrights, film and drama critics, and screenwriters, Kiran Nagarkar, conscious of the prominent position he enjoyed in Indian civil society, opened his essay, "Alone-ness of being Palestine," in the newspaper *The Indian Express*, with a disclaimer, which read, "Perhaps at the outset, I should make it clear that I am a quarter Jewish." As his essay progresses, he mentions how the Israeli prime minister Benjamin Netanyahu reminds him of Adolf Hitler. "The force of the 'as a Jew' preface is to bear witness against the other Jews," as David Hirsh puts it (228). Its basis is the presumption that being Jewish provides a sort of privileged insight into what is antisemitic and what is not—"the claim to authority through identity substitutes for civil, rational debate" (Hirsch 228). Hirsh observes that "antizionist Jews do not simply make their arguments and adduce evidence; they mobilize their Jewishness to give themselves influence. They pose as courageous dissidents who stand up against the fearsome threat of mainstream Zionist power" (Hirsch 228). It must be noted that one of the several examples with which the International Holocaust Remembrance Alliance (IHRA) illustrates the definition of antisemitism it adopted in 2016 and which has since been adopted or endorsed by the United Nations, European Union, and 33 countries, including three permanent members of the United Nations Security Council (France, UK, and USA), is "drawing comparisons of contemporary Israeli policy to that of the Nazis" (IHRA). Gunther Jikeli explains that it:

> obviously depends on what kind of Nazi policies are compared with Israeli policies ("the overall context needs to be taken into account") and "drawing comparisons" should be understood in the colloquial sense of equating and not stressing differences. However, equating Nazi genocidal policies with policies of the Israeli government—what scholars have termed Holocaust inversion—is not only bad taste but false to an extent that it can only be regarded as a form of libel, not criticism. For those who still wonder what the difference is between criticism of Israel and antisemitic accusations against Israel, it might be helpful to think of it in terms of the difference between criticism and defamation or libel. In some cases, it is difficult to distinguish between the two but in most cases, it is pretty clear.
>
> (Jikeli)

Conclusion

Widespread ignorance of the Holocaust, craving for strong leadership, and the traditional Hindu nationalist admiration for Hitler and Nazism account for Hitler's popularity in India (Aafreedi, "The Paradox of the Popularity of Hitler in India").

The fact is that we not only require Holocaust education but also education in Jewish history to make students completely understand why the colossal tragedy took place. It is because of this widespread ignorance of the Holocaust and of Jewish history that people fall so easily for the antisemitic propaganda aimed at denying or minimizing or trivializing or inverting the Holocaust.

Taking stock of this, Presidency University in Kolkata launched an undergraduate course in global Jewish history and a Holocaust-focused postgraduate course, the only such courses in all of South Asia, in 2016. Publication of literature on global Jewish history and the Holocaust in all those 22 major languages of India that are recognized under the eighth schedule of its constitution, and the introduction of Holocaust and Jewish history at the secondary level of education can go a long way in remedying the situation in terms of raising awareness of the Holocaust and eliminating antisemitism.

Absence of the education of Jewish history and the Holocaust, compounded by the lack of credible sources of information on Jews in vernaculars has led to widespread ignorance of who the Jews are and how they suffered during the Holocaust. The domestication, normalization, popularization, and commercialization of Hitler only aggravates the situation, leading to the justification of the perpetration of the Holocaust in public perception. This makes the ignorant masses particularly susceptible to the antiminority propaganda unleashed by the right wing, inspired by Nazi and Fascist ideologies. Together these factors provide conditions conducive for antisemitism, xenophobia, and communalism to thrive in India.

We need to make efforts to raise historical awareness via education as well as Popular Culture to combat the rising popularity of Hitler. We can hope that this would work as a deterrent to a certain degree to the several problems just mentioned and to the occurrence of mass violence, but at the same time, we must be cautious of what Rosenfeld has pointed out:

> The very success of the Holocaust's wide dissemination in the public sphere can work to undermine its gravity and render it a more familiar thing. The more successfully it enters the cultural mainstream, the more commonplace it becomes. A less taxing version of a tragic history begins to emerge—still full of suffering, to be sure, but a suffering relieved of many of its weightiest moral and intellectual demands and, consequently, easier to bear. Made increasingly familiar through repetition, it becomes normalized.
>
> (Rosenfeld 11)

He implores us to be conscious of the fact that:

> The Nazi genocide of the Jews will not soon be forgotten, but how it is retained in memory and transmitted depends overwhelmingly on what we choose to recover from the past, on what we choose to ignore or suppress, and on what we choose to remodel or newly invent.
>
> (Rosenfeld 31)

Notes

1 An example to illustrate this phenomenon is how *#NathuramGodseZindabad* (Long Live Nathuram Godse) was one of the top trends on Twitter for several hours on M. K. Gandhi's birth anniversary, 2 Oct. 2021. Godse was Gandhi's assassin. Please see The Wire Staff, "On Gandhi Jayanti, 'Nathuram Godse Zindabad' Trends on Twitter in India." *The Wire*, 2 Oct. 2021. Accessed 16 Oct. 2021, https://thewire.in/communalism/on-gandhi-jayanti-nathuram-godse-zindabad-trends-on-twitter-in-india; Rakesh, K. M., "Nathuram Godse becomes top Twitter trend on Gandhi Jayanti", *The Telegraph*, 3 Oct. 2021. Accessed 16 Oct. 2021, www.telegraphindia.com/india/on-mahatma-gandhis-birth-anniversary-worship-of-nathuram-godse/cid/1833190

2 The present author has deliberately spelled 'antisemitism' without hyphen, conscious as he is of the scholarly arguments in favor of doing so. However, the hyphenated form has been retained in quotes.

3 Translated from Hindi by the present author.

4 Following are URL links to the Facebook profiles of some of them:
www.facebook.com/profile.php?id=100023033134362,
www.facebook.com/htler.mahakul.9,www.facebook.com/adolf.saroj,
www.facebook.com/profile.php?id=100051366497429,
www.facebook.com/profile.php?id=100035550557153,
www.facebook.com/profile.php?id=100018048877292,
www.facebook.com/govind.kmr.988, www.facebook.com/hitlor.singh.1,
www.facebook.com/hitlor.singh.75,
www.facebook.com/profile.php?id=100024380910915,
www.facebook.com/hitlor.singh.5, www.facebook.com/hitalar.singh.3,
www.facebook.com/hitlar.singh.7, www.facebook.com/hitlear.singh.7,
www.facebook.com/hitlor.singh.3, www.facebook.com/hitlir.singh,
www.facebook.com/profile.php?id=100050188902501,
www.facebook.com/rishu.gujjar.10048,
www.facebook.com/profile.php?id=100008491722043,
www.facebook.com/hitalarrajput.rajput, www.facebook.com/hit.yadav.9,
www.facebook.com/hitlar.yadav.9, www.facebook.com/hitlar.yadav.92,
www.facebook.com/profile.php?id=100014988489709,
www.facebook.com/harish.hindustani.12, www.facebook.com/hitlarkumar.yadav,
www.facebook.com/hitalar.yadav.52,
www.facebook.com/profile.php?id=100034096356815,
www.facebook.com/profile.php?id=100050663072590,
www.facebook.com/Hitler-Khan-1607943762857559,
www.facebook.com/oriflamebykiran

5 Some of the most significant responses are the letters written to Gandhi by Yehuda Leon Magnes; Martin Buber; Hayim Greenberg, the editor of the American Zionist Socialist newspaper *The Jewish Frontier;* and Avraham Sohet, the editor of the Indian Jewish newspaper from Bombay *The Jewish Advocate.*

6 See also Bhattacharjee, Anuradha. *The Second Homeland: Polish Refugees in India.* Sage, 2012; Bhatti, Anil and Johannes H. Voigt. *Jewish Exile in India, 1933–1945.* Manohar, 2005; and Robbins, Kenneth X. "The camp for Polish refugee children at Balachadi, Nawanagar [India]." *The Journal of Indo-Judaic Studies*, vol. 4, 2001, http://mei.org.in/jijs/k4. Accessed 16 Oct. 2021.

Works Cited

Aafreedi, Navras Jaat. "India's response to the Holocaust and its perception of Hitler." *Cafe Dissensus*, vol. 31 (Guest Edited Special Issue), Jan. 2017, https://cafedissensus.

98 Navras J. Aafreedi

com/2017/01/20/contents-indias-response-to-the-holocaust-and-its-perception-of-hitler-issue-31/. Accessed 10 Nov. 2021.

———. "Jewish-Muslim relations in South Asia: Where antipathy lives without Jews." *Asian Jewish Life*, no. 15, 2014, pp. 13–16.

———. "Muslim antisemitism and anti-Zionism in South Asia: A case study of Lucknow." *Anti-Zionism, Antisemitism: The Dynamics of Delegitimization*, edited by Alvin H. Rosenfeld. Indiana University Press, 2019, pp. 454–480.

———. "The paradox of the popularity of Hitler in India." *Asian Jewish Life*, no. 14, 2014, pp. 14–16.

ADL. "Decision by India's Zee TV to Broadcast Soap Opera with Hitler Title to Arab World "Unfortunate and Disturbing"." *ADL Says*, 30 Dec. 2014, www.adl.org/news/press-releases/decision-by-indias-zee-tv-to-broadcast-soap-opera-with-hitler-title-to-arab. Accessed 15 Oct. 2021.

Arjunpuri, Chaitra. "'Hitler's shop sends India shockwave." *Al Jazeera*, 3 Sept. 2012, www.aljazeera.com/indepth/features/2012/09/2012927558327565.html. Accessed 11 Aug. 2020.

Banerjee, Basabi Khan and Georg Stober. "'Hitlermania': Nazism and the Holocaust in Indian history textbooks." *Journal of Educational Media, Memory, and Society*, vol. 12, no. 1, 2020, pp. 43–73.

Bhattacharjee, Anuradha. *The Second Homeland: Polish Refugees in India*. Sage, 2012.

Bhattacharjee, Anuradha and Anushi Agrawal. "Mapping the power of major media companies in India." *Economic & Political Weekly*, vol. 53, no. 19, 2018, pp. 48–57.

Bhatti, Anil and Johannes H. Voigt. *Jewish Exile in India, 1933–1945*. Manohar, 2005.

Casolari, Marzia. "Hindutva's foreign tie-ups in the 1930s: Archival evidence." *Economic and Political Weekly*, vol. 35, no. 4, 2000, pp. 218–228.

Chettiar, Blessy. "Review: 'Gandhi to Hitler' is an assault on senses and cinema." *DNA*, 29 Jul. 2011, www.dnaindia.com/entertainment/review-review-gandhi-to-hitler-is-an-assault-on-senses-and-cinema-1570795. Accessed 15 Oct. 2021.

David, Robin. "Fear your friend Hitler!" *The Times of India*, 16 Jun. 2010, https://timesofindia.indiatimes.com/blogs/On-the-bounce/fear-your-friend-hitler/. Accessed 28 Nov. 2021.

Dhawan, Himanshi. "Why Hindutva's foreign-born cheer leaders are so popular." *The Times of India*, 9 Apr. 2017, https://timesofindia.indiatimes.com/home/sunday-times/why-hindutvas-foreign-born-cheerleaders-are-so-popular/articleshow/58085790.cms. Accessed 20 Aug. 2020.

Egorova, Yulia. *Jews and India: Perceptions and Image*. Routledge, 2006.

———. *Jews and Muslims in South Asia: Reflections of Difference, Religion and Race*. Oxford University Press, 2018.

———. "Memory of the Holocaust in India: A case study for Holocaust education." *Holocaust Memory in a Globalizing World*, edited by Jacob S. Eder, Philipp Gassert and Allan E. Steinweis. Gottingen, 2017, pp. 215–227.

Gandhi, Mohandas Karamchand. *Complete Works of Mahatma Gandhi*, vol. 76, www.gandhiashramsevagram.org/gandhi-literature/mahatma-gandhi-collected-works-volume-76.pdf. Accessed 4 Nov. 2019.

———. *How to Combat Hitlerism*, 22 Jun. 1940, www.mkgandhi.org/mynonviolence/chap44.htm. Accessed 28 Nov. 2021.

———. *Letter to Adolf Hitler*, 24 Dec. 1940, www.gandhiashramsevagram.org/gandhi-literature/gandhi-letter-to-adolf-hitler1.php. Accessed 28 Nov. 2021.

Gautier, Francios. "Mr Francios Gautier, Author & Journalist address on 76th Holocaust Memorial Day; IIC New Delhi." *Jammu Kashmir Unity Foundation [YouTube Channel]*, 6 Feb. 2021, www.youtube.com/watch?v=SJzjge9EJNk. Accessed 15 Oct. 2021.

Golwalkar, Madhav Sadashivrao. *We or Our Nationhood Defined*, 1939, https://sanjeev.sab-hlokcity.com/Misc/We-or-Our-Nationhood-Defined-Shri-M-S-Golwalkar.pdf. Accessed 28 Nov. 2021.

Gramlich, John. "How countries around the world view democracy, military rule and other political systems." *Pew Research Center*, 30 Oct. 2017, www.pewresearch.org/fact-tank/2017/10/30/global-views-political-systems/. Accessed 28 Nov. 2021.

Hirsch, David. *Contemporary Left Antisemitism*. Routledge, 2018.

IHRA. "What Is Antisemitism?" *International Holocaust Remembrance Alliance*, www.holocaustremembrance.com/resources/working-definitions-charters/working-definition-antisemitism. Accessed 28 Nov. 2021.

"India is Now World's Third Largest Internet User after U.S., China." *The Hindu*, 24 Aug. 2013, www.thehindu.com/sci-tech/technology/internet/india-is-now-worlds-third-larg-est-internet-user-after-us-china/article5053115.ece. Accessed 20 Aug. 2020.

"Indian MP shocks with Hitler costume protest in parliament." *BBC News*, 10 Aug. 2018, www.bbc.com/news/world-asia-india-45140801. Accessed 28 Nov. 2021.

Jikeli, Gunther. "Why Is There Resistance to a Working Definition of Antisemitism?" *Jew-Think*, 15 Jan. 2021, www.jewthink.org/2021/01/15/why-is-there-some-resistance-to-a-working-definition-of-antisemitism/. Accessed 16 Oct. 2021.

Johnson, Alan. "Intellectual incitement: The anti-Zionist ideology and the anti-Zionist subject." In *The Case against Academic Boycotts of Israel*, edited by Nelson Nelson and Gabriel Brahm. MLA Members for Scholars Rights and Distributed by Wayne State University Press, 2015, pp. 259–281.

Kumar, Rakesh Ranjan, dir. *Gandhi to Hitler*. By Rakesh Ranjan Kumar. Dir. Rakesh Ranjan Kumar. Perf. Raghubir Yadav. Prod. Dr. Anil Kumar Sharma. "Amrapali media vision Pvt. Ltd., 2011." *YouTube*, 14 Oct. 2021, www.youtube.com/watch?v=oRS1-zIqDkw

Kumaraswamy, P. R. "India and the Holocaust: Perceptions of the Indian National Congress." *Journal of Indo-Judaic Studies*, vol. 3, 2000, pp. 117–125, www.mei.org.in/up-loads/jijscontent/95-1550426856-jijsarticlepdf.pdf. Accessed 28 Nov. 2021.

Lev, Shimon. " 'Can the Jews resist this organised and shameless persecution?'—Gandhi's attitude to the Holocaust." *Gandhi Marg*, vol. 35, no. 3, 2013, pp. 347–373.

———. "Melting Hitler's heart of stone: Gandhi's attitude to the Holocaust." *The Journal of Indo-Judaic Studies*, vol. 13, 2013, pp. 37–55.

Livak, Meir. "The Islamic Republic of Iran and the Holocaust: Anti-Semitism and Anti-Zionism." In *Anti-Semitism and Anti-Zionism in Historical Perspective: Convergence and Divergence*, edited by Jeffrey Herf. Routledge, 2006.

Masani, Zareer. "English or Hinglish—which will India choose?" *BBC News*, 27 Nov. 2012, www.bbc.com/news/magazine-20500312. Accessed 20 Aug. 2020.

Mishra, Atul Kumar. "Newspapers in India and their political ideologies." *Rightblog.in*, 13 Jul. 2015. https://rightlog.in/2015/07/newspapers-in-india-and-their-political-ideologies/. Accessed 20 Aug. 2020.

Nagarkar, Kiran. "Alone-ness of being Palestine." *The Indian Express*, 12 Apr. 2018, https://indianexpress.com/article/opinion/columns/alone-ness-of-being-palestine-jounalist-yasser-murtaza-death-5133603/. Accessed 20 Aug. 2020.

National Archives of India (NAI). File No. "88/33." 1933.

Pattanaik, Smruti S. and Ashok K. Behruria. "Media-scape in South Asia and the issue of regional cooperation." In *The Role of Media in Promoting Regional Understanding in South Asia*, edited by Priyanka Singh. Pentagon Press, 2016.

Porat, Dina. "Holocaust Denial and the image of the Jew, or 'they boycott Auschwitz as an Israeli product.' " In *Resurgent Antisemitism: Global Perspectives*, edited by Alvin H. Rosenfeld. Indiana University Press, 2013, pp. 467–481.

100 *Navras J. Aafreedi*

PTI. "Better not be in Delhi, it's like a 'gas chamber': Supreme court." *The Economic Times*, 18 Jan. 2019, https://economictimes.indiatimes.com/news/politics-and-nation/better-not-be-in-delhi-its-like-gas-chamber-supreme-court/articleshow/67590551.cms. Accessed 28 Nov. 2021.

Purandare, Vaibhav. *Hitler and India: The Untold Story of His Hatred for the Country & Its People*. Westland Non-Fiction, 2021.

Robbins, Kenneth X. "The camp for Polish refugee children at Balachadi, Nawanagar [India]." *The Journal of Indo-Judaic Studies*, vol. 4, 2001, http://mei.org.in/jijs/k4. Accessed 16 Oct. 2021.

Rosenfeld, Alvin H. *The End of the Holocaust*. Indiana University Press, 2011.

Rothe, Anne. *Popular Trauma Culture: Selling the Pain of Others in the Mass Media*. Rutgers University Press, 2011.

Sareen, Tilak Raj. "Indian responses to the Holocaust." In *Jewish Exile in India, 1933–1945*, edited by Anil Bhatti and Johannes H. Voigt. Manohar, 2005, pp. 55–83.

Sarma, Dibyajyoti. "39% of Indians read newspapers: IRS 2017 Report." *PrintWeek India*, 19 Jan. 2018, www.printweek.in/News/-indians-read-newspapers-irs-2017-report-27836. Accessed 28 Nov. 2021.

Schweitzer, Frederick M. "Antisemitism and law." *Antisemitism in North America: New World, Old Hate*, edited by Steven K. Baum, et al. Brill, 2016, pp. 225–300.

Sharma, Manimugdha S. "Why Hitler is not a dirty word in India." *The Times of India*, 29 Apr. 2018, https://timesofindia.indiatimes.com/india/why-hitler-is-not-a-dirty-word-in-india/articleshow/63955029.cms. Accessed 28 Nov. 2021.

Siddiqui, Sarah. "Indian Films Named After Hitler." *Cafe Dissensus*, vol. 31 (Guest Edited Special Issue), Jan. 2017, https://cafedissensus.com/2017/01/19/india-films-named-after-hitler/. Accesssed 28 Nov. 2021.

Sivaraman, Satya. "Musings on the popularity of Mein Kampf." *Infochange India*, no. 16, 2009, pp. 51–52, www.ccds.in/download/publication/agenda/agenda_16.pdf. Accessed 28 Nov. 2021.

Suhrud, Tridip. "'You are today the one person in the world who can prevent a war.' Read Gandhi's letters to Hitler." *Time*, 25 Sept. 2019, https://time.com/5685122/gandhi-hitler-letter/. Accessed 10 Nov. 2021.

Thakurta, Paranjoy Guha. "Media ownership in India—An overview." *The Hoot*, 30 Jun. 2012, http://asu.thehoot.org/resources/media-ownership/media-ownership-in-india-an-overview-6048. Accessed 20 Aug. 2020.

Uniyal, Vijeta. "Why findings of ADL's Global anti-semitism Survey should bother Hindus." *The Times of Israel*, 16 May 2014, https://blogs.timesofisrael.com/adl-global-100-survey-anti-semitism-hinduism-india/. Accessed 23 Mar. 2020.

Vaidyanathan, Rajini. "Newspapers: Why India's newspaper industry is booming." *BBC News*, 1 Aug. 2011, www.bbc.com/news/business-14362723. Accessed 20 Aug. 2020.

Wald, James. "The new replacement theory: Anti-Zionism, antisemitism, and the denial of history." In *Anti-Zionism and Antisemitism: The Dynamics of Delegitimization*, edited by Alvin H. Rosenfeld. Indiana University Press, 2019, pp. 3–29.

Weil, Shalva. "From persecution to freedom: Central European Jewish Refugees and their host communities in India." *Jewish Exile in India, 1933–1945*, edited by Anil Bhatti and Johannes H. Voigt. Manohar, 2005, pp. 64–84.

Wistrich, Robert S. "Anti-Zionist connections: Communism, Radical Islam, and the left." In *Resurgent Antisemitism: Global Perspectives*, edited by Alvin H. Rosenfeld. Indiana University Press, 2013, pp. 402–423.

Wistrich, Robert S. *Antisemitism: The Longest Hatred*. Pantheon Books, 1991.

6 Decoding Holocaust Narratives in Japanese Pop Culture

Through the Lens of *Anne no Nikki* (1995) and *Persona Non Grata* (2015)

José Rodolfo Avilés Ernult and Astha Chadha

Introduction

Since the end of World War II, the memories of the battles conducted in the Asia-Pacific and their cinematic representation have become increasingly marred with reinterpretations and reimagination grounded in an agenda of historical sanitization. It comes together with the resurgence of historical revisionism proposed by neo-nationalist movements, which have had a significant impact on the reconstruction of narration of Japan's role in the Asia-Pacific war. In this context, the reemergence of historical war films about the Holocaust and the exodus of the surviving Jews is significant.

Besides being reflective of Japanese feelings on the European conflict and the image of the Jews, these productions were deployed following an agenda of sanitization and image control of the Japanese involvement in the Holocaust. Sanitization, context omission, and distancing the portrayed narratives from the Asia-Pacific war are characteristics of Japanese war-related films dealing with the exodus of the Jews from Europe, following the Western Hollywood trend of creating heartwarming movies that focus on Gentile characters who provide help to the persecuted community. Alongside these heartwarming flicks, another trend is the dilution of on-screen violence or conflict, steering away from full-blown depictions of the war efforts and the coupling of Japan and the Axis Powers.

That Popular Culture media addressing the Holocaust is produced and consumed in Japan is not surprising given the historical involvement of the country in World War II and the investment and focus of the nation in disseminating diverse products of its culture industry.

While on the surface Japanese films depicting the Holocaust intend to inform the viewer about the specific underpinnings of the Jewish experience, Japanese cinematic representation of the Holocaust is grounded in preconceived narratives aligned to their local media genres and well-established narrative devices and conventions. As Akiko Hashimoto states when discussing the encoding of narrative conventions used to compose and produce Holocaust media, three types of narratives dominate Japan's war memories—perpetrator narratives, which emphasize the role of Japanese as aggressors; narratives of fallen national heroes; and emotional

DOI: 10.4324/9781003251224-9

102 *José Rodolfo Avilés Ernult and Astha Chadha*

emphatic narratives, which strive to achieve identification with victims (Hashimoto 7–8). This chapter argues that *Persona Non Grata* (originally, *Sugihara Chiune*, 2015) and *Anne no Nikki* (1995, based on *The Diary of Anne Frank*), nicely fit into the last two narrative types as they respectively present Chiune Sugihara as the Japanese Oskar Schindler, who sacrificed his diplomatic career and personal safety to save thousands of Jewish refugees, and Anne Frank as a child victim of the Holocaust and a paragon of courage, innocence, and hope for the children of the world to learn from. It questions the compatibility between the Holocaust and the narrative types and genres these productions fall into and explores how the narratives employed in *Anne no Nikki* and *Persona Non Grata* depict the Jewish experience of the Holocaust and their representation of Japanese war memory.

Silence and Selective Portrayal of the Holocaust in Japanese Popular Culture

Anne no Nikki and *Persona Non Grata* are two films released years apart. The former being an animated version of the literary text *The Diary of Anne Frank*, while the latter is a motion picture about the former Japanese diplomat Chiune Sugihara, who is referred as the Japanese Schindler—the savior of the Jews. While *Anne no Nikki* shows the life of a victimized Jewish family, *Persona Non Grata* is the perspective of a Japanese about not just the victimization of the Jews in Europe but also of him. Both the films depict different characters but narrate a very similar story through a diluted portrayal of antisemetic atrocities in Europe as in *Anne no Nikki*, as well as a sort of equalization of the Jewish Holocaust and the Japanese situation in World War II. Both Japan and Jews emerge as victims of World War II, which is quintessential to the creation of a war narrative for Japan—one that allows Japan to distance itself from its imperialist past and its participation in World War II and to feel the pain of the defeat through atrocious bombing of Hiroshima and Nagasaki.

The cognitive dissonance in Japanese Popular Culture manifests itself as the cultural silence of the Japanese regarding the contexts and causes of the Holocaust in Europe. This silence can be noticed in the way the Popular Culture sanitizes the war history and selectively maintains silence on the atrocities toward the victims of the war. This chapter argues that the movies *Anne no Nikki* and *Persona Non Grata* are also selectively omitting as well as sanitizing the facts related to the Holocaust by maintaining differing degrees of silence on the crimes against the Jews. This is referred to here as the silence of Japanese war cinema regarding the Holocaust. Despite being a movie on the theme of the Holocaust, *Anne no Nikki* is set in Amsterdam during the time of Jewish persecution, where most of the background of the movie is conveyed though exposition (i.e., the movie does not show to the viewers most of the cruelty and suffering of the Jews). Though the movie does acknowledge the Holocaust as something that "happened" and caused "suffering," it is only either implied or mentioned by the characters, without showing the gravitas of the situation in the movie. The presence of the Holocaust is there, hanging, but none of the violence or its consequences are dealt with.

Decoding Holocaust Narratives in Japanese Pop Culture   103

The directors deliberately selected to show less powerful ways of conveying or portraying the Holocaust in a movie. This chapter argues that this is because there is no coherent national memory in Japan; Japan as a nation needs to fill that void with the products of the culture industry and war cinema. Such cinema is a way of telling the Japanese that they are victims, though in reality, they were partially, if not greatly, perpetrators. The incoherence or disruption displayed by the directors of the movies generate a sanitizing effect on the viewers with regard to the Holocaust. The attempt to show Japan as a victim makes it impossible to implicate Japan for any consequences of the cruelty of the Holocaust.

Both films show the distorted collective memory of what befell Jews during the years of the Holocaust in the same way that Japanese culture industry could not make sense or find the words and the images to explain the wounds of the defeat of the empire at the end of the war. Symbolically, the Japanese silence on the Holocaust is a way to cope with their own wounds and identify themselves with the Jews as victims while at the same time separating themselves from the painful memories of this condition by sanitizing and diluting the violence of the experience. Such internal tension is similar to what the Germans experienced as the guilt for the war and their suffering at the hands of the Allies (Assmann 193). Japanese exculpate themselves as perpetrators of war crimes in the Asia-Pacific war by concentrating on the Holocaust committed by the Germans, thus linking Japanese and Jews as victims—one victim of the Germans and the other of the Allies.

Through an analysis of *Anne no Nikki* and *Persona Non Grata,* this chapter aims at identifying how the Japanese use Holocaust cinema to relate to the Jewish experience of victims of World War II as a symbolic device to make sense of the trauma of the war and the dissonant and contradictory narrative created by their historical revisionism. It will be argued that the vision of the Holocaust has been produced through ideological compromises to avoid the guilt of their bellicose role during World War II. The analysis of these texts will be done to understand this dissonance in their national memory and the historic narrative embedded in it.

Akinori Nagaoka, the director of *Anne no Nikki*, seems to have elected to represent the Franks and the Van Pels families as victims while at the same time not showing their suffering and constant fear and tension of being found by the Dutch police and the Gestapo, with the goal to maintain at the appearance of a bourgeois family who are soft-spoken and respectable—traits relatable to the Japanese middle class this film is directed at. Missing is the combination of despair, fatalism, and hope of Western portrayals of the Franks hiding. The film's producers rejected the genre conventions of Hollywood Holocaust and war movies and, instead, opted to present a tale of naïve innocence and coming-of-age themes with powerful resonance among the Japanese audience of 1995 to make sure that the film had both popular domestic and international appeal.

Japanese Popular Culture is known to be controversial in its projection of World War II and the Japanese role in it. For instance, the depiction of events surrounding World War II in Japanese anime has aimed at sanitizing the Japanese role in the war, Japanese war movies have been frowned upon for being biased toward

104 *José Rodolfo Avilés Ernult and Astha Chadha*

recreating war memory, and Japanese cosplay has been deemed insensitive for accepting Nazi cosplay (Jaworowicz-Zimny 14).

For example, the peculiarity of Japanese Popular Culture is manifested as Anne Frank is not just seen as the memory of a teenage girl being persecuted for being a Jew at the hands of the Nazi Germany but as a symbol of things she has in common with Japan. This chapter elaborates on two such aspects. The first is Japan's view of Anne Frank's experience of victimhood in World War II in the Holocaust, which Japan experienced through the Hiroshima and Nagasaki bombings (Goodman and Miyazawa 178). Drawing a parallel in their experiences gives more weight to the Japanese narrative of being a survivor of the atrocities, a nation that has been devastated and has risen from ashes of destruction caused in the war, against the version of Japan being an aggressor in the war.

This chapter argues that the film *Anne no Nikki*'s portrayal of the Jewish experience and Holocaust is done through the lens of the *shoujo* genre as a gendered narrative focused on innocence and childhood in a walled and safe space for young girls, which explores intimacy and inner exploration, thus relegating the Holocaust to the backdrop of the narrative. It uses Shinji Miyadai's model of *shoujo* categories to show how *Anne no Nikki* uses the conventions of the style to focus on monologues and the inner emotional world (Miyadai et al. 18). This is important mainly because of the still ongoing discussion about reception and impact of several adaptations of the diary in properly contextualizing the historical legacy of the Holocaust for the Japanese audience. In one camp, scholars like Hema Ramachandran argue that the impact of Anne Frank's narrative has been positive in contextualizing the Jewish experience and facilitating an awareness of sociocultural specificity contrasted with that of the Japanese (Ramachandran 80). However, in the other camp, authors Goodman and Miyazawa identify any adaptation of the diary into popular media as systemic diluting of the Jewish experience into an amalgamation of helplessness and hope, tempered by universal goodwill, in which the ideological program of the Holocaust gets diminished or deemphasized (Goodman and Miyazawa 178–179).

Anne no Nikki as a Japanese Interpretation of Victimization in the Holocaust

The movie *Anne no Nikki* was released on 19 August 1995 in the year marking half a century since the end of World War II. The movie revolves around the time when Anne Frank was forced into hiding along with her family in Amsterdam due to the ensuing Jewish Holocaust in Europe and ends with the scene where they are all arrested to be taken away to concentration camps by the army. This section analyzes *Anne no Nikki* as a text to uncover certain similarities in the movies and the other dominant Japanese war film narratives of the time that put Japan in the position of a defenseless victim of war. But since this movie is about Anne Frank, and not Japan, the same effect is achieved through the story of struggle and survival of the teenage Holocaust victim, who is cornered into submitting to the draconian anti-Jew laws in Europe passed under the Nazi regime. At the same time, by softening the tone of the struggle of the Jews and maintaining silence on their suffering, it

Decoding Holocaust Narratives in Japanese Pop Culture   105

pushes the Holocaust into the background and highlights daily/usual struggles of people in "hiding."

The main thing *Anne no Nikki* achieves is to adapt Anne Frank's concrete specific struggle and the backdrop of Jewish Holocaust into Japanese audience's preconceptions of what a young girl's struggles in life should be. These categories have been informed by diverse styles and modes of *shoujo* manga and animation in Japan. This section argues that the background of Jewish experience of the Holocaust is lost in the very concrete and specific emotional experience of confinement of Anne (i.e., by focusing on internal world of Anne Frank through walled space and dreamscape of her affective inner world), making the film forget about the more dark and somber crude realities of Holocaust. By doing so, *Anne no Nikki* conforms to the emotional emphatic narratives which strive to achieve Japan's identification with Holocaust victims.

Anne no Nikki inserts itself in the otometic style[1] of *shoujo* visual narrative as a faithful adaptation of Anne Frank's 1942–1944 *The Diary of a Young Girl*. There are several factors that illuminate the continued popularity of Anne Frank's story among Japanese audience, such as it being a required reading in elementary schools throughout Japan. Another factor is that Anne Frank's narrative fits nicely into the several types of war narratives established in Japan, which focus on emotional connection and personal identification with the people of a defeated nation, grounded in a discourse of the universality of suffering; the importance of love, kindness, and resilience; as well as antimilitarism (Hashimoto 56). Unsurprisingly, by 1969, there were more than 10 different adaptations in *shoujo* magazines catering to young female readership, which established Anne Frank's narrative as a canonical text belonging to the girl's culture in Japan (Whaley 730).

Anne no Nikki is full of genre properties of *shoujo* otometic narratives—a visual awareness of the mood of characters, the appearance of dreamscapes or walled safe spaces, and a narrative dependent on inner monologues or voice-overs.

Very early in the movie, right after receiving her diary as a birthday present, the film offers the first exploration of Anne's environment, and we see the emergence of identifiable properties from *shoujo* narratives. Anne mentions how difficult life has become for the Jews under German occupation of Amsterdam, but the next scene shows her riding a bicycle (Jews are banned from riding bikes) and even shouting a carefree and excited "yahoo!" while crossing a bridge (*Anne no Nikki*, 11:54–11:55). Anne mentions, "Jews are not allowed to go to see movies, get on trains, drive cars, go out after 8 o'clock in the evening, go to swimming pools or tennis courts, and even ride bikes" (*Anne no Nikki,* 12:40–13:10). She says this as she passes by an army truck while on bicycle by merely pulling her cardigan over her dress to hide the yellow Star of David. This scene in the movie is an early indication of how easy it was to hide their Jewish identity by a simple act of cloaking, as shown in the movie hereafter till the very end. The deliberate juxtaposition of Anne reciting the rules for Jews in 1943 Amsterdam with an act of equal defiance by her or occurrence of chance events is a depiction of innocent "delinquency" being undeterred and unconfronted. The scene is handled with a wide shot of the streets of Amsterdam while a minimalistic piano melody lingers above the scene, disarming the threat that the army soldiers imply. The scene is the most dynamic of the film and uses an abundance of soft colors ubiquitous in *shoujo* manga to the effect of an idyllic urban landscape in which the female lead's mobility and sense of freedom is not thwarted.

However, viewers are informed of impending threats to Anne's experience of infancy, with dark shades and the presence of male authority as tokens of the danger that draw close to the idyllic city. Early in the film Anne is still wandering through a safe open space as her presence within Amsterdam is acceptable. In subsequent scenes of animated indoors, the film focuses more and more on subdued and darker shades of brown and gray, which oppose the more ubiquitous soft blue and warm grays. At the end of this sequence, the film shows Frank's balcony overflowing with an all-pervasive flower arrangement and decorations, which are a staple of *shoujo* visual media. Here, Anne is depicted enjoying her free time, reading among blooming flowers, accompanied by her cat, just being a kid, the dire threat of the concentration camps unbeknown to her. This theme is repeated throughout the film, the emotional state of the characters reflected in their space and the objects surrounding as a way to pay attention to Anne's affections and feelings.

It is characteristic of *shoujo* narratives to illustrate the life story of a character, to be followed vicariously by the readers. Since these characters are usually depicted as children and young girls, it serves a proxy experience for the Japanese viewers/ readers, where physical conflict and emotional distress are toned down to fit the constraints of the genre.

However, while we still see decorative flowers and urban dream spaces, as mentioned previously, there is a certain amount of emotional distress in the original material, which is adequate for *shoujo* narratives. Her intense and emotionally complex inner self, which shows through her monologues and the melodrama interlaced in the walled space of the setting, reveal Anne as a young, vibrant, and dramatic protagonist who strives to survive against the impending doom of the Holocaust. This presents an incompatibility between *shoujo* and the Anne Frank narrative because the style so deeply engrained into Japanese conceptions of Anne requires a tragic heroine who, nevertheless, finds peace or love after her turbulent process of maturing is completed. The source material and the historical circumstance of the Holocaust preclude any such conditions for it to fit into the *shoujo* genre; so, instead, it doubles down on walling down into a dreamscape and the concealment of trauma.

Right after showing Anne struggling to keep quiet in the new hideout due to the fear of being caught, she asks her sister, "Margot, don't you think this is like an adventure?" (*Anne no Nikki*, 30:54–30:58) to which the sister replies, "You are a happy-go-lucky person" (*Anne no Nikki*, 30:58–31:01). Anne again replies, "But, being upset won't make anything better. I love a thrill!" (*Anne no Nikki*, 31:02– 31:06), once again referring to her "suspense film" adventure like exclamation, quite contrary to the experience of Anne Frank in the book (diary entry of Friday, 10 July 1942) wherein she is extremely exhausted with the day's hard work and does not feel at home (Frank 21–22). The movie smoothly hides other conflicts in the annex, such as the tense relationship with her mother, her dislike of Mrs. van Daan, her difficult life in the annex amid food shortage and constant fear of being discovered, and the necessary claustrophobic daily life.

In comparison, the most celebrated film adaptation of the source material, *The Diary of Anne Frank* (1959) directed by George Stevens, presents confronting images of intense inspection and anxious visuals that convey the claustrophobic space together with well-timed close-ups, which present an emotional tension and psychological torture. *Anne no Nikki* almost never allows such close-ups or medium shots; instead, stationary wide shots are employed to reduce tension to great effect. Similarly, dialogues hang in the air to move forward with dates in Anne's diary, with no effect on the scenes that roll thereafter.

The movie ends up dissociating the Holocaust from Anne's narrative by making it a story of secret hideout, family struggles, and events that cause a stir in Anne's life, which fit the *shoujo* genre. The film's focus is on presenting her as an otometic and tragic heroine, rather than a victim of the Holocaust. The confrontational style of other adaptations of *The Diary of Anne Frank* are not present in this film. Such priority of the film inspires courage and hope for the viewers to identify with the character, resulting in the Holocaust falling between the cracks of the genre. So, even though the otometic *shoujo* style is compatible with the Anne Frank narrative, overall, it struggles to inform the viewer about the Jewish experience of the Holocaust.

Anne's diary, Kitty, claims that since it survived instead of Anne, it would never give up Anne's ideals and would want to continue to speak of her wish forever (*Anne no Nikki,* 1:36:20–1:36:35). The diary, Kitty, is a living memory of a girl who felt and wrote things from her own perspective. A depiction of the same on screen gives the required liberty of sanitization of the events for giving a larger humanitarian purpose to the memory of suffering. The diary, too, is synonymous with Japan's presence as a nation that was a silent witness to aggression by Allied forces and a living memory of the pain it went through. Japan identifies with the similar feeling of isolation and forced submission it went through as a result of losing in World War II.

As Hashimoto has argued, the narratives that Japanese media have employed to talk about Japan's war past are deeply entwined into the anti-militaristic and pacifist identity that the Japanese population assumed during the postwar period (Hashimoto 11–12). While the victim narrative seeks to diffuse Japan's own war guilt by showing the Jewish Holocaust experience through the *shoujo* children narrative, there are several problems with this approach such as the viewership expectation of the material of the Anne Frank narrative, which has been used in Japan as educational texts through comics, manga, cinema, etc. (Waley 752). This has created viewership expectations around the Anne Frank narrative (i.e., the centrality of infancy, childhood, and courage in the face of adversity instead of the Holocaust itself).

Persona Non Grata as a Japanese Hero's Sacrifice During the Holocaust

The movie *Persona Non Grata* was released in 2015, about seven decades after the end of World War II. It is based on the life of the Japanese diplomat Chiune Sugihara, who served in the Ministry of Foreign Affairs of the Japanese empire and was sent to Kaunas, Lithuania, as the empire's vice-consul to gather intelligence on Russia. Though the movie intends to hail the "Japanese Schindler" for

108   *José Rodolfo Avilés Ernult and Astha Chadha*

his humanitarian act of issuing visas to many thousands of Jews in Lithuania and helping them evade the Holocaust, it is worth noting that he was dismissed from government service for the same.[2]

Unlike the movie's Japanese title *Sugihara Chiune*, which is the name of the Japanese diplomat and the protagonist of the movie, the English title *Persona Non Grata* makes a wider reference to people who are unwelcome—who have been expelled or forced into refuge—the Poles, who fled from their homeland taken over by the Nazi Germans; the Jews from other parts of Europe, who were being persecuted by Nazi Germans and were desperately searching for a place to go to; and the Japanese diplomat Chiune Sugihara, who is unwelcome in Manchuria, Russia, and later even in Japan. In that sense, Japan, through Sugihara, has been depicted as an entity caught up between aspirations, politics, and the reality of being unwelcome, despite his "efforts to keep his beloved Japan from becoming entangled in an inevitable worldwide conflict" (*Persona Non Grata*, 0:40–0:51).

The film depicts the Japanese hero Sugihara, who is driven by his resolve to serve his country while also gathering intelligence for his nation. He is a man with relatively less dilemma, strong character, and high intelligence, which leads him to raise his voice against his superiors (very un-Japanese behavior) when he realizes that Japan might lose the war. Employing the national hero narrative of the existing Japanese Popular Culture, the hero oversteps his official orders, sidesteps the protocols, and sacrifices his diplomatic career for the future of his nation, which he was not a part of after his dismissal. Like the fallen hero narrative, which interweaves a contradictory logic linking unforeseen progress to present sacrifice to project the Japanese belief of hopeful recovery (Hashimoto 8–9), Sugihara embodies the Japanese valor that stands strong for national service, without culpability or resentment toward the state leadership for their harsh orders.

The condition of the Jews has been portrayed with utmost caution to not depict anything graphically too violent. Concentration camps are hinted at in words. There is hope that survivors can flee when fortunately left unnoticed by aggressive Nazi soldiers, and the general antisemitism is shown only either by being shooed away by soldiers or through mere bullying of a Jewish male on the street by few other guys who punch/kick him a couple of times before they disperse. The overall atmosphere of the life-and-death situation for the Jews is diluted extensively and made to look like a displacement rather than an exodus to avoid persecution. Adherence to the sacrificing hero narrative enables the film to evade a graphic depiction of Jewish experience of the Holocaust by focusing on the hero, maintaining an incongruence with the historical narrative in Europe.

The Japanese innocence is more clearly portrayed through Sugihara's wife Yukiko, who has not seen the realities of the war firsthand until she marries Sugihara and comes to Lithuania. She is shaken by the "account" of a Jewish man who flees with his granddaughter from an encounter with Nazi Germans in occupied Poland where others are shot down mercilessly while only this pair survive miraculously. She is also rattled by the "condition" of the Jews, when she sees a Jewish man being bullied by few people in Kaunas and asks her driver, Pesh:

Decoding Holocaust Narratives in Japanese Pop Culture   109

Yukiko: Do you think he is alright?
Pesh: He's a Jew, he is used to it.
Yukiko: Why?
Pesh: They are pests, that's why. They take our money but keep to themselves. I wouldn't worry too much, madam. There is no point in getting involved with them.

(Persona Non Grata, 53:23–53:48)

The distorted memory of the Holocaust manifests itself unconsciously in lines such as: "It is so strange, isn't it—the world is so big and though the people in it have different shade of skin or color of the eyes, yet the hearts are all the same," implying that Yukiko is not actually aware of the cruelty being inflicted on the Jewish people by Japan's allies and is looking at the atrocities in a larger context of discrimination, instead of antisemitism (*Persona Non Grata*, 1:12:01–1:12:11). She also seems to reflect the Japanese voice when she asks her husband if he still thinks about "changing the world" after which the movie shows him issue visas to the Jews. The stakes for issuing these visas are very different for the Jews and Sugihara—for the former, it is their lives and for the latter, it is his diplomatic career. However, the equalization of both is done when Pesh warns Sugihara: "If you issue visas against the government order, you will be finished as a diplomat. It will affect our intelligence activities and I am not exaggerating when I say your family may be in danger" (*Persona Non Grata*, 1:03:45–1:03:58).

The genre comes to the rescue of the empathizing bystander and Nazi Germany ally, Japan, through Sugihara who decides to act against all odds, disregarding the consequences. Japanese relentlessness as a nation that supports war refugees or immigrants is strengthened with the film's depiction of Sugihara realizing the value of his act of kindness against all odds—the transit visa he issued on paper against the orders and the lives he saved going against what Nazi Germany was convinced of. The movie places Japan as a kind intermediary through Sugihara who tells the Jews, "This is just a visa. It may not be worth the paper it's written on. It will not guarantee that you will reach the other side. Expect a tough trip ahead of you. Just do not give up hope" (*Persona Non Grata*, 1:15:20–1:15:35).

The movie is a constant reminder of how Japan changed lives—first and foremost for the Jews, who were saved by Sugihara, then for Sugihara himself, who took a step toward "changing the world" as he wanted to, then for the Poles through Pesh, who got help from Sugihara in returning to his homeland to fight for its sovereignty in exchange for collecting intel about Russia, and finally for Wolfgang Gudze (a Lithuanian man of German descent, working in the Japanese consulate at Lithuania), who tells Sugihara before parting, "If not for this, I wouldn't have known the joy of being thought of as a good man" (*Persona Non Grata*, 1:30:31–1:30:39).

To avoid any regrets, Japan becomes the supporting force for Jews throughout their journey from Kaunas, Lithuania, until the coast of Japan. The Jews traveling with transit visas issued by Sugihara are stranded at Vladivostok, Russia, where they are stopped from boarding the ship to Japan. It is portrayed as an emotional

110   *José Rodolfo Avilés Ernult and Astha Chadha*

dilemma for Tetsuo Osako, who first stops the Jews but eventually allows them to board the ship, as he tells his superior:

Tetsuo Osako: Even if you do not help, you will not be blamed by other countries … however, today, a little child was among them. Her eyes were as if I was looking at my daughter. I want to save them.

(Persona Non Grata, 1:42:18–1:42:25)

The film ends up showing several Japanese, whose courage made them "heroes" not just for their nation but also for the Jews, who at every point during the journey from Lithuania to Japan received help; for Yukiko, because she empathized with a Jewish mother of two children hoping for life; for Sugihara, because he wanted to change the world; and for Tetsuo Osako, who allowed the Jews to board the ship against orders and traveled back to Japan with them.

There is another construction of similarity between the struggles of the rescued Jews, Sugihara, and Japan. Sugihara is dismissed from the Ministry of Foreign Affairs and later begins a new life in another land (Moscow) where his idea of the world he is trying to save is far from achieved. This is similar to the Jews, who were displaced from their homes and were either executed or had to build a new life elsewhere. This, in turn, is akin to Japan, as a nation, preparing its rise in the aftermath of the lost war.

Conclusion

The chapter has explored how Japanese Popular Culture portrayed the Holocaust through the animation *Anne no Nikki* and motion picture *Persona Non Grata.* The films offer similar depictions of the Jewish experience during the Holocaust and comprise similar characteristics: a) the persecution of the Jews during World War II is not shown or depicted on screen to provide context; rather it is described in dialogue or as exposition The films do not show, they only tell; b) embedded in both films is the implicit identification of the Japanese audience with the protagonists in their role of victims as well as depiction of hope for the rise of a postwar Japan built on the sacrifices of its heroes.

Anne no Nikki is a niche production that enjoys the distinction of being the first and only animated adaptation of the source material, which is positioned at the intersection of historical drama and Japanese *shoujo* animation on the otometic style with all the common conventions of the genre: emotive character driven storyline, stationary wide-shots, emphasis on inner monologues, and diegetic voice-overs. *Shoujo* is ill-equipped to represent and depict the gravitas of the Jewish experience. The reason is that in Japanese Popular Culture, the genre was developed to provide safe place for a female audience, devoid of assertive and aggressive male intervention. The dreamscapes and emphasis on sartorial clothing might not seem very compatible with a more somber theme like the Holocaust. But on a close inspection in the case of *Anne no Nikki*, certain elements of the dramatic bent of *shoujo* manga are found conducive to a portrayal of the Holocaust as per the Japanese

Decoding Holocaust Narratives in Japanese Pop Culture 111

sensibilities, informed by categories and genres they have locally produced. In the case of *Persona Non Grata*, the film is less sanitized than *Anne no Nikki* toward the Jewish experience of the Holocaust; however, it shows a disconnection of the Japanese from the war in Europe. Time and time again, Sugihara and his wife get surprised by the persecution on the Jews, to the point that their humanitarianism is awoken; they pity and help the Jews, justifying their actions in their identification as humans.

The *shoujo* style of *Anne no Nikki* to emphasize the victim narrative of Japan and the sacrificing hero narrative of *Persona Non Grata* require very specific narrative commitments and devices, leaving no room to focus too much on creating awareness for or contextualizing the Jewish experience of the Holocaust. Assuming Popular Culture to be sets of practices and texts which are neutral, there is no topic then which is inherently incompatible with Popular Culture. But it is true that due to the specific categories and genres found within the production and consumption of popular media (such as *shoujo* for Japanese viewership), that assumptions and expectations of the viewership render some topics and narratives decontextualized, thus made incompatible. In other words, as with all cultural phenomena, no topic has an inherent incompatibility with Popular Culture, but it is in preconceptual tone or requirements that certain narratives are associated with the collective consciousness of the viewership. In that sense, the Holocaust and the Japanese war memory narratives seem incompatible from exogeneous readings such as from a Western perspective but are very coherent from a Japanese war memory outlook.

Notes

1 Style of *shoujo* or young girls' manga, which appeared in publications at the beginning of 1970, centers on creating awareness of reality through relationships with other characters. Central to this style is identification of the reader with the protagonist, her emotional world, and the complexity of relationships which may befall the individual. The fulcrum of the style is the acceptance of an understanding of a social setting in an otometic narrative and the possibility of extrapolating it to the reader's own reality so navigation through the real world is facilitated (Miyadai et al. 15).

2 It was only a year before his death, in 1985 that Chiune Sugihara was recognized for his effort and awarded "Righteous Among the Nations" by the State of Israel, being the only Japanese person to have been awarded so. Additionally, Lithuania declared 2020 as the Year of Chiune Sugihara to commemorate 80 years since his service in Kaunas (Embassy of Republic of Lithuania to Japan).

Works Cited

Assmann, Aleida. "On the (in)compatibility of guilt and suffering in German memory." *German Life and Letters*, vol. 59, no. 2, 2006, pp. 187–200.

Embassy of Republic of Lithuania to Japan. "The year 2020 declared as the year of Chiune Sugihara." *Embassy of Republic of Lithuania to Japan*, 13 Oct. 2019, jp.mfa.lt/jp/en/news/the-year-2020-declared-as-the-year-of-chiune-sugihara.

Frank, Anne. *1929–1945 The Diary of Anne Frank: The Revised Critical Edition*. Doubleday, 2003.

Gluck, Cellin, director. "Persona Non Grata: The Chiune Sugihara story." *Netflix*, 2015, www.netflix.com/watch/81153961?trackId=13752289&tctx=0%2C0%2C4d04fba5eac5 34c16b572ab77be552d29fa62727%3A73c538726be24dffcc39ef79adf5dbd7f27fbb5d% 2C4d04fba5eac534c16b572ab77be552d29fa62727%3A73c538726be24dffcc39ef79adf5 dbd7f27fbb5d%2C%2C. Accessed 18 Jun. 2020.

Goodman, David, and Masanori Miyazawa. *Jews in the Japanese Mind: The History and Uses of a Cultural Stereotype*. Lexington Books, 2000.

Hashimoto, Akiko. *The Long Defeat: Cultural Trauma, Memory, and Identity in Japan*. Oxford University Press, 2015.

Jaworowicz-Zimny, Aleksandra. "Nazi Cosplay in Japan." *Journal of War & Culture Studies*, vol. 12, no. 1, 2018, pp. 37–52.

Masuda, Nozomi. "Shojo Manga and its acceptance: What is the power of Shojo Manga?" In *International Perspectives on Shojo and Shojo Manga: The Influence of Girl Culture*, edited by Masami Toku. Routledge, 2015, pp. 23–31.

Miyadai, Shinji, Ishihara Hideki, and Otsuka Akiko. *Sabukaruchā shinwa kaitai: shōjo, ongaku, manga, sei no 30-nen to komyunikēshon no genzai*. Paruko Syuppa, 1993.

Nagaoka, Akinori, director. *Anne no Nikki*. Madhouse, 1995.

Ramachandran, Hema. "The animation of Anne: Japanese anime encounters the diary of a Holocaust icon." *Post Script: Essays in Film and the Humanities*, vol. 24, no. 1, 2004, pp. 71–81.

Schilling, Christopher L. "On symbolic philosemitism in Japan." *Journal of Modern Jewish Studies*, vol. 19, no. 3, 2019, pp. 297–313. DOI: 10.1080/14725886.2019.1688461.

Stevens, George, director. *The Diary of Anne Frank*. Twentieth Century-Fox Film Corporation, 1959.

Whaley, Ben. "When Anne Frank Met Astro Boy: Drawing the Holocaust through Manga." *Positions: Asia Critique*, vol. 28, no. 4, 2020, pp. 729–755.

7 Holocaust Representations Through Popular Music
Ferramonti di Tarsia Amidst Documentation, Commemoration, and Mystification

Silvia Del Zoppo

Holocaust Representations Through Popular Music: A Dichotomic Approach

The ineffability of Holocaust representations in Popular Culture has been largely underlined in Holocaust scholarship by emphasizing the limits of any representational capability as well as the paradoxical nature of any artifact attempting to "capture" the Holocaust in an artistic concept and offer it to nonspecialized public:

> These works span a range of media and art forms . . . with their divergent aesthetic strategies bound together by a common willingness to speak the unspeakable and their uniform rejection of the idea, dominant within post-Holocaust intellectual discourse, that fictional and experimental forms of Holocaust representation constitute basic violations of the historical record and moral law.
>
> (Boswell 4)

When facing Holocaust representations in the realm of music, it seems relevant, for the scholarly investigation on their definition, features, and meanings, to divide them into two broad categories: namely, on the one hand, the so-called "Lagermusik" (i.e. music composed, arranged and/or performed within concentration camps, which included, among others, folk songs, cabaret, entertainment music, jazz, etc.) and, on the other hand, musical representations as commemorative portraits of the Holocaust victims. Such a distinction mirrors the dichotomy introduced by Alan Mintz between "exceptionalist models" and "constructivist models" of Holocaust representations, where the first one "is rooted in a conviction of the Holocaust as a radical rupture in human history that goes well beyond notions of uniqueness." In this meaning, art forms from the Holocaust are provided with authenticity, as rare and "true artistic responses to the catastrophe . . ., necessarily bleak and unadorned and resist[ing] the temptation to uplift or to offer false comfort in its many forms." The "constructivist model," conversely, "stresses the cultural lens through which the Holocaust is perceived" as it necessarily involves a process of cultural appropriation of the phenomenon (Mintz 39).

DOI: 10.4324/9781003251224-10

114 *Silvia Del Zoppo*

This distinction is applicable to Holocaust popular music, too:[1] On the one hand, popular music coeval to the Holocaust is a multifaceted source from which to draw information on everyday life in the camps. Indeed, such a repertoire of folk and entertainment music could be easily understood and shared also by musically uneducated inmates and through active or passive partaking in performances. It became a way to preserve collective (religious, national, ethnical) identities. On the other hand, the musical artworks retrospectively representing the Holocaust (i.e., as a commemoration) do not belong exclusively to the realm of "art music" but also to the popular one and strongly contribute to forge common sense and actual representations and appropriations of the Holocaust. Both categories present ambiguities and aporetic characters while addressing crucial issues, such as their ontological dimension: Is any (re)presentation always an *a posteriori* "presentation"? Therefore, is its mimetic faculty toward the reality it portrays always trustworthy? What are its ethical and aesthetical constraints? The list of philosophical queries could, of course, be continued.

Though popular music and art dealing with the Holocaust highly differ in aesthetical conceptions, stylistic approaches, and underlying meanings, even more problematic seems the abundant documentation concerning musical forms (lyrics, compositions, formal and informal testimonies of performances, etc.) generating from the Holocaust itself as a sort of "self-portrait" coeval to historical events, which includes music occurring in both concentration camps and ghettos, under absolutely peculiar and often extreme circumstances.

Popular Music From the Holocaust

Popular Music in Lager: Historical Evidences and Unexplored Testimonies

There is a growing interest in the previously mentioned musical repertoire, especially intensifying over the last decades. Actually, the first documentations concerning musical expressions in concentration camps started to appear during the war, in the form of diaries and memories, such as the renowned testimony by German actor and film director Wolfgang Langhoff, arrested by the Gestapo in 1933 and taken to Börgermoor concentration camp. Released after 13 months as part of the so-called Easter amnesty, he published in Zurich *Die Moorsoldaten: 13 Monate Konzentrationslager. Unpolitischer Tatsachenbericht.* The book title refers to the protest song *"Moorsoldaten"* ("Peat Bog Soldiers") that had been written by him on revised lyrics by Johann Esser and melody composed by the fellow inmate Rudi Goguel. After the book was translated into English the same year, it became one of the earliest internationally renowned eyewitness accounts of brutality in the Nazi concentration camps.

Soon after the war, several collections of songs started to be published as well: An exhaustive account is provided by Guido Fackler in his seminal work, *Die Lagers Stimme. Musik im KZ: Alltag und Häftlingskultur in den Konzentrationslagern 1933 bis 1936*, and in his further articles.[2] Most of the early publications were in Yiddish, focusing on folk repertoires of Central and Eastern European

Jews. Some collections of Lieder from displaced persons' camps, for instance, were included in two monographs in English written by the British psychological operation officer Lt. Derrick Sington, while documenting war crimes in Bergen-Belsen after the liberation of the camp. At the same time in Eastern Germany, the musicologist Inge Lammel pioneered the research concerning *Arbeiterlieder*, founding and leading the Arbeiterlieder Archiv at the Universität der Künste in the German Democratic Republic. Her research concerning *Lagermusik* generally assumed strong anti-fascist connotations and work and concentration camps tended to be assimilated, furthermore letting emerge a non-homogeneity on this repertoire: Lieder, which, from Lammel's viewpoint, could constitute a genre by no means, were catalogued according to their functions or lyric contents rather than musical features. One of the earliest editions of songs composed and performed in concentration camps appeared in 1968, when Carsten Linde[3] published the first collection of songs composed by Alexander Kulisiewicz, a key figure for the musical life in the Sachsenhausen camp. Kulisiewicz himself was very active from the '70s onwards in collecting a large archive of Lagerlieder in addition to those he composed and learned by heart while being interned in the camp as well as performing them on international stages to preserve their memory, reaching recognition in Germany, Italy, and in the USA but scarcely in communist Poland.[4] Furthermore, in countries such as Czechoslovakia and Poland, scholarly research and musical revivals highlighted national musical traditions: Pivotal studies concerning Terezín[5] started to appear when the world première of Viktor Ullmann's opera *Der Kaiser von Atlantis, oder Der Tod Verweigerung* took place in 1975 in Amsterdam (Del Zoppo 31–36).

According to this synthetic framework, such research concerning music in Lager has conveyed "fuller recognition of the role of music-making in Nazi camps," as Fackler remarks. Nevertheless, musicological investigations have driven attention to particular areas and cases:

> The focus remains primarily on a few well-known topics concerning the war years, such as Theresienstadt (Joža Karas, Ulrike Migdal, David Bloch, Musica Reanimata Society and others), prominent ghettos and concentration camps (Gila Flam, Gabriele Mittag, Bret Werb, Richard Newman, Juliane Kunze and others), . . . [while] music-making among prisoners in other concentration camps and ghettos, by comparison, remains largely unexplored, especially in English-language scholarship.
>
> (Fackler 604)

Secondly, wide interest was paid to classical music composed and performed within camps as well as folk songs—especially resistance songs, "commonly understood as 'Erinnerungsträger' ("vessel of memories"), respectively as means of 'entertainment and witnessing'" (Fackler 605–606). Other forms had been in comparison less systematically investigated (jazz, Viennese Kabarett, dance and musical theatre, etc.). A further aspect to be considered is the delay with which musicological investigations into lesser-known concentration camps and ghettos

116 *Silvia Del Zoppo*

have often started, preventing it from precise historical reconstructions and reliable personal witnesses.

A Neglected Case Study: Music and Civil Internment in Southern Italy 1940–43

With reference to Italy, for instance, internment phenomena, occurring in the central and southern peninsula from the beginning of World War II (which Italy entered on 10 June 1940) to the fall of the Fascist government (on 25 July 1943), have never undergone a thorough historical reconstruction and for decades have been downgraded and mystified as "secondary facets" of the Holocaust, due to the alleged negligibility of persecutions in Italy, in absurd comparison to the figures and severity of the atrocities perpetrated by the Nazi regime. And yet, understating Fascist camps on Italian soil as an epiphenomenon of the Holocaust would be highly misleading, since they directly or indirectly contributed to the systematic state-sponsored process of persecution and annihilation of human beings. The presence of at least 48 centers of civil internment existing in Italy before July 1943, out of which 14 counted more than 50 prisoners, in a few cases reaching some hundred and even thousand inmates (see Antoniani Persichilli 77–96), has been underestimated—if not completely ignored—in the aftermath of the war. Most camps were just reconverted to other destinations and historical testimonies scattered or destroyed. In such a scenario, apart from few exceptions, the first studies on civil internment in Italy were started as early as the '80s by Capogreco and Folino; therefore, it would be particularly hard to make any attempt at reconstructing internment phenomena in terms of everyday life and inmates' personal experience without the impressive collection of official documents and eyewitness reports carried out between the '50s and the '70s by Israel Kalk, a Jewish engineer to whom research sources on civil internment in Italy are owed.

By analyzing a case study like Ferramonti di Tarsia (near Cosenza), it can be easily detected how Italian camps presented absolutely *sui generis* features. Ferramonti, the largest Fascist internment camp in Italy, established in June 1940 with an average presence of 2,000 internees, not only differed from any other Fascist or Nazi Lager but also faced substantial changes before and after September 1943, namely through the transition from an internment camp controlled by the Fascist regime to a DP-camp under British mandate. If its very existence and the historical events concerning it—i.e., its establishment before the Italian entry into World War II, its liberation in September 1943 until its final closure in December 1945—represent an almost forgotten chapter of Italian history, the no less significant musical activities which took place within the camp have been completely neglected until the most recent years.

Briefly, the camp was characterized by the presence of exclusively foreign prisoners, especially Jews from Germany and countries under Nazi occupation (mainly Poland, Austria, Czechoslovakia), from the Balkans (relevant presence of Croats and Serbs) or deported from Italian possessions in the Mediterranean Sea (Rhodes and Benghazi) and served as an accidental meeting place for cultures, languages, traditions, and religions in the inaccessible Calabrian hinterland infested by malaria. The extreme cultural diversity was reflected in the different aspects of the musical production, which was made possible also thanks to the presence, among the prisoners—often with a very high level of education—of several professional musicians:[6] Concerts and variety programs taking place in a barrack used as a theatre; the establishment of a choir accompanying both Jewish, Catholic, and Greek Orthodox rites (a unique case not only in the field of Lagermusik); and musical education offered to interned children were just few of the most surprising aspects of the musical life in Ferramonti. Distinctive traits of the camp also included the tolerant administration by the appointed militia; prisoners were exclusively interned due to security reasons and neither forced works nor their physical elimination were planned in Ferramonti in the beginning. However, as soon as war events turned against Italy, internees' lives were at risk of meeting tragic fates through deportation or extermination. This fortunately was not the case of Ferramonti; still, inmates' experiences of deprivation, future uncertainty, displacement, and loss of roots and ties show analogies with the ones experienced by internees in other Fascist and Nazi camps, thus involving comparable behaviors and (self)-representational tendencies, for instance, through music.

Indeed, music performances within Ferramonti camp presented noteworthy characteristics. Most outstandingly, the participation in musical practices was always on voluntary basis, excluding any form of coercion or use of music as a means of torture and humiliation perpetrated by the militia against the prisoners. Furthermore, performances occurred in both formal events (such as Jewish, Catholic, and Orthodox religious offices) and informal contexts (such as classical concerts, cabaret, entertainment, theatrical sketches). Music was employed for educational purposes in the classes of the Ferramonti-Schule and also for the entertainment of a highly differentiated audience, including both inmates, guards, staff in service in the camp, and possibly (surely after September 1943) external civilians. Collective practices (such as choral and chamber performances) and specific groups identifiable through religion, nationality, or language were actively engaged. Most relevant, borders amid different musical genres ("art" or "popular" music) as well as between professional and amateur performers often lost any meaning within the thin perimeter of the camp, and musical as well as cultural practices found their value as performances of collective identities and shared values within certain groups of prisoners.

Popular Tunes Within Ferramonti: Folk Songs, Cabaret, and Entertainment Music

Numerous concert programs preserved in the Kalk Archive attest to formal and informal practices of *zusammen musizieren* ("making music together"), organized by musicians from different educational and cultural backgrounds, who brought multifaceted repertoires and artistic experiences into the camp. The so-called "art music" was, therefore, not the only one to be performed and listened to in Ferramonti: On the contrary, the inmates also managed to introduce folk and popular repertoire

118   *Silvia Del Zoppo*

of the early twentieth century, especially linked to singing and vocal music, which could be easily remembered, transmitted by heart and performed with occasional arrangements, often imposed by the contingent availability of musical instruments and musicians. In its eclecticism and adaptability to a context of extreme deprivation of freedom and fundamental human rights, music in Ferramonti shows similarities with several Holocaust camps. As an example, the concert program on 8 March 1942, probably the largest ever organized in Ferramonti, features classical repertoire in the first and second part, sets Jewish and non-Jewish composers, sacred and secular music, side by side, while Polish and Slovenian folk songs close the third part.

A further exhaustive example is the "Concert of the Austrians," performed in March 1944, whose program is saved in the Kalk Collection. The musical event, so named due to the wide participation of Austrian and, in particular, Viennese artists, has substantial affinities with the *Bunte Abende* and the German-speaking Kabarett. A Walzer and a potpourri of Viennese Lieder by Hermann Leopoldi, the famous Jewish-Viennese *Klavierhumorist*, according to Traska and Lind's epithet borrowed from the coeval press, author of Schlager and popular songs with often playful and parodic tones, were featured in the program, together with sketches and variety numbers. The theatrical staging *Die Versteigerung von Castans Panoptikum* ("The Auction of Castan's Panopticon") represented the program core: a comedy written by Egon Kisch in 1925, which takes its cue from the events linked to the bankruptcy and consequent auction sale of the panopticon (i.e. a wax museum) inaugurated in 1875 in Berlin by the brothers Louis and Gustave Castan. The protagonists of Kisch's comedy are, among others, the simulacra of historical figures such as King Edward VII, Johann Wolfgang Goethe, August Sternickel (an assassin made famous by the chronicles of the time), and Mayer Amschel Rothschild (a rich Jew, founder of the bank of the same name). The narration, divided into three scenes, is oriented according to a climax of growing comedy toward an unexpected epilogue. The representation, performed by ex-interned Jewish actors in the Ferramonti camp, takes on a strongly self-deprecating character toward atavistic stereotypes associated with the figure of the Jew. In addition, the text shows the use of different linguistic and dialectal registers: a parodic mirror of the multiethnic and multilingual reality of the camp. The sense of parodic self-representation of everyday life in the camp is increased by the use of meta-theater both in the central scene (in which the wax statues come to life and discuss each other) and in the epilogue.

Returning to music, in the documentation transmitted by Sonnenfeld himself to Kalk in view of a documentary project relating to Ferramonti and other Italian camps, the texts of five Lieder performed during the evening or also on the occasion of other variety programs were also found in Ferramonti. These songs, set to music by Hermann Leopoldi, Hans Lang, and Fritz Spielmann, are actually *contrafacta*: Each text, in fact, presents deviations from the respective original Lied in a further parody, mocking sense, mostly adapting and re-setting original narratives and contents to the context of Ferramonti and civil internment in southern Italy.

Popular Music Representing the Holocaust

Popular Music and Commemoration

If one of the earliest and probably most renowned compositions representing the Holocaust in the realm of postwar music is Schoenberg's *Survivor from Warsaw Op. 46* (1947), scored for narrator, men's chorus, and orchestra, several compositions followed in the second half of the twentieth century (Arnold 335 and f., Klokova 173 and f.), such as Steve Reich's *Different Trains* (1988).[7] Other works alluded to the Holocaust as an inspiration source or through literary references: This is the case, for instance, of the oboist and composer Heinz Holliger's *Psalm* (1971), based on the homonymous lyrics included in Paul Celan's *Die Niemandsrose* (1963).[8] Poetry from concentration camps has been often used as a basis for vocal compositions, too: for instance, the outstanding oratorio *Holocaust Requiem* for cantor, children's and adult choir, and orchestra by Roland Senator (1986), based on children's poems from Terezín, as well as *Songs of Remembrance* (1995–1996) by Ruth Lomon, referring to sets of poems written by Holocaust survivors and death camp victims. More recently, operatic works dealing with Holocaust made their appearance, such as Chaya Czernowin's avant-gardist opera *Pnima . . . ins Innere*, inspired by the encounter between a young Israeli boy and his grandfather, a Holocaust survivor as it is narrated in David Grossman's first novel *See Under: Love* (1986).[9]

Of course, not only "art music" has been concerned with Holocaust representations: The American composer, improviser, and saxophonist John Zorn released in 1993 the album *Kristallnacht*, which over the course of seven movements explores the twentieth -century Jewish culture and history, from the klezmer-influenced "Shtetl (Ghetto Life)" to the overdriven guitar and percussion improvisations of "Garin (Nucleus—The New Settlement)." The core of the recording is the central movement ("Never Again"), mainly consisting of high frequency samples of shattering glass, as an onomatopoeic rendering of the "Night of Broken Glass" from which the album takes its name (Schlüter 301 and f.).

However, according to Stratton, it was punk music that firstly marked "the confrontation with the Judeocide in popular culture, and popular consciousness" (200) and even less "extreme" statements acknowledge American and British punk as "an underground movement that rapidly took a hold on mainstream culture and, to some degree, foreshadowed the increased cultural engagement with the Holocaust that took place throughout the 1980s and 1990s" (Boswell 98). Although by the mid-1970s, World War II and Nazism were already staple subjects for Hollywood films and crime fiction, it was only with rock bands like Ramones, Sex Pistols, and post-punk Joy Division that the imagery linked to the Nazism, its gruesome atrocities, and symbols was enhanced and that new narrative paradigms of the Holocaust were traced. Sometimes, punk song openly adopts cinematographic techniques: This is the case of "Atrocity Exhibition" by Joy Division, which, similarly to "Ludovico's technique" in Anthony Burgess's *A Clockwork Orange*, compels the listener (a sort of Alex DeLarge) to a macabre journey through a modern-day hell.

120   *Silvia Del Zoppo*

Additionally, popular music contributed to the critical and public success of several feature films in the form of soundtracks. This is the case of Oscar-awarded movies such as *Schindler's List* by Spielberg (1993, soundtrack by John Williams), *Life Is Beautiful* by Benigni (1997, soundtrack by Nicola Piovano), and *The Pianist* by Polanski (2002, original score by Wojciech Kilar; the soundtrack also includes pieces by Ludwig van Beethoven, Frédéric Chopin, and Johann Sebastian Bach).

Ferramonti in Popular Culture: Commemorations or Canon Variations?

The rising interest in studies on Italian concentration camps in the last decade has led to some attempts at onscreen representations of musical life in Italian camps. However, given, on the one hand, the scarcity or incompleteness of historical sources concerning everyday life in the camp and, on the other hand, the adherence to cinematic conventions, these multimedia modern representations and commemorations risk completely reinventing cultural practices, by associating different meanings and responding to audience's expectations rather than historical reconstructions. The extreme dangerousness of such an attitude was pointed out, among others, by Jeroen van Gessel, remarking the risk, run by both scientific literature as well as artistic representations concerning the Holocaust, of falling in the same aesthetical categories of their representational object (56), identified by Saul Friedländer as "Kitsch" and "Death," respectively defined as "the cult of symbols' purity" and "the (almost) religious glorification of giving life for a cause."[10] As far as the Ferramonti case study is concerned, the category of "Death" does not seem to be strictly relevant, since violence in southern Italian camps surely played a less dramatic role than in most other European camps, and death was definitely not present except as an ordinary accidentality. Therefore, in the case of Ferramonti, where no slaughters occurred, the second of Friedländer's categories might be more reasonably replaced with "trivialization": the need for traces of the human within inhuman phenomena can be here easily satisfied through trivializing narratives. The "mild nuances" of Ferramonti seems to legitimize soft versions of otherwise unbearable truths: a brilliant exception in the universe of concentration Lager, which sounds consolatory or even reassuring and especially commits to condoning self-acquittal, suitably meets spectacular purposes and, in contrast, exorcizes the problematic coexistence of art, culture, and barbarism—if a traditional definition of these concepts is assumed.

Over the years, several biographic novels came to terms with internment experience in Ferramonti, often reporting musical events and narrating cultural practices according to fictional-fantasizing schemes. Actually, fiction preceded historical investigation on Ferramonti through an eponymous novel published in 1953 under the pseudonym of Peter Geörg.[11] Other novels and diaries followed, often narrating complementary stories, especially concerning Jews' attempted escapes from their countries of origin and their captures and deportations to Ferramonti.[12] However, a gallery of representations within Popular Culture portrays Ferramonti's musical practices by means of cinematographic formats, television shows and educational projects, as three case studies reveal: the movie *Oscar* (Dellai, 2016);[13] the show

"Serata colorata. Musiche dal campo di internamento di Ferramonti,"[14] which was broadcast on the Remembrance Day 27 January 2016, on Rai5;[15] and the short film "Il sesto senso della memoria," an educational project addressed to the students of local secondary schools.

As far as *Oscar* is concerned, the film is focused on the biographical experience of Oskar Klein (1934–2006), interned with his family in Ferramonti when he was about 6 years old and who later became an internationally renowned jazz poly-instrumentalist. Apart from some inaccuracies, such as Oskar's name (correct spelling with "k") and age (the protagonist of the movie is a resourceful good-looking youngster), numerous changes are deliberately operated by the film director. Most astonishingly, the whole plot is set in the small village of Asiolo (Vicenza), where the Kleins hid for some time, while no reference is given to the internment period in Ferramonti. The whole script actually unfolds through the love story between Oscar and the daughter of the fascist chief magistrate (it. "podestà"), who both do not seem to adhere at all to fascist ideals. Absurd stereotypes taint the screenplay, particularly celebrating the almost ubiquitous myth of the "good Italian and the bad German," as Focardi summarizes in his book title. The only exception is represented by an innkeeper, who seems the only character among the poor peasants with a deep fascist belief: however, his murder, perpetrated by some partisans as a revenge for his betrayal, soon restores a comforting sense of "justice." On the other hand, the Carabinieri (police force), the local clergyman, and some noons living in a cloister nearby are all represented as extremely collaborative with Jews fleeing to Switzerland, quite coherently with Oskar Klein's memories (Schwamenthal 23–26). Eventually, the quotation of Spielberg's little girl in red coat from *Schindler's List* in a scene at the railway station during mass deportation appears simply pathetic and unfounded, not least because *Oscar* is a color film. Similarly, no mentions of Oskar Klein's postwar life are offered, as a world-renowned musician, who notably performed with, among others, jazz pianist Romano Mussolini (Benito Mussolini's third son) in the '90s. Most relevant, the soundtrack is merely functional to the development of the plot and no emphasis is put on music itself as a possible realm of comment or contrast to verbal interactions among characters.

"Serata colorata," on the contrary, is explicitly focused on Ferramonti. Though based on documentary materials, in this case historical sources have been partially misinterpreted and deformed, for instance, presenting late testimonies by pianist and composer Kurt Sonnenfeld (1923–1997) as a prison diary[16] and performing, during the TV show, musical pieces which were by no means attested to in Ferramonti. The TV show puts emphasis on eclecticism of genres and repertoires but makes use of ad hoc arrangements and amplified instruments, and it offers a narrative that overall unfolds according to audience's expectations rather than historical accuracy, resulting in a mystified representation of Ferramonti as a peaceful—if not pleasant—"summer camp."

Finally, "Il sesto senso della memoria" is a short film directed with the participation of secondary school students, who were involved in the filmmaking by two directors, Nicola Rovito and Fabrizio Nucci. Characterized through the intensive use of music as a *fil rouge* (rather than dialogues, which are rare) and a tendency to

122   Silvia Del Zoppo

anonymize characters (the protagonist is highly inspired by the figure of Kurt Sonnenfeld, though in the film we ignore his name), the short movie tends to actualize the act of commemorating and to actively involve young generations in it. Music is highly "fictionalized" and general meanings (over)simplified, yet still they emphasize the connection between past and present through the temporal dimension and the intergenerational discussion.

Conclusion: Music Performances as a Cultural Behavior Opposing Holocaust Iconoclasm

As the case studies reveal, the main risk of Holocaust representations consists of different forms of memory distortions, eventually leading to its destruction, paradoxically in the very moment of its pretended taking place. In this light, Holocaust music—intended as both postmodern music dealing with the commemoration of the Holocaust and the study and of the music from the Shoah itself—"is not about accurately representing facts, but an attempt to come to terms with how these facts continue to affect us" (Schwab 8): Surely distortion is not always intentional and not necessarily connected to Holocaust negationism; often it represents a means to make a phenomenon "assimilable and easier to bear" (Gilbert 2). Then, representations through music may become an unconscious process of "normalization," particularly in front of phenomena perceived as incomprehensible or unbearable.

Popular music plays a relevant role in such a discourse due to its eclecticism and pervasiveness, from self-standing artwork to soundtrack, from TV show to pedagogical content. On the one hand, founded skepticism should arise in connection with naïve representations and oversimplified interpretations of the Holocaust often occurring in Popular Culture, which not only threaten to trivialize historical events and mislead their understanding toward accommodating forms of "redemptive narratives" (5), satisfying public expectations, but especially result in a double mystification: with regard to both victims' fate—who are pretended to contrast and defeat mistreating or dehumanization processes through redeeming musical art ("heroical narratives")—and to the superimposition of a narrative (i.e. meaning-oriented processes) relieving post-Holocaust generations of harsh reflections on issues like personal responsibility and (in)significance of suffering. In this respect, scholarly investigation on Lagermusik spotlights the necessity of preventing homologation of memory and collectivization of testimony, on the contrary, focusing on everyday contingency as specific boundary conditions in each camp.

On the other hand, however, since the relevance of such a repertoire is mainly due to its performative character as a cultural behavior within the society of inmates' community, musical sources and material evidences are crucial, but the active partaking of young generations in commemorative actions is also fundamental. Moreover, considering musical practices are often collective (both in the camp as, for instance, in today's schools), they show the strict interconnection with processes of preserving individual and collective identities and values: Together with surviving musical testimonies from the Holocaust, they act as self-representational, restlessly questioning response to statements of Holocaust iconoclasm,

Holocaust Representations Through Popular Music

most noteworthily raising individual and public awareness of the threshold of understanding and the never-ending discourse on the nature of human being.

Notes

1 A broad definition of "popular music" is adopted here, considering the richness of semantic nuances associated with the term "popular," its historical shifting and the hazy boundaries of its genres. See Middleton, Richard and Peter Manuel, "Popular music." In *Grove Music Online*. Oxford University Press, 2001.

2 Guido Fackler's doctoral dissertation, focusing on a prewar period, provides scholars with a large-scale collection and critic analysis of Lagerlieder, on the basis of archival research, reports, and interviews with contemporary witnesses, with vast primary and secondary literature references. Among his numerous articles, a source overview is provided in "Cultural behaviour and the invention of traditions: Music and musical practices in the early concentration camps, 1933–6/7." *Journal of Contemporary History*, vol. 45, no. 3, 2010, pp. 601–627.

3 Linde, Carsten, editor. *KZ-Lieder: Eine Auswahl aus dem Repertoire des Polnischen Sangers Alex Kulisiewicz*. Sievershütten Verlag Wendepunk, 1972.

4 Kulisiewicz also published scholarly articles concerning music in the camps. His almost-finished collection including typescript of song lyrics, musical scores and annotations has been preserved after his death at the United States Holocaust Memorial Museum in Washington, D.C.

5 Among the first, most influential Czech musicologists who led researches on this topic, Milan Kuna definitely deserves to be mentioned.

6 Some inmate musicians had already taken up international careers or would have done it after the war: among others, Lav Mirski, Kurt Sonnenfeld, Isak Thaler, Paul Gorin, Oscar Klein, Leon Levitch, Ladislav Sternberg. For prosopographical reconstructions see Del Zoppo, ch. 8.

7 An extensive investigation in Schoenberg's and Reich's works is provided for instance in Wlodarski, Amy Lynn. *Musical Witness and Holocaust Representation*. Cambridge University Press, 2015.

8 Cf. Schlüter, Bettina. "Mediale Substitutions- und Transformationsprozesse in musikalischen Repräsentationen der Schoah." In *Verbot der Bilder—Gebot der Erinnerung: mediale Repräsentationen der Schoah*. edited by Bannasch, Bettina and Hammer, Almuth. Campus Verlag, 2004, pp. 293–297. This psalm is written in memory of Nelly Sachs, who died in 1970, and Paul Celan and Bernd Alois Zimmermann, who both committed suicide in the same year. Though, Celan's work most frequently set to music by composers is surely *Todesfuge*: non-exhaustive list of its orchestrations would include, among others, works for four voices and string quartet by Boris Porena (1957), for soprano and chorus by Tilo Medek (1967), for alto, chamber orchestra and tape by Peter Ruzicka (1969) and lately, for voices, flute, cello and saxophone by Lori Laitman (2010, presenting an English translation of the lyrics).

9 Brown, Eliza. *A Narratological Analysis of Pnima . . . Ins Innere by Chaya Czernowin*. 2015, PhD Dissertation, Northwestern University Evanston. Noteworthily, since the trauma suffered by the ex-inmate does not allow dialogues amid protagonists, the opera is actually lacking a libretto and the four characters in the work sing phonemes and other nonverbal sounds rather than words.

10 A paradigm which was introduced by Hollywood movies and American TV mini-series like *Holocaust*.

11 Georg, Peter. Ferramonti: Romanzo. Tr. from German by Ernesto Peternolli. Ed. Valmartina, Giuntina, 1952. According to Klaus Voigt, the real author under the pseudonym is Karl Bloch, a doctor interned in Ferramonti. Cf. Voigt, Klaus. "La memorialistica dei profughi ebrei in Italia dopo il 1933." Sechi, M. and Santoro, G., editors. *L'ombra lunga dell'esilio: ebraismo e memoria*. Giuntina, 2002, pp. 167–187: 174.

124 *Silvia Del Zoppo*

12 Koch, Rita. "Una lontana estate: [diario da Ferramonti di Tarsia]." *Calabria sconosciuta*, n. 27–28, 1984, p. 67–70; Weksler, Nina. *Con la gente di Ferramonti: Mille giorni di una giovane ebrea in un campo di concentramento*. Progetto 2000, 1992.
13 *Oscar*. Directed by Dennis Dellai, performances by Leonardo Pompa and Sara Lazzaro, Progetto Cinema A.V., 2016.
14 "Serata colorata. Musiche dal campo di internamento di Ferramonti." BrainCircle Italia and Musa Doc, RAI, Rome, 27 Jan. 2016.
15 The cultural channel of public broadcasting service in Italy.
16 ASCDEC/Kalk Archive, II. Ferramonti-Tarsia, b. 2, fasc. 25, fl. 37–46.

Works Cited

Antoniani Persichilli, Gina. "Disposizioni, normative e fonti archivistiche per lo studio dell'internamento in Italia (giugno 1940-luglio 1943)." *Rassegna degli Archivi di Stato*, vol. 38, nos. 1–3, 1978, pp. 77–96.
Arnold, Ben. "Art Music and the Holocaust." *Holocaust and Genocide Studies*, vol. 6, no. 2, 1991, pp. 335–349.
Boswell, Matthew. *Holocaust Impiety. In Literature, Popular Music and Film*. Palgrave Macmillan, 2012.
Brown, Eliza. *A Narratological Analysis of 'Pnima . . . Ins Innere' by Chaya Czernowin*. 2015, PhD Dissertation, Northwestern University Evanston.
Capogreco, Carlo Spartaco. *Ferramonti. La vita e gli uomini del più grande campo d'internamento fascista (1940–1945)*. La Giuntina, 1987.
Del Zoppo, Silvia. *Ferramonti. Cultural Behaviors and Musical Practices in a Southern-Italian Internment Camp*. Peter Lang, 2021.
Fackler, Guido. "Cultural behaviour and the invention of traditions: Music and musical practices in the early concentration camps, 1933–6/7." *Journal of Contemporary History*, vol. 45, no. 3, 2010, pp. 601–627.
Finkelstein, Norman. *The Holocaust Industry. Reflections on the Exploitation of Jewish suffering*. Verso Books, 2002.
Focardi, Filippo. *Il cattivo tedesco e il buon italiano*. Laterza, 2013.
Folino, Francesco. *Ferramonti: in Lager di Mussolini. Gli internati durante la guerra*. Brenner, 1985.
Friedländer, Saul. *Reflections of Nazism: An Essay on Kitsch and Death*. Harper & Row, 1984.
Gilbert, Shirli. *Music in the Holocaust: Confronting Life in the Nazi Ghettos and Camps*. Clarendon Press, 2005.
Klokova, Antonina. " 'Meine Moralische Pflicht' Mieczysław Weinberg und der Holocaust." In *Die Macht der Musik. Mieczysław Weinberg: Eine Chronik in Tönen*, edited by Manfred Sapper and Volker Weichsel. Osteuropa, 2010, pp. 173–182.
Lammel, Inge. *Kampfgefährte—unser Lied*. Tribüne Verlag, 1978.
Lammel, Inge. "Lieder im faschistischen Konzentrationslager: Aus der Tätigkeit des Arbeiterliedarchivs der Akademie der Künste der DDR." *Musik und Gesellschaft*, vol. 33, no. 1, 1983, pp. 16–20.
Langhoff, Wolfgang. *Die Moorsoldaten. 13 Monate Konzentrationslager. Unpolitischer Tatsachenbericht*. Schweizer Spiegel Verlag, 1935.
Middleton, Richard and Peter Manuel. "Popular music." In *Grove Music Online*. Oxford University Press, 2001.

Mintz, Alan L. *Popular Culture and the Shaping of Holocaust Memory in America*. University of Washington Press, 2001.

Schwab, Gabriele. *Haunting Legacies. Violent History and Transgenerational Trauma*. Columbia University Press, 2010.

Schlüter, Bettina. "Mediale Substitutions- und Transformationsprozesse in musikalischen Repräsentationen der Schoah." In *Verbot der Bilder—Gebot der Erinnerung: Mediale Repräsentationen der Schoah*, edited by Bettina Bannasch and Hammer Almuth. Campus Verlag, 2004, pp. 293–297.

Schwamenthal, Riccardo. "Oskar Klein. Storia e cronaca." *Il Sismografo: Bollettino della SISMA—Società Italiana per lo Studio della Musica Afroamericana*, no. 29, 1999, pp. 23–26.

Stratton, Jon. *Jewish Identity in Western Pop Culture: The Holocaust and Trauma through Modernity*. Palgrave Macmillan, 2015.

Traska Georg and Christoph Lind. *Hermann Leopoldi. The Life of a Viennese Piano Humorist*. Ariadne Press, 2013.

Van Gessel, Jeroen. "Holocaust compositions from recent decades: Between 'imagined victims' and the quest for being 'virtually jewish.'" *Partituren der Erinnerung: Der Holocaust in der Musik/Scores of commemoration: The Holocaust in Music*, edited by Verena Pawlowsky and Béla Rásky. New Academic Press, 2015, pp. 41–57.

Wlodarski, Amy Lynn. *Musical Witness and Holocaust Representation*. Cambridge University Press, 2015.

8   Holocaust Museums
A Study of the Memory Policies of the USA and Poland

Adriana Krawiec

Auschwitz in Polish Collective Memory

"When killing stops, only sites remember it"—writes James E. Young (145). Auschwitz is the most significant memorial site of the Holocaust, but it was the state's initial move to preserve the ruins, thus it was a political will to remember the Nazi crimes under the The Act of 2 July 1947 on the commemoration of the martyrdom of the Polish Nation and other Nations in Oświęcim (Journal of Laws of 1947, No 52, item 265). Auschwitz is a place commemorating the tragedy of Nazi victims, and despite being partially reconstructed, it is still a place of historical importance because of its authenticity. The museum is included among historical and martyrdom museums and is considered to hold a symbolic meaning connected with certain kinds of memory policy. In postwar Poland, the authorities of the People's Republic of Poland (PRL) blocked access for Poles to a complete knowledge about World War II. The narrative of Nazi war crimes served the communists in their anti-German propaganda.

During the Cold War, the museum depicted the United States and West Germany as the heirs of German fascism. The Jews were also recognized by the USSR as an agency of Western imperialism, and the Holocaust was treated as the extermination of millions of nations. Throughout the period of the Polish People's Republic, Auschwitz distorted its history. In Poland, it became socially synonymous with the extermination of Poles, and at the international level, it emphasized the suffering of other nations under German occupation, without specifying that it concerned their Jewish citizens (Huener 123). The exhibition at the museum started with "Introduction," unveiling in Block 15 and its main overarching theme was the danger of German imperialism (Huener 121). It clearly showed why the Soviet regime agreed to the development of this area of the former camp.

Auschwitz is a symbol of the extermination of Jews everywhere except in Poland. This is because many Jews managed to survive Auschwitz. Few survived Treblinka or Sobibor (Forecki 174–175). In Poland, Auschwitz has been a symbol of Polish martyrdom from the very beginning. "We will avenge Auschwitz and Pawiak"—Polish people wrote on the walls in occupied Poland (Greń 105). In addition, the museum documented the crimes of the Nazis, which from the beginning was divided into two periods. The first period involved the biological destruction

DOI: 10.4324/9781003251224-11

of Poles lasting from the beginning of the camp until 1942. The second period involved the biological destruction of Jews from 1942 until the liberation of the camp ("The Auschwitz-Birkenau State Museum Archives").

Interestingly, Pope John Paul II on 7 June 1979 metaphorically described Auschwitz as "the Golgotha of the contemporary world." Many Poles used to understand such metaphors as an invitation to see Auschwitz as a figurative Calvary (Young 145). They even started erecting some hundreds of crosses near Auschwitz. The Jews, to whom Auschwitz symbolizes the uniqueness of the Holocaust strongly opposed this practice (Young 144–145). Nevertheless, the reason for the conflict derived from a misunderstanding of the Holocaust among Poles. It was also due to the fact that the Communist authorities turned the memory of the Holocaust and Auschwitz into a political weapon. Poles were mostly unconscious about the uniqueness of the Holocaust of the Jews. Auschwitz fit into the metaphor of "the Christ of Nations," so Poles regarded themselves as a nation who suffered the most during the World War II. What is more, Poles used to think that Poland, as Christ, could not bear any blame. There was only one book, titled *Neighbors: The Destruction of the Jewish Community in Jedwabne, Poland* by Tomasz Gross, that has changed their thinking. The author explored the July 1941 Jedwabne massacre committed against Polish Jews by their non-Jewish neighbors in the village of Jedwabne in Nazi-occupied Poland.

The systemic transition in Poland after the collapse of the USSR was also associated with the new narrative of the past adopted by the new political elites, and the myth of Poland as the "Christ of Nations" was no longer needed in a free, democratic country. In sovereign Poland, Auschwitz stopped serving as the metaphor of the "Christ of Nations." The remembrance of the Holocaust in Poland gives Poland the opportunity to focus on the future, not on the past. The policy geared to the past is understood as a means, not an end in itself, and it is linked to the need to legitimize the actions of political authority, whose aim is to disseminate its own visions about the past times. Its antithesis is the policy of memory shaped in a way that takes into account the influence of history and memory on current problems: the condition and image of the state. Since 1989, the Polish memory policy in terms of Holocaust is also focused on the future as it tries to provide answers to future problems such as racism and xenophobia. There are a number of such projects organized by the International Center for Education about Auschwitz and the Holocaust operating within the museum. An example would be the Summer School for Teaching about the Holocaust in cooperation with the Center for Holocaust Studies of Jagiellonian University. Its goal is to build a fair, open, and tolerant society by incorporating Holocaust education into the Polish education system ("The 2006 Annual Report of the Auschwitz-Birkenau State Museum").

Democratic Poland is no longer isolated; therefore, certain cultural phenomena observed in the West in the middle of the twentieth century such as the memory boom have finally arrived. The phenomenon of memory boom is associated with the emancipation of minorities demanding the reconstruction of their history and activities aimed at their commemoration in the public sphere. Thanks to this, a Romany exhibition was created in Auschwitz. It is a historical narrative, following

128   *Adriana Krawiec*

Hayden White (11), showing history from the perspective of Romany. It is worth recalling that the extermination of the Romany did not exist or was blurred in the People's Republic of Poland. On the other hand, it would not be possible to create such an exhibition without the actions of the authorities. From the beginning of the appointment of the first democratic government in Poland, the so-called matter of Auschwitz has been raised, as evidenced by the team for the future of the museum, whose main postulates from its first meeting in December 1989 were to extend the elements of the specificity of the Shoah (a synonym of the Holocaust, the genocide of six million European Jews by the Nazis) and to create a Romany exhibition (Cebulski 165). What is more, Blocks 4 and 5 are entirely devoted to the annihilation of Jews and do not distort anymore the number of Jews killed in Auschwitz-Birkenau. An inscription in Block 4 states that: "1,100,000 of . . . people died in Auschwitz. Approximately 90% of these victims were Jews."[1] This is a big change, as in the People's Republic of Poland, the museum distorted the information as 4 million victims of various nationalities.

From the 1980s, the aversion to the Germans as the descendants of the Nazis has not been attributed to Polish memory anymore. Jan Lipski wrote then about Auschwitz: "Are only Gestapo and SS men supposed to be Germans?" (Lipski 14–15). Moreover, equating the fate of Poles with the fate of Jews was also eliminated from the discourse (Trojański 135). Currently, Poland faces other problems in the context of the memory of the Holocaust. The memory of the Holocaust in the public space functions more and more not thanks to Auschwitz or historical studies, but thanks to, inter alia, Popular Culture and mass media, becoming a regrettable struggle against symbols. Nobody asks open questions relevant to new contexts but manifests their positions. This was the case with the debate on Jedwabne, triggered by the publication of the book *Neighbors: The Destruction of the Jewish Community in Jedwabne, Poland* by Tomasz Gross. For the left-wing newspapers (e.g. *Gazeta Wyborcza*), it became clear that the murder in Jedwabne, although it was the result of German inspiration, was committed by Poles. According to *Gazeta Wyborcza*, the murder would not have been possible without the general acceptance of this shameful act of the inhabitants of Jedwabne, which resulted from antisemitism. In an interview for the newspaper, Maria Janion noted that the aversion to Jews as strangers is inscribed in Polish culture (Goźliński 6). The far-right-wing journals (e.g. *Nasz Dziennik*) took the position that Gross's book was an accusation, not supported by any evidence, because testimonies forced by the Security Office were certainly not such (Rzeczkowki 12, Pawlas 11). Thus, everyone was entrenched in their positions. It is sad that Poles learned about the collaboration of neighbors in Poland and the whole territory of the former USSR from the media and Popular Culture, and not from history books, although such research has been conducted since the 1990s.

Along with the collapse of communism in Eastern Europe in 1989 and opening of Poland to the rest of the world, it also absorbed more and more what was happening with the Holocaust in Popular Culture. In terms of the memory of the Holocaust, Popular Culture is stuffed with a happy ending. *Schindler's List* (1993) shows the memorable story of the rescue of 1,100 Polish Jews who were not killed.

Life Is Beautiful (1997) presents the unique story of a boy who survived in the concentration camp and was not killed. *Train of Life* (1998) shows the extraordinary story of the deportation train that carries out Jews to freedom, not to an extermination camp. All these films simplify the real horror of the Holocaust and offer something more attractive about it. Offering an unrealistic or Hollywood Holocaust, they also contributed to people's blurred knowledge of the Holocaust. On the other hand, the new statements are noteworthy, as they introduce a certain distance to the existing discourse. One of them is made by Zbigniew Libera in his work "Lego Concentration Camp." Thanks to it, Libera asked about the place of the Holocaust in mass culture. Certainly, mass culture contributes to memory loss. One image quickly replaces another and there is no time for reflection. In this context, there is a talk of dark tourism and even tourists whose visits are touristic. Such visits are motivated by voyeurism, curiosity, and even enjoyment. They are driven by Popular Culture, the popular images of Holocaust, which once most remarkable, now become clichés through familiarity, due to the commercial world we live in. In the modern era of mass travel, it clearly became easier for people to visit these places. Auschwitz becomes another destination to add to and tick on the travelers' list. Travelers left it without proper reflection. The museum itself contributes to this as it presents the crimes committed in Auschwitz as something completed and independent of our experiences in the world.

Until this day, the most important discursive formation[2] in the Auschwitz-Birkenau Museum pertains to the documentation and exhibition of Nazi crimes against humanity at Auschwitz-Birkenau. Statements within this formation emerge, for example, in Block 6. The phenomenon referred to is the extermination of prisoners by starvation (Room 2 and Room 4). In Room 3, the objects serve the discourse of extermination through work. In Room 2 visitors can see photographs of starving children and women along with information boards. With their help, terms such as the extermination of prisoners through insufficient food and devastating amount of work are introduced. In Room 4, the phenomenon referred to is the deadly policy of the Nazis toward children deported to Auschwitz. On the display, there are photos of emaciated children, their wardrobe, and photo captions, alluding to the fact that, in Auschwitz, the children were also the victims of the Nazis who conducted experiments on them and murdered them and the fact that most children did not survive the liberation of the camp. The exhibition is limited to the factual sphere. The discursive strategy in Rooms 2, 3, and 4 of Block 6 involves the following: The exhibition highlights that the prisoners of Auschwitz were subjected to extermination through the Nazi policy of imposing hard work and hunger on them. This history, as exhibited, has no happy ending. It may be hard for many to visit an exhibition that does not promise a happy ending usually found in Popular Culture representations of the Holocaust. But such was the history.

On the other hand, a new aura around the work of memorial site museums such as Auschwitz is a conflict between postmodern culture and traditional culture. The former is largely popular, promoting the joy of life, hedonism, and consumption. Its advantage is the improvement of living conditions and the weakening of nationalist sentiments (Stępnik 71–79).

130   *Adriana Krawiec*

Auschwitz as a museum is not in tune with the postmodern culture and postmodern museum, and it is a modern museum dominated by object-based epistemology. Such a museum aims to classify and show objects as scientific evidence. Postmodern museums no longer deal with describing and classifying certain units. The postmodern museum does not serve the formation of power and knowledge but dialogue (Ziębińska-Witek 85). Rigid classification is anathema to postmodern notions that sees objects in modern museums as victims of a frame-of-government mind (Keene 4–5).

Furthermore, such an exhibition might raise questions, like, to what extent these concern a specific viewer, but it might not offer any answers to the challenges of the postmodern world such as the Rwandan civil war or Burma's path to genocide. However, postmodern culture becomes a culture of play and fragmentation. The traditional hierarchies of values and the patterns of behavior are disintegrating and redefining. People in postmodernity select those values that are convenient for them (Stępnik 70–71). Thus, the authority that arises from the scientific paradigm and a conviction about universal and unquestionable rules that direct nature, societies, and history ensures accurate behavior. Meanwhile, a characteristic feature of the postmodern episteme is a set of different views. In the postmodern episteme, there is no such term as objective truth; no one can tell anyone what is accurate without their acceptance (Belsey 3, 75). It focuses on pleasure and individualized identity building. Yet, the entire area of Auschwitz with its exhibition setting—the ruins of gas chambers, gallows, and buildings affect the senses. Unprepared for such traumatic experiences, young people may not know what to do with this knowledge of the camp and the traumatic experience (Kucia and Stec 86). The responsibility for that is certainly not a martyrdom museum (Kucia) but postmodern Popular Culture (Stępnik 70). Postmodernism's impact on Popular Culture is responsible for the fact that life is reduced to an aesthetic experience; so the aestheticization of reality takes place. In some circles, martyrdom museums are becoming an element of taboo. In Popular Culture, there is no place for enslavement and suffering. Martyrdom museums are either trendy or they do not exist (Stępnik 70).

An interesting move by the museum in the context of postmodern changes is the exhibition "Face to Face. The Art in Auschwitz." Museum workers have collected very interesting documents on art in the camp. They showed them outside the museum through traveling exhibitions, which made history accessible to those who, for various reasons, couldn't visit the site personally or those who have forgotten about Auschwitz. The exhibition was in line with postmodern culture, according to which objects in museums should encourage discourse; they should not serve to impose discourse (Stępnik 77). It was in accordance even with widespread expectations for a happy ending. That may be why we are witnessing a flood of guides to positive thinking, but this is the issue for another essay. There must be a happy ending, and this is what happens in this unusual exhibition, which does not simplify the topic. It appeared in 2017 as part of the Auschwitz-Birkenau Museum exhibition. This utterance falls within the discursive formation: permanent threads of historical narrations concerning the recollection of the Nazi crime against humanity in Auschwitz. This is the exhibition of the former camp prisoners' paintings. This exhibition was held in the branch of the National Museum in Kraków in the Feliks Jasieński Szołayski House. The National Museum in Kraków collects and presents the pieces of art. The former prisoners' works are made from everyday use materials. It is hard to interpret this art in detachment from the memorial site that is the former concentration camp. Hence, it is connected with the memorial site through placing the replica of the inscription at the entrance gate to the former camp: *Arbeit macht frei*. The exhibition's theme is based on the historical testimony created by the prisoners themselves in the form of art concerning the cruelty of the Nazi crime in Auschwitz, whose victims could save only the remnants of human dignity. That was possible, among other things, owing to the artistic works. The discourse that unfolds comprises the moral victory of the Auschwitz victims through depicting the enslaved prisoners who demonstrate the fundamental element of humanity— feelings which the slaughterers could not deprive them of. The exhibition apparently reaches beyond the scientific and specialized discourse toward the testimony from the position of artistic works which, by themselves, do not constitute any historical knowledge, but in combination with exhibition techniques (i.e., inscription replica), generate truth of a historical value. The strategy here includes the recollection of the Nazi crimes in Auschwitz, revealed through the selection of the venue. When visiting the Szołayski House, which seats the exhibitions of art, lectures, concerts, and theatre performances, a visitor may be astonished by the confrontation with this extremely painful theme that undoubtedly contributes to memorializing this exhibition. It is also about presenting the victims as the symbolic winners and the slaughterers as the defeated. The aim here is a tribute paid to the victims through recovering their dignity.

Certainly, similar exhibitions were organized in the PRL (e.g. "Auschwitz in Art" from 1966), but today it has a different meaning. It helps to remember about Auschwitz and about the Holocaust, not in the form of clichés known from pop culture. It is a response to the challenges of the present day, especially it prevents the blurring of the image of Auschwitz and the Holocaust in common consciousness. This "blurring" seems particularly important as most people do not learn about the Nazi crimes from historical studies, but from films, the press, television programs, websites, or other forms of public life.

Another utterance as part of similar formation—that is, the new approach to the permanent threads of historical narrations concerning the recollection of the Nazi crime against humanity in Auschwitz—is the exhibition titled "I Survived the Camp" (2017). This is an exhibition of 34 large-format photos of former prisoners of KL Auschwitz camp. The author of these photos is German photographer Stefan Hanke. For this purpose, in the years 2004–2014, the artist visited seven European countries and met survivors of the concentration camps. The narration consists of the portraits of the former prisoners made in a home setting as well as in the historic places of their torment, a former prisoner's biography, his short utterance, and additional information concerning the making of a photo. There are no grand narratives about heroes, and no enslavement, and no horror of the war. There are even no passive victims of the Holocaust in this story, but this exhibition does not contribute to blurring the Holocaust. Therefore, it is not the narration of remembrance but

132   Adriana Krawiec

historical narration because the former prisoners are as if documented by means of photos and presented as the historical testimony of the truth about Auschwitz. The memoir comprises witnesses who survived Auschwitz concentration camp. This demonstrates their strength because they constitute a living example of moral victory of the truth about Auschwitz. Even though the exhibition fits the postmodern episteme, the discourse does not go beyond the scientific one and power knowledge formation because photography is not only a visual text here but also a technique by means of which the institution, through its authority, convinces that the photos are the image of the truth. The strategy of these utterances is testifying about Auschwitz, counteracting oblivion, and providing a lesson that truth always wins because its witnesses always remain. The objective is also to depict the moral victory.

An incentive to conduct such discourses is to provide a continuous reminder regarding the atrocity of the Nazi crimes. The activities of bodies forming the museum entity—at that time the Polish People's Republic—were responsible for the production of such discourses. They differ a lot from what we could see in the Polish People's Republic as well as they differ from the contemporary exhibition in Block 6. This would not be possible without postmodern changes and Popular Culture; yet, they are far away from the clichés of Popular Culture. The Auschwitz-Birkenau Museum can fit into postmodern culture. Its workers probably realized that if the museum did not do this, it could become a relic, not a living memorial. Meanwhile, places such as Auschwitz are to uphold the principles and institutions that support human freedom and protect it from totalitarian enslavement. They can and should do it in tune with world challenges (Krantz).

Popular Culture in the USA in the Context of the Appropriation and Promotion of the Memory of the Holocaust

On April 22, 1993, the Holocaust became officially incorporated into the American memory (Novick 2). It took 15 years of hard work to open the United States Holocaust Memorial Museum (USHMM) as a physical container to preserve the memory of the Holocaust for all Americans. Its location on the Washington Mall, which contains a number of cultural institutions and various memorials, emphasized the Holocaust's place in the official memory of the nation (Novick 2). It all started on 1 November 1978 when then-President Jimmy Carter established the President's Commission on the Holocaust and charged it with the responsibility to submit a report with respect to the establishment and maintenance of an appropriate memorial to those who perished in the Holocaust. Since then the museum has gained the status of international bestseller. The Holocaust took place far from the United States and involved few Americans, yet it has been transmitted to the American culture, and the American culture has made the Holocaust an issue concerning democratic values.

Owing to the American cultural system, the memory of the Holocaust is one of the most readable cultural codes in the history of mankind. The process of the Americanization of the Holocaust began in the late 1970s when American TV station NBC broadcast a miniseries titled *Holocaust* (*Holocaust: The Story of the*

Family Weiss). The story of Anne Frank was also appropriated in the American Popular Culture. Her diary invited Americans to look beyond the number to see the victims as real people—human beings with passions, beliefs, and fears. There was no more depersonalized mass. Americans created Anne Frank as a perfect victim of the Holocaust by matching her "Diary" to commercial matrices. Then one of the biggest living memorials was built. One may say that it was thanks to authorities, others can argue that it was due to the Popular Culture. The fact is, that since then, the Holocaust has become a central issue of worldwide culture and a universal metaphor for evil, and in the USA, the memory was created from scratch. The United States Holocaust Memorial Museum, on the one hand, renders the past of the Holocaust but, on the other hand, is the rationale for the American memory in the context of the Holocaust. The interpretation of the Holocaust in the USA has gone through many metamorphoses and there have existed many approaches toward the Holocaust and its importance. For this purpose, Jews and American intellectuals and scientists reach to antiquity, and just like in the case of ancient Greeks and Greek tragedy, the immersion of Western citizens in the tragedy of the Holocaust brought catharsis, purification, and forgiveness for the perpetrators. A tragic narrative offered "no happy ending, no sense that something else could have been done, and no belief that the future could, or can, necessarily be changed" (Alexander 32). The message that all of us can be victims or perpetrators make us realize that we cannot distance ourselves or cut ourselves off from the victims' suffering and the responsibility of the wrongdoers. The narration makes the Holocaust an issue of importance for all the Americans as well as the American government. The education on the Holocaust, which from now on has become also an American task, is listed on the public agenda. As a result of public policy, the commemoration of the Holocaust, as well as its education, have been meant for all Americans. This was the purpose of Carter's President's Commission and Holocaust Memorial Council. The effect of its work was the form of the United States Holocaust Memorial Museum (Linenthal, *Preserving Memory* 3, 13).

From the very beginning the aim of the museum was to make the history of the Holocaust widely available and, at the same time, unique and understandable. The first goal was achieved by having the museum in a popular public place—on the National Mall, home to iconic monuments. Then it was considered how to make every American understand the Holocaust—an event unique and terrifying in its scale. The best designers, architects, and screenwriters worked on it. They even designed it in a way that visitors were to feel what the Jews felt. The museum undoubtedly drew on Popular Culture—from Disneyland and Hollywood. For decades now, huge Hollywood film studios have been creating sets against which great historical scenes and screenings of great novels were played out. Disney parks are the world's most popular theme parks, which offer unique experience of a fairy tale. There are claims that the Holocaust Memorial Museum is one more American theme park (Gourevitch 58). The United States Holocaust Memorial Museum has often been accused of "Disneyfying" the Holocaust (Bernard-Donals 25), or of producing a spectacle of suffering by giving visitors access to the modes of experience that the victims also must have experienced. And there is no example more

134 *Adriana Krawiec*

cited than the railway boxcar through which visitors walk as part of the permanent exhibition's third floor (Bernard-Donals 25). Visitors are pulled out of the normal world into the created world of oppressed Jews and authoritarianism, one has the feeling that there is no escape from here; it is cramped and traumatic, there are no windows here. This is an analogy to what Jews experienced when they were deprived of their normal lives and imprisoned in ghettos. It is the American way of understanding the Holocaust (Linenthal, "The Boundaries of Memory" 406–433). Popular Culture helped with that.

As far as the discourse of the building architecture is concerned, its designer, James Freed, insisted on transitioning visitors from official Washington into a world of the Holocaust (Linenthal, *Preserving Memory* 102). He created the world of the Holocaust, a raw building with no windows overlooking the National Mall. Thanks to the previously mentioned narration and architecture, the Holocaust Museum is associated with the American democratic tradition, but in a complex way. First of all, the story itself is alien to American life, and it reinforces the American identity by revealing what America is not. And that is why this is the American tale. What is more, the location of the building among the monuments of glory in the USA showed that the meaning of the museum would be about freedom, tolerance, and pluralism.

In a combination of historical storytelling and an experiment in subjecting the visitor to the experience, USHMM seeks an emotional response from visitors, not just the intellectual input. The architecture and scenery of the museum became a kind of expression. It belongs to the discursive formation: the responsibility of visitors for the fate of the world. Its significance is also included in the propagated statement "Never again" by Elie Wiesel (Novick 239–240), who helped establish the United States Holocaust Memorial Museum and thanks to whom the uniqueness of the Holocaust was stressed. Executive Order 12169 offered a definition of the Holocaust as "the systematic and State-sponsored extermination of six million Jews and some five million other people by the Nazis and their collaborators during the Second World War" (Linenthal, *Preserving Memory* 41). Due to Wiesel's intervention the Report defined the Holocaust as the "systematic, bureaucratic extermination of six million Jews by the Nazis and their collaborators . . . during the Second World War" (*Report to the President*). The Report laid the foundations for the construction of the museum.

By appropriating the Holocaust, American culture has transformed it into a "cosmopolitan memory" that creates a transnational and transcultural "memory imperative" that shapes how individuals, groups, and societies around the world remember their own violent pasts and those of others. Thanks to American Popular Culture, it was possible to spread a human rights discourse globally, and today it dominates local and global politics (Sodaro 15).

Conclusions

For a long period of time, one of the determinants of the Polish national identity was the national narration regarding war losses, in which Polish victory was moral

(Mach 64–66). An essential part of this narration became Auschwitz, where the Nazi crimes were thought to be directed against and only against the Polish nation, then a patriotic-heroic image of the Holocaust was created. As a result of the gradual decomposition of the Polish People's Republic in the mid-1980s, and thanks to the film *Shoah* (1985), it has become possible to debate the passive roles of Poles during the Holocaust, and the Auschwitz-Birkenau State Museum has started to teach about the tragic fate of Jews, Poles, Romany people, and Soviet prisoners of war as well as about the fate of all other groups of victims incarcerated and murdered in Auschwitz.

Today, movies like *Shoah* are less popular than *Schindler's List* or *Life Is Beautiful*. Finally, the change in the status of memory and reflection on the Holocaust is influenced by the contemporary phenomena of the medialization of images, transformations of the culture, and postmodern episteme, which is responsible for sometimes trivial representations of the Holocaust within Popular Culture and the clichés of pictures of views taken in Auschwitz. It makes visitors admire the idealized representations known from postcards and films. This is trendy, and thanks to the trend, many people are more eager to visit Auschwitz. Even if they are motivated by voyeurism, they can get to know something more than from popular movies. On the other hand, the museum imposes discourse and does not relate the past with the present within exhibitions. It does it through the International Center for Education about Auschwitz and the Holocaust, but its seminars do not concern every visitor. Thus, the museum of Auschwitz should do as much as possible to be in tune with the world's challenges and reach a new generation of visitors. Otherwise pop culture and the media alone will educate about the Nazi crimes. Behind the rash of Popular Culture presentations, traditional museums are rubbing against the crisis of attractiveness. The position of traditional museums is also weakened by competition with electronic media. However, the problem may be Polish law, which clearly defines what the museum is supposed to do. In Poland, in accordance with the Act of November 21, 1996 on Museums, museums are controlled by the minister responsible for culture and the protection of national heritage, who supervises museums. By the decision of the Polish parliament, in the times of the People's Republic of Poland, the remains of the former Nazi concentration camps in Oświęcim and Brzezinka (Auschwitz-Birkenau) were to become the Monument to the Martyrdom of the Polish Nation and Other Nations in 1947. In the light of this law, the Auschwitz-Birkenau State Museum also operated on the basis of the statute issued by the entity that created it, in agreement with the Minister responsible for culture and the protection of national heritage. The statute until this day defines the scope and manner of the museum's operation. The law specifies the function of the museum, which is to commemorate and document the Nazi crimes—primarily under the Act establishing the center.

Today, thanks to postmodern culture and new episteme, that is, a set of relations which may be discovered for a given epoch (Howarth 83–84), the museum proposes some new threads of historical narration concerning the Nazi crimes against humanity in Auschwitz. Surely everything that emerges from this museum must be legal. Therefore, it should be expected that under the influence of cultural changes,

136 *Adriana Krawiec*

the museum will change, otherwise it will lose customers and its raison d'être. Time will also show whether postmodern culture is as powerful as Polish law and can establish new discursive formations.

There is no Ministry of Culture in the USA, which does not mean that the cultural system does not exist here. Moreover, it is extremely effective in multiplying the sources of funding and spreading the products of the American culture around the world. The expansion of American culture is the result not only of the American economic power but also mass grassroots culture support as well as outstanding artistic creativity, companies' patronage, and favorable tax policy, together with close cooperation between nonprofit cultural institutions and commercial culture, from which the latter draws its inspiration. We can also observe in the USA close connections in the culture of the public sector, civil society, and the market. This combination manifests itself in the fact that the state acts as a regulator, foundations correct the system, industry promotes and distributes the American culture around the world, and rich donors defend an elite culture.

Owing to the American culture, the memory of the Holocaust has been popularized and has become a central issue of worldwide culture. However, it would not be possible without the actions of the authorities. The question is whether the founder of the discursivity was the US president—Carter, Jews and American intellectuals and scientists, or Popular Culture. Carter's idea to commemorate the Holocaust in America as a confirmation that the US, as the world leader of democracy, was to set an example for others but also as a result of the struggle for the votes of American Jews was controversial. It was known that the monument would not serve as a lesson, hence, the idea of a living memorial emerged. It was supposed to act as a moral compass for the US and the rest of the world.

All in all, thanks to the USA, the memory of the Holocaust became the basis of democracy. It became also the basis for the rest of the world to build and maintain political structures straight from American democracy. However, the lesson of the Holocaust has not been learned, as evidenced by the subsequent crimes of humanity, such as in Burma, where Myanmar's military committed ethnic cleansing, crimes against humanity, and genocide against the Rohingya (*Burma's Path to Genocide*). As it turned out, Popular Culture did not help. The popular slogan "Never again" is an empty slogan in the face of what happened in Burma. After the Cold War, the entire world, or at least the greater part of it, was to move toward a new era in which the idealized versions of American political institutions would emerge everywhere. Unfortunately, it did not happen. Likewise, the lesson of the Holocaust has not been learned for the entire world.

To sum up, the two museums differ in certain respects. Whereas the Polish museum documents the Nazi crimes, the American museum creates a spectacle of suffering, all in order to prevent crimes in the future, and the prevention of crimes against humanity, is guaranteed by democracy. The discourse of both museums depends on who has the power. Popular Culture affects both centers. So do politicians. Who has more power—culture or politicians? Popular Culture surrounds us and influences us; politicians, on the other hand, create norms and institutions. It seems that the discourse depends on the episteme of the epoch in which both

Holocaust Museums 137

centers operate. And all this goes into the archives and in some time it will be also possible to reconstruct who shapes the memory of the Holocaust or Auschwitz—popular media and photos or these centers or maybe politicians who institutionalize the discourse on the Holocaust?

Acknowledgment

The work is based on the author's visit to the United States Holocaust Memorial Museum funded with a grant from the Faculty of International and Political Studies of the Jagiellonian University for research activities.

Notes

1 Data collected by the author during a visit to the Auschwitz-Birkenau Museum and to the United States Holocaust Memorial Museum.
2 This chapter has benefited from Michel Foucault's theorization of archive, social memory, discursive formations, archaeology, genealogy, truths, and episteme. Michel Foucault introduces the term *archive* in order to embrace the collections of rules that in a given epoch and society determine discourses, which is what can be talked about and how it can be done. The archive also defines what will not be made public and, therefore, preserved in social memory as important and legally valid (*Archaeology of Knowledge*). Foucault (*Society Must Be Defended*) connected discourse with power, because, according to him, the meaning of discourse is strictly connected with power mechanisms. In The *Archaeology of Knowledge*, Foucault explains discourses as practices forming objects with specific rules, it means discursive formations, which allow for the emergence of specific truths. Discursive formations are social formations (Bińczuk). In his archaeological analysis, Foucault describes relations among utterances which occur in the discourse field. When we are successful in determining any regularity within objects, concepts, modes of expression, we can talk about discursive formation. The conditions which they are subject to will be called not ideology, theory or science, but formation rules that is conditions for their existence (Foucault, *Archaeology of Knowledge* 56–64). Foucault's discourse archaeology describes formation rules which determine a discourse structure; whereas, genealogy researches the historical conditions of discursive formations emergence, that is, how power relations affect the discourse (Howarth 80–121). In genealogical analyses, discourses are related to non-discourse practices and processes, (e.g., political changes) (Howarth 83). In *Archaeology,* the discourse refers to practices which govern the utterance. The basis of discourse practices unity is constituted by episteme, a set of relations which may be discovered for a given epoch, times (Howarth 83–84).

Works Cited

Alexander, Jeffrey C. "Culture Trauma, morality and solidarity: The social construction of 'Holocaust' and other mass murders." *Thesis Eleven*, vol. 132, no. 1, 2016, pp. 3–16.
Belsey, Catherine. *Postructuralism. A Very Short Introduction.* Oxford University Press, 2002.
Bernard-Donals, Michael. *Figures of Memory: The Rhetoric of Displacement at the United States Holocaust Memorial Museum.* SUNY Press, 2016.
Bińczyk, Ewa. "O czym szepcze władza (w ujęciu Michela Foucaulta) [What power whispers about (in Foucault's approach)]." *Przegląd Artystyczno-Literacki*, no. 9, 1999, pp. 67–72.

138   Adriana Krawiec

Burma's Path to Genocide. *The United States Holocaust Memorial Museum*, https://exhibitions.ushmm.org/burmas-path-to-genocide. Accessed 27 Nov. 2021.

Cebulski, Tomasz. *Auschwitz po Auschwitz. Historia, Polityka i Pamięć wokół Państwowego Muzeum Auschwitz-Birkenau 1980–2010*. Wydawnictwo Libron, 2016.

Forecki, Piotr. *Od Shoah do Strachu. Spory o polsko-żydowską przeszłość i pamięć w debatach publicznych*. Wydawnictwo Poznańskie, 2010.

Foucault, Michel. *Society Must Be Defended* (Translated by M. Kowalska, Warsaw). Wydawnictwo KR, 1998.

Foucault, Michel. *The Archaeology of Knowledge* (Translated by A. Siemek, Warsaw). Państwowy Instytut Wydawniczy, 1977.

Gourevitch, Philip. "Behold now behemoth: The Holocaust Memorial Museum: One more American theme park." *Harper's Magazine*, Jul. 1993, pp. 55–62.

Goźliński, Paweł. "Trzeba opowiadać inaczej." *Gazeta Wyborcza*, 15 Feb. 2001, p. 6.

Greń, Paweł. *Pamięć a media. Obchody wyzwolenia KL Auschwitz-Birkenau w dyskursie prasowym*. Wydawnictwo Aureus, 2017.

Howarth, David. *Discourse* (Translated by A. Gąsior-Niemiec A.). Oficyna Naukowa, 2008.

Huener, Jonathan. *Auschwitz, Poland, and the Politics of Commemoration, 1945–1979*. Ohio University Press, 2003.

Keene, Suzanne. "All that is solid?—Museums and the postmodern." *Public Archaeology*, no. 5, 2006, pp 185–198.

Krantz, Tomasz. "Miejsca pamięci czy pamięć miejsc. Rozważania o roli upamiętniania w przekazie społeczno-historycznym." *Pro Memoria. Biuletyn Informacyjny Państwowego Muzeum Oświęcim-Brzezinka, Fundacji Pamięci Ofiar Obozu Zagłady Auschwitz-Birkenau*, nos. 13–06, 2000, pp. 75–78.

Kucia, Marek. *Auschwitz jako fakt społeczny*. UNiVERSITAS 2005.

Kucia, Marek and Katarzyna Stec. "Edukacja o Auschwitz i Holokauście w perspektywie badań społecznych." *Edukacja o Auschwitz i Holokauście w autentycznych miejscach pamięci. Stan obecny i perspektywy na przyszłość*, edited by Piotr Trojański. Państwowe Muzeum Auschwitz-Birkenau, 2019, pp. 51–90.

Linenthal, Edward. "The boundaries of memory: The United States Holocaust Memorial Museum." *American Quarterly*, vol. 46, no. 3, 1994, pp. 406–433.

———. *Preserving Memory: The Struggle to Create America's Holocaust Museum*. Columbia University Press, 2001.

Lipski, Jan. "Dwie ojczyzny, dwa patriotyzmy. Uwagi o megalomanii narodowej i ksenofobii Polaków." *Otwarta Rzeczpospolita*, http://otwarta.org/wp-content/uploads/2011/11/J-Lipski-Dwie-ojczyzny-dwa-patriotyzmy-lekkie3.pdf. Accessed 27 Nov. 2021.

Mach, Zdzisław. "Poland's national memory of the Holocaust and its identity in an expand Europe." In *The Holocaust: Voices of Scholars*, edited by J. Ambrosewicz-Jacobs. Centrum Badań Holokaustu, 1999, pp. 61–70.

Novick, Peter. *The Holocaust and Collective Memory: The American Experience*. Bloomsbury, 2001.

Pawlas, Jerzy. "Dialog." *Nasz Dziennik*, 19 Apr. 2001, p. 11.

Rzeczkowski, Sebastian. "Oskarżenia bez dowodów." *Nasz Dziennik*, 30 Jan. 2001, p. 12.

Sodaro, Amy. *Exhibiting Atrocity: Memorial Museums and the Politics of Past Violence*. Rutgers University Press, 2018.

Stępnik, Andrzej. "Dydaktyka historii wobec wyzwań edukacyjnych w muzeach." In *Edukacja muzealna w Polsce*, edited by Wiesław Wysok and Andrzej Stępnik. Państwowe Muzeum na Majdanku, 2013, pp. 69–83.

The 2006 Annual Report of the Auschwitz-Birkenau State Museum, http://auschwitz.org/en/museum/news/the-2006-annual-report-of-the-auschwitz-birkenau-state-museum, 477. html. Accessed 27 Nov. 2021.

The Auschwitz-Birkenau Museum Archives. *Projekt ramowy i założenia ogólne Muzeum oświęcimskiego, opracowane m.in. przez dr. Heina, T. Hołuja 1946–1947.* The Auschwitz-Birkenau Museum Archives, 1947.

The Government of the People's Republic of Poland. "The Act of 2 July 1947 on the commemoration of the martyrdom of the Polish Nation and other Nations in Oświęcim." *Journal of Laws*, no. 52, item 265, 1947, pp. 1–2.

The President's Commission on the Holocaust. *Report to the President*, 1979.

The Senate and House of Representatives of the United States of America in Congress assembled. "An act to establish the United States Holocaust Memorial Council." *Public Law*, 1980, pp. 96–388.

Trojański, Piotr. "Edukacja o Holokauście w Polsce. Próba krytycznego bilansu." In *Edukacja muzealna w Polsce*, edited by Wiesław Wysok and Andrzej Stępnik. Państwowe Muzeum na Majdanku, 2013, pp. 129–150.

White, Hayden. "Polityka interpretacji historycznej dyscyplina przeciwko wzniołości." *Porównania*, vol. 7, 2010, pp. 7–32.

Young, James E. *The Texture of Memory*. Yale University Press, 1993.

Ziębińska-Witek, Anna. *Historia w muzeach. Studium ekspozycji Holokaustu.* UMCS, 2011.

9 Trace and Trauma
Early Holocaust Remembrance in American and Canadian Popular Culture

Roger Chapman

In a 2001 Days of Remembrance address at the United States Holocaust Memorial Museum (USHMM) in Washington, D.C., Elie Wiesel discussed the importance of "trace" with respect to the Holocaust (US Holocaust Memorial). "How does one mourn for six million people who died?" Wiesel asked, adding: "Do we know how to remember the victims, their solitude, their helplessness? They left us without a trace, and we are their trace." Those who act as a "trace" honor the individual Jews who perished in the Shoah or, as Jon Stratton calls it, the Judeocide (146). The term "trace" is useful for its range of meanings. To trace is to search and discover. To trace is the act of copying for making a record, such as preserving history. To trace is to follow the contours of a shape, like following a narrative. If following many narratives, a common pattern might be traced. Trace is also a term about the faint or minute. A trace amount is seemingly imperceptible, requiring special effort for detection. A trace can be a hint, a subtle awareness. By linking the remembrance of the Holocaust with a simple word of multifaceted dimension, Wiesel points to the complexity of remembrance about the Shoah.

Wiesel's "we are their trace" admonishment is a challenge to not allow the Holocaust to remain abstract. The question about knowing the victims, their solitude and helplessness, demands answers derived from research and empathy. Implicit in the concept of trace is hiddenness. Related to the hiddenness is the lingering cultural trauma, as experienced by Holocaust survivors and their immediate families and down to the second and third generations, and also to those Jews who have no direct connection to the Shoah. Jack Herskovits, the son of two Holocaust survivors, recalls how "my psychological development was that of wanting to know and wanting to not know my parents' unbearably painful histories and emotional realities" (36). Though that horrific past was the "overriding force in shaping my identity," Herskovits continues, "my knowledge of their actual experience during the Holocaust is limited to a scaled-down, somewhat vague, skeletal version of their histories" (36). Even when Herskovits' parents tried to share their Shoah stories, all they could share was trace—"jagged and confusing fragments" often delivered in Yiddish, a language utilized "when they wanted me to understand and not understand when they didn't want me to understand" (36). Interwoven in the personal history and extending to the broader history of the Holocaust is trace and trauma. In his 2004 speech, Wiesel continued his theme by stating, "All those who have no

DOI: 10.4324/9781003251224-12

tombs: our heart remains their cemetery" (US Holocaust Memorial). For hearts to remember enough to become cemeteries, the challenge will always be the trace.

Another observation to be made, one of the purposes of this chapter, is the Jewish aspect of the trace versus universalization. Though speaking at the Holocaust Memorial Museum, Wiesel clearly had a general audience in mind. He was not addressing Jews alone. So, when he said, "We are their trace," he meant all of the living irrespective of ethnicity. Yet, Wiesel's "we" was also royal. In Popular Culture, the trace has generally been offered by Jews. This chapter will overview the early Holocaust trace in American and Canadian culture as presented by Jews, specifically a Marc Chagall painting, Anna Sokolow's choreography, Leonard Cohen's writings, and the labels of Dr. Bronner's Magic Soaps. This trace represents Popular Culture offerings by Jews who did not directly experience the Holocaust, but it is, nonetheless, representative of the personal as well as expressive of lingering psychological trauma. In this case, the literature, paintings, choreography, songs, and aphorisms on soap labels all constitute Popular Culture in that they were intended for an audience broader than the Jewish one.

The condition for remembering the Holocaust in a universal manner—and as a metaphor for "collective suffering"—was largely advanced by the four-part NBC-TV miniseries *Holocaust*, which was first shown in the United States in 1978 and afterward across Europe (Mintz 26). According to Jon Stratton:

> The miniseries helped to establish the Holocaust as having a Western universal, that is no longer specifically Jewish, theme. The Western world could now think of the events of the Judeocide as the Holocaust, as a morality story about Good and Evil. At the same time, in its new discursive form the Judeocide could be thought of as a total entity rather than in terms of concentration camps, massacres, ghettos and so on. More, the discourse satisfied [Hannah] Arendt's concerns, the Holocaust was thought of as unique and unprecedented—at least in part no doubt a consequence of the championing of the term in the 1960s by writers such as Elie Wiesel. The Holocaust also embraced another of Arendt's preoccupations, that the Judeocide be thought of as genocide. Genocide could now be the key for understanding the horror of the Holocaust—that the Nazis had aimed for the destruction of an entire people.
>
> (151–152)

Stratton's argument about the miniseries making Holocaust history universal yet at the same time a Judeocide underscores the ambiguity of Wiesel's "we." Also, as important as the miniseries *Holocaust* was, it should be pointed out that other films preceded that production, including *The Diary of Anne Frank* (1959), *Judgment at Nuremberg* (1961), and *The Pawnbroker* (1964). With the exception of *The Diary of Anne Frank*, all of these film works are Jewish creations. In other words, the film producers were Jewish. As for the film on Anne Frank, the non-Jewish producer George Stevens, who as a US Army officer had participated in the liberation of Dachau, was obviously using material produced by a Jewish girl who died

142 *Roger Chapman*

in the Shoah. The most popular Holocaust film, produced much later, *Schindler's List* (1993), was also a Jewish work—its famous producer, Steven Spielberg, has shared that between 16 and 20 relatives in Ukraine and Poland had perished in the Holocaust (McBride 22), adding, "My life has always come back to images surrounding the Holocaust" (qtd. in McBride 44). With the exception of George Stevens, all of these film producers represent a Jewish "we"; as for Stevens, his "we" is associated with the remembrance of being a firsthand witness of the Holocaust.

Prior to any of those films, there was the Holocaust rumination by Holocaust survivor Elie Wiesel. When one thinks of the Shoah being communicated to a popular audience, at or near the top of the list will be Wiesel's novel *Night*, which was first published in Yiddish in Argentina (1956), followed by a translation in French for France (1958), and then a translation in English for the United States (1960). Though an early trace, it was not part of American Popular Culture until 15 years after World War II. Prior to *Night*, there were other representations of the Shoah in American and Canadian Popular Culture. These works of early Holocaust trace were trace in that they were less explicit than Wiesel's eloquent and moving but, nevertheless, blunt account. These representations were by Jewish creators.

One of the earliest, if not the first, examples of Holocaust trace in North American Popular Culture was Marc Chagall's *White Crucifixion* (1939), an example of "exemplary Jewish martyrology" (Meyer 414). A Jew from Belarus, exiled sometime after the Soviet takeover, Chagall was living in France when he made this painting of Christ on the cross as an emblem of Nazi-persecuted Jews. Like many of Chagall's dreamlike works, the center image is surrounded by smaller corresponding images. In this case, the crucifixion scene is encircled by incidents telling the story of the Jewish persecution in Europe (a synagogue in flames, a wandering Jew with a sack, a bearded figure fleeing with the Torah, refugees in a boat, a marauding band of soldiers presumably on the hunt for Jews, etc.). In a bold move, Chagall had the painting exhibited in Paris in 1940. After the Nazis invaded France, the painter fled to America, arranging for that painting to later be smuggled out of the German-occupied country. In 1944, prior to the liberation of any Holocaust camp and a year prior to Victory in Europe Day, the painting was part of the *Religious Art of Today* exhibit at the Dayton Art Institute in Dayton, Ohio (Art Institute of Chicago). The first Americans viewing this painting, an early Holocaust trace, likely missed its full import. But later in 1946, when it was exhibited at the Museum of Modern Art in New York, the audience would have been more aware. The painting, Popular Culture in that it is shown to the masses, is an example of Holocaust trace produced before most people clearly understood the horrifying magnitude of the Final Solution. By turning the Holocaust victim into a Christ figure, Chagall universalizes the Holocaust victim.

Remarkably, the same year Chagall painted *White Crucifixion*, Anna Sokolow presented her chorographical work *The Exile* (1939), reflecting on the plight of her people by the Nazis. Later, as she continued to reflect on her ethnicity and the resiliency of the Hebrews over the centuries, it is believed Chagall's painting served as inspiration for her further dance expressions on the theme (Kosstrin, *Honest Bodies: Revolutionary Modernism* 150). A Jewish American whose parents had

Trace and Trauma 143

emigrated to New York from Russia, Sokolow contributed to the early Holocaust trace, offering the choreography performances *Songs of a Semite* (1943), *Kaddish* (1945), *Dreams* (1961), *Steps of Silence* (1968), and *In Memory . . . 543246* (1973). Sokolow emerged from the Martha Graham Dance Company during the 1930s and was active in the Popular Front in opposition to fascism and war. After the war broke out, she offered performances in Mexico and the United States, focusing a body of her art on peace as well as the suffering of the Jews. Most significant of her early Holocaust trace was *Kaddish*, about the Jewish prayer for the dead. *Kaddish*, it is interesting to note, preceded Wiesel's *Night* by almost a decade. In *Night* and its sad commentary on the Kaddish in the context of the Final Solution, with families split apart and sons unable to perform their filial duties, Wiesel lamented, "I don't know whether, during the history of the Jewish people, men have ever before recited Kaddish for themselves" (51).

In Sokolow's *Kaddish*, it is a woman who offers the prayer for the Holocaust dead. In the five-minute performance, the female dancer, representing the universal human, is wearing the *tefillin* (phylacteries), the vestments reserved for males. The first performance occurred in Mexico City on 20 August 1945 and then it premiered in the United States in New York City on 4 May 1946—this period coincided with the early reports of the Holocaust death camps. In her analysis offered in a PhD dissertation, Hannah Kosstrin observes that the solo performance was subtle, which was in keeping with early Holocaust trace: "*Kaddish* does not depict concrete images of the Holocaust, but nonetheless shows understanding and accusation of its atrocities" (*Honest Bodies: Jewishness* 218). The dance includes the beating of the breast and the shielding of one's eyes from the heavens, traditional acts of Jewish contrition to Yahweh. The wearing of the *tefillin* is consequential, as Kosstrin in her dissertation explains: "The *tefillin*, while a marker of Otherness, were also a tool of agency and empowerment" for being "a marker of Jewishness" (222–223). In the Nazi death camps, the goal was not only human genocide but cultural genocide—thus, in the camps the inmates were stripped of all trappings of Judaism, including the *tefillin*, and reduced to wearing a Star of David for the strictly malevolent purpose of being othered. Afterward, by having a dance in which these special vestments are publicly displayed to a mixed audience of Jew and Gentile, there is a statement of triumph about continuity. Despite Sokolow's usage of religious symbolism and of strong figures (often female) from the stories of the Hebrew Bible, her worldview was secular—the trauma she exhibited was Jewish humanism.

The Montreal-born poet/novelist/singer Leonard Cohen, who grew up in a devout Jewish household, was attuned to the cultural trauma of the Holocaust from a more mystical approach. By the end of World War II, he was 11 years old, too young to have fully comprehended the magnitude of what had happened yet old enough to have lingering impressions to reflect upon in adulthood. At some point, he undoubtedly realized he might have been sent to the gas chambers had his paternal grandfather not chosen to leave Lithuania and emigrate to Canada. Cohen's father died when he was 9 years old and the first images of the Holocaust were being shown around the time he was 10 or 11. He referred to his parents' era as "THE DACHAU GENERATION" (Simmons 119). As a young man, he became

144   *Roger Chapman*

very critical of the values of the older generation of his synagogue community in Montreal, believing they were insular, materialistic, and void of transcendence—in his own words, "afraid to be lonely" as "witnesses to monotheism" and oblivious of how "their nobility was insecure because it rested on inheritance and not moment-to-moment creation in the face of annihilation" (qtd. in Simmons 122–123). Cohen's youthful denunciation of the elders seems to betray elements of personal survivor guilt. Perhaps such sentiments carried over during the Yom Kippur War, when in solidarity with the Jewish struggle for survival, Cohen went to Israel and entertained the Israeli troops as a sort of Jewish Bob Hope (Kubernik 99)—perhaps more than anything this was a gesture of taking a little risk, setting an example of what he believes was not shown in his community while growing up. In his poetry collections and novels, there can be found Holocaust trace, suggesting Cohen's lifelong trauma over the Shoah.

In an early volume of poetry, *Let Us Compare Mythologies* (1956), Cohen reflects on life in French-speaking Canada and its cultural diversity. Part of the reflection was his self-examination of how, after the Holocaust, he, as a Jew, could fit in where Catholicism dominated. Like Chagall and like Sokolow, who explored Mexican culture and at times utilized Catholic symbols for expressing herself, Cohen is often friendly and at ease with the figure of Christ. Also, he rejected the view that the death of Jesus of Nazareth was the fault of the Jewish race; like Chagall, he regarded the crucifixion as a component of the history of Jewish persecution and perhaps, too, a universalizing story. In the second poem of the volume, it reads:

When young the Christians told me
how we pinned Jesus
like a lovely butterfly against the wood,
and I wept beside paintings of Calvary
at velvet wounds
and delicate twisted feet.

(Let Us 16)

But the poem ends with him rejecting the myth about the Jewish Christ-killer, calling it an "elaborate lie" that led to "a hollow yellow sign" (a reference to the Star of David patch Jews wore during the Holocaust)—as this thought continues in the poem, Cohen suggests dialogue when he presents the theme of the anthology, writing, "Then let us compare mythologies" (*Let Us* 16–17). Comparing mythologies is an exercise of universalizing. In "Saviors," Cohen presents "the Roman sport of crucifixion" as part of the long narrative of persecution of the Jews (*Let Us* 73–74). In perhaps one of the more Holocaust-explicit poems—"Lovers"—the Shoah is rendered as an extension of the long history of pogroms; there is a cryptic reference to "the first pogrom" and then later "the hot ovens" before the man and woman "Kiss before the soldier came/ To knock out her golden teeth" (*Let Us* 40). Finally, in the poem "Warning," Cohen offers a chastisement of those who said nothing as neighbors around them disappeared, advising that "it can spread" and might someday lead to the disappearance of the loved ones of those who had earlier remained silent (*Let Us* 68).

When addressing the Holocaust in his work, Cohen worried about his romantic style producing a form of aesthetic pleasure. Such concern harmonized with Theodor Adorno, who quipped, "To write poetry after Auschwitz is barbaric" (34). But inspired by Charles Baudelaire's *Flowers of Evil*, Cohen produced *Flowers for Hitler* (1964) and utilized an anti-art style in order for the poems not to act as "a collaborator in the world's insincerity" (Wynands 206). Cohen deplored the quick return to normality after the atrocity of the Shoah, recognizing it as a type of suppression, which was his awareness of trauma and trace. But normality was even sought by the camp survivors; of the children who later became young adults, about 40 percent admitted to having suffered from PTSD but they refused mental health services because "the struggle for normal life could not accommodate asking for therapy" (Cohen et al. 615). Contrary to convention, perhaps a luxury due to not having had any direct or indirect experience of the camp horrors, Cohen thought it was important to bring the Holocaust into people's living rooms.

In his novel *Beautiful Losers* (1966), Leonard Cohen gives a second look at the colonial past of his own country and "recognizes the unsettling fact that a holocaust lies at the beginning of Canadian history" (Mannani and Thompson 177). Here he universalizes the Holocaust, an example of multidirectional memory with "the emergence of Holocaust memory on a global scale [that] has contributed to the articulation of other histories" (Rothberg 6). When Cohen writes, "I accuse the Church of killing Indians" (Cohen, *Beautiful* 47), he is referring to the genocidal campaigns against the indigenous people of the northern part of North America. Also, he laments Christianity's displacement of the native religion and the gradual loss of transcendence as religion waned under modernism. One must wonder, though, if he ever considered the Hebrew conquest of the Promised Land in the same vein.

The early Holocaust trace provided by Cohen was the beginning of lifelong reflection. Like Wiesel, who explored the mysticism of other religions, Cohen in various ways sought to find transcendence, even devoting most of the 1990s as an adherent of Zen Buddhism and becoming a monk, despite struggling with strong libidinal urges. An experiment of mixed results, Cohen in *Book of Longing* (2006) conceded after coming down from the mountain: "I finally understood/I had no gift/for Spiritual Matters" (22). But his Jewish identity is apparent throughout the volume with his drawings that include the Star of David, as if maintaining solidarity with the Shoah victims. In "Not a Jew," Cohen suggests any Jew lacking Jewish identity is not really a Jew and that is "final" (perhaps suggesting a type of Final Solution self-renunciation) (Cohen, *Longing* 158). As if still trying to grapple with the why of the horror, late in life he mused:

German puppets
burnt the Jews
Jewish puppets
did not choose.
(Cohen, *Longing* 160)

146 *Roger Chapman*

Embedded in that trauma trace is an unexpected, and even charitable gesture, of equalizing both the Germans and Jews as "puppets" in the tragedy.

After his period of seclusion, Cohen returned to giving concerts, until the end of his life touring worldwide while singing his repertoire, including "Dance Me to the End of Love" (1984). So subtle about the Holocaust, the song remains a trace, popular at weddings even though it was inspired by the poignant true story of Jews at a camp being marched off to execution accompanied by live classical music being played for the occasion (Simmons 337). Such a mental image that should produce lasting cultural trauma: "Dance me to your beauty/with a burning violin"; "Dance me to the children/who are asking to be born"; "Dance me through the panic/till I'm gathered safely in"; and "Raise a tent of shelter now/though every thread is torn" (Cohen, *Leonard* 161–162). For those who have read Wiesel's Holocaust memoir, the song will remind them of the Polish character Juliek playing the violin at Buchenwald and "bidding farewell to an audience of dying men" (Wiesel, *Night* 112). Also, the song connects with Sokolow's *Kaddish* being accompanied by Maurice Ravel's *Deus Mélodies Hébraiques*, which included a solo violin performance about a last dance in Vienna before the Nazis took over (Kosstrin, *Honest Bodies: Revolutionary Modernism* 131). Cohen's song, with its pleasurable aesthetic, is in contradiction with the earlier aim of *Flowers for Hitler*, just as most people fail to recognize it is reflecting on the Holocaust. Though this song would not be classified as early Holocaust trace, it demonstrates the change over time as Cohen continued to reflect on the genocide, suggesting a sense of lingering trauma. When not recognized for what it is about, the song literally represents just a trace— and that must have added to Cohen's trauma, perhaps because it somehow, in part, violated the ethic of a more idealistic past.

Cohen, who was a fixture in the Canadian and American postwar counterculture movement, no doubt was familiar with Dr. Bronner's Magic Soaps. This soap product, which comes in liquid and bar form, was popular in hippie circles for its natural ingredients and for not being produced by a big corporation. Equally attractive to the counterculture mindset was the labeling of Dr. Bronner's Magic Soaps. In very small lettering was a barrage of idealistic aphorisms, many of them quirky, emphasizing the need for peace and universal brotherhood with nonstandard word capitalization and numerous exclamation points. Though some have regarded the aphorisms on the soap labels as nonsensical, they, in fact, were the serious and long-thought-out compilation of the "All-One-God-Faith" of the soap maker, Emanuel (Emil) Heilbronner (Chapman 288). During the interwar period, Heilbronner emigrated to America from Germany. Wishing not to be associated with "Heil Hitler," at some point he dropped the Heil from his name and, at the same time, adopted an honorific title, thus retooling himself as Dr. Bronner. Despite his pleadings after seeing the worrisome developments beginning in the 1930s, he was unable to convince his parents to leave Germany—in the end, they became victims of the Holocaust. The last correspondence he received from them was a postcard from the father, which tersely read, "You were right" (Chapman 290). Around the same time, Dr. Bronner's wife died, leaving him a widower with children. The death of his wife and parents deeply impacted his psychological equilibrium, perhaps

Trace and Trauma   147

exacerbating preexisting mental problems, prompting him to carry on as a type of holy fool in pursuit of the "Moral ABC."

As he later explained, "And now in 1944, as I buried my wife . . . I swore to God within me and within every living being on this planet that . . . I'd become the servant of God." When he got his finances in order:

> I quit my job and became a searcher for truth. True to my name, Emanuel, search for truth—*emmis* is truth in Hebrew. And so I learned beginning in 1944, that what causes all the trouble on this earth, the past 2000 years, is the lack of rabbis, the failure of rabbis to teach every twelve-year-old boy on God's spaceship earth the "Moral ABC," without which none survive free.
>
> (*Dr. Bronner's Magic Soapbox*)

In 1948 when he started a soap business, he peddled his product on the street while preaching his "Moral ABC." Desiring only the homemade soap, most customers balked at listening to his sermons. Refusing to be stymied, he began printing his message on the soap labels—if they would not listen to him directly, they would at least take the message home and perhaps at odd moments read and reflect (Chapman 291). Having much to say, the text was rendered in tiny font in order for everything to fit. Over the course of time, he developed six types of soap—peppermint, almond, eucalyptus, lavender, tea tree, and unscented baby mild—and he had enough preaching material for each label of 3,000 words to be distinctive (Chapman 292). Later, his aphorisms were published as a book (Bronner, *The Moral ABC*), and years after his death, in 1997, an LP record album of his spiritual statements and aphorisms was produced by the soap company that still exists as a family-run business (Rowe).

Though over the years some have regarded the writings as gibberish, they actually possess a molecular structure of Judaism, in certain respects paralleling the basic teachings of Rabbi Hillel and in its broadest sense harmonizing with the Hebrew concept *tikkun olam* ("repairing the world") (Chapman 293). Like Leonard Cohen, Dr. Bronner had been raised in an Orthodox Jewish household. And also like Cohen, as an adult, he remained strongly anchored in Jewish identity while abandoning worship rituals without loss of otherworldliness. An early embracer of Zionism, Dr. Bronner purposely chose a dark–sky blue label for his first soap product, the liquid 18-in-1 Hemp Peppermint Pure-Castile Soap, in order for it to match the color of the flag of modern Israel. Dr. Bronner would have approved of Cohen playing songs for the Israeli forces during the Yom Kippur War, but first and foremost, he wanted world peace. The impulse behind his *tikkun olam* message was finding a way to go forward after World War II and the Holocaust.

From the perspective of Dr. Bronner, the problems of the twentieth century, including Nazism, communism, and the nuclear age, were the failure of passing on the "All-One-God-Faith" (monotheism) and the *universal* moral code associated with it (the "Moral ABC"). The Shoah and the death of six million Jews was one of the consequences of this overall neglect to pass on the timeless moral values. Dr. Bronner argued, "What an apology we Rabbis owe" to the victims (the millions

148   *Roger Chapman*

dead, *and not Jews alone*) and the victimizers (including Marx, Lenin, Hitler, Stalin, and Mao) for the collective failure to teach the "Moral ABC" (Bronner 2, 15, 18, 28, 40, 48, 51). The nuclear age, he warned, meant that henceforth the truth needed to be taught for the sake of humanity's future survival: "For with Bomb & Gun we're All-One or None!!!" (Bronner 3).

Broadly universal, Dr. Bronner saw an interconnectivity between Judaism and other religions, believing over the ages there were astronomers who as spiritual leaders received revelation from each passing of Halley's Comet. The revelation over time was progressive, contributing to an evolutionary growth of humankind. But unfortunately, during the modern era, parents and teachers neglected to pass on to their children the universal values of the accumulated wisdom (Chapman 291). This universal moral code consisted of good behavior at the individual level, which provides the foundation for world peace. The code required free speech and a free press, a strong work ethic, and a desire for what is best for self as well as others. In the fourth maxim on the peppermint soap label, it reads in part: "God's Law can save us, but if we teach only our clan? We're all hated then! So, we must teach friend and enemy, the whole Human race, the full-truth, hard-work, free speech, press-and-profitsharing Moral ABC's All-One-God-Faith" (Chapman 293).

Though consistent in its message, Dr. Bronner's jeremiad was (and is) hard to follow. In the jumble of words, the Holocaust trace is not readily discernible. Though the All-One-God-Faith message lacked the eloquence of Leonard Cohen, its embedded Holocaust remembrance was probably no less distinguishable than what was in the song "Dance Me to the End of Love." While Dr. Bronner's soap labels did not connect Jesus with Jewish martyrdom the way Marc Chagall did, he, nonetheless, regarded Christ as having been a student of Rabbi Hillel and, thus, part of the Jewish tradition, part of the "Moral ABC" (Chapman 295). Those early purchasers of Dr. Bronner's Magic Soaps would have probably thought the Holocaust context to be a little creepy, but like much of the early Holocaust-related postwar Popular Culture, it was less than overt. The life story of Dr. Bronner can only be understood as a personal struggle to overcome the trauma of the Holocaust; it could be argued that his preaching was a form of kaddish. Just as in Holocaust remembrance the common refrain is the purpose of remembering is to prevent genocide of a race of people from ever being attempted again, the imperative rationale of Dr. Bronner's preaching was to prevent the extermination of the human race.

In the immediate years following World War II, the Holocaust did not get the amount of attention one might have expected. Perhaps this was due to the utter shock, like a sudden cut that takes a long moment for the blood to start oozing. By the 1970s, however, a new emphasis took shape, fostered in part by new research and the television miniseries *Holocaust*. Hitler's Final Solution came to be regarded "as a unique defining moment in Western civilization, a transcendent manifestation of moral evil" (Jenkins 90). It has also been observed that "the Holocaust is a pervasive optic through which all people in the West, not just Jews, or for that matter Germans, since the 1980s have come to see the world" (Stratton 6). As this chapter has shown, in the immediate postwar period, there were examples of Holocaust trace in American and Canadian Popular Culture, often subtle as it

Trace and Trauma 149

represented individuals quietly working through their sense of personal trauma. Arguably these traces, Jewish in their origin, contributed toward a broader form of rumination, opening a space for multidirectional memory that includes "other histories of collective violence" (Rothberg 9). According to Jon Stratton, "Memory might appear to be a personal matter, born out of one's own individual experience but it is located in the ways the society as a whole remembers, and makes sense of things" (146–147). The "we" of Elie Wiesel's "we are their trace" can only take on a universal aspect after those who knew the shape provided an outline for the rest to follow in order to arrive at understanding. Marc Chagall, Anna Sokolow, Leonard Cohen, and Emanuel Bronner were Jews who did not experience the Holocaust directly (though Chagall had to flee Europe), but they left for posterity some examples of response from their secondhand trauma. The debates of the future will certainly be about finding the right balance between regarding the Holocaust as a crime against humanity versus the Shoah as a crime against Jews (Magid 109), which will largely determine the precise meaning of Wiesel's "we."

Works Cited

Adorno, Theodor W. *Prisms* (Translated by Samuel and Shierry Webber). Cambridge University Press, 1981.

Bronner, Emanuel. *The Moral ABC I & II* (4th ed.). Bronner's All-One-God-Faith, 2006.

Chapman, Roger. "Dr. Bronner's 'magic soaps' religion: A tikkun olam response to the Holocaust, the atom bomb, and the Cold War." *Journal of Religion and Popular Culture*, vol. 25, no. 2, 2013, pp. 287–301 (*Project Muse*). DOI: 10.3138/jrpc.25.2.287 (Accessed 16 Jun. 2020).

Cohen, Estel, et al. "Posttraumatic stress symptoms and fear of intimacy among treated and non-treated survivors who were children during the Holocaust." *Social Psychiatry & Psychiatric Epidemiology*, vol. 38, 2003, pp. 611–617 (*ProQuest*). DOI: 10.1007/s00127-003-0681-9 (Accessed 16 Jun. 2020).

Cohen, Leonard. *Beautiful Losers*. Vintage, 1993.

———. *Book of Longing*. Ecco, 2006.

———. *Leonard Cohen: Poems and Songs*. Alfred A. Knopf, 1993.

———. *Let Us Compare Mythologies*. Ecco, 2007.

Dr. Bronner's Magic Soapbox (Director Sara Lamm). Reckon So Productions DVD, 2007.

Herskovits, Jack. "On being a psychoanalyst who grew up in the shadow of the Holocaust." *Issues in Psychoanalytic Psychology*, vol. 33, 2011, pp. 35–41.

Jenkins, Philip. *Decade of Nightmares: The End of the Sixties and the Making of Eighties America*. Oxford University Press, 2006.

Kosstrin, Hannah. *Honest Bodies: Jewishness, Radicalism, and Modernism in Anna Sokolow's Choreography from 1927–1961*. 2011, PhD dissertation, The Ohio State University, http://rave.ohiolink.edu/etdc/view?acc_num=osu1300761075

———. *Honest Bodies: Revolutionary Modernism in the Dances of Anna Sokolow*. Oxford University Press, 2017.

Kubernik, Harvey. *Leonard Cohen: Everybody Knows*. Backbeat Books, 2014.

Magid, Shaul. "The Holocaust and Jewish identity in America: Memory, the unique, and the universal." *Jewish Social Studies*, vol. 18, no. 2, 2012, pp. 100–35 (*JSTOR*), www.jstor.org/stable/10.2979/jewisocistud.18.2.100. Accessed 16 Jun. 2020.

Mannani, Manijeh and Veronica Thompson. *Selves and Subjectivities: Reflections on Canadian Arts and Culture.* Athabasca University Press, 2012.

McBride, Joseph. *Steven Spielberg: A Biography.* Simon & Schuster, 1997.

Meyer, Franz. *Marc Chagall.* Harry N. Abrams, 1981.

Mintz, Alan. *Popular Culture in the Shaping of Holocaust Memory in America.* University of Washington Press, 2001.

Rothberg, Michael. *Multidirectional Memory: Remembering the Holocaust in the Age of Decolonization.* Stanford University Press, 2009.

Rowe, Peter. "Dr. Bronner speaks! North County's late eccentric soap maker returns on new LP." *San Diego Union-Tribune*, 23 Jan. 2017, www.sandiegouniontribune.com/lifestyle/people/sd-me-bronner-abc-20170117-story.html

Simmons, Sylvie. *I'm Your Man: The Life of Leonard Cohen.* HarperCollins, 2012.

Stratton, Jon. *Jewish Identity in Western Pop Culture: The Holocaust and Trauma through Modernity.* Palgrave Macmillan, 2008.

The Art Institute of Chicago. *Exhibition History of White Crucifixion*, www.artic.edu/artworks/59426/white-crucifixion. Accessed 26 Jun. 2020.

United States Holocaust Memorial Museum. "Elie Wiesel: Days of Remembrance excerpts." *The Holocaust Encyclopedia*, https://encyclopedia.ushmm.org/content/en/article/elie-wiesel-days-of-remembrance-excerpts. Accessed 16 Jun. 2020.

Wiesel, Elie. *The Night Trilogy.* Hill and Wang, 2008.

Wynands, Sandra. "The representation of the Holocaust in Flowers for Evil." *Essays on Canadian Writing*, vol. 69, 1999, pp. 198–209, http://search.proquest.com.proxy.pba.edu/docview/197242063?accountid=26397. Accessed 16 Jun. 2020.

Part III

In Defense of Popular Culture

10 Mothers, Daughters, and the Holocaust

A Study of Miriam Katin's Graphic Memoirs

Sucharita Sarkar

Recent Holocaust scholarship shifts the focus from "massive" analyses to more microscopic, "intimate history" sourced from, among other documents, testimonies (Kunzel and Galimi 335). Such testimonies—which may be oral, written, or verbal-visual—can be considered potential sources of "microhistory," which is defined as "the intensive historical investigation of a relatively well-defined smaller object, most often a single event, or a village community, a group of families, even an individual person" (Magnusson and Szijarto 4). Considered as microhistory, Holocaust survivor memoirs document not only experiences but also the affective dimension of feelings, perceptions, and beliefs. Graphic memoirs can become a "rich location for the work of documentation," as they "push on conceptions of the unrepresentable and the unimaginable" with their hybrid verbal-visual language (Chute 17). Art Spiegelman's *Maus* (1986, 1991) remains the best-known graphic memoir of the Holocaust, but there have been several others that have deployed the diagrammatic language of comics to engage with the fraught process of remembering and documenting the Holocaust. This chapter studies two graphic memoirs of Miriam Katin, a self-taught artist and Holocaust survivor, *We Are on Our Own* (2006) and *Letting It Go* (2013).

In her first memoir, *We Are on Our Own*, Katin remembers how her mother Esther and she—as a child—escaped the Nazi invasion of Budapest and how both subsequently grapple with issues of faith. In her second memoir, *Letting It Go*, Katin—now a mother residing in America—struggles to forgive the past and accept her adult son's decision to relocate to Germany, partly because of her anxiety about her mother's response to this relocation. Katin's works form a significant counterpoint to Spiegelman's *Maus* in multiple ways. Katin's works, which centralize maternal relationships—her relationship with her own mother in *We Are on Our Own* and her relationship with her son and, also, her mother in *Letting It Go*—contrast with the father-son relationship that undergirds *Maus*, where Spiegelman's narrative is sourced mostly from his conversations with his father, Vladek. From a feminist perspective, Katin's matricentric works are a significant insertion in Holocaust literature, as the mother-daughter dyad is often the "unspeakable" story that is "neglected by psychoanalytical theories and submerged in traditional plot structures" (Hirsch, *The Mother/Daughter* 3). Not just in her focus on the maternal, Katin's works engage with margins in other ways, too. Her memoirs are

DOI: 10.4324/9781003251224-14

154   *Sucharita Sarkar*

located at the spatial and temporal margins around the concentration camps. Unlike Spiegelman's parents' traumatizing captivity at Auschwitz, the horrors Katin and her mother encounter are situated outside the camps. Katin's memoirs—like many others located outside concentration camps—reveal the spread and pervasiveness of the persecution of Jews and others under the Nazi regime.

In *We Are on Our Own*, Katin documents her and her mother's story of living in Budapest in 1944, when Hitler's forces occupied Hungary; Katin's father had already fled the country to avoid persecution. The oblivious child Katin plays with her dog, Rexy, at a street café, while her mother's conversation with her friend reveals their initial stunned belief at the planned persecution of the Jews, who are required to give up their pets to the Nazis (*We Are* 8). The consequent escalation of persecution is shockingly swift. After Esther gives up Rexy to the German authorities, she returns home to find that her Hungarian landlord has given her a week's notice to leave. He claims to be "only following orders" but mutters "dirty Jews" when his back is turned; the extra-narrow panel where the muttering landlord is drawn emphasizes the sly, narrow-minded, everyday racism that Jews had to endure (Katin, *We Are* 13). To avoid being ghettoized, Esther flees to the countryside disguised as "a village girl with an illegitimate child" (Katin, *We Are* 18). She stays with an old couple in the wine-making countryside, working as their servant, until she is spotted by a Nazi officer who comes there to buy wine. She is forced into sexual relations with him and has to endure sexual abuse for months. Such routine exploitation of vulnerable women forms the often-silenced periphery of all wars, and here, too, it happens outside the concentration camps, at a time when the war is almost ending and Russian troops are entering Hungary. These are the marginal stories uncovered through microhistorical documentation, stories that nuance the generalized, collective history of the genocide.

In the visual aesthetics of Katin's memoirs, margins (and the lack of them) play a significant role. In *We Are on Our Own*, the rectangular frames are mostly drawn within clear, straight borders. In one strikingly impressionist page—a rare colored page in a mostly-monochromatic memoir—comprising six equal-sized rectangular panels, the reader sees a Nazi flag appear outside a window, gradually obscuring the view till the black color of the swastika covers the window almost entirely, while the text in the gutters states, "And then one day, God replaced the light with darkness" (Katin, *We Are* 5). The visual symbolism is direct and powerful: the Nazi flag obliterating the sunlit view outside the window and converting the lives of Jews into a dark, hellish existence and the six rigid panels paralleling the ruthless rule enforcement by the German military. In *We Are on Our Own*, sometimes these straight borders are broken through, and these visual interruptions indicate a sudden spike in the horrors encountered. For instance, when the married German officer sexually abuses Esther, he gradually grows attached to her and gifts her luxuries like silk stockings during his visits. When Katin draws this scene, the stockings drip outside the margins of the panel, mimicking the violation of ethical and personal boundaries that this scene represents (*We Are* 43). Katin's memoir sensitizes the reader as to how suffering is deeply personal and not objectively

Mothers, Daughters, and the Holocaust 155

scalable, even though Esther does not suffer the inhuman tortures and unimaginable deaths of concentration camp victims.

As a child caught in the vortex and aftermath of Nazi and postwar violence, Katin's most concrete anxieties are centered around the disappearance of her dog Rexy and the other dogs she substitutes for her pet instead of having any concrete memories of Russian soldiers who rape her mother and the other women (and also try to rape her) when they get drunk in the wine cellar of their host (*We Are* 58–59). Some of her clearest memories are aural; she remembers the violence of the Russian soldiers through the sound of bomb explosions, in a panel where the "boom boom crash" of Russian bombs jolt her awake from the safety of sleep (onomatopoeically represented by the jagged sound effects bursting the orderly borders of the panel) (Katin, *We Are* 48). Just as the trauma of violence is not perpetrated by the Nazis alone and is continued, in different ways, by the Russians in this case, the victims of violence are also not only the Jews. When the Russians march into the village where Katin and Esther have taken refuge, "looting and burning," they take away all the men to "work" and leave "only the women and children" (*We Are* 53). The Russian soldiers rape the women, most of whom are Hungarian non-Jews. Even Esther is forced into a relationship with the German officer not because she is a Jew, but because she is a woman. Katin's memoir demonstrates how violence is often gendered, and not just racial—how it seeps beyond racial identities and oppresses all those who are powerless, especially women.

While Katin's first memoir, *We Are on Our Own*, is located outside the spatial boundaries of the concentration camps, her second memoir, *Letting It Go*, is positioned beyond the historically defined temporal borders of the Holocaust (1941 to 1945). The cover of this second memoir references the child-self of Katin's first memoir: It depicts an adult Katin letting go of a balloon with the Nazi swastika symbol painted on it, a child-like gesture both linking and separating the times and spaces of the two memoirs. *Letting It Go* is set in the present century, and Katin emphasizes this temporal distance when she draws her visits to Holocaust memorials when she is in Berlin. The memorials and memorabilia from the past (tombs and nameplates of murdered Jews) are in black-and-white, juxtaposed with multicolored intrusions from the present (the visitors, including, Katin; food vendors for tourists). The clashing juxtaposition and the accompanying text expose the ironic rupture and reductive banality of commodifying past trauma: "Wish you were here!," "Holocaust memorial with pretzels," "With ketchup and mustard," "With soft ice cream" (Katin, *Letting* 99). Yet, despite the temporal distance of so many decades, the Holocaust persists as a lived, marked present in the survivors' minds and, often, bodies. In Berlin, when a tour guide tries to persuade Katin and her spouse to visit Holocaust memorials by insisting that "if we don't visit those places they will be forgotten," an angry Katin retaliates, "I don't need you to tell me where I should go and what I should see. I live with this stuff every day. That's enough for me. You go" (Katin, *Letting* 84). The Holocaust spreads, sticks, and infects sites beyond the officially determined spatial and temporal boundaries. Microhistories uncover and document these liminal spaces and times where the

156   *Sucharita Sarkar*

Holocaust is experienced—"lived with"—beyond borders, outside camps, after the war, in new countries, "every day."

In *Letting It Go*, apart from a few exceptions (for instance, in panels memorializing the past), Katin opts not to use borders. The colorful, borderless frames represent the chaotic quality of Katin's present life as an artist and a mother/daughter in New York. Her settled life in her adopted country is disrupted by the sudden intrusion of Berlin, a city that she continues to associate with Nazi oppression. Her son informs her of his decision to "settle in Berlin" with his Swedish partner, Tinet, and he requests her help in translating his Hungarian citizenship documents, which will permit him to reside in Germany: However, he is aware that Katin will "probably hate" the idea (Katin, *Letting* 25). Berlin interrupts not just her personal life as a mother but also Katin's professional life as an artist when she is invited to visit the Jewish Museum of Berlin, where her work will be exhibited (Katin, *Letting* 114–115).

The absence of borders diagrammatically metaphorize the blurring of identity categories (artist/mother/daughter/spouse), temporalities (past/present/future), and spatiality (Hungary/Israel/United States/Germany) that has shaped Katin's experiences and subjectivity. As the story progresses, Katin's creative decision to erase rigid boundaries for the panels becomes a visual representation of her subjective choice to "let go" of the animosity and anger she fixates upon Berlin and of her choice to free her present self from being restricted by her past trauma. An embodied metaphor of letting go is the severe diarrhea Katin suffers during her first visit to Berlin to see her son and his partner. Katin draws herself with diarrhea—suffering through the night, exhausted and shivering—across several wordless, borderless panels, and the foul-smelling bodily fluids leaking out of the boundaries of her tired, ill body are an embodied, visual parallel for the painful, torturous process of letting go of the traumatic past of the Holocaust. The process of letting go is agonizing, and Katin also indicates that this process is never completed. During her second visit to Berlin, when she is looking at her own artwork display, she starts itching badly. The itching worsens throughout the night and lasts up to the time she departs, although her spouse is unaffected. Katin draws some bugs hopping on the doormat of the hotel where they stayed, and then, she enlarges these bugs and draws them on the pages after the graphic narrative has formally ended (*Letting* 147–148). These anthropomorphized bugs are humorously drawn, with glasses, briefcases, and umbrellas, parodying urban commuters, and they converse among themselves about how the blood sucked from Katin's body "will be all over the city. That will call her back" (*Letting* 147). The bugs also disclose that two of them—"Klaus and Monika"—have been "sent" to New York "with" Katin, thus suggesting that Katin will carry memories of the past on her body, and inside, even in the future (Katin, *Letting* 148). Reminiscent of Spiegelman's framework of animal allegory in *Maus*, Katin's bugs are inserted not at the center like in *Maus*, but at the periphery, at the end of the narrative. These bugs—and the itching and rashes that erupt on Katin's body because of them—visually represent the continuing, indelible pain of surviving the Holocaust. The Holocaust can be lived with or adjusted to, or even forgiven with temporal distancing, but it cannot be forgotten.

Mothers, Daughters, and the Holocaust   157

Katin's son's decision to relocate to Berlin initiates this process of partially letting go, and one of Katin's concerns when her son, Ilan, informs her is how her own mother, Esther, will react. When Esther learns about Ilan's decision, however, she is much less agitated than Katin expects her to be: "What's the difference? Berlin, Paris, London. He's far away. He's not here" (*Letting* 31). Katin initially contests her mother's equanimity—"Not for me. The fact that he's in Berlin, it's a horror"—but later, after a prolonged, intense, internal struggle, embraces her mother's acceptance of Ilan's choices (*Letting* 31). In both her memoirs, the relationship between Katin and her mother, Esther, is crucial to the narrative. In *We Are on Our Own*, the "we" of the title directly refers to the mother-daughter dyad. In *Letting It Go*, the overt focus is on Katin, but her mother remains a significant thematic presence. The omission or marginalization of the mother or of mother-daughter relationality has been examined by feminist scholars like Marianne Hirsch. Graphic microhistories of the Holocaust also often fail to recover stories of the absent mother(s). In *Maus*, Spiegelman foregrounds the lost story of his mother, Anja, who has committed suicide, by narrating how he wants to read his "mom's diaries" to "have some idea of what she went through" after his parents were separated inside the concentration camp; however, he is unable to do so because his father admits to having "destroyed" all of them when he had a "very bad day," post-trauma (*Maus I* 158). Spiegelman can access his parents' shared past only through the words of his father. Vladek, his father, is, however, unable to even remember the content of Anja's diaries, except for her stated wish: "I wish my son, when he grows up, he will be interested by this." The first book of *Maus* ends with Spiegelman accusing his father of being a "murderer" of his mother's wishes and words (Spiegelman, *Maus I* 159). Spiegelman's anger at his father's act of wanton destruction emphasizes the lost or unrecoverable maternal microhistories of the Holocaust and also reveals the role of the patriarchal father in silencing the mother's voice.

Katin's *We Are on Our Own* resists and reverses this process of silencing the mother. Here, it is her father who is mostly absent throughout large parts of the narrative, entering it only after the war has ended and Esther and Katin are being safely sheltered by a mutual acquaintance. Although Katin does not include the story of her father during the historical period of the Holocaust, she does trace his exhausting journey to find his wife and daughter and the reunion of their family. The mother-daughter relationship is central to the memoir; however. Katin writes in the afterword that "this book is the story of our escape and life in hiding during the year of 1944–1945," and she sources the content of her story from both by imagining "the places and people my mother told me about" and also from "reading the last few letters and postcards my mother had written to my father" (*We Are* 125). Although Katin writes/draws this survivor memoir, she does not consider her own memories as her primary source material, as her young age made her memories incomplete and unreliable. This is emphasized visually through Katin's absence in several incidents: Even when present, she would often be oblivious to her surroundings. Thus, she could only have represented those situations through other people's memories, in this case, her mother's. For instance, in the crucial frame where Esther and her friend are conversing about Esther's plans to escape from

158 *Sucharita Sarkar*

Budapest, Katin draws herself running around the peripheries of the panel, happily searching for her dog Rexy without paying any attention to this conversation which will determine the course of her life (*We Are* 14). It is her "imagination" and her access to her mother's written records (in the letters/postcards) and oral testimonies (stories that Esther tells Katin) that enable Katin to process and represent these maternal memories through the visual-verbal format of the graphic memoir. Katin's memoirs, especially *We Are on Our Own*, are produced through intersections of her own memory and "postmemory," which is defined as the "overwhelming inherited memories" of individual and collective trauma that the "generation after" mediates not through "recall" but through "imaginative investment" in their parents' stories and behaviors, and this is a process wherein one risks "having one's own life stories displaced, even evacuated" by one's ancestors (Hirsch, *The Generation* 5). As a child born before the Holocaust, Katin has her own memories, but she is too young for cogent meaning-making. So, as the visual tension in her narrative often reveals, she conjuncts memory and postmemory, even when they contradict each other in ironic and poignant ways. For instance, the child Katin calls Esther's Nazi abuser the "chocolate god" and "nice man" and tries to reassure her mother when he leaves: "He will come back Mommy. Don't cry" (*We Are* 42–43). The panels that reveal Esther's abuse are developed via postmemory, and Katin herself is absent. However, the panel where the Nazi gifts Esther silk stockings in return for sexual favors is positioned next to the panel where Katin comforts Esther: The gutter is partially absent as the panels bleed into each other in a visual simulation of the juxtaposition and blending of memory and postmemory in Katin's narrative (*We Are* 43).

A feminist reading suggests that Katin, in *We Are on Our Own*, "speak[s] for the mother" and this is problematic because this "is at once to give voice to her discourse *and* to silence and marginalize her" (Hirsch, *The Mother/Daughter* 16; italics in original). The complex nature of mother-daughter relationality that reticulates all memoirs of mothers written by daughters is suggested through Katin's mother's covert fears and helplessness, although such fears are also traceable to the lingering paranoia of persecution survivors. Katin recounts: "She watched me creating this book with apprehension. When I would tell her, 'Mom, everyone from this story is either dead or too old to care,' she would reply, 'You never know. Someone might see it, take offense and come after us'" (*We Are* 127). Esther and Katin's mother-daughter relationship outside the graphic memoirs reveals the fragile dynamics of power and trust that form the substratum of the memorializing project. Feminist scholar Marianne Hirsch suggests a third alternative to the silencing of mothers/mothers-and-daughters, and to the one-sided representation of mothers by daughters. Hirsch writes, "Rather than daughters having to 'speak for' mothers, mothers would be able to speak for themselves, perhaps with 'two voices,'" as mothers are always both mothers and daughters (*The Mother/Daughter* 197). It may be argued that Katin is able to speak for herself as mother/daughter in her second memoir, *Letting It Go*. In this work, Katin writes/draws both as a mother (worried about her son's relocation to Berlin) and as a daughter (worried about her mother's reactions to this relocation): Beyond these two voices, however, Katin is also able to write/draw about her individual, creative selfhood. Significantly, it is during her second visit to Berlin as an invited artist whose artwork is being exhibited, that she learns the German word for "coming to terms with the past": her son's partner tells her, as they follow the visible traces of the demolished Berlin Wall stretching across the city, "They even have a word for it. *Vergangeheitsbewältigung. . . . Vergangenheit* is past. *Bewältigung* is mastering. Coming to terms with" (Katin, *Letting* 137). A collective reading of Katin's memoirs discerns not only the complex, often-gendered, and braided processes of remembering, sharing, recording, and representing that produces memoirs of the Holocaust but also the processes of reintegrating fractured subjectivities (mother/daughter/survivor/artist) that enables Katin to understand and live with the Holocaust.

In this long, fraught process of reintegration and rebuilding, Katin again centralizes her mother's contribution. Her first memoir is dedicated to her mother: "For my mother, who taught me to laugh and to forgive" (Katin, *We Are* 1). Laughter and forgiveness are immensely difficult lessons for Holocaust and trauma survivors to learn, yet Katin's mother passes on this healing matrilineal legacy to her daughter. Esther's deep personal faith is the bulwark of her emotional strength, and Katin memorializes her mother's faith as well as her own ambiguity toward the concept of a benevolent God. *We Are on Our Own* begins with a reference to the primeval *tehom* (Hebrew for "abyss or deep") of the Bible, written on a full-page black panel: "In the beginning darkness was upon the face of the deep" (Katin, *We Are* 3). Katin's innocent world of Bible readings and stories of a benevolent God is destroyed ruthlessly by the Nazi invasion, and Katin blames the same God for this destruction: "And then one day, God replaced the light with the darkness" (Katin, *We Are* 5).

As their persecution escalates, Esther stubbornly clings to her faith even as a curious Katin increasingly questions the existence and purpose of God. There is an episode where a figurine of St. Anthony that Esther gives to Katin gets lost, and Esther tries to comfort her, saying, "Child, child, he did help you to safety. Perhaps somebody else needs him now" (*We Are* 73). Katin visualizes this moment in a panel where the mother holds the daughter in a close embrace, although they face in opposite directions, Katin wide-eyed and wailing, Esther sorrowful but calm. This panel represents both the closeness of the mother-daughter bond and the difference between them. All through the story, Esther finds God in unfamiliar spaces. On one occasion, sheltering from Russian fighter planes bombing the village, Esther—along with the benefactors who have given her refuge—go down to hide in the wine cellar, where she is forced to sedate a crying Katin by giving her wine. An exhausted, inebriated Esther discovers that "God is red. God is in the glass. . . . God lives inside the big barreeellsss" (*We Are* 50). Katin, on the other hand, becomes increasingly suspicious and skeptical even as a child. Traveling through icy fields, a dead dog reminds Katin of her vanished pet dog, Rexy, and "somehow she knew that God was not the light and God was not the darkness, and not anybody at all. Maybe God was not" (*We Are* 69). This doubt—"maybe"—and questioning persists throughout her life.

160   *Sucharita Sarkar*

As the war ends, and Katin's father, Karoly, returns, Esther's faith reverts to more conventional dimensions. Karoly is an atheist. He believes in a "deadly sky," but Esther refuses his atheism, asking, "Because then, how can we go on?" and Karoly answers, "The same way you have arrived here. On your own. We are on our own, Esther. That's all there is" (Katin, *We Are* 118). Karoly and Esther represent two divergent responses of Holocaust survivors to faith: While many lost their belief in a merciful God because of the immeasurable scale of human evil they witnessed under the "deadly sky," many others like Esther were able to survive this evil through their dependence on a consolatory divinity who would enable them to "go on." Sitting on her father's lap, shaken by the inexplicable death of her pet dog, Rexy, although she had "prayed and prayed," Katin ends her childhood narrative with the question, "What if Mommy burned that God after all?" (*We Are* 122). Beginning with Biblical lessons and ending with a questioning of divine existence, *We Are on Our Own* narrates the problematic, divergent, yet intermeshed spiritual journeys of Holocaust survivors, journeys of belief or disbelief that also shape their post-traumatic subjectivities.

In the afterword, Katin explains how she has absorbed her "father's atheism at home and secular education at school" (*We Are* 126). Reconciling her Jewish identity with her lack of faith in a Jewish God becomes more problematic while living as a scrutinized immigrant in the United States. At school, her children are given Bibles, which the parents are expected to read to them (Katin, *We Are* 101). Paralleling earlier frames of Esther teaching the *Book of Genesis*, Katin repeats the maternal pattern, reading the *Bible* aloud to her child. However, when her child questions whether the story of creation is true, Katin says, "Well no. . . . This is just a sort of a story" (*We Are* 103). Unable to replicate her mother's sturdy faith, Katin regrets that she "could not give this kind of comfort, a comfort of faith in the 'existence of God,' to my children. I was unable to lie" (*We Are* 126). In this confession, Katin is both acknowledging how her mother's faith had comforted her as a child, and she is also differentiating herself from her mother's legacy of faith. However, despite her regret and divergence, Katin, too, is passing on valuable life lessons from her lived experiences to her children. By being "unable to lie," she transmits to her children the necessity to be true to one's selfhood and to resist normative cultural expectations that force one to live a lie. This authenticity—seen in both Esther's faith and in Katin's skepticism—is a significant maternal legacy for Katin because it accommodates and includes differences. The persecution of Jews was based on ethnic and religious differences, and the militaristic Final Solution was aimed at annihilating these differences and establishing the dominance of one race/religion. Katin suggests an alternative politics: a mutual coexistence where differences of faith or opinion can still allow for caring relationships. Katin's alternative to Nazi intolerance is limited to the microcosm of her family, yet the matrilineal legacy that she receives, modifies, and passes on to her children can also be rescaled to macroscopic dimensions. Feminist scholar Sara Ruddick proposes "maternal thinking" and "caring labor" as strategies against the militaristic: a maternal politics that can create a "sturdier, more reliable instrument of peace" (136). Esther's protective labor, rooted in her faith, and Katin's maternal thinking routed

Mothers, Daughters, and the Holocaust 161

through her spiritual questioning are authentic, interconnected, life-affirming, and inclusive. In *Letting It Go*, Katin performs the "caring labor" of translating citizenship documents for her son, despite her personal opposition, to accommodate his choice of settling in Berlin. The microhistory of Katin and her family demonstrates a pacifist, alternative politics to the intolerant, exclusionary, life-destroying, violent history of the Holocaust. Also, by including and opposing the violence inflicted by the Russians, Katin positions her "instrument of peace" as an alternative to, not just the Holocaust, but to all wars and violence.

Increasingly consumed by a receptive public, Holocaust narratives have to grapple with two interlinked debates: First, how are these situated in the domain of Popular Culture; and second, how do these texts address the thorny issue of the (in)compatibility of Popular Culture and the Holocaust. Although "comics" originated in mainstream American superhero culture, by the 1960s, it evolved into a versatile, hybrid, "word-and-image documentary" medium that could express and accommodate a range of trauma-related experiences in direct and precise as well as universal and symbolic ways (Chute 261). However, the treatment and production of the graphic medium—as well as other media such as film—sometimes slip over into sentimentalizing and sensationalism, producing what Spiegelman terms as "Holokitsch," for instance, the multiple "comics work about Anne Frank" (Chute 261). To explain how "Anne Frank the victim became Anne Frank the phenomenon," Magilow and Silverman use the term "Americanization" to describe a "certain way of presenting the history of the Holocaust such that its overwhelming horror becomes more palatable and more redeemable via its commercialization" (45). Many popular trauma cultural texts glorify the child Holocaust victim/survivor, not just Anne Frank, but several other "misery memoirs," which "fuse Holocaust victimhood with child abuse" in unethical and incongruous ways, like "representing genocide as a children's adventure story" (Rothe 139). The forms of Popular Culture produce and consume Holocaust narratives as vicarious spectacles of suffering and redemption, often without any ethical responsibility to the victims/survivors.

Although an immigrant American by choice and although her first memoir represents herself as a child survivor, Katin creates works that are markedly different from spectacularized, sentimentalized, and simplified "Holokitsch" texts. Authentic survivor testimonies—in graphic or other media—counteract the "over-exposure," superficiality and misrepresentations of dominant Popular Cultural texts on genocide (which are often fictional or forged and fake) and, instead, offer the "only way to reinvest the Holocaust with its rightful weight" (Marshman 18). Katin's survivor testimonies also deviate from, and subvert, the dominant pop-cultural Holocaust tropes. Katin's memoirs do not sensationalize the Holocaust; on the contrary, they are located on the temporal and spatial periphery of Holocaust experiences. In *We Are on Our Own*, Katin layers her own testimony as a child survivor with her adult mother's testimony. This layering produces a confusion of perspectives, for instance, Esther's Nazi abuser is the chocolate-provider to Katin. The narrative arc of Katin's first memoir embraces this confusion, and it is not "a melodrama of suffering and redemption around ethically simplified conflicts of good versus

162 *Sucharita Sarkar*

evil" (Rothe 88). Katin's interlacing of memory and postmemory complicates and resists the oversimplification of pop-cultural Holocaust representations. Instead of the depoliticization symptomatic of such narratives, Katin offers a matricentric alternative politics.

The anthropomorphic bugs in *Letting It Go* wittily subvert the kitschy trope of talking animals in Popular Culture comics, like Disney's Mickey Mouse. Katin also satirizes her own anger and ambivalence toward Berlin. While visiting Berlin, Katin's husband's wedding ring is lost and then found, but Katin tells her son that she is altering the truth to make the ring "stay lost" to make her story of Berlin "as nasty as possible" (*Letting* 111). Her son's partner says, "This whole thing says it all about a Jewish American couple visiting Germany for four days: They don't see enough to get past their own prejudice" (Katin, *Letting* 112). Here, Katin mocks her own touristy and sometimes inappropriate approach to Berlin and its history. She also exposes the processes of inauthentic populist Holocaust kitsch memoirs that falsify or sensationalize detail. By ultimately revealing the truth of the ring being found in the text of the memoir, Katin is also positioning her own memoirs as authentic. Katin's anxiety regarding her son's shift to Berlin mediates her own rage and anxieties about the city itself. Berlin is not only the city that shaped her Nazi-shadowed past, but it is also the city where her son lives at present, and the collision of her multiple anxieties after she meets her son in Berlin is followed by the late-night burst of diarrhea, which symbolizes the messy process of letting go, both of maternal frustrations and of past trauma. It is through her matricentric approach and focus that Katin's memoirs differentiate themselves from standardized pop-cultural Holocaust kitsch.

Conventional historical studies dismiss memoirs and autobiographies as the "least convincing of all personal records" because these are based on personal memories, which are often not "available to public scrutiny" (Popkin 49). However, the scale and enormity of Holocaust trauma cannot be adequately expressed through official records because the lived experience of trauma is often absent in, and inaccessible through, such records. This is why the microhistorical turn in Holocaust Studies is crucial, as the change of scale can accommodate intimate, microcosmic experiences that pluralize the homogenous, collective "great history"; microhistory aims to "bridge the gap between the deeply personal approaches of the Holocaust . . . and the collective destiny of vast numbers of communities and immense populations" (Zalc and Bruttmann 6). The graphic medium—a "seriality" of frame-gutter sequences that literalize the process of representation through presences (frames/panels) and absences (gutters)—is capable of engaging with the overt and covert details and depths of trauma. "Movingly, unflinchingly, comics works document, display, furnish" (Chute 17). In spite of its origins and continuing entanglements with Popular Cultural stereotypes, the genre of graphic narratives—and the medium of comics—do not need to be limited by the forms and stereotypes that dominate Popular Culture. Katin's graphic memoirs add her matricentric perspectives to counter stereotypes and fill absences in popular Holocaust discourse. Her memoirs unpack her personal and familial Holocaust experience from multiple spatial and temporal perspectives; they expand our understanding of the Holocaust's spread and persistence. In spite of their associations with pop-cultural "Holokitsch," such resistant memoirs are an emerging and legitimate part of the ongoing project of Holocaust sense-making: the documenting of its trauma and the search for healing from this trauma.

Works Cited

Chute, Hillary. *Disaster Drawn: Visual Witness, Comics, and Documentary Form*. The Belknap Press of Harvard University Press, 2016.

Hirsch, Marianne. *The Generation of Postmemory: Writing and Visual Culture after the Holocaust*. Columbia University Press, 2012.

———. *The Mother/Daughter Plot*. Indiana University Press, 1989.

Katin, Miriam. *Letting It Go*. Drawn & Quarterly, 2013.

———. *We Are on Our Own*. Drawn & Quarterly, 2006.

Kunzel, Geraldien von Frijtag Drabbe, and Valeria Galimi. "Microcosms of the Holocaust: Exploring new venues into small-scale research of the Holocaust." *Journal of Genocide Research*, vol. 21, no. 1, 2019, pp. 335–341. DOI: 10.1080/14623528.2019.1631517. Accessed 19 Nov. 2021.

Magilow, Daniel. H. and Lisa Silverman. *Holocaust Representations in History: An Introduction*. Bloomsbury Academic, 2015.

Magnusson, Sigurour Gylfi and Istvan M. Szijarto. *What is Microhistory? Theory and Practice*. Routledge, 2013.

Marshman, Sophia. "From the margins to the mainstream? Representations of the Holocaust in popular culture." *E-sharp*, vol. 6, no. 1, 2005, pp. 1–20, https://gla.ac.uk/media/Media_41177_smxx.pdf. Accessed 19 Nov. 2021.

Popkin, Jeremy D. "Holocaust memories, historians' memoirs: First-person narrative and the memory of the Holocaust." *History & Memory*, vol. 15, no. 1, 2003, pp. 49–84. DOI: 10.1353/ham.2003.0005. Accessed 19 Nov. 2021.

Rothe, Anne. *Popular Trauma Culture: Selling the Pain of Others in the Mass Media*. Rutgers University Press, 2011.

Ruddick, Sara. *Maternal Thinking*. Beacon Press, 1995.

Spiegelman, Art. *Maus, A Surivivor's Tale I: My Father Bleeds History*. Pantheon, 1986.

———. *Maus, A Survivor's Tale II: And Here My Troubles Began*. Pantheon, 1991.

Zalc, Claire and Tal Bruttmann, editors. *Microhistories of the Holocaust*. Berghahn, 2017.

11 Superheroes and the Holocaust in American Comics

Michaela Weiss

The Holocaust has become a significant part of American cultural discourse despite the fact that Holocaust survivors and their descendants form only 1 percent of the population (Novick 2). The immense impact of the Holocaust's legacy and the extent of its domestication in American literature and (Popular) Culture are reflected in the structure of literary and cultural production: Out of the 100 best-selling books by American Jewish writers, 92 deal with the Holocaust (Merwin). However, the beginnings of literary representations of the Holocaust in America were conflicted. While in Europe the first Holocaust testimonies were published during the 1940s and 1950s, American writers were largely unaware of what was happening in Europe and focused more generally on the depiction of war, or the effects of the prewar economic depression.[1] Equivalent thematic tendencies dominated the Popular Culture, especially comics, which featured a rapid "increase in violence and unpunished crime" (Bower 184), as well as an excessive ferocity and gore (Pecina), be it *War Comics*, *Young Men on the Battlefield!: The Story of a Massacre*, or *Combat Kelly*. Besides the lack of information and the economically and politically turbulent era of the late 1930s, marked by the end of the Great Depression, the rise of fascism, and the outbreak of World War II, writers and artists alike doubted their ability to represent the Holocaust in a truthful and authentic manner, as they had to rely on the translation of memoirs, historical studies, testimonies, and autobiographies that started to appear in the late 1950s (Kremer, 15, Budick 212–230, Kolář 14–17). This sense of inappropriateness, as well as the debates concerning the suitable art form, were further reinforced by contemporary critical studies such as Theodor Adorno's *Kulturkritik and Gesellschaft* (1951), George Steiner's *Language and Silence* (1967), or Elie Wiesel's *A Jew Today* (1978). While the critics and consequently the writers were preoccupied with discussing the limits and (im)possibility of aesthetic reproduction of the Holocaust or its utter unspeakability, American artists of Jewish origin addressed the tragedy in a manner that would capture the interest of American readership and in a medium they had access to: the critically dismissed (though immensely popular) superhero comics.

While the majority of writers of Jewish origin of that time struggled with marginalization, antisemitism, and anti-immigrant sentiments, comic artists additionally faced hostility and contempt. Paul Buhle finds parallels between the dismissive attitudes toward comics and Yiddish. They both entered the American cultural

DOI: 10.4324/9781003251224-15

Superheroes and the Holocaust in American Comics 165

scene at the same time and were disregarded as "bastard form[s]," joining image and text on one side and merging Hebrew, German, and Russian on the other (5). The presence of Jews in the medium was, therefore, no coincidence, as Will Eisner claims: "There were Jews in the medium because it was a crap medium. And in a marketplace that still had racial overtones, it was an easy medium to get into" (Brownstein and Schutz 211). The (Jewish) superheroes not only attracted young readers because of their strength and heroism but primarily embodied and voiced their creators' social and political concerns. It is, therefore, no surprise that most American superheroes are patriots who addressed the issue of Nazism[2] and, since the late 1960s, the Holocaust. Since its beginnings, American superhero comics, thus, adopted several functions: They served as entertainment for young readers, were employed as a motivational tool for American army personnel,[3] and provided a platform for marginalized immigrant artists to address their anxieties and, simultaneously, manifest "solidarity with an idealized America, pluralistic and undivided" (Devarenne 48).

In the 1960s, the interest and public awareness of the genocide were sparked by the 1962 airing of the Eichmann trial, followed by Hannah Arendt's study *Eichmann in Jerusalem: Report on the Banality of Evil* (1963). In American culture, the Holocaust was turning into a trope often used to highlight the injustice and minority oppression in America, especially during the Civil Rights Movement. In the year of Arendt's publication, Martin Luther King, Jr., in his "Letter from Birmingham Jail" analogically linked the persecution of Jews with his call for equality. The shift of social climate in the shadow of the Cold War is reflected in the superhero comics, which, unlike the prewar narratives, introduced heroes with "believable human qualities and failings" (Wright 207). The distrust of authorities resulted in a blurring of the boundary between the hero and the villain, which most visibly resonates in the (superhero) comics featuring the Holocaust. The critical invisibility of the graphic medium allowed the artists to mirror the conflicted public attitudes toward history and portrayal of victims and perpetrators and was aimed at a mixed audience, not only kids.

As most American (Jewish) writers of the 1950s and 1960s were still avoiding the fictional rendering of the Holocaust, it was primarily the comic books that taught the American public, especially the youth, about the genocide, shaping the thematic and formal trends of future American Holocaust fiction. The first comic artists to introduce the Holocaust into American culture were Al Feldstein and Bernard Krigstein, whose graphic narrative *Master Race* (1955) portrayed an encounter between a Holocaust survivor and a traumatized Nazi war criminal from the perpetrator's perspective. To make the story more attractive and relatable to the American audience, they set the story in an American subway. The indirect representation of the Holocaust, relying chiefly on traumatic memories and flashbacks, has been widely adopted not only by other comic artists but also fiction writers and filmmakers. When discussing the contribution of comics to Holocaust representation, Neal Adams observes that

it wasn't like seeing a powerful documentary, or visiting high-tech museum, or reading a scholarly treatise. [It was] a time when it fell to humble comics

166 *Michaela Weiss*

book writers and artists to give voice to something that too few people wanted to talk about.

(11)

Even though comics was the first medium to feature the Holocaust, the critical acceptance of the ability of the medium to do such representation justice took another 40 years; only after the mainstream appreciation of Art Spiegelman's *Maus* (1980 to 1991) did the critics gradually accept comics as a medium capable of addressing sensitive issues and of providing an authentic and inoffensive treatment of the Holocaust. That, however, does not apply to superhero comics, which is still largely underresearched. What shall not be forgotten, however, is the ability of Popular Culture to reflect current social issues and structures and, due to its flexibility, to mirror pressing social issues in a form accessible to wide audiences.

While the representation of the Holocaust in (superhero) comics was, until recently, perceived as irreverent and, in James Dittmer's words, "beneath the gaze of most cultural critics" (628), the popular graphic rendering of the genocide can translate the past into a more relatable and graspable narrative. In the same vein as Kurt Vonnegut's employment of science-fiction elements in his famous war novel *Slaughterhouse-Five* (1969), the fantastic elements of the superhero comics serve to present what is often marked as unspeakable, surreal, or unimaginable. The unrealistic story lessens the emotional suspense by providing a distance between the reader and the events, while at the same time, it promotes a wider understanding of the scope and impact of the genocide by embedding it into collective national cultures and narratives. The superheroes and villains provide an adequate and palatable representation of human monstrosity: While the characters are intentionally "surreal," their deeds and emotions are not.

The first representation of the Holocaust in superhero comics appeared in Captain Marvel's story *The Mad Master of the Murder Maze!* (1969). Inspired by the Feldstein and Krigstein's *Master Race* and the mad scientist trope, Gil Kane and Dan Adkins featured writer and sociologist Cornelius Webb, who is trying to explore people's reaction to terror to gain inspiration for his new book on race enhancement. He sets up a Lower East Side housing project, where the tenants are selected according to age, social status, and ethnicity, hoping to scientifically prove that fear and torture effectively reduce people to animals. Rick Jones, Captain Marvel's sidekick, unwittingly rents one of the apartments and, together with Captain Marvel, becomes part of the monstrous experiment.

While, at first sight, the block seems idyllic and peaceful, at night, the place turns into hell. Rick is confronted by giant rats and is saved by Captain Marvel. While the superhero engages in the fight to save the tenants, Jacob Weiss, a Holocaust survivor, discovers a parallel between the mental state of the tormented inhabitants and the prisoners in the concentration camp; the analogy is then further emphasized when the tenants are herded by use of gas. Weiss overhears Dr. Webb exclaim that this experiment would contribute to the "betterment of the race" (19) and suddenly feels it is his duty to fight Webb, as the situation mirrors his experience from Auschwitz: "Those **words** . . . like living ghosts from my **past**! Can I stand **by** . . . and

Superheroes and the Holocaust in American Comics   167

hear them uttered **again??** Such barbarity must **never** happen again . . . **NEVER!!**"
(19, original emphasis and spacing). After stopping the machinery that terrorized
the captives, Weiss dies, with his tattooed hand outstretched, unlike Webb, who is
horrified that the subject of his experiment is dead: "If G-K is **dead** . . . then, the
researches . . . the work of a **lifetime** goes up in **smoke!**" (20, original emphasis
and spacing). In the end, the whole place explodes, so this time it is the perpetrator
and, metaphorically, his ideology that eventually go "up in smoke."

Despite the presence of Captain Marvel, the true hero is the Holocaust survivor
who actively resists fear and racist ideology and is willing to sacrifice his life for
the safety of others. Even though Weiss hesitates whether to tackle the scientist
with bare hands, he eventually overcomes his fear and passivity, challenging the
perception of a victim as weak and incapable of action.[4] Kane and Adkins not only
featured a moral and brave survivor, but they also included one major concern of
the survivors: the loss of identity. Many Jews were buried under Christian names or
in unmarked (mass) graves or were identified by a number. At the end of *The Mad
Master of the Murder Maze!* Dr. Webb gets to learn Weiss's name. Jacob Weiss is,
therefore, finally recognized as a human being, not as a mere number denoting an
anonymous part of an experiment.

In 1971 another superhero and Holocaust survivor fought the Nazis in America,
this time without the scientist trope. In the issue *Night of the Reaper* (1971)
of *Batman with Robin, the Teen Wonder*, the superhero hunts war criminals in
Vermont. Like Kane and Adkins, Denny O'Neill made the fight against Nazism
more immediate by setting the plot in America. The story takes place during a
traditional Halloween parade in Rutland that featured superhero costumes and, in
the 1970s, served predominantly as a meeting of the comics creators. Today, the
event has become more general and has reached a cult position among the comics' fans (Thomas 73–77).

Batman and Robin meet Dr. Gruener, a Holocaust survivor who discloses to
them that Dr. Schloss, a former concentration camp supervisor known as "the
Butcher" for his brutality, has arrived at Rutland. Gruener warns them that the
Nazis have found out that Batman and Robin are searching for them to put them
on trial, which is why Schloss's collaborators are trying to kill anyone in their superhero costumes.

Yet unexpectedly, it is also the Butcher whose life is in danger. Despite Batman's attempt to save the man to deliver him to court, he comes too late and only
watches Schloss's car explode. Both heroes now have to investigate the Butcher's
murder as well as the attacks on their impersonators. After gathering sufficient evidence, Batman confronts a mysterious figure in a Reaper costume, who confesses
not only to telling the Nazis that Batman had arrived at Rutland but also to his decision to take personal vengeance on Schloss. To the superhero's surprise, the Nazi
killing reaper is Dr. Gruener, who feels justified to kill the Butcher:

And who has **better** right? My father and mother, my sisters . . . I saw the
Butcher empty his pistol into their bodies . . . I heard him **laugh** when
their blood poured onto the filth of the camp! Who are **you** to judge me?

168 *Michaela Weiss*

> You—who have not witnessed the **horror** of those days! Still, I wake from sleep **screaming**! I feel the agonies . . . smell the smoke of the **execution** chamber . . . listen to the helpless cries of babies.
>
> (21, original emphasis and spacing)

On his escape from Batman, the Reaper runs into an innocent man whom he pushes aside. When he lifts his scythe to slay him, his Star of David pendant gets caught in the weapon. The symbol reminds him of his cultural belonging and values. With horror, he repents, realizing that he has violated the values of his ancestors and community. At that moment, he loses balance and falls off a cliff. The Holocaust victim, in this case, the murderer, is driven by revenge and takes justice into his hands, yet he is not portrayed as purely evil, as his violent acts are explained (though not justified) by his traumatic past. Alongside the critical dismissal of the survivors as weak and passive (Auron 16–18), there ran a parallel belief that was deeply embedded in American culture: the belief in inherent immorality of Holocaust survivors. Deborah E. Lipstadt manifests how most people reading the testimonies documenting the fight for survival concluded that those who survived must have performed immoral acts (27–28). While the moral integrity of Dr. Gruener was not revealed until the end of the story, his capability of violence and murder stems from his refusal to remain a passive victim, or a prey hunted down by the Nazis, yet unlike Jacob Weiss, who fought for the safety of others and was willing to sacrifice his life, Dr. Gruener becomes obsessed with personal retaliation.

The growing preoccupation with the Holocaust and its domestication in American culture is documented in Betty Friedan's famous feminist study *The Feminine Mystique* (1974), where she compared the confinement of American suburban housewives to "a comfortable concentration camp" (298). Yet the major step of Americanization of the Holocaust turned out to be the airing of the NBC series *Holocaust* (dir. Marvin Chomsky, 1978), followed by President Carter's Commission on the Holocaust that was chaired by Elie Wiesel and led to the establishment of the United States Holocaust Memorial Museum in 1993.

The continuous rise of visibility of the Holocaust inspired many comics artists to revisit their superheroes' war-time battles. While Captain America punched Hitler already in 1941—addressing the dangers of war and Nazism rather than the suffering of the Jews—Chris Claremont and Roger McKenzie explored the Holocaust-related dimension of Captain America's heroism in issues *From the Ashes* (1979) and *The Calypso Connection* (1980). *From the Ashes* opens with Captain America at a press conference, denying charges of the Nazi party and the Ku Klux Klan of violating their right to free speech. When asked if he still finds himself useful at times of peace, Rogers decides to give up his superhero role and return to a career as an artist. He finds a new apartment and meets its owner Anna Kapplehaum, a Holocaust survivor. She remembers how he saved her and other prisoners from the Diebenwald death camp, which was scheduled for mass execution, by charging into the camp on a motorcycle. She is grateful that somebody is interested in her story: "Thank you for listening to an old woman, Steve. It helps to remember, to talk, sometimes" (30). Due to the previously mentioned American perception of

Superheroes and the Holocaust in American Comics 169

the survivors as immoral or weak, many remained silent. As Lipstadt documents, the repression of the past was encouraged by the survivors' fellow Jews, who felt that Americans did not want to hear the traumatizing stories or, worse, that nobody believed them (28–29). Anna only shared her story with Captain America because she knew he would understand. Her moving narrative persuades Rogers to accept another mission as Captain America. Claremont and McKenzie, thus, not only followed the most common line of Holocaust representation in American culture (i.e., representation of the Holocaust via memories of the survivors) but, at the same time, added a new dimension to the 1940s Captain America stories by not hiding the ethnicity of the prisoners and explicitly presenting the superhero's involvement in the liberation of concentration camps.

Anna Kapplehaum's story is further expanded in *The Calypso Connection*, depicting her forced participation in the camp's orchestra that accompanied the death of other prisoners as well as abuse from Dr. Klaus Mendelhaus, dubbed the Butcher. During one of her traumatic flashbacks on a street, Anna meets the dreaded doctor and faints. The old man examines her tattooed number and sighs: "Gott in Himmel . . .! Everywhere I go . . . it is always the same . . . There is no escape from the past and no hope for the future!" (Claremont *Calypso*, original spacing) The former camp supervisor is, therefore, not presented as a dangerous or evil monster but rather as a traumatized old man who cannot escape his past. The human side of the perpetrator and his desire to leave his tormenting past behind are further revealed after he and Anna are kidnapped by Nazi sympathizers, who plan to transport them to South America on the steamboat *Calypso* to establish a new Nazi regime. Mendelhaus is forced to kneel in front of Hitler's portrait and hopes that Anna understands that, this time, they are both in the victim position. Yet, Mendelhaus refuses to remain passive, confronts his captors, and even saves Anna's life after she is taken hostage by a commander. When Captain America appears on the scene, he finds Anna enraged and ready to shoot her former tormentor, ignoring the superhero's pleas to grant him a regular trial.

The depiction of the drastic treatment of the camp prisoners at the beginning of the story served the creators as an explanation for Anna's desire for revenge. Interestingly, she uses Nazi terminology, highlighting the immorality of her act: "Murder is the only solution left. The final solution. This . . . this butcher . . . taught me that, at Diebenwald, when he murdered my parents . . . my family. I still carry the scars. And he's going to pay for that" (Claremont *Calypso*, original spacing). The Butcher pleads for forgiveness but to no avail. Captain America, holding Anna in his arms realizes that despite the death of one former Nazi, this struggle is not over, and "will never be over. Not until we learn to temper justice . . . with mercy" (Claremont *Calypso*). This issue problematizes the role of a victim, negotiating the thin line between victim and perpetrator as well as representing the traumatizing psychological impact of the Holocaust, reflecting the official recognition of PTSD in 1980.

The American preoccupation with the Holocaust, the immorality of the survivors, and PTSD are perhaps most visibly reflected in the popular superhero comics series *X-Men* (originally created in 1963 by Stan Lee and Jack Kirby) featuring a

170   *Michaela Weiss*

diverse group of ethnically unmarked mutants who were targeted for their otherness. In issue *Gold Rush!* (1982) of *Uncanny X-Men*, Chris Claremont used the Holocaust as a universalist image of evil that would explain the concept of the mutants as persecuted outcasts (Malcolm 144), relying on flashbacks to reveal the traumatic past of one of the chief villainous mutants, Magneto. Like Jacob Weiss, Dr. Gruener, and Anna Kapplehaum, Magneto is driven by his desire for personal vengeance. Disregarding the moral aspects of his deeds, he refuses to remain a helpless victim and passively watch his tribe be threatened or oppressed. In *Gold Rush!* Magneto confronts the former camp supervisor, the Butcher, who is now a member of the Nazi-related Hydra organization and admits that while he does not care for Nazism or humanity, he is ready to kill anyone who threatens the mutants: "Hate is more popular than love, fear more prevalent than trust. If humanity wishes to follow you to its damnation, so be it. I care nothing for you, or them. And when *Homo Sapiens* are no more, *Homo Superior* will claim their right, full place" (Claremont, *Gold Rush*, original italics). His revolt rises from similar sentiments as Jacob Weiss's, Dr. Gruener's, or Anna's, yet unlike them, Magneto could rely on his superpowers: "Mutants will not go meekly to the gas chambers. . . . We will fight and we will win" (Claremont, *Gold Rush*, original spacing).

Twenty-six years later, a more detailed and accurate depiction of his childhood was revealed in *X-Men: Magneto Testament* (2008–2009). Magneto, born Max Eisenhardt, was a German Jew who was deported to Auschwitz; yet Dr. Mengele spared him due to his superpowers that were, however, not fully developed. By framing the villain's immorality by Holocaust narrative, Claremont turned Magneto from an evil, revenge-driven antihero, into a traumatized survivor with complex motivations. The retrospective alterations of the character's past had a major impact on the critical recognition of *X-Men*. The intricacy of Magneto's heritage has been thoroughly discussed by many (Malcolm 144–160, Bangert 122–123, Lund 10–12 and Werbe 302–313). While issues of X-Men, Batman, and Captain America feature a traumatized survivor who turns from a victim into a perpetrator, Captain Marvel featured a heroic survivor who resorts to violence only when facing immediate danger. What all these stories emphasize is the ominous presence of the Holocaust and its impact on the lives of the survivors, challenging the image of America as a safe space.

A different approach to Holocaust representation was adopted by Jon Bogdanove and Louise Simonson in *Superman: The Man of Steel* (1998). Issues #80–82 commemorate the 60th anniversary of Superman and provide more detail into Superman's interventions during the Holocaust and against Nazism. In issue #80, Clark Kent joins Lois Lane, who investigates American neo-Nazis who terrorize the locals. While the word "Jew" never comes up, the people tell the reporters they were told to go back to Europe, "where the Reich knew how to deal with people" like them (Bogdanove and Simonson 80). The only allusion to their Jewishness is one old man's stereotypical crooked "Jewish nose" and yarmulke. In this story, Superman interrupts an alt-right meeting and reminds the crowd that being an American means primarily to be "a champion of tolerance and diversity—justice and kindness" (Bogdanove and Simonson 80). In issue #81, Clark Kent is appointed to

Superheroes and the Holocaust in American Comics   171

cover the Nazi occupation of Poland. While Superman is fighting the Nazis, Lois Lane flies to Poland and is immediately captured and sent on a death train to Treblinka. Superman, who could not prevent the burning of the Warsaw ghetto, rushes to save Lois. Before he can return to fight the Nazi regime, he suddenly appears back in Metropolis. Superman, thus, cannot change history but is able to prevent worse-case scenarios.

Soon after its publication, *Man of Steel* faced severe criticism, mainly from Jewish commentators for omitting the words "Jews" and "Germans." This controversial decision, made by the editors of DC Comics, was supposed to make the stories more universal and accessible for young readers (Greenberg). In 1998, six years after *Maus* received a Pulitzer Prize, there was hardly a need for such reduction. Still, *Man of Steel* represents the first attempt in superhero comics to present wartime Poland directly from the hero's perspective and not from the survivors' memories or flashbacks.

While nowadays, there are Holocaust-related museums, scholarly studies, documentaries, and movies, the medium of comics has not lost its educative role and potential. Rubin explains that, especially for the younger generations, Holocaust literature, including comics, "taps into a kind of 'Hunger Games' scenario of survival in a world that's out to destroy you" (Merwin). The representation of the Holocaust, thus, merges with the current sweeping popularity of dystopia. The interest in superheroes has not diminished, and due to the growing influence of social media, the audience closely scrutinizes and evaluates new issues and projects concerning superheroes and is not afraid to voice concerns or severe dissatisfaction with their development. In *Captain America: Steve Rogers* (2017), Cap discloses his connection to the criminal and white supremacist organization Hydra and utters "Hail Hydra," and in the subsequent limited series *Secret Empire*, Cap becomes the dictator after Hydra takes over the United States. The connection of the Nazi fighter superhero with his primary enemy met with huge resistance from both fans and critics. Aliza Weinberger believes that by this decision, Marvel not only reflects current political tendencies but contributes to the general conservative mood:

> There's been a rise in white supremacy and hate crimes, and the country is embroiled in populist bordering on fascist sentiment. . .. People are getting hurt, and Marvel is giving the Alt-Right neo-Nazis of 2017 a co-opted symbol for their hate.

Marvel's *Secret Empire* project appeared in the same year as Frank Spotnitz's Amazon Series adaptation of Philip K. Dick's *The Man in the High Castle* (2015–2019) that depicted a world after the Nazis won the war. As a part of the advertisement, the New York subway was covered in Nazi-motivated symbols, including the American flag with swastikas replacing the stars, or an adapted imperial Japan flag ("Nazi-inspired ads"). Amazon was asked to remove the offense-causing adverts, while the content of the series was found disturbing, yet not faulty. Marvel, however, continued its controversial project for two years, featuring the other Captain America who has been a secret agent of Hydra. Moreover, it is hard to tell whether such an ending was

172 Michaela Weiss

Marvel's plan or whether they reconsidered their original plan due to fan pressure. The public resistance reflects the visibility of the superhero comics and their ability to mirror current social and political issues. More importantly, it further documents the lasting existence of historical awareness and sensitivity to the presentation of alt-right ideology and the Holocaust even in Popular Culture and establishes the emphasis on moral obligations of artists, regardless of genre.

Funding Acknowledgment

This chapter is a result of the project SGS/1/2020, Silesian University in Opava internal grant *Twenty-first Century Perspectives on Text Analysis.*

Notes

1 With the exception of several writers of Jewish origin, see Lillian Hellman's play *Watch on the Rhine* (1941), Arthur Miller's essay "Hitler's Quarry" (1941), or Saul Bellow's debut novel *Dangling Man* (1944).
2 See Jerry Siegel and Joe Schuster, "How Superman Would End the War" (1940); Joe Simon and Jack Kirby, *Captain America* (1941); Charles Biro and Bob Davis, *Daredevil Battles Hitler* (1941); Bill Finger and Jack Burnley, *Crime of the Month* (1943).
3 Copies of *Captain America*, *Superman*, *Captain Marvel*, and *Batman* were shipped to Allied soldiers as the "the portrayal of these enemies as almost 'sub-human' reassured Allied soldiers . . . that the enemy was indeed beatable" (Miles 79).
4 The criticism of the survivor who did not actively fight was common not only in America but also in the early years of the State of Israel, where the survivors were often seen as "human dust," "rejected," and, above all, passive (Auron 16–18).

Works Cited

Adams, Neal. "Speaking about the unspeakable." In *We Spoke Out: Comic Books and the Holocaust*, edited by Neal Adams, Rafael Medoff and Yoe Craig. Yoe Books, 2018, p. 11.
Adorno, Theodor. "Kulturkritik und Gesellschaft." In *Prismen, Gesammelte Schriften*, vol. 10.1, edited by Rolf Tiedmann. Suhrkamp, 1977, pp. 11–30.
Arendt, Hannah. *Eichmann in Jerusalem: Report on the Banality of Evil.* Viking Press, 1963.
Auron, Yair. *The Holocaust, Rebirth, and the Nakba: Memory and Contemporary Israeli-Arab Relations.* Lexington Books, 2017.
Bangert, Axel, Gordon S. C. and Libby Saxton, editors. *Holocaust Intersections: Genocide and Visual Culture at the New Millennium.* Legenda, 2013.
Bellow, Saul. *The Dangling Man.* Vanguard Press, 1944.
Biro, Charles and Bob Davis. "Daredevil battles Hitler." In *Darevil (no. 1).* Lev Gleason Publishing, 1941.
Bogdanove, Jon and Louise Simonson. *Superman: The Man of Steel* (vol. 1, nos. 80–82). DC Comics, 1998.
Bower, Kathrin M. "Holocaust avengers: From 'the master race' to magneto." *International Journal of Comic Art*, vol. 6, no. 2, 2004, pp. 182–94.
Brownstein, Charles and Diana Schutz, editors. *Eisner/Miller: A One-on-One Interview Conducted by Charles Brownstein.* Dark Horse, 2005.
Budick, Emily. "The Holocaust in the Jewish American literary imagination." In *The Cambridge Companion to Jewish American Literature*, edited by Michael P. Kremer and Hana Wirth-Neshner. Cambridge University Press, 2003, pp. 212–230.

Superheroes and the Holocaust in American Comics   173

Buhle, Paul, editor. *Jews and American Comics: An Illustrated History of an American Form*. The New Press, 2008.

Claremont, Chris, Cockrum, Dave and Wiacek, Bob. *Gold Rush! Uncanny X-Men* (vol. 1, no. 161). Marvel Comics, 1982.

Claremont, Chris and Roger McKenzie. *From the Ashes. Captain America* (vol. 1, no. 237). Marvel Comics, 1979.

———. *The Calypso Connection. Captain America* (vol. 1, no. 245). Marvel Comics, 1980.

Devarenne, Nicole. "'A language heroically commensurate with his body': Nationalism, fascism, and the language of the superhero comic." *International Journal of Comic Art*, vol. 10, no. 1, 2008, pp. 48–54.

Dittmer, Jason. "Captain America's empire: Reflections on identity, popular culture, and post-9/11 geopolitics." *Annals of the Association of American Geographers*, vol. 95, no. 3, 2005, pp. 626–643.

Feldstein, Al and Bernard Krigstein. *Master Race. Impact* (no. 1). EC Comics, 1955.

Finger, Bill and Burnley Jack. *Crime of the Month. World's Finest Comics* (vol. 1, no. 9). DC Comics, 1943.

Friedan, Betty. *The Feminine Mystique*. Dell, 1974.

Greenberg, Eric. "Superman editors sorry about omission: Comic erases Jews from Holocaust (Review of Superman: Man of Steel, by Jon Bogdanove and Louise Simonson)." *New York Jewish Week*, 10 Jul. 1998, www.jweekly.com/article/full/8618/superman-editors-sorry-about-omission-comic-erases-jews-from-holocaust/. Accessed 28 Apr. 2020.

Hellman, Lillian. *Watch on the Rhine: A Play in Three Acts*. Random House, 1941.

Kane, Gil and Dan Adkins. *The Mad Master of the Murder Maze! Captain Marvel* (vol. 1, no. 11). Marvel Comics, 1969.

King, Martin Luther, Jr. *Letter from Birmingham Jail*. Penguin, 2018.

Kolář, Stanislav. *Seven Responses to the Holocaust in American Fiction*. Ostrava University Press, 2004.

Kremer, Lillian. *Witness Through Imagination: Jewish American Holocaust Literature*. Wayne State University Press, 1989.

Lipstadt, Deborah E. *Holocaust: An American Understanding*. Rutgers University Press, 2016.

Lund, Martin. "The mutant problem: X-Men, confirmation bias, and the methodology of comics and identity." *European Journal of American Studies*, vol. 10, no. 2, 2015, pp. 1–18, https://journals.openedition.org/ejas/10890. Accessed 18 Nov. 2021.

Malcolm, Cheryl Alexander. "Witness, Trauma, and remembrance: Holocaust representations in X-Men comics." In *The Jewish Graphic Novel: Critical Approaches*, edited by Samantha Baskind and Ranen Omer-Sherman. Rutgers University Press, 2008, pp. 144–160.

Merwin, Ted. "Too many Holocaust books?" *The New York Jewish Week*, 18 Jan. 2016, jewishweek.timesofisrael.com/too-many-holocaust-books/. Accessed 1 May 2020.

Miles, Johnny E. *Superheroes and Their Ancient Jewish Parallels: A Comparative Study*. McFarland, 2018.

Miller, Arthur. "Hitler's quarry." *Jewish Survey*, no. 1, 1941, pp. 8–9.

"Nazi-inspired ads for The Man in the High Castle pulled from New York subway." *The Guardian*, 25 Nov. 2015, www.theguardian.com/us-news/2015/nov/25/nazi-inspired-ads-for-the-man-in-the-high-castle-pulled-from-new-york-subway. Accessed 11 May 2020.

Novick, Peter. *The Holocaust in American Life*. Houghton Mifflin, 1999.

O'Neill, Denny, Neil Adams and Dick Giordano. *Night of the Reaper. Batman with Robin, the Teen Wonder* (vol. 1, no. 237). DC Comics, 1971.

Ordway, Jerry, Janke Dennis and Karl Kesel. *Time and Time Again. Superman* (vol. 2, no. 54). DC Comics, 1991.

Pak, Greg, Carmine Di Giandomenico and Matt Hollingsworth. *X-Men: Magneto Testament*. Marvel Publishing, 2009.

Pecina, Jozef. "Two-fisted tales and frontline combat: EC's comics contribution to war comics." *Americana: E-Journal of American Studies in Hungary*, vol. 21, no. 1, 2016, http://americanaejournal.hu/vol12no1/pecina. Accessed 18 Nov. 2021.

Siegel, Jerry and Joe Shuster. "How Superman would end the war." *Look Magazine*, 27 Feb. 1940, https://archive.org/details/HowSupermanWouldEndTheWar. Accessed 18 Nov. 2021.

Simon, Joe and Jack Kirby. *Captain America* (vol. 2, no. 1). Timely Publications, 1941.

Spencer, Nick and Jesús Saiz. *Captain America: Steve Rogers* (vol. 1). Marvel Comics, 2017.

Spiegelman, Art. *Maus: A Survivor's Tale*. Pantheon Books, 1991.

Steiner, George. *Language and Silence: Essays on Language, Literature, and the Inhuman*. Atheneum, 1967.

Thomas, Roy. "Hi! I'm Your Host, Tom Fagan!: An interview with the man who led the parade." In *Alter-Ego: The Comic Book Artist Collection*, edited by Roy Thomas. DC Comics, 2001, pp. 73–77.

Vonnegut, Kurt. *Slaughterhouse-Five*. Delacorte, 1969.

Weinberger, Aliza. "Marvel Comics has taken this Nazi Captain America thing too far." *Mashable*, 25 Apr. 2017, https://mashable.com/2017/04/25/captain-america-hydra-nazi-marvel-comics/?europe=true. Accessed 11 May 2020.

Werbe, Charlotte F. "Retroactive continuity, Holocaust testimony, and X-Men's Magneto." *The Journal of Holocaust Research*, vol. 33, no. 4, 2019, pp. 302–313.

Wiesel, Elie. *A Jew Today* (Translated by Marion Wiesel). Random House, 1978.

Wright, Bradford W. *Comic Book Nation: The Transformation of Youth Culture in America*. The Johns Hopkins University Press, 2001.

12 Unearthing the Real in the Magical

Holocaust Memory and Magic Realism in Select Post-Holocaust Fictions

Tiasa Bal

Magic as a literary trope is as old as humanity itself. Fairy tales, legends, and myth-making have been instrumental in depicting sociopolitical changes as well as serving as a source for alternative histories of the margins. This chapter addresses the use of magic realism in literature to critique privileged histories and reinstate the narrative agency of disempowered communities and their pasts. It focuses on the representation of the Holocaust in Popular Culture, particularly in post-Holocaust fictions, and inspects magic realism as a narrative mode that resists the sly omission and papering over of the brutalities of the genocide. The study takes into comparison three texts each dealing with death, intergenerational trauma, and Jewish folk beliefs that are allegorically shaped by the usage of spectacular, fantastical, and inexplicable elements of magic realism.

Popular Culture and magic realism bear an intrinsic relationship with each other. Although there does not exist any strict definition of Popular Culture, it is widely accepted as "folk" or "popular" beliefs, embodied practices, and objects rooted in local traditions as well as those with a "mass" following generated from political and commercial events (Mukerji and Schudson 47). Chandra Mukerji and Michael Schudson speak of two branches of anthropology that inform Popular Culture. First, the structural approach asserts that people perceive their world through binary opposites—good/evil, pure/impure, secular/religious, etc. This is the operative principle of the natural order, and people, places, or events that seemingly challenge these binaries are considered extra-natural or supernatural and potentially dangerous or even magical (Mukerji and Schudson 49). The second branch, the interpretivist approach, was made popular by Clifford Geertz. Geertz explained that humans assign a symbolic meaning to everything around them. It is by reading culture itself as a text and analyzing its symbolic influence on human behavior that one can bridge the gap between event time and discourse time and reconstruct meaningful histories of inexplicable events (Mukerji and Schudson 49).

Magic realism espouses both these lines of reasoning. It incorporates the presence of everything unfamiliar or uncanny into quotidian life and makes use of signs, symbols, and beliefs rooted in long-term cultural practices to explain how people imagine the world around them. It embodies elements that not only dilute the distinctions between the ordinary and the fantastical but also emerge from specific spatial and temporal contexts in various communities and are epiphenomenal to the cultural

DOI: 10.4324/9781003251224-16

176   *Tiasa Bal*

practices of the same. By Abner Cohen's definition, a community is a group of people who owe their identity to an organically shared set of experiences, beliefs, and practices (Street 282). In effect, Popular Culture is a manifestation of popular consciousness, and magic realism is one such expression of that consciousness.

The origin of the term "magic realism" harks back to the Weimar era in Germany. "Magischer Realismus" or magic realism was coined as a new movement in the German art world during the roaring '20s to capture the mystery of life behind the surface reality. Coined by Franz Roh, the "magic" element of magic realism lay not in the supernatural but in a latent quality of mystery that pervades every object yet remains hidden in plain sight. The second wave of magic realism flourished in Central America in the 1940s, and the third, beginning in 1955 in Latin America, soon came to establish itself across the world. Magic realism and magical realism gravitate toward fiction that relies upon the factual, unvarnished tone of its narrative when presenting magical occurrences. Besides being an instrument of locating self-identity, such as in Borges' "The Aleph," magic realism carves out a space for lived experiences on the other side of silence and bridges the blank spaces between histories from the top and those from below. It rescues these difficult histories from erasure and reinforces the narrative agency of voices that are lost in the echo. Magic realism is a common narrative mode in fiction written from the perspective of the politically or culturally disempowered.

In the information age, instruments of mass media are often controlled, censored, and moderated to preserve the official narratives of the state and designed to manufacture consent in favor of the government's role in them. As John Street argues, the existence of Popular Culture implies the existence of an elite culture that is created and preserved by institutes of power. It is further propagated by discursive and pedagogic practices which privilege some forms of culture as worthy of study over others, thereby marginalizing the communities that created them (Street 303–304). Theodor Adorno and Max Horkheimer have made an important distinction between mass media or mass culture and Popular Culture. The former is generated by structures of power and imposed upon the masses with the aid of media or pedagogy, whereas the latter is an organic exercise created by the people themselves from a set of shared values and beliefs that allow them to carve an identity out for themselves. Adorno and Horkheimer highlighted the use of the radio, film, and television in postwar America as a vehicle of disseminating state propaganda and conditioning the masses to accept the watered-down version of international events without engaging with it critically (Street 307–308).

The Birmingham School of Cultural Studies, led by Stuart Hall, regarded Popular Culture as practices of resistance and subversion of the codes of oppression. The Holocaust survivors had no material culture to preserve except the everyday items they could escape with. The United States Holocaust Memorial Museum houses a collection of artifacts ranging from sewing machines used in the ghettos to dolls and other playthings. Survivors have donated family pictures, children's drawings, pocket watches, wedding canopies, and more that are the only remaining evidence of the reality of the genocide. Holocaust memory is shaped by these artifacts, and the meanings attached to them were created by the survivors themselves (Street 308).

In the context of representing the Holocaust in writing, magic realism becomes a vehicle of communicating the inexpressible horror of genocide and dislocation, which have been papered over by mainstream or state-sponsored histories. It represents a counternarrative written from the testimonies of the survivors and their families and is an act of resistance against the suppression of their past. Furthermore, it is established in certain shared beliefs and practices of the Jewish community across the world and is an intrinsic part of how the Holocaust survivors and their successors express their altered realities. Therefore, the representation of the Holocaust informs or gives rise to a Popular Culture that is both rooted in a community's local traditional values, practices, and consciousness as well as born from the global tragedy of a community that was brought to the brink of extermination.

In Holocaust studies, both the limits and challenges of representation are vastly deliberated. It is believed that certain core aspects of the extermination of European Jewry defy our powers of depiction and narrative. The question of whether histories such as that of the Holocaust can be written empirically and impartially gives rise to another one: What should be the archives of such histories? The twenty-first century marks a watershed moment in the development of the field of Holocaust studies that has registered a generational shift marked by the departure of eyewitnesses, the digital archives occupying a status of dominant power or influence, and the institutionalization of a global Holocaust memorial culture. Moral, epistemological, and aesthetic limits inform any representation of the Nazi atrocities. The distinction between the indescribable and appalling events of the Holocaust and the limitations of its literary reconstructions has not escaped the historian's gaze, who remains cautious of the potential displacement of empirical history by its fictionalized versions. The conundrum of reconciling the historian's standpoint and the novelist's perspective is an ongoing one. Michael Rothberg observes:

> Within Holocaust studies broadly defined, two approaches to the question of genocide have dominated, which I will call realist and antirealist. By realist, I mean both an epistemological claim that the Holocaust is knowable and a representational claim that this knowledge can be translated into a familiar mimetic universe. . . . By antirealist I mean both a claim that the Holocaust is not knowable or would be knowable only under radically new regimes of knowledge and that it cannot be captured in traditional representational schemata.
>
> (Rothberg 3–4)

In positing that it is offensive and undesirable to gain aesthetic pleasure from a Holocaust-related work of art, Adorno rejects a sanitized and palatable representation of the genocide (Adorno 34). His dictum in the essay "Cultural Criticism and Society" does not, in itself, refute the view that he thought that poetry was impossible after Auschwitz. Adorno's proclamation was largely taken to mean that the Holocaust was "indescribable" or "ineffable" and any attempt to represent it in Popular Culture is a debasement of the event (Lang 6). There is also a parallel concern on the politics of Holocaust denial and that historically inaccurate portrayals of the Holocaust even for the sake of artistic license may be marshaled in favor of refuting the gravity of the event altogether. The popular representations of the Holocaust might erringly homogenize the Jewish identity altogether. Secular Jewish identity has over time become inextricably bound with the Holocaust (Stratton 99). While the majority of the German Jewish diaspora in America that emerged in the mid-nineteenth century had no experience of the Holocaust, almost all Polish Jews had vivid memories of not just concentration camps but the carnage that unfolded under the Nazi regime. Minimizing these nuances is what gives rise to the "desanctification of the Holocaust" (Stratton 101). The dilemma of representing the Holocaust as an event of fatality or as one of survival has often led to a reductive portrayal of the event altogether sidestepping the ethical responsibility of narrating these events for the commemoration of the countless lives that were lost in the genocide.

Texts such as Christopher Browning and Jürgen Matthäus's *The Origins of the Final Solution* (2003), Daniel Mendelsohn's *The Lost: A Search for Six of Six Million* (2006),[1] and Saul Friedländer's *The Years of Extermination* (2007)[2] raise questions about the status of Holocaust historiography, the limits of representation, and the ethics[3] of discursive practices around the Holocaust. Literary critic Geoffrey Hartman, in his collection of essays *The Longest Shadow*, discusses several issues related to reminiscing and representing the Holocaust. His essays are a nuanced critique of realism's refusal to set limits to representation, in that they denounce a certain kind of historical narrative that gives priority to realistic overimaginative interpretation or literary narratives (Hartman 119). The extensive corpus of literary works on the Holocaust is composed against an insidious background of unprecedented and systematic genocide. This literature addresses the trauma of human existence in the face of that doom and its aftermath. Whether and to what end the Holocaust can be represented in fiction raises the question of navigating the difference between exercising creative liberties and propagating misinformation. The scholar must be cautious to winnow the interpretation from the fabrication without trivializing the objective reality of the Holocaust as a historical event.

Alan Mintz notes that there are two models of Holocaust remembrance—the constructivist model, which stresses the cultural lens through which the Holocaust is perceived, and the exceptionalist model, which centers on the grim reality of the Holocaust as it had taken place (Mintz 38–40). He elaborates that though there was a surge in the production of Holocaust literature, some even acquiring a cult status, its initial acceptance was slow and distorted in mainstream consciousness. This was mainly for two reasons: The first was an aversion toward using any creative license in the retelling of the event. The only appropriate way to commemorate the Holocaust was to depict its naked horror (Mintz 42). The second reason was a reservation against the dispassionate assessment of an event of incalculable loss and destruction. It was felt that the Holocaust should not be a testing ground for honing academic prowess and literary criticism (Mintz 43). Despite both restrictions, the production of Holocaust writing kept getting subsumed over time into popular consciousness in America. The Eichmann trial, the Civil Rights Movement, the Six-Day War, all gave an impetus to the generation of Holocaust literature and its

Unearthing the Real in the Magical 179

adaption across a plethora of Popular Cultural mediums such as films, novels, and others (Mintz 37).

Over the years, the memory of the Holocaust has become more complex, nuanced, and rooted in the phenomenology of remembrance. As the first generation of survivors departs, the ways of remembering also change. The direct, experiential memories make way for new embodied practices. Wulf Kansteiner describes this as: "Collective memories from shared communications about the meaning of the past that are anchored in the life-worlds of individuals who partake in the communal life of the respective collective" (Kansteiner 188). Why do succeeding generations continue to hold on to the memory of an imagined homeland, a sense of loss, particularly as the loss is but a memory borrowed from their parents and grandparents? These recurrent questions inform the changing historiography of the Holocaust. In Andreas Huyssen's estimation, generations that are described as indirect witnesses to the Holocaust have laid claim to it (Huyssen 251). The Holocaust has affected the lives of countless Jews who are removed in time and space from the original scene of trauma. Survivor testimony is the most conclusive proof of the cataclysm of the event. But Holocaust-inflicted trauma continues long after the historical event had passed. The intergenerational transmission of trauma attendant on the Holocaust, a reality of the Jewish experience, has remained one of the central experiences that undergirds Jewish identity in North America. The impact traumatic histories have on ensuing generations is well articulated by Marianne Hirsch, who used "postmemory" as a method. Postmemory defines:

the relationship that the generation after those who witnessed cultural or collective trauma bears to the experiences of those who came before, experiences that they "remember" only by means of the stories, images, and behaviors among which they grew up. But these experiences were transmitted to them so deeply and affectively as to seem to constitute memories in their own right.

(Hirsch 106–107)

In the context of the third-generation Jewish writings, postmemory broadly refers to a collective, cultural memory that sustains the aftereffects of the Holocaust.

The shift in the vocabulary of Holocaust memory, trauma, and representation is marked by the movement from survivor testimonies to post-Holocaust accounts of the genocide. Hirsch argues, "To grow up with such overwhelming inherited memories, to be dominated by narratives that preceded one's birth or one's consciousness, is to risk having one's own stories and experiences displaced, even evacuated, by those of a previous generation" (107). The retrieval of their past becomes central to their identity formation. Unlike the second generation, who grew up with the survivors and struggled against the pervasive shadow of the Holocaust, the third generation bears the onus of recasting narratives from the emotional debris of the past. The geographical and temporal space—the dynamic of distance—that separates contemporary Holocaust fiction from the historical event provides a powerful and sustainable groundwork.

180   *Tiasa Bal*

Third-generation novelists revisit and revise classical archetypes for understanding the dehumanization and suffering of the European Jewry under the state-sponsored genocide. Yerushalmi suggests that "even where the Jews do not reject history out of hand, they are not prepared to confront it directly, but seem to await a new, metahistorical myth, for which the novel provides at least a modern temporary surrogate," (98) leaving the contemporary Jews to choose "myth over history" (99). In being chronologically disconnected and shielded from the horrors of the historical realities of the Holocaust, the third-generation writers rely upon tropes of magical realism, Jewish myth, mysticism, and folktales to confront the effects of Holocaust-induced trauma. They are aware of their inability to recreate the horrors of the Holocaust without having an unmediated experience of the mass murder. Alan Itkin reflects, "Holocaust mimesis rather than Holocaust testimony and memory are central to the way that they address the Holocaust—questions that become more relevant for Holocaust literature and scholarship as the era of survivor testimony recedes into the past" (Itkin 108). Nonetheless, they are cognizant of its resounding impact and try to comprehend and reproduce the varied but sharply felt predicament of contemporary Jews who have inherited the traumatic legacy of the Holocaust.[4]

The literary and artistic representations of the Holocaust seek to enunciate how disorienting the genocide was for those suddenly caught in the fray of Nazi atrocity. They confront the linguistic, stylistic, and ethical difficulties inherent in representing this catastrophe in fiction,[5] the act of remembering, and of repeating an inherited memory through narrative. The Holocaust is an event archived by its representations and magic realism provides a means to understand its multifaceted realities. These fictional representations seek to verbalize that which defies comprehension—the occurrence of the uncanny in the everyday.

The literary works of Jonathan Safran Foer, Nicole Krauss, Michael Chabon, Alison Pick, Julie Orringer, and Erika Dreifus mark the ongoing legacy of the Holocaust and relentlessly explore how the genocide continues to define our collective consciousness. Their narrative territory is situated in a post-Holocaust world infiltrated by the memory of the Holocaust. These writers deal specifically with the fictional retelling of the Holocaust and the ways that the Holocaust influences and determines the lives of many Jews[6] and non-Jews born after 1945. Replete with a variety of innovative narrative techniques, their writings reject a tokenistic, moralizing, and sentimental use of the past. While treating highly personal and individualized experiences, these authors also promulgate a sense of communal or collective trauma—a memory that is transferred, undertaken, and performed.

Thane Rosenbaum's *The Golems of Gotham* (2002) is a post-Holocaust "romance" in which the ghosts of notable concentration camp survivors haunt the streets of Manhattan, imploring its populace never to forget. *The Golems of Gotham* opens with the suicide of Holocaust survivors, after succumbing to the insurmountable grief of losing their loved ones to genocide. In Joseph Skibell's *A Blessing on the Moon* (1997), the recently murdered Chaim Skibelski climbs out of a mass grave to witness Polish peasants usurping his house and possessions. Anne Michaels's *Fugitive Pieces* (1996) illustrates the rescue of Jakob Beer, a boy whose

Unearthing the Real in the Magical   181

parents and sister were killed by the Nazis in Poland, by a Greek archaeologist, Athos Roussos; Beer's adult life in Canada; and, after his demise, the search for his diaries and papers by a young disciple, himself the son of Holocaust survivors. *Fugitive Pieces*, the first novel of a poet, (re)inscribes human loss and memory into descriptions of landscape, weather, and ancient history. The novel is written in "strange episodic images," and it diverts its attention to the world of the spirit and the transcendent.

These texts reflect the use of magic realist techniques, gothic, and horror genres in the representation of the Holocaust, challenging the idea that the Holocaust is overwhelmingly represented by historical realism. They offer a critical approach to continue the project of Holocaust representation into the post-testimonial era, permitting a form of literary engagement with the event that, nevertheless, acknowledges the ethical, temporal, and experiential distance from the real. The sensibilities of our era invest the fantastic element with meaning signifying the emergence of the unconscious, that which is repressed and forgotten. The problem of the reality we experience—both extraordinary things, which may be phantasms projected by our mind, and ordinary things, which conceal beneath their banal appearances a second nature that is more ominous, mysterious, and terrifying— defines the essence of the fantastic literature, whose effects are continually negotiated in the interstices of these conflicting versions of reality.

In *The Fantastic: A Structural Approach to a Literary Genre* (1970), Tzvetan Todorov posits that what distinguishes "the fantastic" in fiction is the bewilderment in the face of an implausible experience, manifested in the hesitation between the rational, realistic explanation and acceptance of the supernatural or spectral. He tentatively defines "the fantastic" in literature as the occurrence of an event that cannot be explained by the laws of the world with which we are accustomed. Subsequently, he proposes the terms "fantastique-étrange" (fantastic-uncanny) for events that the reader initially perceives as manifestations of the supernatural but which, in the end, have a rational explanation and "fantastique-merveilleux" (fantastic-marvelous) for those happenings that have no such explanation, compelling the reader to accept occurrences that are not governed by the known laws of Nature (Todorov 46–62). A text is only fantastique (fantastic) for as long as it sustains a hesitation between these two genres that form its borders. In *The Fantastic in Literature*, Eric S. Rabkin argues that not only representations of reality but reality itself is a matter of perspective. Although there is no uncontested definition of the fantastic, almost all critics agree that it incorporates into the narrative elements that may strike the reader as supernatural, transcendental, or inexplicable and that unsettle the reader into doubting the coherence of the text they are reading.

The magic realist representation, with its alleged uneasy relationship to history and its immediacy to the mode of the grotesque, has, nevertheless, aided in reconstructing the events of the Holocaust from a post-memorial perspective. David Punter drew attention to the fact that the recurring terms (such as ghosts, crypt, phantom, dead, hauntology, telepathy) in Gothic culture and spectral criticism serve as useful instruments for literary-historical research and theoretical reflection. He raised the example of Maurice Blanchot's metaliterary reflection. For

182   *Tiasa Bal*

Blanchot, contact with literature was inseparably associated with a unique kind of impossible encounter with someone who, while dead, continues to be, in a way, alive. According to the author of *The Space of Literature* (1955),[7] a relation with literature presupposes contact with something which lasts in a particular form of suspension, in a shape that does not directly refer to a clearly defined condition, assuming an intermediary form of existence in the space between death, spectral presence, and resurrection.

There needs to be a regular acknowledgment of the persistent, discursive enigma around the Holocaust. Beyond its tangible damage as recorded in official documents, the Holocaust had incapacitated many of the survivors for life. Unlike the rest of humanity, the Holocaust for the survivors did not end with the defeat of the Nazi regime. The specter of death continues to haunt beyond the visible structures of the concentration camps and gas chambers. As Rodolphe Gasche has shown, depicting the Holocaust in ontic terms would be doing injustice to its memory. It is no surprise that the Holocaust resists attempts at being decoded by the wider readership. The precipitate of such incalculable violence cannot be objectively recorded into history without underestimating its enormity. Yet there are more ways than one to talk about trauma, to read into literatures of silence, and to exhume those experiences impervious to vocabularies of standardized languages. Superseding the strict demarcations and conventionally accepted definitions of the real and the supernatural, magic realism acts as an infallible conduit to preserve the phenomenology of the Holocaust.

Rosenbaum's *The Golems of Gotham,* while establishing the silence surrounding the Holocaust, precludes the possibility of overcoming its trauma. Rosenbaum's golems are shades of Oliver's parents along with six iconic writers of the Holocaust who had all committed suicide, unable to work through its traumatic memories. A golem, much like the survivor, while being able to vocalize, is not comprehensible. It cannot express itself in speech. The crippling of language that renders one mute is, therefore, not only the aftermath of violence but a condition of extreme distress that engenders violence. This source of violence results in the lack of possession of the faculty of speech and, by extension, the capability of producing only inarticulate sounds. The muteness visited on the victims by the unspeakable events and the attendant disorientation of reality they suffer cannot be retrieved by grammatical constructs or narrative linearity. Magic realism creates that space through its agency of myths, motifs, and memory and empowers the survivors to address themselves as active subjects rather than mere objects in their history.

A Blessing on the Moon takes this discussion further by mediating the experience of the Holocaust through one of its victims, Chaim. His consciousness of the event and the metaphor and history of the Holocaust continue beyond his corporeality. Yet Chaim's mangled and bleeding body remains above ground, invisible to others, paradoxically capable of functioning for both the living and the dead. The looming impermanence of life that the survivors experience and the inability to articulate such death-in-life vision manifests into their narrative reticence. Even in survival, death becomes ingrained in their psyche—a pervasive reality that cannot be exorcised. While negotiating the inalienability of death from a survivor's

Unearthing the Real in the Magical 183

memory, Joseph Skibell makes use of fantastical elements from Jewish folklore without estranging it from the reality of the Holocaust. For instance, he likens the persecution of the Jews to the waning moon, the moon itself being an emblem of Israel due to its monthly reappearance. The waning and eventual waxing of the moon during the Holocaust symbolizes an unprecedented threat to the Jews, followed by a restoration of hope for their survival. Chaim spends much of the novel longing for that "World to Come," only to leave his corporeal form when the moon waxes. Furthermore, the importance of the moon in the Jewish calendar provides an antidote to the horrors of the Holocaust. Like the moon that rules the heavens during the day and at night, the Jews are promised liberation from their sufferings and a newer, happier world.

The experience of the Holocaust is historical, collective, and autobiographical all at once. Anne Michael's *Fugitive Pieces* deftly negotiates this phenomenon. Michaels relies on language, specifically poetic language, to forge her links with the past and, thereby, engages with the ethics of representation within the field of Holocaust studies. The novelist, in directing her ruminative inquiries into the nature of memory, guilt, atrocity, love, and restoration, elides the Holocaust itself. Shortly before his death, renowned poet Jakob Beer had begun writing his memoirs of surviving the Holocaust. Yet its fragmented, imagistic recollection requires chronological assemblage to be understood by the wider public. Jakob here is not remembering things for the reader's benefit but for his own sake. Escaping death at the hands of the Nazis at 7, Jakob lived from one day to the next, through the vast darkness of a Polish forest, slept at night inside the burrows he dug into the earth, and ate grass to stay alive. Despite being rescued, he remained tethered to the memories of his murdered parents and sister. Jakob's mental life had become a nightmarishly unfinishable excavation of a past that intrudes into the present. The extent of Jakob's work provides a space for Ben, the child of Holocaust survivors, to understand "the influence of the dead in the world of the living" (53). Jakob's testimony emphasizes that trauma is not an appendage that can be excised. It is an all-pervasive disorienting force that leaves irreconcilable grief in its wake. However, magic realism, in the form of phantom pain and spectral chasm, makes it possible for alternative histories to coexist without diminishing the survivor's agency and lived experience.

The three depictions of death—Oliver's parents' death by suicide years after their escape, Chaim's death leading to an afterlife, and Jakob's near-death experience and eventual survival—highlight that regardless of the fate of the Jews, death is a shared omnipresent reality of the Holocaust phenomenology. Death is the link that binds the experience of the Holocaust irrespective of what gap intervenes between the event and the time after it becomes discourse. As Yehuda Amichai explains in his poem "The Diameter of a Bomb," the fallout of violence, especially as pathological and calculated as the Holocaust, is an infinite ripple across time and its effects do not stop with the victims alone (118). Death follows the survivor and leaves a trail for the following generations who inherit that memory.

The catastrophic legacy of the Holocaust has cast a long shadow on the lives of the Jews, those who lived through or were claimed by it as well as their successors.

184   *Tiasa Bal*

For Jews, the necessity of remembering was a way of keeping alive a history that stretched its arm into their present and, indeed, into their future. However, remembering the Holocaust meant revisiting the darkest side of World War II and their incalculable personal tragedies through it. The Holocaust was in its essence an unspeakable act of violence that shattered the idea of a normal life for its survivors. To navigate through the testimonies that bear no formal structure, linearity, and, at times, coherence, magic realism serves as a rudder to comprehend belated memory and its impact upon the lives of the survivors. The agony of remembering traumatic pasts is twice as brutal as experiencing it. Magic realism is a preliminary means of ameliorating that agony. It circumvents the existing ableism in historical narration without taking away the gravity of the survivor's experience. Magic realism is indispensable to narratives that transcend the confines of structured language or linear history. It tears down the supremacy of objective historical narration through its liminality and enforces the agency of the survivors as an essential and inseparable part of the history of the Holocaust. Magic realism, as Jenni Adams argues, serves as an important breakthrough in retrieving accounts of the Holocaust in the post-testimonial era. It permits a form of literary engagement with these events even while retaining the gravity of its trauma and acknowledging its ethical and experiential distance from the real. The element of consolation or escape present in these works immunizes the testimonies of the haunting and the haunted from the erasure of temporality.

Magic realism simultaneously operates within literary realism and reorients its conventions, thus problematizing not only realist discourse but also the Western rationalist ontological framework of the genre. It canonizes alternative forms of experience, knowledge, and truth. It gives victims of inconsolable tragedies a means of coping with the past discursively without sanitizing their experiences or making them more palatable. The magical event cannot be subsumed within realist parameters, thus resisting subordination to the structures which it breaches. Magic realism cannot be seen in isolation vis-à-vis the vagaries of its immediate political rhetoric. Whether from an overtly anti-imperial, postcolonial, feminist, or Marxist approach, or a combination of these, or whether its politics is interlaced symbolically through the tension between written western European culture and oral- or mythic-based cultures, these writers position the narrative outside the dominant power structures and cultural centers.

Genocide, refugee crises, war, and xenophobia continue to influence our worldview and the universal perceptions of faith and humanity. Fictional narratives suggest possibilities concerning the inheritance of trauma—this inheritance must be worked through so that an individual is able to function in the present and face the future with some degree of hope. To educate the masses about both the historic as well as the moral significance of events of catastrophe requires a pedagogic tool of its own. New Literacy theorists suggest finding a connection between local literacies and the prevalent academic literacies. Following suit from Adorno, Horkheimer, and Gramsci, Popular Culture can be seen as a site of struggle between dominant and marginalized groups. And therefore, the pedagogic exercise must be done in the interest of the disempowered. There is no paucity of literature on the Holocaust. A sincere study of fiction, especially produced by the second- and third-generation survivors can break the long spell of the enigma that surrounds the Holocaust and consecrate into cultural remembrance its rightful narrative agency. The process may be a long-term one; however, it is a human calling to return these histories to the people who had experienced them with a solemn resolution to never see them being repeated. In his essay "Trauma and Narrative," Joshua Pederson asserts that "indeed, it is a widely accepted therapeutic truth that the stories we tell about the catastrophes that beset us—both individual and collective—can be crucial tools for recovery" (97). These narratives skillfully integrate the tragedy of the Holocaust with a sense of hope, no matter how improbable this may sound, and mediate the moral obligation to remember with the equally moral responsibility to reconcile with the past and aspire to a life filled with meaning and possibility.

Notes

1 A nonfiction memoir, *The Lost,* tells the story of Mendelsohn's travels in search of details about the lives of a maternal great-uncle, his wife, and their four daughters who were killed by the Nazis.
2 In the second volume of the history of Nazi Germany, Friedländer pieces together personal testaments of the victims, perpetrators, and bystanders.
3 Avishai Margalit explores the ethics of remembrance and representation in *Ethics of Memory* (2000). He makes a distinction between ethics and morality.
4 Jeffrey C. Alexander's concept of "cultural trauma" argues that a shocking event leaves ineradicable marks upon the group consciousness of a collectivity.
5 Trauma theorists such as Cathy Caruth hold that a traumatic experience escapes language. Caruth designates trauma as a crisis of representation (4).
6 In "Notes on Trauma and Community," Kai Erikson eloquently describes the concept of collective trauma and its impact on the self (460).
7 The translation of *L'espace littéraire.*

Works Cited

Aarons, Victoria and Alan L. Berger. *Third-Generation Holocaust Representation: Trauma, History, and Memory.* Northwestern University Press, 2017.

Adams, Jenni. *Magic Realism in Holocaust Literature: Troping the Traumatic Real.* Palgrave Macmillan, 2011.

Adorno, Theodor W. "Cultural criticism and society." In *Prisms* (Translated by Samuel and Shierry Weber). MIT Press, 1983, pp. 17–34.

Amichai, Yehuda. "The diameter of the bomb." In *The Selected Poetry of Yehuda Amichai* (Translated by Chana Bloch and Stephen Mitchell). University of California Press, 1996.

Bar-On, Dan. *Fear and Hope: Three Generations of the Holocaust.* Harvard University Press, 1995.

Berger, Alan L. "Unclaimed experience: Trauma and identity in third generation writing about the Holocaust." *Shofar*, vol. 20, no. 3, 2010, pp. 149–158.

Bowers, Maggie Anne. *Magic(al) Realism: The New Critical Idiom.* Routledge, 2004.

Caruth, Cathy. *Unclaimed Experience: Trauma, Narrative, and History.* John Hopkins University Press, 1996.

Crownshaw, Richard. *The Afterlife of Holocaust Memory in Contemporary Literature and Culture.* Palgrave Macmillan, 2010.

186 *Tiasa Bal*

Erikson, Kai. "Notes on Trauma and community." *American Imago* (vol. 48, no. 4). Psychoanalysis, Culture and Trauma: II, 1991, pp. 455–472.

Faris, Wendy B. *Ordinary Enchantments: Magical Realism and the Remystification of Narrative*. Vanderbilt University Press, 2004.

Gasché, Rodolphe. *Storytelling: The Destruction of the Inalienable in the Age of the Holocaust*. State University of New York, 2018.

Grimwood, Marita. *Holocaust Literature of the Second Generation*. Palgrave Macmillan, 2007.

Hartman, Geoffrey. *The Longest Shadow: In the Aftermath of the Holocaust*. Indiana University Press, 1996.

Hirsch, Marianne. *The Generation of Postmemory: Writing and Visual Culture after the Holocaust*. Columbia University Press, 2012.

Huyssen, Andreas. *Twilight Memories: Making Time in a Culture of Amnesia*. Routledge, 1995.

Itkin, Alan. "Bring up the bodies: The classical concept of poetic vividness and its reevaluation in Holocaust literature." *PMLA*, vol. 133, no. 1, 2018, pp. 107–123.

Kansteiner, Wulf. "Finding meaning in memory: A methodological critique of collective memory studies." *History and Theory*, vol. 41, no. 2, 2002, pp. 179–197.

Kaplan, Brett Ashley. *Landscapes of Holocaust Postmemory*. Routledge, 2011.

LaCapra, Dominick. *Writing History, Writing Trauma*. Johns Hopkins University Press, 2014.

Lang, Berel. *Holocaust Representation in Art: Art within the Limits of History and Ethics*. John Hopkins University Press, 2000.

Lang, Berel. *Post-Holocaust: Interpretation, Misinterpretation and the Claims of History*. Indiana University Press, 2005.

Langer, Lawrence L. *Admitting the Holocaust: Collected Essays*. Oxford University Press, 1995.

Margalit, Avishai. *The Ethics of Memory*. Harvard University Press, 2002.

Marshman, Sophia "From the margins to the mainstream? Representations of the Holocaust in popular culture." *E-Sharp*, vol. 6, no. 1, www.gla.ac.uk/media/Media_41177_smxx. pdf. Accessed 27 Nov. 2021.

McCarten, Edward. "Magic realism." *Ambit*, no. 168, 2002, pp. 76–81.

Mendelsohn, Daniel. *The Lost: A Search for Six of Six Million*. HarperCollins, 2006.

Michaels, Anne. *Fugitive Pieces*. Alfred A. Knopf, 1997.

Mukerji, Chandra and Michael Schudson. "Popular culture." *Annual Review of Sociology*, vol. 12, 1986, pp. 47–66.

Pederson, Joshua. "Trauma and narrative." In *Trauma and Literature*, edited by Roger Kurtz J. Cambridge University Press, 2018, pp. 97–109.

Rabkin, Eric S. *The Fantastic in Literature*. Princeton University Press, 1976.

Reed, Jean-Pierre. "Theorist of subaltern subjectivity: Antonio Gramsci, popular beliefs, political passion, and reciprocal learning." *Critical Sociology*, vol. 39, no. 4, 2012, pp. 561–591.

Rosenbaum, Thane. *The Golems of Gotham*. Harper Collins, 2002.

Rothberg, Michael. *Multidirectional Memory: Remembering the Holocaust in the Age of Decolonization*. Stanford University Press, 2009.

Rothberg, Michael. *Traumatic Realism: The Demands of Holocaust Representation*. University of Minnesota Press, 2000.

Skibell, Joseph. *A Blessing on the Moon: A Novel*. Algonquin Books, 1997.

Stratton, Jon. *Jewish Identity in Western Pop Culture: The Holocaust and Trauma through Modernity*. Palgrave Macmillan, 2008.

Street, John "Politics and popular culture." In *Blackwell Companion to Political Sociology*, edited by Kate Nash and Alan Scott (3rd ed.). Wiley Blackwell, 2001, pp. 302–311.

Todorov, Tzvetan. *The Fantastic: A Structural Approach to a Literary Genre* (Translated by Richard Howard). Cornell University Press, 1975.

White, Hayden. *The Practical Past*. Northwestern University Press, 2014.

Yerushalmi, Yosef Hayim. *Zakhor: Jewish History and Jewish Memory*. University of Washington Press, 2011.

Young, James E. *Writing and Rewriting the Holocaust: Narrative and the Consequences of Interpretation*. Indiana University Press, 1990.

13 "Once-upon-a-very-real-time"

Fairy Tales and Holocaust in Jane Yolen's Novels

Anisha Sen

The term "fairy tale," now used as a generic label for magical stories for children, comes from the French term *Conte de fées*, coined for a group of seventeenth century tales written for adults, as pointed out by Jane Yolen. Over the years, fairy tales have been revised, simplified and, "purged" of explicit contents to an extent where people nowadays do not know that the old tales have been different. In a bid to make the stories suitable for children, the popular versions have significantly diluted the greater implications and complexities that lay latent in the fabric of the older narratives. In modern times, the term "fairy tale" has come to stand for a lie or fanciful untruth. Terri Windling and Ellen Datlow believe that this has simplified the old tales of "anguish and darkness" by reducing the trials and tribulations of the characters; in the old tales, "Happy endings, where they exist, are hard won and at a price" (Windling and Datlow 87–88). This discontent with the popular fairy tales (as written by Charles Perrault, Brothers Grimm, and Hans Christian Andersen) led to their subversion toward the end of the eighteenth century, to bring out the strands that had been neglected for long. The period from 1960 to the present has particularly witnessed several experimentations with the genre of fairy tales, ranging from political fairy tales written during the Vietnam War to their feminist reworking. These literary adaptations took away the abstract temporality that began with "once upon a time" and ended in "ever after"; instead, they located the stories within particular historical moments or in modern times. The world of fairy tales is filled with violence, death/killings, scheming family members, cannibalistic witches, and so on. The old tales already have ingredients that can be rearranged against the backdrop of dark, disturbing times. Apart from this, the German origins of the Grimm brothers, the source of numerous fairy tales, provide an inevitable connection to one of the darkest chapters of history—the Holocaust.

In 1999, historian Tim Cole wrote, "At the end of the twentieth century, the 'Holocaust' is central to modern consciousness. . . . [It] has emerged as nothing less than a ruling symbol in our culture . . . a dominant icon" (Cole 12, 18). World War II, the Holocaust, and the resultant horrors shook the world to its core and cast a tall shadow over the literature produced in the postwar world. But, a blend of fairy tales and the Holocaust seems paradoxical until one considers Jack Zipes' statement:

DOI: 10.4324/9781003251224-17

"Once-upon-a-very-real-time" 189

Both the oral and the literary forms of the fairy tale are grounded in history: they emanate from specific struggles to humanize bestial and barbaric forces, which have terrorized our minds and communities in concrete ways, threatening to destroy free will and human compassion. The fairy tale sets out to conquer this concrete terror through metaphors.

(1–2)

It is challenging to depict history in terms of fiction as its accuracy is often questioned. Depicting a dark chapter of history in terms of the "juvenile" genre of fairy tales should prove to be an even greater challenge. However, for an author or a reader who does not have any firsthand experience of the Holocaust, the familiar fairy tales can provide a palimpsest on which the unfamiliar history can be inscribed. Besides being the common point of reference for everyone, fairy tales also make the process of narrating the trauma of the Holocaust easier by aesthetically distancing the tale from its narrator, subsuming it into a greater metanarrative. Anna Hunter explains this amalgamation of the apparently incongruous narratives of fairy tales and the Holocaust—"Consider, however, that both are highly informed by generic convention; consider further that both are dependent for their meaning upon the reader, who must recognize the relationship between signifier and signified within narrative frames that very often mask the true content of the text" (60).

Sabrina Ora Mark in her article "Cracked Fairy Tales and the Holocaust" recounts an interesting personal experience where she visits the Holocaust Museum Yad Vashem to see murals of fairy tales painted by the Jewish writer Bruno Schulz. A Gestapo officer, Felix Landau, had asked Bruno to paint the walls of his son's nursery in exchange for protection from the Nazis. Shortly after the mural was complete, Bruno was shot and killed by another Nazi on the streets. Through this real incident, art links up the Holocaust and fairy tales in a poignant way, through the brushstroke of a victim.

Even after exploring the various points where we can connect the Holocaust with fairy tale narratives, a question remains—if the old fairy tales had to be diluted for the children, then how can one make such a dark chapter of history fit for their ears? The Holocaust, in itself, poses a difficulty in explicating the horrors, and this is where the role of fairy tales come in—talking about the horrific time in terms of "stories" makes it easier to narrate and also more suitable for young readers. Imre Kertész, a Holocaust survivor, felt compelled to write in *Gályanapló* (1992), "The concentration camp is imaginable only and exclusively as literature, never as reality" (qtd. in Sanyal, 56). To explore this idea, I would like to focus on how the fairy tales "Sleeping Beauty" or "Briar Rose" and "Hansel and Gretel," have been used as narrative frames to relate Holocaust experiences. "Hansel and Gretel" specifically has quite a few retellings set in the backdrop of the Holocaust, and all these narratives weave the trauma of the Holocaust deftly into the fabric of the original tales. However, this study will be limited to a detailed account of only Jane Yolen's novels and how they use fairy tales to talk about the Holocaust.

190 *Anisha Sen*

Eric A. Kimmel, in his 1977 article "Confronting the Ovens," tries to explain why no children's author had yet penned down "the ultimate tragedy" of the Holocaust:

> This situation is due not to any dearth of able writers, but to the collision between the subject and some of our basic beliefs about the nature of literature for children and adolescents. To put it simply, is mass murder a subject for a children's novel?
>
> (Kimmel)

However, he anticipated that it was only a matter of time before a novelist found a way to portray the Holocaust in all its horror for young readers. Jane Yolen did find one, and it all began with her 1988 publication, *The Devil's Arithmetic*. Though the two later novels are related more closely to fairy tales, it is imperative to start by discussing her very first Holocaust novel briefly, as they all come together to form a pattern. *The Devil's Arithmetic* is the only one among the three novels that does not use the frame of any fairy tale, yet it carries within it certain unmistakable allusions to the tales. Later on, in *Briar Rose* (1992), based on the story of "Sleeping Beauty," and *Mapping the Bones* (2018), based on the story of "Hansel and Gretel," Jane Yolen sets off to fully explore this apparently paradoxical nexus between fairy tales and the Holocaust.

The Devil's Arithmetic does not adapt any fairy tale, but Yolen chooses to use magic or fantasy as a framing device to narrate an otherwise grim tale. The protagonist Hannah is a reflection of Yolen's childhood, as she "hated the idea of having to remember so much Jewish history and ritual" (Yolen, "If the Muse Comes Calling"). At a family Seder (a Jewish ritual service and ceremonial dinner), while performing the symbolic ritual of opening the door to the prophet Elijah, Hannah suddenly finds herself magically transported back in time to Nazi-occupied Poland. Later, after experiencing firsthand the horrors of a labor camp run by the Nazis and on the verge of being killed, she is transported back to America and the present. The trope of transportation is a common feature in fantasy stories, but in this novel, Yolen gives it a playful twist. Hannah is no Alice going down a rabbit hole or a child about to discover the phantasmagorical world of Narnia. The transportation is similar to the one we find in the novel *Kindred* by Octavia E. Butler, where a young African-American woman writer time travels back to the dark years of slavery. Ironically, Hannah's magical transportation brings her face to face with the harsh realities to an extent where the normal life she had been leading seemed to be a mere fantasy. Moreover, unlike the protagonists in fantasy stories, Hannah (transformed to Chaya) already knows about the world she is entering from her history books and family stories. But her bookish knowledge is ineffectual in the face of real danger; she must experience reality firsthand to understand the value of the rabbi's words, "And the past tells us what we must do in the future" (Yolen, *Arithmetic* 78).

This fantastical device in *The Devil's Arithmetic* is used to tone down the impact of the firsthand experience of the Holocaust for the young readers, without

"*Once-upon-a-very-real-time*" 191

trivializing it. It is also a comment on those dark times where nothing except magic/miracle could save you. Besides this, the novel makes use of certain fairy tale references that are worth mentioning. After Hannah goes back in time, she narrates a muddled version of the "Hansel and Gretel" story to her friends, significantly while traveling through a forest. Shortly after that, she realizes that she is trapped in a nightmarish world without any means of going back—"Where was her home?" (Yolen, *Arithmetic* 57). Her predicament at this point is very similar to that of Hansel and Gretel, who lost their way in the forest and could not find their home. The leitmotif of the "Hansel and Gretel" story becomes more prominent upon Hannah's arrival at the labor camp, where they learn about the gas ovens in which Jews are burnt. This place is euphemistically termed Lilith's Cave, a reference to Jewish folklore where Lilith was a female demonic figure. When Hannah learns that the commandant of the camp comes on rounds to choose people for "processing" or death, she jokes about the situation saying, "Hansel, let out your finger, that I may see if you are fat and lean" (Yolen, *Arithmetic* 128). Through this comment, the Nazis assume the role of the cannibalistic witch, who came to check every day if Hansel had fattened up enough to be her meal. The chores they had to complete at the labor camp are also reminiscent of how the witch used to make Gretel work hard for her. But the cruelty and the overwhelming number of Nazis at the camp are enough to tell us that in this world, Gretel aka Hannah does not have a chance against them. So, instead of incinerating the evil force, she is compelled to walk toward the ovens, albeit in an attempt to save a friend. It is clear right from this novel that Yolen has noticed certain similar patterns between the story "Hansel and Gretel" and the harrowing accounts of the Holocaust; this strain is developed further in her final Holocaust novel *Mapping the Bones*. Besides the prominent reference to the "Hansel and Gretel" story, *The Devil's Arithmetic* also has a passing reference to the tale of Red Riding Hood. In a moment of deep despair at the labor camp, Hannah muses, "That's where we are now. In the belly of the werewolf" (Yolen, *Arithmetic* 143), and just like the old version of this fairy tale, there is no redemptive ending for the girl.

Even while Yolen uses fairy tale tropes in her Holocaust narrative, she takes care to point out that the historical reality was far grimmer than the Grimms' tales. Before they are taken to the labor camp, Hannah tries to alert everybody about the reality of the Nazis and tries to differentiate the reality from her stories: "The gas ovens I mean are no fairy tale" (Yolen, *Arithmetic* 67). Hannah's aunt interestingly has the name Gitl, which is confused at this point with the name Gretel, once again pointing to the popular fairy tale. By the time they are herded into trucks for resettlement, Gitl has realized that the future holds nothing bright for them: "This is not one of your stories that ends happy-ever-after. There are not imaginary bullets in those guns" (Yolen, *Arithmetic* 70). Yolen herself admits in her epilogue to the novel that fiction cannot come close to the actual horrors of the camps, but it can still become a witness and a device to remember.

Yolen's first Holocaust novel is also about memory and the importance of remembering the past to understand the present. The story becomes like a Holocaust memorial, which stresses the importance of not only commemorating but

192   *Anisha Sen*

also sympathizing with the survivors. *The Devil's Arithmetic* begins with Hannah grumbling, "I'm tired of remembering" and ends with her declaring, "I remember, Oh, I remember," and throughout the novel, Yolen plays around with the idea of remembering. This idea encapsulates not only the need to remember the past but also the difficulty of narrating the traumatic past. It is significant that Hannah, who carries the memory of the future while she is transported to the past, is shorn of all her memories soon after she enters the labor camp. This signifies that for the Jews who entered those horrific camps, their memories of happy days simply became fanciful stories. But Hannah remembers everything once she returns to her world, proving the words of Rivka to be true: "We forget because remembering is so painful. But memory will return, when you are ready for it" (Yolen, *Arithmetic* 119). As painful as it might be, forgetting is not an option because the victims must be commemorated and lessons must be learned from history: "As long as we can remember, all those gone before are alive inside us" (Yolen, *Arithmetic* 112).

Jane Yolen draws upon and elaborately shapes this concept of memory in her second Holocaust novel, *Briar Rose*. This novel is a part of the *Fairy Tales Series*, edited by Terri Windling. It is a brilliant take on the "Sleeping Beauty" story where the fairy tale is initially used as a leitmotif but goes on to have a bigger implication. Yolen weaves the actual fairy tale delicately into the fabric of her own story about a Holocaust survivor. The concentration camp of Chelmno was in a castle, and this led her to make the seemingly impossible connection between a "happily ever after" tale and one of the darkest chapters of history. Sleeping Beauty's story had once been quite different from the Grimms' version that we know now. There have been several old versions of the tale involving the rape of the sleeping princess (in Giambattista Basile's *Sun, Moon, and Talia*) leading to the birth of her two children and a cannibalistic queen/ogress (in both Basile and Perrault's tales). If one remembers the use of these dark and disturbing themes in the old narratives, Yolen's decision to use this particular fairy tale as a framing device for a Holocaust narrative does not appear too surprising.

Briar Rose is divided into three parts—Home, Castle, and Home Again, and this reflects Yolen's partiality for the number three, especially in her fairy tale adaptations. Three is the number of magic and finds recurrent mention in the fairy tales. There are multiple stories that are narrated within the frame of the "Sleeping Beauty" story. Becca's grandmother Gemma is fond of telling the story of Sleeping Beauty to her grandchildren, but that is the only story she ever tells them. She keeps on narrating the story obsessively, to the point where only Becca remains interested in it. Though the grandchildren notice that certain parts of Gemma's narrative depart significantly from the well-known fairy tale, what they do not realize is that she is actually narrating a personal experience of deep trauma, which the fairy tale enables her to express through symbols. The process of remembering and recounting becomes important once again, however difficult or fragmented that experience might be. Cathy Caruth, an influential voice in trauma theory draws upon Freud as she points out that "the impact of the traumatic event lies precisely in its belatedness, in its refusal to be simply located, in its insistent appearance outside the boundaries of any single place or time" (196). This explains Gemma's

"*Once-upon-a-very-real-time*"   193

tendency to dislocate her experience and graft it into another story for the sake of narrating it, over and over again. This is similar to what happens in Lisa Goldstein's story "Breadcrumbs and Stones," where the narrator's mother, a Holocaust survivor, tries to define her story in terms of the story of "Hansel and Gretel" before she could finally bring herself to narrate her experience.

In *Briar Rose*, the way Gemma's version of the story departs from the actual fairy tale constitutes an important aspect of the novel. There was no spindle on which the princess was supposed to prick her finger but a great mist that put the entire kingdom to sleep: "A mist. A great mist. It covered the entire kingdom. And everyone in it—the good people and the not-so-good, the young people and the not-so-young, and even Briar Rose's mother and father fell asleep" (Yolen, *Briar Rose* 43). The mist becomes a symbol for the Nazi domination, and the hundred years' sleep stands for their sleeping conscience. This sleep is also equated to the final sleep, which millions of Jews were put into, during the Nazi domination. The time is accursed, just like the princess, and though she will be eventually rescued, the experience will have a cataclysmic effect: "A hundred years is forever" (Yolen, *Briar Rose* 44). In the novel, the ending of the survivor's story witnesses the birth of the daughter of Gemma (who is the self-proclaimed Briar Rose of the novel). This is reminiscent of the older versions of "Sleeping Beauty" where the princess gives birth in her sleep. Gemma's narrative runs throughout the novel, in between the actual story of the novel and her grandchildren's interruptions. But the simple childhood tale starts to take on a deeper meaning as Gemma, on her deathbed, extracts a promise from Becca that she will find the castle and the prince. "I am Briar Rose" (Yolen, *Briar Rose* 17) were Gemma's last words.

Becca begins her research, trying to find the real-life connection between her grandmother and the fairy tale. Her investigations take her to Chelmno, a Jewish extermination camp in Poland, and she discovers that Gemma had been a Holocaust survivor. The trail leads her to Josef Potocki, who narrates Gemma's story of survival. She had been a victim of gassing by the Nazis and was left to die in a pit. A gang of Holocaust survivors on the run had chanced upon her while she was still alive. Aron, a member of that group, had revived her with the help of Josef. Even while drawing upon the well-known images of "sleep" and the revival of the "princess," Yolen decides to give a slight twist to her narrative—it was Josef who gave Gemma a mouth-to-mouth resuscitation, but it was Aron whom Gemma married eventually. Josef was under Nazi persecution for being a homosexual, and he had simply shared a bond of companionship with Gemma. His kiss was the "kiss of life" rather than the "kiss of love," as is clear from Gemma's unique "Sleeping Beauty" narrative: "And as he did so, giving her breath for breath, she awoke saying 'I am alive, my dear prince. You have given me back the world'" (Yolen, *Briar Rose* 238). Yolen intentionally lets the romance bleed out from the famous kiss in the fairy tale, probably because it never occurred in the old versions and also because she wanted to realistically depict a world where survival is of supreme importance and romance a mere luxury.

With the ambiguity surrounding the "kiss" in the novel, it becomes difficult to answer the question—who is the "prince" in this story? It was Josef who "kissed"

Gemma awake, but she was equally grateful to Aron for her life. This question is intentionally left unanswered, as Josef is clear on one point: "You must understand (he said) that this is a story of survivors, not heroes" (Yolen, *Briar Rose* 16). Gemma is as much the hero of the story as the two men who saved her. The predominance of heterosexual love in our fairy tales is also implicitly questioned through Josef's love life. Heterosexual love is not excluded from the novel though—there is Gemma's marriage at the center of the story and Becca's love life, framing the narrative. While Aron was killed off, putting an abrupt end to Gemma's fairy tale, Becca kisses her man in the end, signifying the beginning of her "happily ever after."

Yolen's last novel on the Holocaust named *Mapping the Bones* draws upon yet another well-loved fairy tale by the Grimm brothers. The Grimms' story of "Hansel and Gretel" also has other versions preceding it, just like the "Sleeping Beauty" story. Among these, the noteworthy ones are Perrault's "Le Petite Poucet" and Madame d'Aulnoy's "Finette Cendron." What remains common across these narratives is the child's/children's anxiety regarding abandonment, starvation, and a fight for survival. The ogre/witch is defeated by being pushed into the oven. It is a tale of bravery and a rite of passage into adulthood, but on a closer look, the themes of cruel betrayal, cannibalism, and brutality also begin to emerge. Once again, Yolen discovers the dark strands in the fairy tale which she can use to develop her own Holocaust narrative. The fairy tale is used more loosely in this particular novel as compared to *Briar Rose*. The life of the twins Chaim and Gittel mirrors the experiences of Hansel and Gretel to some extent and the literary allusions to fairy tales are strewn around in the novel. Chaim (pronounced as Hayim) and Gittel are Jewish names, which are phonetically similar to the names of the protagonists of the fairy tale.

Yolen persistently uses her favorite number three yet again, and she explains the tripartite structure of her novel in the afterword. The life of Chaim and Gittel is divided into three sections—their difficult life in the Lodz ghetto, their escape into the Bialowieza Forest, and their harrowing experiences at the Sobanek labor camp. These three sections correspond to the three important points in the fairy tale—starvation and poverty that force the children to leave their home, their abandonment in the forest, and their days at the witch's house. Despite the presence of violence in both, Yolen tries to echo the happy ending of the original story by giving the survivors a future. The novel is a masterfully crafted piece of art, blending the elements of history, myth, and poetry together: "My soft spot as a writer is the place where history, poetry, and legend combine to tell a deeper truth" (Yolen, "If the Muse Comes Calling"). This story is also about remembering, not only the horrifying incidents of the labor camp but also the idyllic life that the twins had led before the Nazis took over. The narrative is interspersed with sections headed "Gittel Remembers," where Gittel's perspective and memories are narrated.

Yolen finds an innovative way to recount the Holocaust experience in the course of this novel. Chaim faced problems of articulating himself. He stuttered and could not speak more than five words at a time. His stutter is a physical manifestation of the psychologically difficult process of narrating trauma and the hesitation connected to it. However, he was able to express himself eloquently through poetry,

"Once-upon-a-very-real-time"   195

and this becomes his voice throughout the novel. He scavenges for scraps of paper even under the direst circumstances and writes down poetry about whatever he encounters. In a historical narration involving the staggering statistics of exterminated Jews and other people who died fighting, there is little scope of giving any recognition to individuals. Yolen attempts to do what history could not, using Chaim's poetry as a vehicle to commemorate individuals who died under the Nazi persecution. Poetry is a way of immortalizing its subject and for each death or horror that Chaim witnesses, he writes a poem. The act of creation also helps him endure and keeps him going—

> Every day I can wake is another day of life.
> Every day I can walk is another day of hope.
> Every day I can sing is another day of grace.
> Every day I can write a poem is another day.
> (Yolen, _Mapping_ 382)

His poems often come to him in fragments, signifying the fragmented consciousness under the horrific circumstances, but in the end, art has the power to turn everything into an aesthetic whole. Reciting the lines of poetry in his head makes the burden of hard labor seem easier to him, just as the act of remembering and recounting lightens the burden of traumatic memories.

The story does a wonderful job of recounting the horrors of the Jewish ghettos and labor camps. Chaim and Gittel's parents are caring and protective, unlike the parents we encounter in the fairy tale, who abandon their children in the woods. However, in a turn of fate, Chaim and Gittel get separated from their parents while trying to escape from the Lodz ghetto. They go into the Bialoweza Forest with Polish partisans, who undertake the task of transporting the children to safety. The forest is a recurrent theme in German tales as it occupies a significant part of the landscape and represents a subversive space. Ironically, the forest, which threatens Hansel and Gretel, bears the promise of safety for Chaim and Gittel, albeit a temporary one. This points out the cruelty of the Nazi regime, where even a forest appears safer for children compared to one of their camps. The forest, however, contains no hope for them to return home—there are no pebbles that can guide them back. When Bruno tries to drop pebbles to find their way home, Chaim realizes its futility: "But he kept silent, thinking bitterly instead, _As if there's a home to go back to_" (Yolen, _Mapping_ 184). Under the Nazi domination, "home" becomes an amorphous concept for the Jews as they are ruthlessly uprooted without a place to return to.

As the children are captured and taken to the Sobanek labor camp, Gittel reflects, "We arrived at the camp under gray skies, and all too soon there was a first frost, a fairy tale world gone mad" (Yolen, _Mapping_ 238). We are prepared to encounter a world of distorted fairy tales, where rather than a single threatening presence of a witch, there are thousands of Nazis, hungry for blood. The ultimate fate in the labor camp is incineration, a punishment meted out to transgressors and people who become unfit for the hard work. The chimney where the bodies are

196 *Anisha Sen*

burnt is compared to the witch's oven in "Hansel and Gretel": "The old witch's ovens never stop smoking; that delectable house reeks of roast pork" (Yolen, *Mapping* 237). The inmates of the labor camp ominously refer to the gas oven by using hand movements, rather than by talking about it openly. This is very similar to how the oven is referred to as Lilith's Cave in *The Devil's Arithmetic*. It becomes easier to talk about indescribable things in terms of myth or euphemism, just as it becomes easier, as the texts indicate, to express the trauma of the Holocaust in terms of fairy tales.

The theme of betrayal occurs in the novel, but it is not the parents anymore who betray their children. Under the Nazi regime, the Jews were encouraged to spill the beans about their kinsmen to curry favor with the Germans. The Sobanek camp is also ironically dubbed the House of Candy because any inmate could give another away in exchange for candies that the soldiers handed out to them. The name House of Candy is as deceptive and misleading as the witch's house of bread and sugar (also represented as a gingerbread house or a house made of candies across versions), which looked inviting but was actually a trap. The doctor von Schneir becomes the metaphorical witch, who initially arrived with medicines to cure the sick children: "His face wreathed in smiles, his hands full of candy" (Yolen, *Mapping* 238). But, ultimately, he turns into a nightmarish Angel of Death (a term which was also associated with the notorious Doctor Mengele). This is very similar to the witch in the fairy tale who invites the children warmly, only to reveal her cannibalistic instincts later. But Yolen purposefully destabilizes the conventional gender specificity of the witch—cruelty is gender-neutral in a world consumed by hatred. But deception is two-fold in the novel—it is not the transformation of apparent goodness into pure evil but also of apparent evil revealing itself to be goodness in disguise. The latter happens in the case of Madam Grenzke, who initially made the children work but was actually a partisan in disguise and ultimately became their savior.

Drawing inspiration from an age-old tale, Yolen modifies its various strands to accommodate the story she wants to tell. She narrates the story of a world run by pure evil and, in the process, presents different shades of evil rather than a single evil figure. The German soldiers and the Nazi regime represent the all-pervasive evil force, with the doctor being the supreme figure of evil. The women who extract work from the children in the factory are ruthless, but they pale in comparison to the psychopathic doctor. One of them even tries to stop the doctor from taking away Chaim as she knew it would endanger him. One of the soldiers collapses on the floor as he could not bear the sight of the doctor mercilessly murdering Gregor under the guise of an operation. Yolen also does not spare the Jews who turn against their own kind; evil is seen as a part of one's nature, rather than a part of a certain nationality or religion. Just as it seems comforting to translate suffering into poetry, it becomes easier to talk about the evil forces in real life in terms of the stock characters found in the folk and fairy tales. In a moment of starvation and despair, Chaim is reminded of the witch in "Hansel and Gretel," a story that forms a bridge between his past (when his mother used to read out the story) and present. Mirroring Hannah from *The Devil's Arithmetic*, Chaim also thinks of the

"*Once-upon-a-very-real-time*"   197

camp doctor in terms of the wolf in "Red Riding Hood,": "There is no wisdom, just cunning: /wolf's quiet padding on the trail . . . There is no atonement, just growling/in the belly of the wolf" (Yolen, *Mapping* 329). The Russian folk tale about the ogress Baba Yaga is referred to when Chaim desperately tries to find some comfort in the idea of the camps and he thinks of the Russian proverb in the tale: "Morning is wiser than evening" (Yolen, *Mapping* 234).

In her stories of horror, Yolen succeeds in incorporating stories of heroism. Here, heroism does not lie in protesting (because that will get you killed instantly), but in endurance and resilience. Here, heroism is about living in the most squalid circumstances and still daring to break into subversive laughter, something that Chaim called "gallows humor." The way the witch in "Hansel and Gretel" fattened up Hansel showed how he was dehumanized like a lamb to the slaughter. The Nazis similarly dehumanized the Jews, numbering them like cattle and using them for experiments like lab rats. A single act of heroism like shoving the witch into the oven is not enough anymore, and the children in these Holocaust novels have to fight a bigger battle against a greater force: "That heroism—to resist being dehumanized, to simply outlive one's tormentors, to practice the quiet, everyday caring for one's equally tormented neighbours" (Yolen, *Arithmetic* 169). Contrary to the usual trend in fairy tales, in each of these novels, Yolen makes the girl her own hero, a damsel who does not rely on the prince/man to save her from distress. In *The Devil's Arithmetic*, Hannah bravely steps toward the ovens to save Rivka's life; in *Briar Rose*, Gemma's "resurrection" resists all attempts of the Nazis to kill her and she lives to tell her tale; in *Mapping the Bones*, Gittel saves the life of her brother and herself, aided by Madam Grenzke. This takes a cue from the actual fairy tale of "Hansel and Gretel," which is one of those rare fairy tales where the girl saves herself and also the man. In these Holocaust novels, heroism, as well as wickedness, are not limited to any particular gender.

Fictional narratives of the Holocaust have often been criticized as inaccurate and inferior to Holocaust survivor literature. Even *The Diary of Anne Frank* has been severely edited to make it more popular and Americanized, as pointed out by Cynthia Ozick. Such Americanization of the Holocaust has been criticized for misrepresenting the deep trauma of the Jewish victims, but it has also helped to establish a sense of pride regarding Jewish heritage in modern-day Jews. At a convention for librarians, soon after the publication of *The Devil's Arithmetic*, an editor of a children's book journal opined that resorting to fantasy "trivialized the Holocaust" (Franklin). The science fiction writer Orson Scott Card retorted that fictions like *The Devil's Arithmetic* allowed the readers to imagine themselves in the protagonist's place, which made them relate to him/her in a better way than they could through a memoir.

Adapting popular fairy tales in the light of the Holocaust adds to this further, as the readers can relate to the adaptations through symbols, characters, and patterns that are already known to them via fairy tales. Adaptation of a particular work of literature gives that piece an afterlife by recalling it to the memory. The process of narrating trauma also seems to be similar, containing the act of remembering. The three novels of Yolen narrate stories of deep trauma, but each novel portrays it

198 *Anisha Sen*

differently. In *The Devil's Arithmetic*, the protagonist has to go through a harrowing experience, albeit temporarily, to understand the importance of recounting and narrating trauma. In *Briar Rose*, there is an attempt to couch the tale of trauma in the vocabulary of fairy tales, which provides an impetus to know the real story. In *Mapping the Bones*, the trauma is expressed through Chaim's poetry and Gittel's memory, even when words fall short. Experiences of trauma tend to resist narration or lead to fragmented, incoherent narration. Ruth Franklin discusses how her family members, who had escaped the Holocaust, could never really escape from the experience: "But they didn't often talk in detail about their experiences. When they did, the stories they told were confusing and full of gaps, and I'd complain at having to hear them" (Franklin). This is not unusual as the problematic relation between narration and trauma, explored by Christa Schönfelder, demonstrates:

> Literary trauma texts often expose and work with the essential paradox that characterizes trauma narratives in general: the attempt to communicate that which resists ordinary processes of remembering and narrating, of representation and comprehension. Trauma narratives raise important questions about the possibility of verbalizing the unspeakable, narrating the unnarratable, and making sense of the incomprehensible.
>
> (30)

Even while the process of narrating trauma is a difficult one, there is, in each survivor, an urge to tell their stories, to defeat the ghosts of the past by facing them. The importance of narration is thus supreme, and relating it through certain symbols of fairy tales renders the process easier. Bruno Bettelheim opines that imaginative stories can help children cope with the emotional and psychological problems. Hence, coming to terms with trauma through fairy tales does not seem an anomalous concept.

Popular Culture, or pop culture, carries a tag of lively informality but also a sense of the trivial. For the longest time, fairy tales have also been trivialized, known to be meant only for children. Peter Arnds writes that in 1945 "the Allied Forces briefly banned the publication of the Grimm's tales in Germany because they associated the horrors expressed in many a fairy tale with violence in the death camps" (423). Fairy tales clearly have an impact strong enough to unsettle and also provide a rich scope of writing back—these German fairy tales are adapted by the Jews (Jane Yolen herself has Jewish origins) into popular Holocaust narratives, where the antagonists are the Germans.

Using Popular Culture to depict the Holocaust, thus, opens it up to a wider audience. Alan Mintz comments upon "the pivotal role of popular culture in spreading awareness of the Holocaust from the Jewish community to the larger American nation" (x). It is also an effective tool when it comes to children or young adults, who get introduced to the concept of the Holocaust through fiction. Anything more realistic would be unfit for their ears and can be introduced at a later stage. However, the optimistic and unrealistic "happy" endings at the end of the stories tend to give the children/young adults an inaccurate picture of the Holocaust. Following Anne

Roth, one could say these generate the ethical dilemma of "the transformation of the pain of others into bestselling mass media commodities" (8). They spell out the message of hope rather than despair.

Blending something as horrific as the Holocaust with something as dreamy as a fairy tale is apparently incongruous, but I have tried to show the various ways in which they are not. A fairy tale can become as horrific as a Holocaust tale with a simple change in the ending—if the prince had not come on time for Sleeping Beauty (which actually happens in an adaptation of the tale, titled "Stronger than Time" by Patricia C. Wrede) or if Gretel had failed to kill the witch, then the fate of the protagonists would have been tragic. On the other hand, the cathartic conclusions that Jane Yolen accommodates in her Holocaust novels make them akin to the fairy tales' "happy-ever-after" endings. The generations that came after the survivors of the Holocaust and their unfamiliarity with the experience are proof that the Holocaust has, in itself, become a kind of dark fairy tale, to be handed down from one generation to the next in the form of stories. All the three novels that I have discussed have fictitious and ambitiously optimistic endings. Unlike Hannah, there was no hope for the Jews to time travel to a better time. No woman could escape Chelmno alive. Gittel's revolt and killing of the doctor inside the camp without any repercussions, sound almost fantastic. As Yolen herself admits in her note to *Mapping the Bones*,

> In the actual Holocaust of World War II, there were many real stories. The vast majority of them did not have a happy ending. Or even a semi-happy ending. Over six million of those Jewish stories ended in brutality, humiliation, torture, starvation and death. But, sometimes, in a novel, the author can save a few lives, can choose who makes it to the end.
>
> (417)

Nevertheless, there were people who did survive those hellish camps. The fact that they could again lead normal lives and start a family was nothing short of a fairy tale for them, as Chaim Abromowitz puts it eloquently in *Mapping the Bones*—

> Think of it: my child's hand in mine
> as she sleeps without fear,
> knowing nightmares always become day.
> This is the true miracle.
> The only one.
>
> (Yolen, *Mapping* 413)

Works Cited

Arnds, Peter. "On the awful German fairy tale: Breaking taboos in representations of Nazi euthanasia and the Holocaust in Günter Grass's 'Die Blechtrommel,' Edgar Hilsenrath's 'Der Nazi & der Friseur,' and Anselm Kiefer's visual art." *German Quarterly*, vol. 75, no. 4, 2002, pp. 422–439.

Baer, Elizabeth R. "A postmodern fairy tale of the Holocaust: Jane Yolen's "Briar Rose." *Studies in American Jewish Literature*, vol. 24, 2005, pp. 145–152.

Basile, Giambattista. *Stories from the Pentamerone*. *Projeect Gutenberg*, www.gutenberg. org/files/2198/2198-h/2198-h.htm. Accessed 4 Dec. 2021.

Bettelheim, Bruno. *The Uses of Enchantment: The Meaning and Importance*. Vintage Books, 1989.

Caruth, Cathy. "Trauma and experience." In *The Holocaust: Theoretical Readings*, edited by Neil Levi and Michael Rothberg. Rutgers University Press, 2003, pp. 192–198.

Cole, Tim. *Images of the Holocaust: The Myth of the 'Shoah Business.'* Duckworth, 1999.

Felman, Shoshana and Dori Laub. *Testimony: Crises of Witnessing in Literature, Psychoanalysis and History*. Routledge, 1992.

Franklin, Ruth. "How should children's books deal with the holocaust." *The New Yorker*, www.newyorker.com/magazine/2018/07/23/how-should-childrens-books-deal-with-the-holocaust. Accessed 4 Dec. 2021.

Frischer, Rita Berman. "Jane Yolen." *Jewish Women's Archive*, https://jwa.org/encyclopedia/article/yolen-jane. Accessed 4 Dec. 2021.

Goldstein, Lisa. "Breadcrumbs and stones." In *Snow White, Blood Red*, edited by Terri Windling and Ellen Datlow. EOS, 2000, pp. 388–406.

Granville, Eliza. *Gretel and the Dark*. Penguin, 2014.

Grimm, Jacob and Wilhelm Grimm. "Rose-Bud." In *Grimms' Fairy Tales*. Penguin, 1996, pp. 48–51.

Hunter, Anna. "Tales from over there: The uses and meanings of fairy-tales in contemporary Holocaust narrative." *Modernism/Modernity*, vol. 20, no. 1, 2013, pp. 59–75.

Kimmel, Eric A. "Confronting the ovens: The Holocaust and juvenile fiction." *The Horn Book*, www.hbook.com/?detailStory=confronting-ovens-holocaust-juvenile-fiction. Accessed 4 Dec. 2021.

Lang, Andrew, editor. "Hansel and Gretel." In *The Blue Fairy Book*. Dover, 1965, pp. 251–259.

Lasner, Phyllis and Danny M. Cohen. "Magical transports and transformations: The lessons of children's Holocaust fiction." *Studies in American Jewish Literature*, vol. 33, no. 2, 2014, pp. 167–185.

Mark, Sabrina Orah. "Cracked fairy tales and the Holocaust." *The Paris Review*, www.theparisreview.org/blog/2018/10/08/cracked-fairytales-and-the-holocaust/. Accessed 4 Dec. 2021.

Martinez-Alfaro, Maria Jesus. "The estrangement effect in three Holocaust narratives: Defamiliarising victims, perpetrators and the Fairy-Tale genre." *Journal of the Spanish Association of Anglo-American Studies*, vol. 42, no. 1, 2020, pp. 37–56.

Mintz, Alan. *Popular Culture and the Shaping of Holocaust Memory in America*. University of Washington Press, 2001.

Ozick, Cynthia. "Who owns Anne Frank." *The New Yorker*, www.newyorker.com/magazine/1997/10/06/who-owns-anne-frank. Accessed 4 Dec. 2021.

Perrault, Charles. "The Fairy Tales of Charles Perrault (George G. Harrap and Co. Ltd., 1922)." *Project Gutenberg*, www.gutenberg.org/cache/epub/29021/pg29021-images.html. Accessed 4 Dec. 2021.

Roth, Anne. *Popular Trauma Culture: Selling the Pain of Others in the Mass Media*. Rutgers University Press, 2011.

Sanyal, Debarati. *Memory and Complicity: Migrations of Holocaust Remembrance*. Fordham University Press, 2015.

Schönfelder, Christa. *Wound and Words: Childhood and Family Trauma in Romantic and Postmodern Fiction*. Transcript, 2013.

Tatar, Maria, editor. *The Classical Fairy Tales*. Norton, 1998.

Weil, Ellen R. "The door to Lilith's cave: Memory and imagination in Jane Yolen's Holocaust novels." *Journal of the Fantastic in the Arts*, vol. 5, no. 2, 1993, pp. 90–104.

Williams, Raymond. *Keywords: A Vocabulary of Culture and Society*. Fontana Press, 1976.

Windling, Terri and Ellen Datlow, editors. *Black Thorn, White Rose*. William Morrow & Co., 1994.

Yolen, Jane. "An experimental act." *The Ethical Spectacle*, www.spectacle.org/396/scifi/exper.html. Accessed 4 Dec. 2021.

———. *Briar Rose*. Tor, 1992.

———. "From Andersen on: Fairy Tales tell our lives." *Marvels & Tales*, vol. 20, no. 2, 2006, pp. 238–48.

———. "If the muse comes calling: Jane Yolen on writing." *Jewish Book Council*, www.jewishbookcouncil.org/pb-daily/if-the-muse-comes-calling-jane-yolen-on-writing. Accessed 4 Dec. 2021.

———. *Mapping the Bones*. Philomel Books, 2018.

———. *The Devil's Arithmetic*. Puffin Books, 1990.

Zipes, Jack. "Breaking the magic spell: Politics and the Fairy Tale." *New German Critique*, no. 6, 1975, pp. 116–135.

14 Retelling the Holocaust With Children

A Pedagogic Study of Stephen King's *Apt Pupil* and Jane Yolen's *The Devil's Arithmetic*

Diganta Ray

"Whoever listens to a witness, becomes a witness," Elie Wiesel commented at the International Conference on "The Legacy of Holocaust Survivors" at Yad Vashem's Valley of the Communities in April 2002 (Wiesel). Wiesel raises two important questions at this conference. First, who will be the last survivor of the Holocaust to retell the stories that keep the memories of the struggle of the Jews alive? And second, what does one do with that memory of violence, and in what context does s/he apply that knowledge? Wiesel's remarks highlight the importance of retelling the Holocaust narrative across generations in order to historicize the Jewish identity. However, issues about retelling and remembrance become problematized as we rethink the question of passing down the memory of torture and suffering to the children of the Holocaust survivors. It is frequently observed that the children of the survivors transpose themselves to their parents' past in order to compensate for their losses, thus living a double life, both in the past and the present (Karpf 9). The issue becomes even more complicated as we move to the second generation who, as Erin McGlothlin notes in his book *Second-Generation Holocaust Literature*, do not have a direct, lived experience of the Holocaust, but whose identity is constantly inflected by the narratives of trauma passed down to them (1–3) This chapter will study this idea of legacy and rupture in Stephen King's novella *Apt Pupil* and Jane Yolen's historical novel *The Devil's Arithmetic*. As the title of the chapter suggests, my central argument is that it is essential to retell the Holocaust narrative *with* children and not just *to* them. I will analyze the pedagogic differences between the two approaches, arguing that the former strategy not only focuses on retelling the narrative of violence but also closely monitors how the children comprehend and register such information and how they utilize that historical knowledge in their own lives.

At the outset, it is essential to observe how *Apt Pupil* and *The Devil's Arithmetic*, as popular fiction, question or subvert the idea that the association of the "popular" with the mass entertainment industry inevitably leads to the creation of a repetitive, commercialized formula that cannot form a part of "respectable" literature. Although any form of popular literature is always tied to the means of production and the chain of distribution through which it travels, I wish to borrow Raymond Williams's understanding of the term "popular" in order to redefine the paradigm against which the discussion of the Holocaust in popular imagination will be

DOI: 10.4324/9781003251224-18

carried out. In *Keywords,* Williams observes that apart from the modern meaning of being "well-liked by many people," the word has always had a political connotation, signifying, for example, a system of governance "belonging to the people" and constituted by them. He also further emphasizes that Popular Culture, in the modern sense, also includes cultural elements created by the people for themselves (Williams 198–199). This renewed understanding of the popular as a dynamic process of cultural formation makes it a site of intense power struggles among the different communities wherein the racial, class, or gender identity of the mass is formed. Therefore, despite following the narrative conventions of the genre as popular fiction, *Apt Pupil* and *The Devil's Arithmetic* do not simply reiterate the dictates of the dominant discourse of the society. Rather, they offer an accessible narrative space wherein the existing social structures and political systems can be questioned, challenged, broken down, and reconstituted. The theorization of the popular as a subversive tool to deconstruct existing knowledge structures radically alters our understanding of the Holocaust in popular fiction. This is because any engagement with the politics of violence within this new idea of the popular as a site of power leads the characters and the readers alike to break through the fictive space and question the mechanisms of culture creation.

Post-truth politics has repeatedly tried to deny, erase, and suppress the memory of the Holocaust as a factually solid and historically specific event. Dismissing the testimonies and documents of the victims, the deniers distort facts, mix truths with convoluted lies, and deliberately disorient the common people to prevent them from understanding the true horrors of the Holocaust. Deborah E. Lipstadt, for example, shows how some of the instructors in educational institutions misguide students with a revisionist model of history, in which Holocaust denial is presented as the "other side" of the story (Lipstadt 12). This attempt to create a false balance not only supports the neo-Nazi political propaganda but also demeans the struggle of the survivors and blinds the students from seeing the actual damage caused by fascist, totalitarian regimes. In the post-truth world where facts and political realities are consciously relegated to a secondary status, it becomes imperative that the pedagogical structures of our society incorporate and situate the Holocaust within its historically accurate context. Therefore, in order to gain a full understanding of this historical tragedy, one has to deconstruct the larger forms of systemic violence against the Jews and the other antisemetic policies designed to oppress them. Michael Gray, for instance, argues that while the study of Auschwitz is crucial to the study of the Holocaust, the curricula for instruction should also focus on other transit camps like Westerbork, where Jews were holed up before being sent to the concentration camps, or on camps like Drancy and Dachau, all of which were significantly different from each other. Furthermore, he suggests that even before the Final Solution was conceived, the Nazis had set up ghettos for Jews in Poland from 1939 onwards and conducted mass shootings of the Jews in the Baltic States, Ukraine, Russia, and other parts of the East (Gray 20–21). Teaching the Holocaust without addressing this larger issue of racial oppression and systemic violence delimits the scope and relevance of the tragedy and situates it in a distant chronological past. Without any

204   *Diganta Ray*

knowledge of this deep-rooted racial politics, the persecution of the Jews will be reduced to a mindless act of violence, whose implications would be oblivious to the students. In *Apt Pupil*, for example, when Todd Bowden sadistically pressures the Nazi veteran Kurt Dussander to tell him the violent details of the camps, he seems unaware of the historic potency of these records of violence; to him, they are mere tales of torture—"the gooshy stuff" (King 159)—in which he takes delight. By dissociating the trauma of the Holocaust from its historic base, Todd fails to see the underlying threat to identity and selfhood caused by this brutal act of racial violence. Similarly, Hannah, in *The Devil's Arithmetic*, fails to grasp the significance of the identification number tattooed on Grandpa Will's arm at the camp and tries to replicate it on her own arms. It is, therefore, misleading to see the Holocaust as an act of mindless and random violence. As Goldhagen argues, "The perpetrators were not automatons or puppets but individuals who had beliefs and values about the wisdom of the regime's policies which informed the choices that these individuals, alone and together, made" (Goldhagen, "A Reply to My Critics" 4). In his book *Hitler's Willing Executioners*, he attributes the cause of this historical genocide to the prevalence of eliminationist antisemetism in Germany, which convinced the people that the Jewish Germans were different from the non-Jewish German and that there existed a "Jewish Problem" which needed to be "solved." Goldhagen observes that the belief in the eliminationist standpoint had grown so powerful that people no longer questioned the verifiability of this notion but merely worried about the nature of the "solution" (Goldhagen, *Hitler's Willing Executioners* 80–81). Therefore, an understanding of the sociological position of the Jews is important in any pedagogical formulation of the Holocaust. Todd, blinded by the spectacle of violence, fails to gain this understanding, while Hannah, despite her Jewish identity, remains unaware of it until she is magically transported to a Polish village in 1942 and forced to be a survivor and witness herself.

In the building of the structure of Holocaust education three crucial factors are involved—the training and ability of the teacher to deal with the subject, the mode of teaching followed while diffusing information, and the nature and extent of the students' receptivity to such knowledge. While studying Jane Yolen's *The Devil's Arithmetic* and Stephen King's *Apt Pupil,* it is essential to analyze the characters as willing or unwilling agents who educate and create an impact, positive or negative, on the lives of the children, Hannah Stern and Todd respectively. The first obstacle faced by anyone broaching the subject is the sheer incomprehensibility that characterizes the barbarity of the act and the emotional costs of reading through it (Schilling 3–4). Even the hardened Nazi veteran Dussander is reluctant to remember and reiterate the details of the event, fearing that the nightmares would occur again. At the same time, the fact that Todd receives an A-plus on his research paper on the Holocaust shows how the subject has gradually moved on the path to "normalization," entering the mainstream of historical research and understanding (Marrus 14). This "normalization," however, has a schizophrenic dichotomy at its core. On the one hand, it can be a positive step toward integrating the historical knowledge of the oppression of Jews within the learning experience of future generations, thus

Retelling the Holocaust With Children 205

keeping the memory of their struggle alive. On the other hand, "normalization" can also mean that there is a blatant dehumanizing of the victims and their suffering by making it a mere "topic" of history. As Todd says:

> You have to write that stuff in a certain way. You got to be careful. . . . Oh yeah. All those library books, they read a certain way. Like the guys who wrote them got puking sick over what they were writing about. . . . They all write like they lost a lot of sleep over it. How we've got to be careful so nothin like that ever happens again. I made my paper like that, and I guess the teacher gave me an A 'cause I read the source material without losing my lunch.
>
> (King 151)

Todd, therefore, sees the disgust of the scholars who write about the Holocaust and the tone of ominousness that the horrific incident inspires in their works as just another academic style of writing, which he pretends to follow to raise his grades. One of the fears of including the Holocaust as a part of a teaching curriculum is that by deriving educational lessons from it there is a risk of explaining it away from the classroom perspective, in accordance with the students' perceptive capabilities. This, in turn, will diminish its importance and desensitize the children toward such historical violence. They would begin to accept it as yet another form of human social behavior instead of questioning the horrors of human history and why they took place (Schatzker 221). Thus, without any humanitarian motive, Todd's apparently harmless research into the history of the Holocaust eventually leads him down to a path of psychopathic murders of homeless vagrants. On the other hand, Dussander, too, "normalizes" and desensitizes Todd toward the horrors of the Holocaust further by indirectly comparing it to other atrocities committed by the American government. The attempt to muffle the severity of the torture carried out on the Jews by comparing it to other incidents of violence committed during the war has been a common strategy among several Hitler apologists. Although it is important to situate the Holocaust within its historic context, any attempt to "normalize" it by comparing it to atrocities committed elsewhere is a mere ploy to diminish one's sense of guilt and responsibility (Fulbrook 316). Dussander's frequent nightmare of "the restless dead" coming after him and pulling him down shows that despite his attempt to explain away the genocide as just another part of the war, he is haunted and hunted by a deep sense of guilt (King 197). Unfortunately, by trying to accommodate that violence into their lives as something common, Todd and Dussander adopt homicide as a psychological defense mechanism. In order to circumvent Dussander's toxic negation of history and Todd's psychopathic normalization of violence, it is essential to engage with the Holocaust in a more emotional and personal manner, as we will see later in Yolen's text.

For Todd and Dussander, the reality of the Holocaust has been erased and supplanted by a hollow image. When the boy first enters Dussander's room, for instance, he feels disappointed because it does not have any portraits of Hitler, medals, swords, or firearms hanging from the wall as he saw in the movies and on

206   *Diganta Ray*

TV (King 141–142). His lack of emotional involvement with the historical tragedy can, therefore, be understood as an outcome of the bombardment of sensationalized images through media, which fail to cultivate a culture of sensitivity among people. By trivializing the horror of the genocide, Todd has turned the "conspiracy of silence" into a "conspiracy of banality" (Schatzker 221). Forcing Dussander to remember and reiterate the records of violent, oppressive history, he has reduced the social and political struggle of the Jews to a meaningless sequence of death. There is, however, a stark reversal of power when he mistakes the SS uniform to be a mere image and reflection of the spectacle of the war. The Nazi uniform, which he gives to Dussander to wear, is not a mere image but a symbol; and as a symbol, it wields a power greater than Todd can comprehend or control. Once the hardened veteran starts marching in his uniform, not only does Todd get frightened and lose a part of the control he exercised on the man, but also the physical horror of it becomes a tangible reality accessible to him:

> For the first time the corpses in the ditches and the crematoriums seemed to take on their own reality for Todd. The photographs of the tangled arms and legs and torsos, fishbelly white in the cold spring rains of Germany, were not something staged like a scene in a horror film . . . but simply a real fact, stupendous and inexplicable and evil.
>
> (King 180)

The power imbalance in the second half of the story is not brought about by Dussander blackmailing Todd into studying so that their secrets are safe but by the symbolical force of the SS uniform that textures their nightmares and actualizes the horrors of the past before them. *The Devil's Arithmetic,* too, brings out the importance of historicizing the contemporaneity of the Holocaust (Snyder, *Black Earth* xv) and understands that "the further we get away from it, the more the Holocaust turns into a symbol which constitutes a reality in our lives and influences our consciousness and reactions in times of crisis, perplexity, and desolation" (Schatzker 219–220). Near the beginning of the novel, as Hannah goes to attend the family Passover gathering, she displays the same ignorance toward the suffering endured by the previous generations of her community, as Todd does in his "research." For Hannah, as she herself tells her mother, "It's all in the past" (King 9). There is, thus, a deep chasm in historical understanding that hinders the first-generation survivors from passing over the knowledge of the Holocaust to their future generations. There are two issues involved in the pedagogic transmission of this information from one generation to the next—the chronological disconnect between the survivors of the past and the current generation and the ethical issue of transferring the painful knowledge of systemic violence to the people who may not have developed adequate intellectual or emotional mechanisms for comprehending it. The first problem is that until Hannah is forced to live through the event herself, she is unable to rationally transpose the suffering and struggle of her community onto the experiences of her daily life. Once she is transported to the past as Chaya, she meets Rivka in the concentration camp who teaches her the tricks of survival and

Retelling the Holocaust With Children   207

the importance of retaining their humanity. When Rivka is about to be sent to the gas chamber, Chaya sacrifices her life for her so that she can live on to remember and recount the past. As Hannah once again returns to the present, she realizes that Rivka is her Aunt Eva and Chaya her dead friend. This overlapping of the past and the present brought about by the fusion of the lives of Chaya and Hannah leads to the creation of an affective history that can easily travel through the communal cultural memory. The pedagogical approach of *The Devil's Arithmetic*, therefore, significantly differs from that of *Apt Pupil* in the way history is revisited. In King's novella, Todd's attempt to recreate the war experience by making Dussander march creates a partial and skewed simulation of history, just like Dussander does by putting the cat in the oven which sounds "almost like a young boy" (King 201). Even before the Nazi veteran's narrative downplays the voice of the victims, Todd himself dehumanizes them by treating them like lifeless meat: " 'Today I want to hear about the gas ovens,' Todd said. 'How you baked the Jews'" (King 165). Hannah's affective engagement with history is efficient in challenging this erasure of identity and selfhood, which such narratives of violence bring about.

The use of magic realism in *The Devil's Arithmetic* also highlights how Yolen diegetically weaves in the problem of comprehending and communicating the knowledge of the Holocaust to future generations. The fact that Hannah has to be transported back to the horrific past in order to understand the gravity of history proves that the ordinary epistemological tools of reality, and thereby of realist fiction, are inadequate when it comes to the question of passing the Jewish legacy and the memory of the Holocaust to later generations. Even language breaks down in the face of the disastrous consequences brought about by this tragedy. This linguistic failure to capture the psychological trauma is evident in the scene where Gitl stares in disbelief at the dead body of the little child Tzipporah who died of starvation: "Yitzchak . . . what will I say . . . Tzipporah . . . he must be told . . . what can I . . . *monsters*" (Yolen 106). The elliptic outburst of Gitl, ending with a fierce denunciation of the barbarity of the oppressors demonstrates how any coherence of thought and action has been shattered by the bluntness of the trauma. In such a context, the magic realist technique promotes a pluralistic view of history prioritizing marginal voices over dominant realities (Adams 13). By tracing Chaya's narrative of resilience over Hannah's modern narrative, Yolen builds a multinodal perspective that leads to a subjective rather than factual understanding of the Holocaust for Hannah. At the beginning of the novel, Hannah and Aaron steal the afikomen of the Passover and hide it, as the adults pretend that they are unaware of the place Aaron was hiding with it (Yolen 16). In a perverted reflection of this scene, later in the story, Hannah learns in the concentration camp that though the children undressed and hid in the garbage pile, the commandant was as much aware of their presence as the guards were (Yolen 123). Apparently, it seems as if the harmless custom of hiding with the afikomen, which Hannah and her brother followed, has been deliberately written over with this life-threatening situation of Chaya's narrative. The purpose of using magic realism in this context is not to fragment reality into two inverted halves that are disjointed from each other but to show how the past and the present constantly intermingle with each other in the cognitive map of the victims.

208   *Diganta Ray*

By transposing Chaya's experiences onto Hannah's life, Yolen does not erase or suppress the latter's identity. Rather she forges a dialogic relationship between the past and the present that stimulates the idea of resistance in Hannah's mind. When Hannah/Chaya chooses to pick up the baby and run into the garbage pile when the commandant arrives or when she sacrifices her life to save Rivka, she is neither a passive victim nor a passive learner to whom the legacy of the Holocaust is blindly handed over. She becomes, instead, a moral agent whose choices influence the way history is written as much as it determines her own identity. Remembering the Holocaust, therefore, must be accompanied by an assertion of this idea of Jewish resistance. Be it Shmuel's attempt to escape from the camp, Rivka's clever mnemonic that converts the dehumanizing number on her arm into a meaningful symbol, or Gitl's charity organization that unites the survivors with their family members, *The Devil's Arithmetic* shows how any narrative that fails to take into account the subversive moral will of those living in the camps and their resistance against the oppressors implicitly participates in the same violent erasure of the Jewish identity at an intellectual level. Once Hannah has completed living through Chaya's life, her selfhood is mapped onto a palimpsest of communal history defined not only by the collective trauma but also by the collective will to survive.

Pedagogically speaking, while (re)envisioning/revisioning human history, it is essential to make the future generations understand their moral freedom and moral responsibility, which empower them with an agency of their own. Hannah learns her position as an active participant within the Holocaust narrative through her interactions with Rivka, who helps others to survive in the concentration camp despite being under duress herself. As Leonard Grob observes:

> We must educate-toward-rescue, I argued. The witness of rescuers can open a clearing within which the young can envision an open moral horizon for their future acts. No longer bound by Freudian and Hobbesian determinist notions of the primacy of self-interest in our conduct, our children and our students can be empowered to see themselves as genuine moral agents. The behavior of rescuers, I argued, is not, as it is often deemed, "heroic"; it is as ordinary—and thus accessible—as are acts of cowardice or silent complicity in the face of evil.
>
> (Grob 85)

In the context of the Holocaust, compassion is not just an emotional state or a sociological construct based on humanitarian principles; it is an ontological truth that reinstates world order by breaking the cult of violence. Even before Hannah experiences the life of Chaya and develops a fresh understanding of Aunt Eva's life, she had felt a connection with her during the family gathering. This preconscious bond that binds Hannah and Aunt Eva hints at the fact that the relationship between the survivors is based on more than a cultural epistemological base; it is forged by the instinctive desire to empathize and help the community to survive as a whole. The "education" of Hannah is completed only when the cultural knowledge of Jewish tragedy is complemented by a solicitude toward the victims and an eagerness to alleviate the same. The politics of compassion, as we will see, is the only viable answer to the exclusionary politics that characterized the Nazi regime's megalomaniac exercise of authority. Being politically compassionate is different from practicing the same virtue at an individual level. It requires one to overcome one's ignorance about history and to actively engage with systems that perpetuate violence at a global level. This means that one has to be aware not only of oppressive structures of power within one's limited geographical and temporal space but across the geopolitical and politico-temporal network. Hannah's relocation to the Polish village in 1941 is significant because it breaks this spatiotemporal understanding of history. Similarly, in Louise Murphy's *The True Story of Hansel and Gretel*, Magda, who is herself socially outcast as a "witch," helps Hansel and Gretel to survive by providing them with a shelter and hiding them in the oven when a Nazi officer comes and takes her away to be killed (Murphy 237).

The pedagogical objective of teaching about the Holocaust, formally or informally, should, therefore, be to excite the moral imagination of the current generation to break the barrier between the Self and the Other. The politics of compassion is beneficial in this context because it follows the logic of the Self-in-excess. That is to say, it is based on the principle that selfhood is not restricted to one's body, community, or nationhood but overflows into other people, ethnic groups, and nationalities. This centrifugal expansion of the Self breaks down the hierarchy of "us" and "them," which is effective in combating the supremacist notions that lead to the Holocaust in the first place. It also implies that all emotional, social, or economic resources accrued by an individual are shareable with others beyond the economy of exchange. When Rivka, for instance, is able to "organize" shoes, sweaters, and other items, she does not hoard them for herself but distributes them to the likes of Chaya (Yolen 115). Similarly, Chaya saves the softer parts of the bread from her own meal for Yitzhak's son until Gitl discovers it and hands over her own share to the little boy (Yolen 125–126). By handing down one's own resources to the other for survival, Rivka, Chaya, and Gitl create a shared identity that is much more inclusive than the polarized identity promoted by the Nazis. Hannah's educational curve, involving her experiences as Chaya, justify the importance of empathy along with critical thinking in learning about the Holocaust (Hilton and Patt 9). The great "visceral" impact that the knowledge of the Holocaust has on the later generations (Tinberg and Weisberger 2) means that there is an ethical conundrum involved in passing over this legacy to children. On the one hand, the shock of violence can affect and permanently alter the psychological configuration of the child, as it does in the case of Todd. But on the other hand, the emotional potency of this knowledge also implies that with the right tools and guidance, the children are able to understand the immediacy of the Holocaust—that demands a constant ethical engagement—as much as they understand its historic past. As opposed to the politics of compassion, which leads to the flourishing of selfhood, fascism is entropic; it ends with the destruction of the fascist self (Finchelstein 67). Todd's attempt to reclaim control over his life by killing the vagrants—like zur Linde's ideological self-determination through violence in Borges' "Deutsches Requiem" (Finchelstein 57)—only hastens the annihilation of his rational self. When his guidance

210 Diganta Ray

counselor confronts him about Dussander, he does not kill him and run away but, as is suggested, goes on to shoot random people by the freeway with his rifle until he is captured by the authorities. Todd's use of violence has, thus, deadened even his instinct of self-preservation, making him his own victim. Although both Todd and the senile Dussander we meet lack the ideological fervor of zur Linde, they share the same fate of self-destruction.

In our final analysis, we will try to understand how certain non-diegetic elements, relating to the status of *Apt Pupil* and *The Devil's Arithmetic* as popular fiction, influence the way the legacy of the Holocaust is constructed and passed on. Anne Rothe notes how the American popular imagination has exploited Holocaust narratives to create a model of modern-day heroism where the metamorphosis from a victim to a survivor is the most crucial accomplishment. By making it a tale of redemption, popular trauma culture created a sentimental story through which the pain of the oppressed could be comfortably packaged and sold to the mass (Rothe 8). However, from the 1970s with works like Marvin Chomsky's TV series *The Holocaust* and William Styron's *Sophie's Choice*, the conventional tone of Hollywood happy ending present in most of the early popular films was replaced by a much more grim, although more realistic, and complex depiction of the life of the victims during the genocide (McDonough 90–92). In *Apt Pupil*, the taut suspense of whether Dussander and Todd will be caught becomes the primary narrative thrust that keeps the readers engaged. Once Dussander commits suicide on realizing that his identity has been revealed and Todd is apprehended for his crimes, the narrative comes to a sudden closure. The fact that the education system's failure to impart the knowledge of the Holocaust in a proper manner created a monster out of Todd is not addressed. Dussander and Todd become mere "villains" whose defeat will return order and peace to the world. It is, therefore, important to highlight how Todd's learning creates a version of history that "entertains" and invites him to play with the past, in ways that gratify his curiosity of knowing how it was to live in those times from the perspective of the perpetrator (Eppert 74). However, it is this omission of the pedagogic relevance of studying the Holocaust as a failure of humanistic sympathy that generates the critical need for addressing the relationship between popular fiction and history. Alan Mintz identifies two opposing models that define Holocaust representation in popular media. The first is an exceptionalist model that recognizes the Holocaust as a singular event in history like no other that creates a chasm between the present and the past—the world before the event and the world after the event. Any faithful artistic response to the event must, therefore, be bleak and without any false uplifting outcome. The second is the constructive model that realizes that despite being an unprecedented event, the history of the Holocaust can be understood only within preexisting cultural and epistemological frameworks; therefore, any representation of the event will inevitably involve an act of appropriation wherein the Holocaust gets linked with other relatable forms of knowledge (Mintz 38–39). *The Devil's Arithmetic* debunks the idea that popular literature uses history only for its "entertainment value," thus co-opting Mintz's constructive model of representation. Hannah's engagement with the past is experiential rather than "entertaining." Unlike King's novel, there are no easy and final victories in Hannah's case. The smooth narrative transition from Chaya entering the gas chamber to Hannah coming back to the empty hall of her own house only hints at the continuity between the past and the present. This passage between the two histories, thus, opens up a psychological channel between the two chronologically distant experiences of Hannah, wherein the repressed, collective trauma of the Holocaust in the past invades Hannah's everyday reality in the present. By reliving Chaya's life, she successfully reconstitutes history rather than just remembering it. It is interesting to note that while going through Chaya's experiences, Hannah revisits the past as it has already occurred; however, the traumatic circumstances which personally involve her and require her to make independent choices as an active participant, collectively form, what Lawrence Langer calls "deep memory" (Langer 6). When Aunt Eva retells the story of their past, Hannah no longer feels disconnected from it like she did when her grandfather had gotten emotionally agitated while recollecting his deep memories of the Holocaust. The cycle of education is, thus, completed. The ethical and physical transformation of Hannah has been seen as problematic by Lassner and Cohen who believe that this adds a note of "hopefulness" to the testimony of victims, which, in reality, was inaccessible to them. They observe, "In contrast to Nazi history, magical transport suggests a narrative power that supersedes that of the Nazis and thus offers an alternative lifesaving resolution where there was neither for the actual victims" (Lassner and Cohen, 172). However, I argue, that her return should not be seen as an escape precisely because she does not forestall the torture of the gas chamber. She emerges back as a witness but only after she has passed through the experience in its entirety, including, I propose, the experience of a horrific death. Moreover, even when Hannah returns to her "normal" world where she is safe, there is a lingering sense of gloom that troubles the readers. The process of recuperating from the horrors of the Holocaust is shown to be a continuous one that takes a toll on one's sanity and sense of self; but at the same time, it is essential to acknowledge that this grief cannot be fought and done away with forever. Hannah's "magical transport" should, therefore, not be seen as a quick getaway from the horrors of reality but as a channel of communication that both burdens her with the knowledge of the suffering and empowers her to speak about them. The "optimistic" ending of *The Devil's Arithmetic* should, therefore, not be seen as a mere narrative tool that palliates the horrors of the Holocaust and mellows down the victims' or survivors' experiences. Rather, it shows that such a representation establishes a continuity between the past and the present filling up the historic divide caused by the Holocaust. It is, therefore, possible to ethically engage with the victims' and survivors' pain by acknowledging that any such understanding and representation will inevitably pass through a dense cultural medium that might alter and distort the authentic experience. However, such distortions are easily overcome, as we have already discussed, by creating an affective continuity between the past and the present.

As our study indicates, it is necessary to understand the difference between Holocaust as history and Holocaust as a pedagogical tool. In the domain of academia, the receptivity of the students and their cognitive and emotional processing power influence the way the knowledge of the genocide is historicized and passed on.

212   Diganta Ray

The distillation of information about the Holocaust should not reduce it to a curricular entity but should recognize the role it plays in altering, whether positively or negatively, the fabric of the current society. Any pedagogical framework involving the Holocaust should, therefore, have three objectives: to contextualize, to commiserate, and to contemporize. First, any discussion of the event has to judiciously examine the systemic structures of oppression that led to Jewish victimization and explain how they relate to other forms of violence. Once this sociopolitical context is established, the need to combine empathetic modes of evaluation and critical, rational ones in the study of the survivors and victims must be emphasized. Lastly, this legacy of painful knowledge must be resituated in the contemporary historic setting so that the ethical agency of the students develops out of the dialectic between the past and the present. Both *Apt Pupil* and *The Devil's Arithmetic* deal with representations of the Holocaust that reorient the understanding of suffering for the protagonists. In the former, the reenactment of the perpetrator's vision of violence transforms the testimony of suffering into a gore galore for Todd's amusement; in the latter, the testimony of Rivka, Chaya, and the others becomes a pulsating, living, open-ended tale that is willing to record and fuse all marginalized voices, past and present, and weave it into the unending yarn of history.

Works Cited

Adams, Jenni. *Magic Realism in Holocaust Literature: Troping the Traumatic Real.* Palgrave Macmillan, 2011.

Eppert, Claudia. "Entertaining history: (Un)heroic identifications, apt pupils, and an ethical imagination." *New German Critique*, no. 86, 2002, pp. 71–101.

Finchelstein, Federico. *From Fascism to Populism in History.* University of California Press, 2017.

Fulbrook, Mary. *A History of Germany 1918–2014: The Divided Nation.* Wiley Blackwell, 2015.

Goldhagen, Daniel Jonah. *Hitler's Willing Executioners: Ordinary Germans and the Holocaust.* Alfred A. Knopf, 1996.

———. "A reply to my critics: Motives, causes, and alibis." *The New Republic*, vol. 215, no. 26, 1996, pp. 37–67.

Gray, Michael. *Teaching the Holocaust: Practical Approaches for Ages 11–18.* Routledge, 2015.

Grob, Leonard. "Reflections of a Holocaust scholar/philosopher." In *Teaching about the Holocaust: Essays by College and University Teachers*, edited by Samuel Totten, Paul R. Bartrop and Steven Leonard Jacobs. Praeger, 2004, pp. 81–93.

Hilton, Laura J. and Avinoam Patt. "Introduction: The challenges and necessity of teaching the Holocaust in the twenty-first century." In *Understanding and Teaching the Holocaust*, edited by Laura J. Hilton and Avinoam Patt. University of Wisconsin Press, 2020, pp. 3–16.

Karpf, Anne. "The war after." *Jewish Quarterly*, vol. 43, no. 2, 1996, pp. 5–11.

King, Stephen. *Apt Pupil. Different Seasons.* Hodder and Stoughton, 2007, pp. 133–382.

Langer, Lawrence. *Holocaust Testimonies: The Ruins of Memory.* Yale University Press, 1991.

Lassner, Phyllis and Danny M. Cohen. "Magical transports and transformations: The lessons of children's Holocaust fiction." *Studies in American Jewish Literature*, vol. 33, no. 2, 2014, pp. 167–185.

Lipstadt, Deborah. *Denying the Holocaust: The Growing Assault on Truth and Memory*. Plume, 1994.

Marrus, Michael R. "Good history and teaching the Holocaust." In *Lessons and Legacies II: Teaching the Holocaust in a Changing World*, edited by Donald G. Schilling. Northwestern University Press, 1998, pp. 13–25.

McDonough, Frank and John Cochrane. *The Holocaust*. Palgrave Macmillan, 2008.

McGlothlin, Erin Heather. *Second-Generation Holocaust Literature: Legacies of Survival and Perpetration*. Camden House, 2006.

Mintz, Alan. *Popular Culture and the Shaping of Holocaust Memory in America*. University of Washington Press, 2001.

Murphy, Louise. *The True Story of Hansel and Gretel*. Penguin, 2003.

Rothe, Anne. *Popular Trauma Culture: Selling the Pain of Others in the Mass Media*. Rutgers University Press, 2011.

Schatzker, Chaim. "The teaching of the Holocaust: Dilemmas and considerations." *The Annals of the American Academy of Political and Social Science*, vol. 450, pp. 218–226.

Schilling, Donald G. "Introduction." In *Lessons and Legacies II: Teaching the Holocaust in a Changing World*, edited by Donald G. Schilling. Northwestern University Press, 1998, pp. 3–9.

Snyder, Timothy. *Black Earth: The Holocaust as History and Warning*. Vintage, 2016.

———. *On Tyranny: Twenty Lessons from the Twentieth Century*. Random House, 2017.

Tinberg, Howard and Ronald Weisberger. *Teaching, Learning, and the Holocaust: An Integrative Approach*. Indiana University Press, 2014.

Wiesel, Elie. "Never shall I forget that night . . .." *Yadvashem*, www.yadvashem.org/holocaust/elie-wiesel.html

Williams, Raymond. *Keywords: A Vocabulary of Culture and Society*. Routledge, 2011.

Yolen, Jane. *The Devil's Arithmetic*. Puffin Books, 1990.

15 "Is It Safe?"

Marathon Man as Holocaust Drama

Douglas C. MacLeod, Jr.

Introduction

According to John Storey, in *Cultural Theory and Popular Culture: An Introduction*, Popular Culture is: well-liked by many; the opposite of high culture; mass produced for commercial purposes and not for creative expression; a form of escapism for the masses; created by those dominant within the culture it is produced in; and, generally comes out of postmodernism (8–13). Most would agree with Storey. Indeed, Popular Culture is manufactured to placate and entertain. But what happens when something as disturbing as the Holocaust becomes part of the Popular Culture industry?

This chapter speaks to this issue, specifically focusing on John Schlesinger's gritty masterpiece *Marathon Man* (1976), a Holocaust drama situated in the American zeitgeist primarily because of its thrilling brutality rather than its subtly overt discussion about the horrors of the Final Solution. I will provide definitions and motifs associated with Hollywood Thrillers and present issues associated with cinematically representing the Holocaust. And, to help argue that *Marathon Man* is a Holocaust drama masked as a Hollywood Thriller, it is important for this essay to make correlations between several key action sequences from the film and the oral testimonies and writings from Holocaust survivors and family members—their testimony now memories of a past most of humanity hopes not to repeat but needs to learn about, whether with nonfictional or fictional narratives.

The Levy/Janeway Chase Sequence: An Introduction

"Babe" Levy (Dustin Hoffman) is constantly on the run. Levy runs to make his graduate class on time, to catch up to an attractive woman on campus; he physically attempts to run from his problematic childhood. And, on several occasions, as the film spirals into homicidal chaos, Levy must run to save himself.

In one set piece, Levy, after getting dentally tortured by the notorious Nazi Dr. Szell (Laurence Oliver), darts away from the secret agent/turncoat Janeway (William Devane) and his two henchmen. He runs through Manhattan's dark and dirty streets in the hopes of finding a savior. The mise-en-scène comprises cobblestone streets and construction sites with steaming pipes and dim emergency lights. The

DOI: 10.4324/9781003251224-19

"Is It Safe?" 215

streets are desolate while our tormented protagonist sprints through an unforgiving metropolis that normally never sleeps. He is naked from the waist up, almost emaciated, screaming into the night while Janeway, biting at Levy's heels like a rabid canine, sprints to catch up with the experienced runner. Janeway almost catches him, but Levy is stealthy and makes it up a rock mound before Janeway can capture him. Levy, by the skin of his teeth, makes it to the empty highway. But, the chase is not over. Janeway and his lackeys drive to the highway and follow our winded and exhausted protagonist until Levy has no choice but to jump from one ramp to another, risking his life for the sake of saving it.

The Levy/Janeway Chase Sequence is one of *Marathon Man*'s most stimulating moments, what Brian Davis in his early work on the subject calls a "popular stock device" (74) of the Hollywood Thriller. And yet something more is taking place: This harrowing and raw chase sequence speaks directly but subversively to the Jewish experience during World War II and to Holocaust victimization.

In *Inside the Concentration Camps: Eyewitness Accounts of Life in Hitler's Death Camps*, Thomas Whissen translates an oral history of one survivor:

> Along the way the SS guards suddenly said to us: "Run away!" You could hear German machine guns firing in our direction. Already there were some dead. The guards cried: "Go on, run, run!" We asked in which direction. The Polish Jews with their five years of experience said, "The end has come. Pray it's over." They knew the Germans' methods. I got away and hid myself in the woods under the snow. My friend and I remained there for three days and nights, while 20,000 prisoners were being gunned down with machine guns.
>
> (141)

Another survivor from Whissen's oral history, which comprises over 200 Holocaust voices, talks about how:

> One night six men succeeded in reaching the barbed-wire and began to climb over. They were spotted in the glare of the floodlights by the guards in the watchtower and surrendered on the spot. In the meantime a sentry had been alerted and, in spite of their begging and pleading, he gunned them down without batting an eye. We all witnessed the scene, which was brightly lit by floodlights.
>
> (113)

These are two testimonies of many camp victims who ran away from their potential killers, a motif of multiple Holocaust dramas.

The chase sequence is shot with muted colors and in darkness. One can barely see the outline of a spotlight and construction stacks billowing smoke; one can hear a dog barking in the distance and the sound of Levy's heavy breathing. Levy's experience is similar to that of other camp victims who arrived at the death camps that housed "screaming guards, loud noises, barking dogs, beatings, and flames from the chimneys of nearby crematoria" (Green and Kumar 104). The city becomes a

216   Douglas C. MacLeod

place of urban entrapment, a sprawling maze. While running away from his captors, Levy thinks about Abebe Bikila, the barefooted Ethiopian marathon runner who won a gold medal in the 1960 Tokyo Olympic Games and died several years earlier than the film, in 1973, after he was hit by a car and became paraplegic. According to Judith Becker, a Holocaust survivor who provided testimony in 1978 of her experience at Majdanek for the Yad Vashem Resource Center:

> Shoes are the most important thing you owned, if you owned it, in the camps because if you didn't have shoes your feet got sore and once you had sores on your feet they didn't heal. You couldn't keep up the pace and you might as well have died. You were finished.
>
> ("From the Testimony")

The Nazis would take their victims' much-needed shoes; the climate was oftentimes unforgiving, and the murderers made sure to take their preys' belongings to keep them passive. In the House of Wander at the United States Holocaust Memorial Museum in Washington D.C., viewers can see thousands of shoes piled up, dusty and smelling of fading rubber, collected from the camps; and, if viewers go to the museum's website and type in "shoes," over 2,200 matches come up, filled with stories of the barefooted and photos of leather, suede, and canvas.

The Levy/Janeway Chase Sequence is powerful not only because of its intensity but also because it uses genre bending by both being a taut example of a Hollywood Thriller as well as an accurate, creative representation of the Holocaust.

Definitions and Motifs

A popular definition of the Hollywood Thriller, coming from Filmsite.com, explains these films promoted "intense excitement, suspense, a high level of anticipation, ultra-heightened expectation, uncertainty, anxiety, and nerve-wracking tension" ("Thriller-Suspense Films"). This tension comes when the:

> main character(s) is placed in a menacing situation or mystery, or an escape or dangerous mission from which escape seems impossible. Life is threatened, usually because the principal character is unsuspecting or unknowingly involved in a dangerous or potentially deadly situation
>
> ("Thriller-Suspense Films")

There are numerous films that have these narrative tropes and would also fall outside of what would be considered the Hollywood Thriller. One thinks of Halloween (any of them), Alien (any of them), and Double Indemnity (1944), all of which have thrilling moments, but none are considered Hollywood Thrillers. So, more motifs have to be presented for any film to be categorized as such.

According to Brian Davis in his book *The Thriller*, "The most routine thriller is likely to contain something to catch the attention: a grotesque villain, a dynamic music score or perhaps an athletic chase sequence which unexpectedly starts the

"Is It Safe?" 217

pulse racing long before boredom has set in" (8). Davis's commentary adds an extra layer in that he writes about set pieces and characterizations but also how cinematic techniques gain audience attention. The Hollywood Thriller, thus, is not just based on story but on what Graeme Turner in *Film as Social Practice* calls "film language," such as the camera, lighting, sound, mise-en-scène, and editing:

> The complexity of film production makes interpretation, the active reading of a film, essential. We need to, and inevitably do, scan the frame, hypothesize about the narrative development, speculate on its possible meanings, attempt to gain some mastery over the film as it unfolds. The active process of interpretation is essential to film analysis and the pleasure the film offers.
>
> (65)

The audience is important to this equation, but so is how the film finds its audience. Turner states:

> A film needs to specify its audience, not only in its text but also in its advertising campaign; in the series of interviews and promotional performances that may surround it; in the selection of exhibition venues (if there is a choice); even in the choice of the distribution company (again if there is a choice).
>
> (98)

Thus, for a Hollywood Thriller to be generic, the production company needs to advertise it as such, the audience has to see it as such, and the film's language has to represent it as such; however, if the audience has not seen the film, the production company releases posters and trailers/previews to ensure audiences know what type of film it is. In the case of *Marathon Man*, it is more obvious than most. The poster has Dustin Hoffman staring straight at us, pointing a gun, and underneath the title it says, "A thriller." And, the trailer/preview is filled with imagery of Dustin Hoffman being thrown into bathtubs, being attacked by Sir Laurence Oliver and William Devane, along with explosions, diamonds, sinister music, and screams. Paramount Pictures spared no expense in making sure the audience was aware of the film's intensity.

In a contemporary article written by Pablo Castrillo and Pablo Echart, they speak about the subgenre, "American Political Thriller," which *Marathon Man* falls under, being still a Thriller but having a narrative that makes it different than general American Thrillers. In "Towards a Narrative Definition of the American Political Thriller Film," the standard Thriler comprises five "approaches":

1) it is a work of crime fiction or a variation of such, that tends to center on the victim of a crime as its protagonist; 2) it presents in the characters, and causes and exploits in the audience, intense emotional estates; 3) it presents a world tipped off its balance, unstable, and ambiguous; 4) such world remains, however, realistic, ordinary, and functioning according to the parameters of real life; and 5) the characters inhabiting this world encounter the extraordinary and

218   *Douglas C. MacLeod*

find themselves disoriented, having to learn how to navigate environments that are new to them.

(112)

Marathon Man falls under each of these "approaches." Fandango, a popular film reviewing website and movie ticket purchasing venue, has a very succinct summary worth presenting:

> Thomas "Babe" Levy (Dustin Hoffman) is a Columbia graduate student and long-distance runner who is oblivious to the fact that his older brother, Doc (Roy Scheider), is a government agent chasing down a Nazi war criminal (Laurence Olivier)—that is, until Doc is murdered and Babe finds himself knee-deep in a tangle of stolen gems and sadistic madmen. Even his girlfriend, Elsa (Marthe Keller), becomes a suspect as everything Babe believed to be true is suddenly turned upside down.
>
> ("Marathon Man Synopsis")

Thus, the film can be considered an American Political Thriller. In fact, *Marathon Man* is mentioned as an example of one of three narrative styles associated with American Political Thrillers called "The Challenge of Active Agency," where the protagonist is "weighed-down, isolated, and underprepared for the task at hand" and is generally hindered by "emotional baggage" (115). In *Marathon Man*, Levy "is deeply traumatized by the death of his father, who committed suicide after becoming targeted by an Anti-Communist witch-hunt in the dark years of McCarthyism" (115), which makes him unequipped for the forces chasing him.

Oftentimes, American Political Thrillers are released at a specific historical time, it is "a consequence of the political and social climate of the United States at a time full of fears associated to the various threats of Cold War scenarios" and at the heart of this type of film "lies a conflict that confronts an individual with the system, the ordinary citizen against the institutions, the human being against the inhumanity of political and/or corporate power" (120). In addition, the protagonist may succeed but may still not understand what or why the actions happened; and these films often "resort to actual events as a basis for their dramatic premises, with a greater or less degree of explicitness in their reference to those events," which involve the government, organizations, or private corporations, and many times a combination of all three (120).

The film is an adaptation of William Goldman's 1974 popular novel and was inspired by the "real-life Dr. Josef Mengele, nicknamed the 'Angel of Death,' who had conducted ghastly medical experiments on prisoners at Auschwitz-Birkenau during World War II" and an article that spoke about "Nazis who got rich stealing gold from the teeth of prisoners"; along with "the memory of a hated dentist from [Goldman's] childhood" (Bettencourt and Kaplan 1). Using real people, he created Dr. Christian Szell (the name based on the conductor George Szell, a fervent Nazi-hater and Holocaust survivor), the sadistic dentist who comes out of hiding to get

"Is It Safe?" 219

his precious diamonds (Mengele himself hid in Paraguay during the time the book was being written). Proof of these actions is regularly written about in Holocaust literature, one of the more recent stories coming out of Luneburg, Germany in 2015, where Max Eisen, an Auschwitz survivor, was a witness put on the stand against Oskar Groning, a member of the SS. Eisen was given the job of breaking gold crowns out of teeth pulled by Nazis:

> Mr. Eisen was recruited by a Polish doctor to clean the sickbay. Any inmate who could not walk after two days in the infirmary was taken by SS guards to the gas chambers, Mr. Eisen said. "Some hours after this, SS soldiers would come back with a bloody rag that was full of gold molars," he said. "I had to remove gold crowns."
>
> (Charter)

Eisen's story is connected to one of the more famous scenes in *Marathon Man*, where Szell (who menacingly and famously says, "Is it safe?") digs into Babe's gaping mouth, held tightly by Janeway's cronies, and tortures both him and the audience with the sound of the dentist's drill hitting a live tooth and its exposed nerve. The screams that come from Babe are sickening. We experience what Babe experiences, the drill coming at us at the same time as it comes for Babe, a moment that has him "manipulated, emotionally crippled" and "dehumanized" (Castrillo and Echhart 116), as are most protagonists in American Political Thrillers. We have all experienced the dentist's chair; we have all been placed in that prone position, ready but not ready to get our teeth cleaned, or pulled, or scraped, or capped, etc. We are trapped like Babe; and, we are placed in the position of Holocaust victims who experienced the pain inflicted upon them. We become like Eva Kor, one of Mengele's twins:

> After one of the injections, I became very ill with a very high fever. My arms and legs were swollen, and I had red spots all over my body. Maybe it was spotted fever; I don't know. Nobody ever diagnosed it. Mengele looked at my fever chart, laughed sarcastically, and declared, "Too bad, she's so young— she has only two weeks to live." At that time, I knew he was right: I was very ill. But I refused to die. I made a silent pledge: "I will prove Mengele wrong. I will survive, and I will be reunited with Miriam." For the next two weeks I was between life and death. I have only one memory: crawling on the barrack floor, because I no longer could walk. There was a faucet on the other end of the barrack. As I crawled, I would fade in and out of consciousness. I just kept thinking, *I must survive. I must survive.* After two weeks my fever broke, and I immediately felt a lot stronger. It took another three weeks before my fever chart showed normal and I was released from the barrack of the living dead and reunited with Miriam. That event—surviving whatever I was injected with—serves as a very big source of strength to me.
>
> ("How I Survived")

220   Douglas C. MacLeod

Based on the scenes and information presented, *Marathon Man* is an example of the Thriller, and even more specifically the American Political Thriller; and, the film resonated with audiences, grossing over $28 million in 1976, and was the 14th top grossing film that year ("Annual Movie Chart—1976"). *Marathon Man* was successful as an American genre picture, but there is more to this film than set pieces.

Genre Breaking and Genre Bending

Although many Hollywood Thrillers use generic motifs, Todd Berliner, in "The Genre Film as Booby Trap: 1970s Genre Bending and *The French Connection*," claims that 1970s American genre pictures are unique in that they are divided into two categories: "genre-breakers" and "genre-benders" (25). The genre-breaker "comment[s] on earlier movies, promoting the notion that Hollywood's standard tropes are now passe" (26) while genre-benders "rework genre conventions . . . without cracking them open," thus "exploit[ing] our habitual responses to generic conventions in order to set us up for their unconventional outcomes" (27). Berliner believes that, although used on several occasions in previous decades, the techniques of genre breaking and genre bending became prevalent in the 1970s because Hollywood conventions were "worn out" and not producing the same effect on audiences they once had. He also claims that genre breaking was a logical progression while genre bending was "not inevitable," but a good opportunity for "a skilled filmmaker . . . to exploit viewers' complacent acquiescence to cinematic tradition" (31). Using *The French Connection* (1971) as an example of the genre bending of Police-Detective Films, Berliner proves that 1970s American generic texts can be manipulative and leave the audience with "inconsistent feelings" (31); however, what happens when a film genre-bends but fulfills its generic obligations to its audience? *Marathon Man* genre-bends by using motifs associated with the Thriller (or the American Political Thriller) while manipulating them to create a Holocaust testimonial; but, rather than the film making us feel "uncomfortable or uncertain of our judgements," (31) at the end, we end up feeling that justice has been done.

Another question needs addressing: Is it ethical to represent the Holocaust using Thriller tropes such as chase sequences, techniques of suspense, a plot device where, "through some chance encounter with a world where things are really happening, where the stakes are big and life is lived at high tension, a man hunts and in turn is hunted, is trapped, caught, escapes, and finally defeats his enemy" (Harper 21), or a specialized "hero" of his/her own learning who has lonely pride, is worldly, and has a passion for action (Harper 25)? There are some, like Ilan Avisar, who claim that the acts performed on camp inmates were so atrocious it presents a problem when attempting to represent them in movies:

In summary, the issue of representing of the actual historical experience is crucial in light of the serious gap between fact and fiction, and in that respect it is connected to the broader issues of the limits of artistic mimesis.

However, in the case of Holocaust representation, the problem assumes a special dimension because of the unique character of the targeted reality whose details are fictionally bizarre and its facts often beyond belief.

(3)

Others, like Geoffrey Hartman, write that the Holocaust was so appalling it should not be represented at all, mainly due to the lack of sympathy toward, and a glorification of, the violence, torture, and tragic deaths of millions:

It is true that movie violence I see on the screen, through real-time reporting or fictional re-creation . . . the more I rediscover the wisdom of a classical poetics that limited direct representations of violence and suffering, especially on the stage, and developed instead to a powerful language of witness or indirect disclosure . . . The idiom of violence . . . will desensitize rather than shock.

("The Cinema Animal" 63–64)

Opposing writers like Avisar and Hartman are writers that believe Holocaust representation can be beneficial to the understanding of what happened during World War II. Barbie Zelizer, for instance, states:

If we are to allow popular culture its own voice in representing the past, there is one distinction that we need to reinstate. We must build again that distinction between the event-as-it-happened and the event-as-it-is-retold. And once we have done so, we need to recognize that we can never do better than the latter. In all modes of historical recounting, including traditional history, the event-as-it-is-retold is as close as we can come.

(30)

With an understanding that the depiction of the Holocaust is both accepted and frowned upon, it would be correct to suggest that *Marathon Man* is not accepted as a proper representation. If one were to use Haim Bresheeth's six category model, *Marathon Man* would be a mismatch Holocaust film that combines the Holocaust with motifs associated with the Thriller, a genre "inappropriate to a subject of such gravity" (203). This chapter suggests otherwise; the film relays the Holocaust must be represented for further study and remembrance.

The Reconstruction of Levy/The Deconstruction of Szell

Marathon Man, on the surface, uses Nazism as part of the storyline; Szell, the villain, is a Nazi. Also, the film begins with a deadly altercation/car chase through Manhattan that leads to the death of Szell's brother, who is a Nazi sympathizer spewing derogatory remarks toward a Jewish man who starts a fight with him. But, *Marathon Man* is more, and one first physically notices this when seeing Levy's pajama pants as he runs away from Janeway and his gun-thugs in the Levy/

222   *Douglas C. MacLeod*

Janeway Chase Sequence. Levy's pajama pants, although at first innocuous, are reminiscent of the pants worn by Holocaust victims working, and dying, in the concentration camps. On the book cover of *We Were in Auschwitz* is a similar image; the book is tinted in a muted blue and gray color, stripes are on both sides, and, in the front, a red triangle (to indicate what type of prisoner the person was) with a number next to it, a number that was tattooed on the victim's body. "Stripes" are defined as "camp clothing made out of special, gray-blue striped material (nettle-fiber, it was said). Well-cut, form fitting stripes were a sign of well-being, function, and self-esteem on the part of the prisoner who wore them" (Siedlecki et al. 194). "Babe" Levy did not have the same "privileges" as, what Margareta Glas-Larsson calls, the "prisoner elite" (91) of Auschwitz. Oftentimes, Babe is cinematically shot alongside or around or behind fencing, a trope connected to concentration camps; and, in the beginning of the film, he is almost attacked by an unleashed German shepherd. On the Holocaust Memorial Center website, there is an oral history by Shmuel Sosnowicz, and he claims, "German shepherd dogs were eating corpses on the streets" and workers "were delivered to the Germans every day to work on the roads and build fence posts" ("Novice"). Many of these tropes of the Final Solution are subtle as to not place Levy (a traditionally Jewish last name) into the overt role of pseudo-Holocaust survivor; instead, they are more meant to enhance the thrilling nature of the script to ensure audiences are feeling on edge, very much like how Levy feels in those chilling moments.

Currently, our discussion is about Levy, but during the film, Szell systematically gets deconstructed and ultimately becomes the victim. For example, Szell walks through the predominantly Jewish Diamond District of Manhattan, trying desperately to appraise his newly acquired diamonds. This makes Szell uncomfortable, his disorientation represented by an ominous leitmotif. Szell is in hiding and trapped by those he persecuted; he, in essence, becomes like the Jews. Robert Weltsch, a Zionist, would agree by stating Jews were forced to think that "the only important thing was not to be recognized as Jews" and "the Jews did not display their Jewishness with pride" allowing them to betray their heritage and religious beliefs (121). Going from store to store, Szell barters with several Jewish salesmen (one having a number tattooed on his wrist), but when scared that one of his prisoners may recognize him, he runs away. While chased by his victim, Szell also gets recognized by an old woman and screams for someone to get him, but no one hears her. The scene ends with the woman almost getting hit by a car and the Jewish salesman getting his throat slashed by Szell's hidden dagger. Szell gets away.

Another deconstructive moment of the film has Szell shaving his head; he is forced to become like his victims, his identity slowly being stripped away. Primo Levi, in *Survival in Auschwitz*, remembers:

Now the second act begins: Four men with razors, soap-brushes and clippers burst in; they have trousers and jackets and stripes, with a number sewn on the front . . . they catch hold of us and in a moment we find ourselves shaved and sheared. What comic faces we have without hair!

(23)

In a final moment of deconstruction, Szell is forced by Levy to swallow his diamonds one by one. "ESSEN!" Levy yells, taking the role of the victimizer. Yaffa Eliach speaks of a similar story:

> At about twelve o'clock noon, the door opened wide and into the room stormed two angels of death, S.S. men in their black uniforms, may their names be obliterated. "Noontime, time to eat bread, soup, and meat," announced the two S.S. men . . . "You must eat immediately, otherwise you will be shot on the spot" . . . Schneeweiss pulled himself to attention, looked the German directly in the eyes, and said in a very quiet tone, "We Jews do not eat today. Today is Yom Kippur, our most holy day, the Day of Atonement."
>
> (155–159)

Due to the man's insubordination, "The German took out his revolver from its holster and pointed it at Schneeweiss's temple. . . . A shot pierced the room. Schneeweiss fell. On the freshly polished floor, a puddle of blood was growing bigger and bigger" (159). Like Schneeweiss, Szell refuses to eat another diamond, and Babe figuratively kills him by throwing the diamonds into the water below. Szell, in his greed, chases after them, falls down the stairs, and stabs himself with his own knife.

Szell's deconstruction runs parallel to the reconstruction of our "hero," Babe Levy. For him to be reconstructed (or liberated), however, Levy must go through literal torture. His compulsion to exercise, the suicide of his father, the stabbing death of his brother, his being forced to become like Szell, and his interrogation, all lead to Levy's sense of satisfaction. The last scene has Levy throwing the gun he used on Szell over a chain-link fence, (a motif of entrapment in the Thriller and, at the same time, an object alluded to by many Holocaust victims), and walks off; his days of running are over. Genre bending, although used to manipulate audiences, does not leave them feeling uncomfortable but relieved that our "hero" gets vindication.

A discussion on *Marathon Man* would not be complete without an analysis of the interrogation scene between Levy, Szell, and Janeway's henchmen. In one of the most disturbing moments in cinematic history, John Schlesinger directed a scene with such blinding violence and torture it led Charles Sawyer, in an *Our Town* review, to claim it would "cut New York dental visits in half" (13). The dental torture scene also led to heated debates on cinematic violence. For example, Frank Rich wrote:

> Still heading toward an unfortunate watershed in movie violence—toward that horrifying point when we're going to be, I think completely immune to screen bloodshed—and once we reach that juncture, there's no turning back. "Marathon Man" [sic] which attempts to give gratuitous film violence a new legitimacy, is a step toward that point.
>
> (20)

224 *Douglas C. MacLeod*

In "The Violence Question," Max Lerner argues people do not become desensitized by the violence so much as rub "away the boundary between the imagined world and the real world" (39). Arguments like Rich's and Lerner's are similar to arguments raised when discussing the Holocaust representation, where theorists like Hartman claim that Holocaust films "desensitize rather than shock" (64) and others, like Barbie Zelizer, understand that the only way to represent the Holocaust is to talk about the "event-as-it-is-retold" (30).

The violence of the dental torture scene in *Marathon Man* is violating but does not desensitize audience members. Rather it forces audience members to learn about what happened during the Holocaust. Robert Jay Lifton states that "there was a constant pressure from above toward a maximum involvement in selections, particularly from the spring of 1944 when dentists and pharmacists were also ordered to take their turns on the ramp" (197) and to make selections. When selected, the prisoners were forced to open up their mouths for teeth extractions. The book *Inside the Concentration Camps: Eyewitness Accounts of Life in Hitler's Death Camps* states:

> "The exact number of gold teeth each prisoner possessed was carefully recorded in a register." . . . "They pulled out the teeth of prisoners in their search for diamonds, claiming they could easily be concealed in a hollow tooth. They also extracted crowns, but they didn't record these extractions in the register." . . . "They used tongs to pull out all my gold teeth."
>
> (Aroneanu 11)

The atrocities that are done to Babe Levy are, thus, very much like those done to Holocaust victims.

Conclusion

Sophia Marshman, in her article "Margins to the Mainstream?: Representations of the Holocaust in American Culture," makes the claim that:

> The Holocaust has become better assimilated into the public consciousness through popular fiction and the resulting films, yet the more "popular" the Holocaust becomes, the less it inspires awe. The Holocaust is thus increasingly appropriated and fiction, to a greater extent than survivor testimony, determines how the Holocaust is transmitted and remembered.
>
> (10)

Because of this, true testimonies of survivors (and those that died) may become sanitized and popularized to the point of distortion and marginalization. That argument can be made about *Marathon Man*, a film recognized more for its performances and its gore than its testimony. But, what it is remembered for is not as important as what it accomplishes. *Marathon Man* uses genre bending by both being an example of a Thriller (American Political Thriller) and an accurate representation of the

"Is It Safe?" 225

savagery of the Holocaust. Although theorists and historians feel that to represent the Holocaust as a Hollywood genre picture is tasteless, immoral, and unacceptable, without representation there can be no remembrance.

Works Cited

Annual Movie Chart—1976. *The-Numbers.com*, www.the-numbers.com/market/1976/top-grossing-movies

Aroneanu, Eugène, compiler. *Inside the Concentration Camps: Eyewitness Accounts of Life in Hitler's Death Camps* (Translated by Thomas Whissen). Praeger, 1996.

Avisar, Ilan. *Screening the Holocaust: Cinema's Images of the Unimaginable*. Indiana University Press, 1988.

Berliner, Todd. "The genre film as booby trap: 1970s genre bending and *The French Connection*." *Cinema Journal*, vol. 40, no. 3, 2001, pp. 25–46.

Bettencourt, Scott and Alexander Kaplan. "Marathon Man: Supplemental liner notes." *Filmscoremonthly.com*, www.filmscoremonthly.com/notes/fsmcd1305_notes.pdf

Bresheeth, Haim. "The great taboo broken: Reflections on the Israeli reception of *Schindler's List*." In *Spielberg's Holocaust: Critical Perspectives on Schindler's List*, edited by Yosefa Loshitzky. Indiana University Press, 1997, pp. 193–212.

Carroll, Kathleen. "The flick that ticks." *New York Daily News*, 7 Oct. 1976, p. 104.

Castrillo, Pablo and Pablo Echart. "Towards a narrative definition of the American political thriller." *Communication & Society*, vol. 28, no. 4, pp. 109–123.

Charter, David. "Auschwitz survivor: I was forced to pull gold from teeth of Jews." *Theaustralian.com.au*, www.theaustralian.com.au/world/the-times/auschwitz-survivor-i-was-forced-to-pull-gold-from-teeth-of-jews/news-story/f8ad3fd109471bf3bfdb59f195736f9d

Davis, Brian. *The Thriller: The Suspense Film from 1946*. Studio Vista/Dutton Pictureback, 1973.

Eliach, Yaffa. *Hasidic Tales of the Holocaust*. Vintage Books, 1982.

Glas-Larsson, Margareta. *I Want to Speak: The Tragedy and Banality of Survival in Terezin and Auschwitz* (edited by Gerhard Botz. Translated by Lowell A. Bangerter). Ariadne Press, 1991.

Goldman, William. *Marathon Man*. Delacorte Press, 1974.

Greene, Josh and Shiva Kumar, editors. *Witness: Voices from the Holocaust*. The Free Press, 2000.

Harper, Ralph. *The World of the Thriller*. The Press of Case Western Reserve University, 1969.

Hartman, Geoffrey D. "The cinema animal." In *Spielberg's Holocaust: Critical Perspectives on Schindler's List*, edited by Yosefa Loshitzky. Indiana University Press, 1997, pp. 61–76.

Kor, Eva. "How I survived Auschwitz's 'angel of death.'" *Vox.com*, www.vox.com/2015/3/19/8235119/auschwitz-survivor-mengele-twin

Lerner, Max. "The violence question." *New York Post*, 9 Oct. 1976, p. 39.

Levi, Primo. *Survival in Auschwitz*. Simon and Schuster, 1958.

Lifton, Robert Jay. *The Nazi Doctors: Medical Killing and the Psychology of Genocide*. Basic Books, 1986.

Marathon Man. Directed by John Schlesinger, performances by Dustin Hoffman, Laurence Oliver, Roy Scheider, and William Devane, Paramount Pictures, 1976.

"Marathon Man." *imdb.com*, www.imdb.com/title/tt0074860/

226 *Douglas C. MacLeod*

"Marathon Man Synopsis." *Fandango.com*, www.fandango.com/marathon-man-58920/movie-overview

Marshman, Sophia. "Margins to the mainstream?: Representations of the Holocaust in American culture." *www.gla.ac.uk*, www.gla.ac.uk/media/Media_41177_smxx.pdf

"Novice (Sosnowicz), Samuel (Shmuel)." *holocaustcenter.org*, www.holocaustcenter.org/visit/library-archive/oral-history-department/novice-sosnowicz-samuel-shmuel/

Rich, Frank. "From gore to bore." *New York Post*, 9 Oct. 1976, p. 20.

Sawyer, Charles. "Marathon Man." *Our Town*, 8 Oct. 1976, p. 13.

Siedlecki, Janusz Nel, Krystyn Olszewski and Tadeusz Borowski. *We Were in Auschwitz* (Translated by Alicia Nitecki). Welcome Rain Publishers, 2000.

Storey, John. *Cultural Theory and Popular Culture: An Introduction* (8th ed.). Routledge, 2018.

"Thriller-suspense films." *filmsite.org*, www.filmsite.org/thrillerfilms.html

Turner, Graeme. *Film as Social Practice* (2nd ed.). Routledge, 1993.

Weltsch, Robert. "Wear the yellow badge with pride." In *Out of the Whirlwind: A Reader of Holocaust Literature* (Revised and Expanded), edited by Albert H. Friedlander. UAHC Press, 1999, pp. 119–123.

Zelizer, Barbie. "Every once in a while: Schindler's List and the shaping of history." In *Spielberg's Holocaust: Critical Perspectives on Schindler's List*, edited by Yosefa Loshitzky. Indiana University Press, 1997, pp. 18–35.

16 Child's Play, Fantasy, and the Holocaust in *Jojo Rabbit* and *The Boy in the Striped Pajamas*

Medha Bhadra Chowdhury

Popular cinema has played a determinant role in the production of Holocaust memory. Cinema has expanded very rapidly as a technological and commercial phenomenon, stimulating public interest in the Holocaust and the lives of its victims and survivors. Films, which are a part of a visual Popular Culture, introduced a new narrative mode that enabled a wide spectrum of representations and discovered a creative language to express the interminable suffering of the Holocaust. Popular Culture when supported by digital technologies and mass media can enable greater communication, connection, and opportunities for participation. After the popular staging and film adaptations of Anne Frank's diary in the 1950s, the trauma of the Holocaust was transmitted to the public consciousness in an unprecedented way. Hollywood films intersected with the larger public sphere and enabled a broader range of reception toward the genocide. In recent times, films such as *Schindler's List* (1993), *The Last Days* (1998) and *The Pianist* (2003) have raised the Holocaust discourse to a paradigmatic status. However, when associated with Popular Culture or "pop culture" as it is often called, the Holocaust may appear to lose its solemn cultural significance. The term "Popular Culture" has evoked conflicting responses with Adorno's theory of the culture industry providing an explosive critique of the homogenization of contemporary culture owing to mass production (12). Popular Culture's relation to mainstream consumerism and forms of capitalist production has also complicated the general conception of the term. Subsequently, its definition has changed over a period of time with the emergence of Popular Culture studies as a field of academic inquiry and research, exploring the intersections of Popular Culture with a number of disciplines such as sociology, anthropology, literature, and art.

Popular Culture, when allied with these disciplines, has a broad range of intellectual and social meanings, but despite its dynamism, there are several contradictions that emerge upon analyzing aspects of Popular Culture and their relationship with the Holocaust. While it eschews notions of elitism, insisting on a democratization of culture and its consumers, the aesthetics of popular films finds it difficult to accommodate the experience of the Holocaust. Alan Mintz remarks that "the enormity of the catastrophe—what it meant for Jews and for the world that a third of the Jewish people had been murdered—simply could not be accommodated by ideas of victory and liberation, no matter what shocking facts

DOI: 10.4324/9781003251224-20

228   *Medha Bhadra Chowdhury*

may have been available by the end of the war" (5). The images of horror and brutal crimes against humanity visualized in Holocaust films typically slip from public memory with an overriding emphasis on themes of collective responsibility and forgiveness (for instance, in *Schindler's List* where Oskar Schindler is given a hero's farewell by the Jewish workers). However, the representation of the Holocaust in popular films has also caused the Holocaust to transcend the circumscribed concerns of one religious-ethnic community into the public arena as a whole, permitting the use of cultural material relating to the Holocaust to reach a global audience. Mintz argues:

> Universalization is, without doubt, the most profound and pervasive mechanism by which the Holocaust was allowed entry into American culture, at the level of popular culture especially but at more exalted levels as well. In the case of the Holocaust, the historical significance of the event is supposedly elevated by virtue of its being taken as an example or illustration of a larger rubric such as the individual's responsibility for other human beings.
>
> (99–100)

While violence in Holocaust films is constructed through a careful process of selection and ordering, which makes its representation visually and morally acceptable to a large audience, the presence of children in these narratives of violence can present even greater challenges because the evidence of an evil and monstrous horror directed toward them often lies beyond the orbit of ordinary experience and imagination and draws a heavy burden of judgment. Nancy Miller states that popular representation in Hollywood films enables audiences "to take pleasure in—or at least be comfortably moved by—the Holocaust as spectacle" (5) but the visual experience changes considerably when the child-as-victim trope comes to dominate a film narrative. Perhaps the idea of the Holocaust as a terribly disquieting and tragic event surfaces more potently through the representation of child victims, establishing a shared condition of guilt, degradation, and loss among the audience. Like the image of the girl in a red coat drifting through the Kraków ghetto pierces through the stark black and white background of Jews being loaded onto wagons in Steven Spielberg's *Schindler's List* (1993), the inclusion of children in Holocaust films sharply cuts through the collective amnesia to remind the audience of the totality of violence.

In *Jojo Rabbit* (2019) and *The Boy in the Striped Pajamas* (2008), the two films under consideration in this chapter, the trauma-laden narrative of the Holocaust is communicated through child protagonists. At the intersection of fantasy and historical representation, the films manifest the Holocaust as a part of a child's experience and capture important nuances that are often missed in films concerned with adult narratives. While the films manifest disparate dimensions of experience, the use of fantasy connects the two films, bringing them into close comparison and portraying various postures of avoidance and denial—for the protagonists, struggling to cope with stress and trauma and for the audience, grappling with the horrifying reality of children living through the genocide.

Child's Play, Fantasy, and the Holocaust 229

During the Holocaust (1933–1945), the lives of millions of Jewish and non-Jewish children were affected by the atrocities that were committed to seek the Final Solution. Jewish children, particularly, suffered persecution, deprivation, and resettlement at the hands of the Nazis and their wartime allies, but a whole generation of young people lost their childhood as a consequence of the war. Many European children of the period knew less about meadows, flowers, pets, and toys than they did about violence, hunger, and death. The harshness of everyday life could hardly be ignored as children were drawn into the conflict and suffered due to the common catastrophe. The disturbing conditions of life would have been impossible for a child to rationalize and would have no doubt contributed to mental confusion and, in extreme cases, deep psychological disorientation. The effects of trauma on children who were victims, survivors, and even perpetrators were complex, and it produced a range of manifestations. It resulted in distortions of memory; deviance from the known world; hallucinations, often bordering on fantastic and absurd creations of the mind; and, at times, a psychological regression into the past.

There is no reason to assume that children and fantasy have a natural connection, although children may be considered as certainly more capable of bridging the gap between the real and imaginary through the discursive processes of cognition. The child may develop a fantasy because he/she perceives the real world as being full of arbitrary, adult-controlled restrictions. The fantasy world provides an alternative where motivations, actions, needs, and gratifications are more uncomplicated and direct than in the desperately complex real world. Although the child's fantasy substitutes violence, pain, and discomfort with friendship, romance, and pleasure, it is not necessarily evasive or irresponsible or straightforward.

Fantasy is often built on truth, and while it may not be related to facts, there is an underlying basis of truth which is drawn from the real world, where the subject unconsciously finds fodder to feed the fantasy. Knowledge of the material world is necessary to invent another one, and fantasy is, because of its relationship to the real world, replete with meaning. While fantasy indulges in a different plane of reality, which bears a tenuous relationship with the real world, it also involves, at times, the idea of escapism from the pressures of real life. The romantic escapism into a substitute world provides shelter to the child, particularly in times of distress. Todorov argues that "it is not possible to define the fantastic in terms of opposition to the faithful reproduction of reality or in terms of opposition to naturalism. The fantastic is a particular case of the more general category of the 'ambiguous vision'" (33). It presents a different approach to reality, an alternative way of apprehending and coping with existence.

In Taika Waititi's Academy Award–winning film *Jojo Rabbit* (2019), the young protagonist, Johannes "Jojo" Betzler, is a member of the *Deutsches Jungvolk*, a separate wing of the Hitler Youth for young boys aged between 10 and 14 years. Jojo takes great pride in his calling as he prepares himself for the "best weekend ever" (3:34) at the Nazi summer training camp and flaunts his new uniform and knife. At the beginning of the film, he is seen standing in front of the mirror addressing himself, "Jojo Betzler. Ten years-old. Today, you join the ranks of the Jungvolk, in a very special training weekend. It's going to be intense. Today, you become a man" (1:02). Confronted by bullies, he desperately tries to convince his mates that he's not a "scared rabbit," (12:36) frightened by the possibility of violent action. In the process, Jojo strikes up a perplexing friendship with an imaginary Adolf Hitler, who soothes his injured ego and feelings of abandonment by providing the young boy his well-intentioned counsel: "Let me give you some really good advice. Be the rabbit. The humble bunny can outwit all of his enemies. He's brave, and sneaky, and strong" (13:17). The playful analogy with the animal world actively extends the fantasy to a reality and betrays the child's vulnerability. However, the fiction, also, enables Jojo to maneuver through the difficulties of socialization, which are typical to children of his age group, and foster a sense of self-identity.

The invented figure of Hitler is a way in which the domain of Jojo's fantasy co-incides with his reality. In fact, the surrealistic presence of Hitler in Jojo's life may be interpreted as a heightened form of reality. His friend Adolf does not inhabit a parallel universe but is intrinsically a part of Jojo's own surrounding. The Nazi ideology is sustained within Jojo's social environment through popular iconography and attitudes, and these aspects of life condition the boy's formative years. His enthusiasm is bolstered by his imaginary friend, who comically exploits Jojo's own insecurities to motivate his desire of being a "good" Nazi. Adolf reassures Jojo, "Sure, you're a little bit scrawny, and a bit unpopular, and you can't tie your shoe-laces, even though you're ten-years-old. But you're still, the bestest, most loyal little Nazi I've ever met" (1:53).

Theorists have argued that play becomes a medium through which the young child can cope with issues of competence and mastery. The make-believe or pretend play enables young children to act out situations involving mastery or competence, additionally allowing them to develop new skills or to compensate for skills they cannot yet demonstrate in the real world (Rubin et al, 65). Within the young Nazi order, the children learn an early lesson in discipline and brutality, but Jojo fails to participate in their ritual of initiation despite his unfaltering belief. This induces in him a sense of helplessness, and the emergence of an imaginary friend specifically reflects Jojo's attempts to secure a measure of his own ability and autonomy.

Jojo's encounter with the Jewish girl Elsa Korr, who has been sheltered by his mother in a secret room in their house, disrupts his happy charade with the imaginary Hitler. Elsa informs Jojo,"I'm not a ghost, Johannes. I'm something worse, but I think you already know that, don't you? You know what I am?" (25:08). Jojo, who has been fascinated by the myth of the Jewish "race" and intends to write a book about them, is thrown into a state of bewilderment as the information he seeks from Elsa illuminates a narrative of suffering and loss, eliciting a curious sense of sympathy from him. Jojo learns that Elsa is not the supernatural presence haunting their house, neither is she the symbolic "ghost" or monster that his people have vilified. The myth of Jews as "demons who love money" (37:55) is ironically undercut by Elsa's seeming "human-ness." Jojo must accommodate Elsa's identity at the cost of an Aryan dream, which has encouraged his feelings of antisemitism and which has been programmed into his mind by the Nazi rhetoric. The discovery of the Jewish girl in the attic, thus, threatens to tear apart Jojo's fantasy, which has developed through a systematic indoctrination of the Nazi agenda.

Child's Play, Fantasy, and the Holocaust 231

Together Jojo and Elsa combat repression, as well as desire, through a common narrative that is exceptional in terms of its constant play between reality and illusion. While Jojo struggles to sustain the fantasy of harmonious coexistence with a Jew in the face of his overwhelming Nazi faith, Elsa dreams of an impossible freedom which is at odds with her present situation. The two children, thus, collectively build a fantasy based on shared secrets to negotiate the cultural tensions and their obvious antipathy for each other. Their mutual engagement in a make-believe world proceeds from an uneasy, brittle peace, ultimately moving toward a final reconciliation and daring escape.

The public hanging of his mother, Rosie, who is identified as a member of the German resistance serves as the final blow to Jojo's fantasy. He runs back home and tries to stab Elsa in a fit of rage but collapses in her arms, utterly disillusioned and heartbroken. The synchronization of the scene with images of war, the devastation of the town, and Allied forces infiltrating the Nazi stronghold suspends the fantasy to focus on the practical realities of the Holocaust. The film ends decisively with Jojo's rejection of the fantasy when he kicks his imaginary friend Hitler out from the window. As Jojo and Elsa dance a sudden, awkward jig on the street, it holds the promise of a breakthrough to a new world we can only imagine. The effervescence of the ending, or what Jacob Heilbrunn suggests the "saccharine promises of redemption," (5) has been regarded as fulfilling the objectives of popular entertainment and mass consumption and, most importantly, as a contradiction to the reality of the Holocaust.

It is interesting to note the critical responses to the film in the context of the discussion on Popular Culture and the Holocaust. The parody implicit in the characterization of Hitler (reminiscent of Chaplin's *The Great Dictator*) has been regarded by a section of critics as trivializing the Holocaust, while others have found it a significant reinterpretation of the horrors associated with it through pseudo-comic art. Writing for the *New York Times*, Anthony Scott supports the former proposition in his review titled " 'Jojo Rabbit': The Third Reich Wasn't All Fun and Games." Scott remarks that the film presents an impressionistic view of evil and the pervading sense of moral goodness seems affected. The antisemitism which is depicted in *Jojo Rabbit* also appears to be "outlandish" and "Elsa's Jewishness has no real content. She exists mainly as a teaching moment for Johannes. Her plight is a chance for him to prove his bravery" (Scott). Echoing Elie Weisel's paradigmatic critique of the 1978 U.S. television miniseries *Holocaust*, in which he disapproved of the "cheapness," the emotional manipulation, and stereotyped characterization of the historical re-creation, Anthony Scott's review draws attention to the melodramatic conventions of cinema as a form of popular Holocaust representation. Henry Gonshak observes that "sentimentalizing the Holocaust in Hollywood has almost been synonymous with 'Americanizing' it" (8). The conflation of the quintessentially American rags-to-riches tale and the Christian suffering and redemption plot in Holocaust survival narratives particularly characterized Hollywood productions. The sentimentality would be encoded into these Popular Culture products at large because it enabled the transformation of the pain of others into best-selling mass media commodities.

232   *Medha Bhadra Chowdhury*

Melodramatic Holocaust-and-redemption kitsch continues to generate highly commercial media interest. Kitsch is symptomatic of mass culture, but a Popular Culture approach to kitsch rejects the distinction between high and low art forms. While critics such as Sam Binkley have argued in favor of kitsch having its own distinct aesthetic, kitsch in popular cinema can potentially reduce the complexity of Holocaust representation by relying on well-rehearsed formulas, clichés, and conventions. As Anne Rothe argues:

> As the mass media rely on melodrama's plot formula for representing victimization and suffering, the trauma kitsch ubiquitously generated in popular culture conveys a sense of comfort, because it asserts that no matter what happens—whether genocide or child abuse or lesser evils—good always wins over evil, and the world is predictable and safe.
>
> (45)

Avishai Margalit maintains that objects of kitsch can produce manipulative emotional responses, enabling and even enforcing the problematic ease with which consumers align themselves with the subject position of total innocence. Kitsch "distorts reality by turning the object (or event) represented into an object of complete innocence" (215). It significantly reduces the intricacy of human emotions to melancholy and nostalgia. The sentimentalizing of the Holocaust so rampant in Hollywood is especially regrettable because of a significant yet subtle connection between fascism and kitsch—between, that is, the irrational, emotion-laden ideologies promulgated by fascist movements and the equally emotional, intellectually simplistic appeals found in most kitschy popular art. Both fascism and kitsch mobilize feelings as opposed to intellectualism, but the quintessence of Hollywood kitsch is the "feel-good" movie, a concoction elaborately designed to tug at the audience's heartstrings. The mass media embodies the optimism of the American culture, and even Holocaust films reflect the intrinsic commercialism of Hollywood and its profit-driven compulsion to entertain. As Alan Mintz remarks, the Holocaust which Adorno had famously regarded as beyond the moral limits of artistic representation "has been admitted into the mainstream media and become the subject of profitable and high profile film and television projects" (4).

Though *Jojo Rabbit* revisits the Holocaust in ways which appeal to a mass consciousness with a fairy tale of hope and redemption, a dramatic climax, and an upbeat ending, I argue that the film cannot be derided as pop cultural trash within the critical framework of the Holocaust. While it is certainly incongruous to the grim reality recorded by historical facts and falls prey to the archetypal trope of the triumph of good over evil, the representation of the Holocaust in *Jojo Rabbit* is essentially an artistic exploration of a young boy's powerful fantasy in the wake of the catastrophic event. The tense dynamic between the reality of the Holocaust and the fantastic world of Jojo ultimately creates an exceptional verisimilitude to a child's psychological conflict and the complex mindscapes that can possibly be produced in contexts of violence and death. The alternative world which Jojo enters is a grotesque parody of the "normal," and the fantasy, at its deepest level, is

Child's Play, Fantasy, and the Holocaust 233

a tool of survival in strange circumstances. Todorov argues that the concept of the fantastic "can be defined in relation to the real" (25) and

> the hero of a narrative continually and distinctively feels the contradiction between the two worlds, that of the real and that of the fantastic, and himself amazed by the extraordinary phenomena which surround him. This extraordinary phenomenon is always a break in the acknowledged order, an irruption of the inadmissible within the changeless everyday legality. When confronted with the inexplicable, men like ourselves who inhabit the real world, experience the sentiment of fear or perplexity together with a sense of irreducible strangeness.
>
> (35)

Play or game is a significant way in which the child interprets his world, and it is artistically and respectfully used to communicate the otherwise unimaginable reality of the Holocaust. Fantasy opens up a space where the child's subjectivity coincides with a sociohistorical reality. This fantasy world often comes to be inhabited by other objects, experiences, and people that the child routinely encounters. Children's play is exciting because they put themselves in a precarious world of shared realities: theirs and what is objectively perceived. For a child, play and reality are one-and-the-same; they often fail to differentiate between the two. D.W. Winnicott, the noted child psychoanalyst, perceived child's play as "the interplay of personal psychic reality and the experience of control of actual artifacts" (47). Winnicott further argued that it is "only in playing [that] the child or adult is free to be creative and that it is creative living that makes life meaningful" (53). Without the creative impulse, meaning can disappear and life can seem worthless. In the film, the physical action of play enables the child to creatively engage with the external world and construct a framework for interpreting his experiences. They are sets of action that are meaningful to the child.

The film accommodates the child's fantasy with his view of the world and the reality of the Holocaust in many ways, though not as explicitly as one might expect. Waititi portrays the child as attempting to assimilate stories or situations to create a broad and flexible image of the living world. For instance, Jojo is fascinated by Elsa's knowledge about the affairs of their country and people. He spends hours listening to her without realizing that he is betraying his imaginary friend, Hitler. As they playfully banter with each other, Jojo hopes they can still be friends although friendship with Jews is forbidden and Elsa is his enemy. The fantastical quality of their narrative is reinforced by Waititi's cinematic technique, through the bursts of color and music. The camera pulls back in the scenes with the adults, while it lingers on the faces of the children. Waititi privileges the affective dimensions of the child protagonists and offers up the pivotal quality of their imagination in the scene where they sit huddled in a dark corner of the house dreaming vividly of the future. Despite the charges of sentimental distortion, the crucial qualification to keep in mind while watching the film is that a certain amount of historical distancing is legitimate in the context of the narrative and, perhaps, even required

234 *Medha Bhadra Chowdhury*

for an aesthetic purpose, since if one presents the Holocaust in all its unmitigated horror, one will almost surely lose the mass audience one is hoping to educate.

In Mark Herman's, *The Boy in the Striped Pajamas* (2008), adapted from John Boyne's novel of the same title, the child's play represents a fantasy bred by innocence and becomes a way of negotiating between perception and understanding in the context of the Holocaust. In the film, Bruno, the son of a high-ranking Nazi official plays a board game with a Jewish boy, Shmuel, across the barbed fence separating his father's property from the concentration camp. He believes Shmuel is one of the farm children dressed in black-striped pajamas like the adults "working" there. From the cracks of the window in his room, Bruno is able to see an enclosed place, which he believes is a farm. The "farmers" are all dressed in black-striped pajamas and work tirelessly through the day in what appears to be a most commonplace scene in the countryside. Bruno mistakes them for wearing uniforms while his parents play along to protect him from the horrifying truth.

Failing to understand the monumental historical change and the ongoing crisis of the Holocaust, the little boys impose their feelings onto the external world in order to make the bizarre conditions of their life intelligible to themselves. The two children find their present situation completely unrealizable, and the stories they tell each other provide a paradigm of meaning to their strange reality. Their forbidden friendship, with its risk of discovery, goes unnoticed, and neither Bruno's father nor his mother intercept their secret meetings by the fence. Their playground marked off both materially and metaphorically is the thin strip of land in between the two spaces: the concentration camp and the home. The boundary is the isolated, consecrated spot, sheltered from the real world, where special rules apply. The children escape from the gaze of the adults to retreat into a temporary sphere of activity. Their play space isn't disciplined and rule-based but capricious and fantastical. While it is true that their friendship grows in extraordinary circumstances, the children's game, though unbelievable, creates a narrative of mutual sympathy and cross-cultural interaction.

The children inhabit a secondary world, which is a realm of endless play and adventure, a neverland where pirates do not exist and one which precludes maturation of consciousness. The game meets their need for companionship and Bruno never discovers the reality of the concentration camp. Shmuel confesses to Bruno that he does not like the soldiers who have forcefully taken away their clothes, and Bruno reassures Shmuel that his father is not that kind: "He's an important sort in charge of making everything better for everyone" (54:41). Even Shmuel is too naïve to understand the significance of the events that occur at the concentration camp, so when Bruno asks him about the two tall chimneys which emit a foul stench, Shmuel informs him that they probably burn "lots of hay and stuff" (53:52). The Holocaust is almost like a palimpsest rendered through the film, and the horrors of the concentration camp are delayed till the end when the security of the home and the wholesomeness of the fantasy are rudely shattered through the climactic experience of being trapped in a gas chamber. *The Boy in the Striped Pajamas* ends with an apocalyptic vision of the barred doors of a gas chamber, which trap the boys in their game. The physical play assumes a moral purpose as Bruno decides to join

Child's Play, Fantasy, and the Holocaust   235

Shmuel on the other side of the border. His expiation for the sin of betraying the trust of a friend presages the issues of reparation, responsibility, and reconciliation, which became of foremost importance in postwar Germany, where the Holocaust notably signified national shame and catastrophe.

In *Creative Writers and Day-Dreaming* (1908), Sigmund Freud suggests that "every child at play behaves like a creative writer, in that he creates a world of his own" (421). Both the child at play and the creative writer are engaged in fantasizing, an exertion of the imaginative capacity. Through his play, the child links "his imagined objects and situations to the tangible and visible things of the real world" (421). From his experience as a psychotherapist, Freud concluded "that the motive forces of phantasies are unsatisfied wishes and every single phantasy is the fulfillment of a wish, a correction of unsatisfying reality" (423).

Although the play world of the two children is unthreatened by the hostilities of the real world, following Freud's interpretation, one might concur that the fantasy originates from a disturbed consciousness and attempts to correct an "unsatisfying reality." The deep psychological malaise caused by the Holocaust was accompanied by an acute realization of collective trauma—whether perceived, imagined, or emphatically known. Bruno's mother shares the guilt of persecution as she learns of her husband's more significant responsibilities as a high-ranking member of the Nazi operation. While Bruno is strictly sheltered from the trauma of guilt and complicity, there are brief collisions which occur through a series of sweeping parapraxes—including overlooked contradictions and incongruities on the part of the adults. The child unconsciously absorbs the conscious and unconscious memories and feelings of the parent and proceeds to enact them in his own life. The process of transference occurs elusively as Bruno absorbs fragments of his mother's psychological distress caused by the unrelenting pressure of bringing up her children at the site of a concentration camp. These sensations percolate in order to produce a deep sense of unhappiness in the child.

The Jewish child, Shmuel, is directly exposed to the trauma of Holocaust brutality at the nearby camp but unable to psychically integrate his experience by way of an associative meaning formation. Although not explicitly indicated, perhaps Shmuel exists in a double state of knowing and unknowing. Confronted with the bleak reality of the concentration camp, there is a possibility that his infantile imagination erects barriers against knowing, to ward off the trauma and de-contextualize tangible experience. The repetition of the game sets into motion a fantasy that is both affective and cognitive. In the shared, symbolically mediated fantasy world, the children negotiate with the unprocessed trauma of loneliness and negative memories associated with the Holocaust.

The final meeting of the two children leads them into the heart of the concentration camp as Bruno crosses over the barbed fence dressed in a pair of striped pajamas. The play space merges with the real world of the concentration camp and the children are set free to explore the wasteland in utter bewilderment and horror. The play ceases to be fun as the children enter a space where their fantasies are deformed into grotesque human shapes and violent images. Bruno wanders through the concentration camp amidst the chaotic preparation of trooping Jews to

236 *Medha Bhadra Chowdhury*

the gas chamber. The unrepresentable Holocaust, which had been looming in the background, makes its presence felt through the dark grey visuals of the ongoing catastrophe. The confusing crowd of the gas chamber with naked bodies pressed against each other in the darkness waiting for a "shower" of the lethal Zyklon B and the human rot of the Holocaust materialize through the shadowy corners of the child's fantasy and completely overwhelm the comfort of imagination.

Unlike Waititi's *Jojo Rabbit,* which ends with an imaginary scene of reconciliation, *The Boy in the Striped Pajamas* registers the external shock of the camps and the Jewish extermination. The image of the children clutching each other as they enter the gas chamber provokes a collective memory of guilt that extends beyond the immediate subject, yet the film has been criticized on account of its use of trauma culture tropes, which unethically ascribe a moral, aesthetic, and educational value to narratives that fuse Holocaust victimhood with child abuse. The incongruity of representing genocide as a children's adventure story and the historical impossibility of the plot about the friendship between a Jewish boy imprisoned in a concentration camp and the son of the camp commandant have been critically examined by Anne Rothe, who remarks

> Boyne [in the novel as different from the film] untenably conflated the genocidal murder of the Jewish boy with the accidental killing of the German one—who functions as a sort of mini-Schindler, an infantilized version of the good-German figure—through the Christian-cum-Holocaust trope of suffering innocents. And likewise in sync with the trauma culture zeitgeist, he invoked the notion of emotional truth, which he juxtaposes to and favors over historical truth, when he argues that to "truly understand the horrors of Auschwitz" one must "uncover as much emotional truth within that desperate landscape" as one can.
>
> (140)

However, the representation of death and devastation in the film avoids a defensive transformation of events but upholds the "banality of evil," to use Hannah Arendt's phrase describing the terrifyingly ordinary aspects of evil in the context of the Holocaust. Till the end, the two children believe that it is all a part of the game, and they play according to the rules of the camp. To slightly revise the implications of Arendt's term and extend it to the present study of children's fantasy and game play, one may argue that through their simple psychological mechanism, the child protagonists naturalize the atrocities of the Holocaust into commonplace, ordinary, and seemingly prosaic events. Yet, the historical value and everlasting ethical dilemma of the Holocaust remain undiminished even through the representation of children and their fantasy.

Despite the existing criticism that emphasizes the incompatibility of the Holocaust experience with Popular Culture, these films undeniably produce a muted sense of trauma, which underlies the playful world of the children and which is very much a part of a Western cultural consciousness that remembers its original encounters with Holocaust atrocities through an artistic secondhand witnessing. Fantasy, which is the central dimension of the two films, creates an aesthetic design that mimics some aspects of a post-Holocaust collective consciousness. As living memories of the Holocaust die out and recent Holocaust memorialization grows in the form of art, literature, and Popular Culture, these films work on the basis of a vicarious form of witnessing and an empathetic identification with Holocaust victims to transmit the traumatic memory of the genocide and ensure its circulation in cultures of waning historicity. Although the two films establish only a referential relation to past reality, they recognize the possibility of the cultural transmission of an affective Holocaust memory, outside the binary of authentic and inauthentic. They mediate between history and Popular Culture through diminutive Holocaust references and images for a wider, if not deeper, historical understanding. Essentially, the fantasy of the children presents the Holocaust to us as we would like to see it, neither too remote nor too immediate.

Works Cited

Adorno, Theodor W. and Anson G. Rabinbach. "Culture industry reconsidered." *New German Critique*, no. 6, 1975, pp. 12–19. DOI: 10.2307/487650.

Arendt, Hannah. *Eichmann in Jerusalem: A Report on the Banality of Evil*. Penguin, 1963.

Freud, Sigmund. "Creative writers and daydreaming." In *Literature and Psychoanalysis*, edited by Edith Kurzweil and William Phillips. Columbia University Press, 1983, pp. 19–28. DOI: 10.7312/kurz91842-003.

Gonshak, Henry. *Hollywood and the Holocaust*. Rowman and Littlefield, 2015.

Heilbrunn, Jacob. "Telling the Holocaust like it wasn't." *The New York Times*, 11 Jan. 2009, p 5.

Jojo Rabbit (Directed by Taika Waititi, performances by Taika Waititi, Scarlett Johansson, Roman Griffin Davis, Sam Rockwell and Thomasin McKenzie). Fox Searchlight Pictures, 2019.

Margalit, Avishai. "The kitsch of Israel." *New York Review of Books*, 24 Nov. 1988, pp. 21–23, www.nybooks.com/articles/1988/11/24/the-kitsch-of-israel/.

Miller, Nancy K. and Jason Tougaw. "Introduction." In *Extremities: Trauma, Testimony, and Community*. University of Illinois Press, 2002, pp. 1–20.

Mintz, Alan. *Popular Culture and the Shaping of Holocaust Memory in America*. University of Washington Press, 2001.

Rothe, Anne. *Popular Trauma Culture: Selling the Pain of Others in the Mass Media*. Rutgers University Press, 2011.

Rubin, Kenneth H., Greta G. Fein, and Brian Vandenberg. "Play." In *Handbook of Child Psychology: Socialization, Personality, and Social Development* (vol. 4), edited by Paul Mussen. Wiley, 1983, pp. 693–774.

Schindler's List (Directed by Steven Spielberg, performances by Liam Neeson, Ben Kingsley, Ralph Fiennes, Caroline Goodall). Amblin Entertainment, 1993.

Scott, Anthony. " 'Jojo Rabbit' review: The Third Reich wasn't all fun and games." *The New York Times*, 17 Oct. 2019, p 13.

The Boy in the Striped Pajamas (Directed by Mark Herman, performances by Asa Butterfield, Vera Farmiga, David Thewlis, Jack Scanlon and Rupert Friend). BBC Films, 2008.

Todorov, Tzvetan. *The Fantastic: A Structural Approach to a Literary Genre* (Translated by Richard Howard). Cornell University Press, 1975.

Winnicott, Donald W. *Playing and Reality*. Tavistock Publications, 1971.

17 *In*correctamundo?

Holocaust, Humor, and Anti-Hate Satire in the Works of Brooks and Waititi

Kyle Barrett

> The unspeakable is not the potentially speakable but the absolute condition upon which speakability depends. Once uttered, then it is no longer unspeakable.
>
> (Bishop 159)

In an age when Donald Trump can become president, the Brexit campaign can secure votes in England and Wales to leave the European Union (forcibly removing Scotland and Northern Ireland against their will), and extreme far-right politics can become somewhat normalized through nationalist, populist parties attaining seats in Europe at the "municipal, regional, national and European Union (EU) levels" (Alvares and Dahlgren 47), one could be forgiven for believing that we are living in a bleak satire. If we consider these tremendously problematic notions in a different way, we can claim a reality television star became the most powerful person on the planet, the British conservative "elite" believe their empire is still alive and well, and White populist nationalism is, worryingly, becoming the "new normal." Mainstream media and Popular Culture have increasingly been attacked by those who believe themselves to be "the victims of a prevailing leftist ideology" (Wilson 1). The rise of "fake news" claims and the generation of far-right "alternative media" platforms also indicate a "triumph of the Trumpians," where the "the weird irony-laden Internet subcultures from right and left . . . equally set themselves apart from this hated mainstream" (Nagle 7). Therefore, Popular Culture, both past and present, requires deeper examination to explore the conflict between progressive attitudes and increasing individualism that wishes to perpetuate intolerance. As for Popular Culture's role in contemporary society, what can it offer? It is here where we can locate cinema as a site of reflective contemplation and a responsible retaliation to the far-right.

It cannot be a mere coincidence that over the past few years there have been a variety of films from around the world that have examined the last great crisis of the far-right attaining control in Europe (World War II) perhaps as a warning that history is repeating itself. Films such as *Son of Saul* (László Nemes, 2015), *Darkest Hour* (Joe Wright, 2017), and *A Hidden Life* (Terrence Malick, 2019) have each explored the horrors of fascism conducted by the German Nazi party from an array of perspectives. Each one of these is firmly located within the dramatic

DOI: 10.4324/9781003251224-21

genre and attained its share of critical accolades. There have also been attempts to approach this shocking period in our history with a sense of humor. Theodor Adorno famously wrote, "Writing even one more poem after Auschwitz is barbaric" (33), and it is here where we can locate Bishop's notions of the "unspeakable." The tension of incorporating humor, or at the very least adopting comedic elements, to balance the horrors of the far-right extremism and the Holocaust is, of course, problematic. For example, despite several Oscar nominations, including Best Picture, and winning Best Adapted Screenplay, Taika Waititi's *Jojo Rabbit* (2019) received a lukewarm reception. Critics believed the film was making light of the Holocaust and was "a sugary fantasy" and "buries the awful truth" (Kohn). Historically, films that have made attempts at incorporating humor with the horrors of the Holocaust have caused controversy, such as Roberto Benigni's *Life Is Beautiful* (1997), which was deemed a sentimental fantasy that "diminishes the suffering of Holocaust victims" (Dawson). Despite objections, the film won Best Picture at the 1998 Oscars.

As the world combats the far-right, *Jojo Rabbit* appears to be too topical. However, its use of satire—the film's tagline is "An Anti-Hate Satire"—is part of wider film history of using humor in fraught times. Satire, as Dustin Griffin comments, "seeks to persuade an audience that something or someone is reprehensible or ridiculous" (1). Indeed, Charlie Chaplin's *The Great Dictator* (1940) famously lampooned Adolf Hitler and demonstrated "the absurdity of intolerance" (Kerner 84). *Jojo Rabbit* has much in common with Mel Brooks' *The Producers* (1967), a film that recognizes the farcicality of the Nazi party and converts the grandeur of propaganda filmmaker Leni Riefenstahl into a Broadway-style musical. This chapter will analyze the use of comedy and satire in *The Producers* and *Jojo Rabbit*, highlighting the tensions between humor and dark subject matter. Each of these films provides a suitable juxtaposition in terms of approach. They both explore similar themes but combine different genre elements. To put it simply, *The Producers* is strictly a comedy and *Jojo Rabbit* a comedy-drama. The films are set in different eras and countries: *Jojo Rabbit* during WWII in a fictional German city, Falkenheim; *The Producers* during the year of its creation, 1967, in New York. This provides a scale in which to discuss the comparable techniques found in Brooks and Waititi's works, both of whom produced the films during substantial political shifts.

There have been numerous volumes published on Holocaust representations in Popular Culture (see Zelizer 2000; Mintz 2001; Magilow and Silverman 2015) that have explored and examined audiovisual depictions in a variety of contexts. However, here, I wish to focus specifically on cinema. It is important to highlight that both *The Producers* and *Jojo Rabbit* are not comedies *about* the Holocaust but rather films that reveal the absurdity of far-right ideology. They do not excuse the heinous actions of Nazis but undermine and attack their capacity of indoctrinating society with a ludicrous, extremist ideology, particularly those in early adolescence. The purpose here is to address the responsibility of Popular Culture when depicting dark subject matter with regard to the Holocaust victims, survivors, and their descendants.

240   *Kyle Barrett*

Cinema, Humor, and Empathy

In 1960, French sociologist Joffre Dumazedier asked, "What fresh resources does the cinema offer to popular culture?" (104). It is a question that remains pertinent. Filmmaker Mark Cousins notes in his epic documentary *The Story of Film: An Odyssey* (2011) that cinema is "an empathy machine." Perhaps this may be the most astute answer. Susan Lanzoni defines empathy as "our capacity to grasp and understand the mental and emotional lives of others" (3). Indeed, we watch films to explore and empathize with cultures, identities, genders, sexualities, and experiences different to our own. I, therefore, believe that cinema is an avenue to deconstruct and counter intolerance and plays a substantial role in generating and perpetuating empathy. In terms of art, perhaps it is the best medium to foster global discourses: It is a universal language. In that regard, I consider all films to be political. Christian Zimmer proclaimed such in 1974, stating that there is "no innocent film . . . no film without political incidence" (124). I draw attention to this as according to Eyal Zandberg, there are two primary concerns regarding the approach to depicting the Holocaust in Popular Culture:

> On the one hand, some creators aim to construct their authority as valid storytellers of the Holocaust through the appropriation of the modes and styles of high culture . . . On the other hand, some creators might choose the opposite solution and emphasize the characteristics of popular culture in order to create a critical point of view.
>
> (Zandberg 568)

In the examples I will examine below, both Brooks and Waititi have adopted the latter approach whereby they utilize characteristics of Popular Culture to create their critical viewpoints. More specifically, they have employed humor, not at the expense of the victims of the Holocaust, but as a tool to undermine fascism. Lawrence R. Mintz states that humor is a central feature of Popular Culture despite differing "significantly from culture to culture" (281). Of course, humor is to one's taste but, in general, we can perceive comedy as an "instinct that can exceed specified boundaries, as a container for expectations and surprises, and as a way of encountering the world" (Beavis 3). Therefore, humor is a powerful tool to ease viewers into specific, often fraught, filmic worlds. Parody and satire are possibly the *most* political forms of comedy. Dentith views parody in terms of linguistics, noting that it "involves the imitation and transformation of another's words" (4) to ridicule and subvert the original incantation. In a comedy film, the most common trope is to ridicule or parody the ways in which we communicate with one another, highlighting society's inability to function without correcting this. When approaching serious, dark, or taboo subject matter, we consider comedies of this ilk to be "black humor," defined as "humor based on horrible, macabre or cruel events, and tragedies (e.g., death, serious disease, insanity, terrorism, murder, war, etc.)" (Martin and Ford 114). Consider the work of Chris Morris who has continually explored controversial subjects. For instance, his *Four Lions* (2010) depicts inept, aspirational suicide bombers. However, there is a sense of compassion toward his characters that while the deadly repercussions of their actions are inexcusable, through comedy, Morris satirizes the increase of post-9/11 paranoia and beliefs of suicide bombers.

Considering the nature of the Holocaust, an event which Alan Mintz notes is of such "awful negative transcendence that it cleaved history into a before and after" (36), how is it conceivable to even dare broach this with a comedic approach? Scholar Sidra DeKoven Ezrahi views that, though not without complications, there is a role for humor, stating: "What is at stake in the reinstatement of laughter 'nach Auschwitz,' after Auschwitz, is not the fidelity of a comic representation of the Shoah but the reinstatement of the comic as building block of a post-Shoah universe" (Ezrahi 287). Indeed, I believe the examples below are examples of "building blocks" that, again, are not "comic representations" of the Holocaust but ridiculing the perpetrators. Consequently, humor has a function in "human relatedness" (Lachmann 93) whereby comedy and Popular Culture (in this instance cinema) are harnessed to delve into dark subject matter that will continually expose the horrors of the Holocaust, reflect upon the capacity of our inhumanity, and express empathy for the victims.

Producing a Bad Taste Flop: *The Producers* and Being a Smarty

Mel Brooks, born Melvyn Kaminsky, began his career as a writer on Sid Caesar's *Your Show of Shows* (NBC, 1950–1954). During this period, Brooks worked with fellow comedian Carl Reiner. Both began a partnership beyond the show, developing a stand-up act that would produce the famous *2,000-Year-Old Man* sketch, wherein Brooks portrayed the titular character, interviewed by the strait-laced Reiner, providing humorous and scathing perceptions of his thousands of years on the planet up to the 1960s. The sketch's surrealism would give an indication of the exaggerated comedy that features in Brooks's films. Brooks's feature debut, *The Producers*, was released at a time of change in North American cinema. The collapse of the studio system resulted in young filmmakers, such as Dennis Hopper, Martin Scorsese, and Elaine May, being given studio support. This period of filmmaking was in response to "a range of social upheavals in the United States in the late 1960s and early 1970s" (King 8). During this time, the Vietnam War was escalating as was public opposition to the conflict resulting a tumultuous social, cultural, and political period in American history.

The year 1967 is key for North American cinema. A handful of films would demonstrate the shift between the conservative 1950s filmmaking to the radical 1960s. This transformation in filmmaking, aesthetically and thematically, is important to highlight for *The Producers*. For instance, the film was released the same year as the genre-bending, rule-breaking *Bonnie and Clyde* (Arthur Penn). Its intense, graphic ending changed depictions of onscreen violence forever. The year 1967 also saw the release of the saccharine musical *Doctor Doolittle* (Richard Fleisher), a complacent, family-friendly film that would not upset the general public. There was also the release of *The Graduate* (Mike Nichols), a comedy that

242   *Kyle Barrett*

explored the alienation of the baby boomer generation. The revisionist gangster homage *Bonnie and Clyde* and the mature comedy *The Graduate* were a truly remarkable step forward in North American cinema, dealing with, at the time, contemporary "adult" issues. Both films deal with outsiders: the characters in *Bonnie and Clyde* rebel against the conservative society in which they live as it is "oppressive and denying" (Kolker 36); *The Graduate*, features a passive protagonist that merely rebels against his conservative parents. Why, then, was *The Producers* released in an era of revisionism in Hollywood cinema? Its exaggerated, outrageous premise is far-removed from the aforementioned films' "maturity." Perhaps that is the very reason. *The Producers* is an interstitial film within this context, a text which operates "both within and astride the cracks of the system, benefitting from its contradictions, anomalies, and heterogeneity" (Naficy 46). To deconstruct this further, the film has a preposterous premise that then segues into a blackly comedic musical. *The Producers* echoes the farcical nature of Marx Bros. films from the 1930s-1940s, with many one-liners similar to Groucho Marx from its star Zero Mostel, portraying greasy producer Max Bialystock. It is also reminiscent of the comedy duo teams of the 1930s and 1940s, with the introduction of the anxiety-laden, strait-laced foil Leopold Bloom (Gene Wilder). The visual references are there in body type: Bialystock is stocky, Bloom is tall and thin, which recalls Laurel and Hardy or Abbot and Costello. The film may not be in the revisionist bracket of *Bonnie and Clyde* or mature comedy of *The Graduate*, but it does make a daring statement by undermining, and satirizing, fascism.

The plot dares to speak the "unspeakable" in numerous ways. When Bialystock learns from Bloom that he could earn more money from a flop than a Broadway hit, they connive to find the crassest, appalling script they can. They discover ex-Nazi officer Franz Liebkind (Kenneth Mars), who has written a play romanticizing the Third Reich entitled *Springtime for Hitler*. Additionally, the film mocks the notion of creativity and its necessary forms of finance, reflecting Brooks's own struggles to get *The Producers'* investment. The film took six years to reach the silver screen, with many unwilling financers considering it "too tasteless, too outrageous" (Kashner). While it could be argued that Brooks, at the time, was a misunderstood genius, he makes no effort to apply that to Liebkind. There is an emphasis on the clownish nature of Liebkind. Mars's acting style would be a precursor to Brooks's own performances in many of his films, for example, portraying the incompetent, buffoonish Governor in *Blazing Saddles* (1974). It is the pursuit of Liebkind's script where the film delivers its first darkly comedic joke: two Jews in league with an unhinged, traumatized, ex-Nazi officer. Frank McConnell wrote that "the 'carnival' atmosphere of satire is both frivolous and deeply serious" (206) and this notion is applicable here. As the characters scramble to get a cast and crew together, it descends into a "carnival." One of the funniest subversive images Brooks achieves in the film is the shot of actors waiting to audition for the role of Hitler. There are numerous actors of several ethnicities. Those we get to witness auditioning (through song!) include a Mexican who all but steals the scene. Brooks's inclusion of this scene not only plays to the broad comedy elements—the producers continually cut off genuinely terrible actors' mid-song—but maintain the undercutting satire:

Incorrectamundo? 243

These are the very ethnicities that the Nazis wanted to obliterate. The producers finally settle on Lorenzo St. DuBois (Dick Shawn), or as he prefers to be called, LSD. The character is an over-the-top exaggeration of the hippy culture in bloom during the 1960s, but he gets the part of Hitler to enhance the chances of the play being a flop. While obviously played for laughs—LSD has no conception of how offensive the play/role is—hippy culture would, unfortunately, become affiliated with murderous atrocities in the form of Charles Manson and his "Family." When the play is finally performed to a packed audience, it is the culmination of the satire, broad humor, and one-liners that are part of Brooks's oeuvre. Henry Jenkins explains:

> The stagecraft is loud, excessive, and what we'd now call "politically incorrect," with goose-stepping chorus girls dressed in Heimlet themed scanties and jokes that evoke but do not acknowledge the horrors of the Holocaust. Brooks dares us to be shocked, while also hoping that we will be sophisticated to be inside the joke.
>
> (154)

The delay of witnessing any of the play until this point is a masterstroke of narrative development. The reaction shots from the audience witnessing the play are an attempt to mirror the film's audience. At the conclusion of the opening musical number, the audience is in shock at what they have witnessed. Enjoyment of the show is not be condoned, and Brooks is teasing the film's audience as to how they should respond as indicated when someone claps out of politeness and is beaten by those around him. More and more of the audience storm out in disgust, as its gleeful lyrics and catchy melody do indeed present an admiration for the Third Reich. Bialystock and Bloom, and by extension Brooks himself, want to offend us. However, when LSD takes the stage, the audience realize the unintentional satire of the play. Effectively, they find Hitler ridiculous, much to Liebkind's chagrin. He then proceeds to stop the play, raging that the scenario has been manipulated and it is indeed meant to be taken seriously. The metacommentary Brooks employs is not meant to be subtle, it is intentionally direct. It is a technique he would utilize throughout his career and "serves as another reminder that the audience is *an audience* and that their otherwise omniscient perspective is constructed in relation to the director" (Meier 150).

The sequence should be given further consideration in terms of its satire. The film is grand, garish, over-the-top. It is designed as a synchronized Busby Berkley number but with Nazi imagery. In many ways, it mirrors Riefenstahl's *Triumph of the Will* (1935). Mary Devereaux writes that Riefenstahl's most famous film is at once "masterful and morally repugnant [that] epitomizes a general problem that arises in art. It is both beautiful and evil" (227). Its operatic scope, depiction of discipline, and furious rhetoric was, in its own way, grand, garish, over-the-top. Perhaps the only thing that was missing was a musical number. The notion of Nazi rallies, discipline, uniforms, and gesturing is ridiculous to Brooks. *Triumph of the Will* is a film that becomes "an overwhelming emotional spectacle of National

244 *Kyle Barrett*

Socialist imagery that mixes the concepts of ideology with mythology to create Hitler's image as a savior: his singular charismatic persona in the film" (Rizvi 79). As *Springtime for Hitler* progresses, it becomes more excessive, in much the same manner as *Triumph of the Will*. The comedy emerges as LSD is supposed to embody this "savior" as depicted by Riefenstahl. LSD's seemingly improvised hippy slang—"I lieb you, I lieb you, baby"—is a far cry from the hate-filled rhetoric of the infamous Nazi leader but illustrates the ridiculousness of the language—the "unspeakable" is literally being "speakable" as it is being subverted. Audiences return in droves and the play becomes a success, defeating Bialystock and Bloom's plans. In essence, Brooks is critiquing himself—and Hollywood—to a certain extent. The idea of a Nazi musical is oxymoronic. It should not be made, yet Brooks has made it. The chief villains of the film, Bialystock and Bloom, who connive to steal vast sums of money from elderly women, represent the greedy nature of Hollywood: Producers are out to exploit anyone, anywhere, using any means necessary, including the Holocaust. Yet, Brooks, in the layers upon layers of metacommentary, is effectively stating "don't shoot the messenger." Indeed, Brooks, himself a World War II veteran (who fought at the Battle of the Bulge) and of Jewish heritage, is claiming the right to mock the perpetrators who committed mass genocide, using humor as his primary tool.

Upon its release, *The Producers* was not an overwhelming success. The film subsequently divided audiences and critics. It made little at the box office, and Brooks "watched his film in an all-but empty New York cinema, assuming by the tepid response that he would never work again" (Symons 26). The film generated positive interest when it was later endorsed by actor Peter Sellers. As noted previously, film culture was shifting in North American cinema and was tackling more serious subject matter that appealed to younger generations. Strikingly, during the World War II period, there were multiple cultural artefacts parodying and lampooning the Nazis that were acclaimed. Chaplin's *The Great Dictator* is perhaps the most well-known example. However, perhaps, in the traumatic aftermath of World War II, those who lived through it or experienced the horrors directly were possibly, and understandably, sensitive to the depiction of the far-right in any form. Brooks, ultimately, has put the responsibility on the viewer to acknowledge, and indeed reflect on, their acceptance of such a difficult issue as a comedic subject.

He's Not the Führer, He's a Very Naughty Boy! *Jojo Rabbit*

Born in 1975, in Aotearoa, New Zealand, Taika Waititi is of Māori, Pākehā (European), and Jewish descent (on his mother's side). One of the leading contemporary filmmakers to emerge from the antipodes, Waititi became known for his distinctive blend of deadpan comedy and dramatic subject matter. However, his humorous take on serious social-cultural-political themes is rooted in his childhood. During his extremely self-exposing TED Talk on humor as a key to creativity, Waititi declared that as a child he was obsessed with swastikas, doodling them on a variety of surfaces and notepads. Knowing this was deeply offensive and feeling incredibly

Incorrectamundo? 245

guilty about his obsession, he would quickly transform them into sketches of windows. This was not a revelation that Waititi was supportive of Nazism but rather that even at a young age there was a need to subvert fascist imagery. Aspects of this have culminated in his most controversial feature film to date, *Jojo Rabbit*. Based on the novel *Caging Skies* by Christine Leunens, the film follows devout Hitler Youth member Johannes "Jojo" Betzler (Roman Griffin Davies). Upon discovering that his mother, Rosie (Scarlett Johansson), has been hiding a young Jewish girl in their attic, Elsa (Thomasin McKenzie), Jojo begins questioning the Nazi regime. Jojo's imaginary friend is none other than Adolf Hitler (played by director Waititi), who counsels him throughout the film and tries to keep him within the far-right. Given the current political climate where most of the world has opted to vote for populist, right-wing governments, it appeared as though Waititi was too timely. He also incorporated a comedic tone. The previous analysis on *The Producers* noted concerns of depicting fascists with a light, satiric tone. This section will consider these elements further with regard to *Jojo Rabbit*.

As noted in the introduction, the film was billed as an "Anti-Hate Satire," perhaps in an attempt to lampoon what the Nazis deemed 1930s anti-fascist cinema as "Hetzfilme" (hate films) (Hake 137). Frank McConnell writes that satire "reexamines and recreates the 'epic' world of high tragedy, but with a view to internalizing its grandeur, teaching us that though the age of the heroes (and of the heroic writers) may be over, our responsibility to the ideal of the heroic is not" (222). The titular character is, at first, completely devoted to the Nazi party and the Hitler Youth. Jojo vehemently believes the anti-Jewish rhetoric, presenting a complex, challenging character to accept and certainly not a heroic protagonist that McConnell refers to. However, Waititi's manipulation of genres is where the film both intrigues and challenges the audience, utilizing tropes found in his previous work. His 1980s-set *Boy* (2010) examines a Māori family on the East Coast of Aotearoa from the perspective of young teen Boy (James Rolleston). When his father, Alamein (Waititi), returns from prison, Boy begins questioning his prior worship of his significantly absent dad. The film, ultimately, reflects the "revelation of the destructive consequences for children of negligence on the part of parents" (Fox et al 39). There are several parallels between *Boy* and *Jojo Rabbit*. In both films, there is a "consistently fluid movement between fantasy and the lived realities of the characters, which is used as part of the humor of the film, but it is also a commentary on the real and perceived inadequacies of their masculinity" (Wright 164). Boy's vivid imagination, obsession with Michael Jackson (another problematic idol), and admiration for his father make him a somewhat outcast among his peers, particularly at school. Jojo is similarly an outcast among his fellow Hitler Youth, deemed more effeminate and incapable of achieving the necessary skills to survive during the tail-end of World War II or, indeed, even not able to take part in it. He attains his nickname when he refuses to kill a rabbit to prove his worth.

The final moment that cements his outsider status occurs when, believing that Adolf is encouraging him to disregard what the others think of him, Jojo takes a grenade during a demonstration on how to use it and runs through the woods before it inevitably explodes. Jojo is scarred and develops a leg injury. Now somewhat

246   *Kyle Barrett*

physically limited, he is given the position of what could be considered a clerk, distributing propaganda leaflets and salvaging any materials that the Nazis can use from air raids. Feeling excluded and emasculated, Jojo finds a way to gain the other Youth members' respect upon discovering Elsa in his attic. He conducts "interrogations"—merely immature interviews—to generate material for a book on Jewish "secrets," twisting Elsa's answers into cartoon drawings of outlandish creatures to demonize Jews even more. *Boy* and *Jojo Rabbit* also contain single parents as Alamein is a widower and Jojo's father is absent, fighting overseas but it is insinuated that he has become a deserter. With only Rosie, a secret anti-Nazi activist, to care for Jojo, tension arises further due to his desire for a strong male role model.

As with *The Producers*, the comedy emerges from the undermining of the Nazis' behavior and beliefs, highlighting their dangerous absurdity. Hitler Youth commander Captain Klenzendorf (Sam Rockwell) and his subordinate Fraulein Rahm (Rebel Wilson) are both buffoonish in their behavior. Rahm, in particular, believes the anti-Jewish propaganda, brainwashing the Youth further by embellishing the notion of Jews having descended from human-animal breeding. Waititi is situating these attitudes, exaggerations, intolerances in an effort to discuss the contemporary political climate. Klenzendorf is one of the most complex characters in the film. He is a contrast to Liebkind, where the latter was a devout Nazi, the former is performing a job in a war that he does not place any value. Klenzendorf satirizes the "just following orders" officers. Responsible for training Jojo's Hitler Youth camp, he facilitates Nazi indoctrination. He develops a rapport with Jojo and becomes intrigued by his book on Jews, not realizing they are based on interviews. Klenzendorf shares with Jojo his desire to roam the battlefield dressed in a flamboyant outfit that would not be out of place in Liberace's wardrobe. Klenzendorf represents the unthinkable: a humanized, multifaceted Nazi officer. Though primarily played for laughs, he is the only male in the film that shows any compassion toward Jojo and treats him as an equal. It is here where we can locate comedy's:

> capacity to speak what is unspeakable is important but dangerous, or important because it is dangerous. And comedy's capacity to link the gravity of existence to the levity of shared misery means that comedy will forever be speaking the unspeakable.
>
> (Bishop 136)

It is unspeakable to consider that a high-ranking Nazi officer could have any sympathy, yet, in a final act of decency, he saves Jojo's life from Allied forces who are rounding up any Nazi officers, young or old, to be executed by firing squad.

Many deriders of the film found that the comedy was misplaced alongside the dark drama. Richard Brody of *The New Yorker* writes, "Waititi displays a sort of wan humanism in which Jojo's fanatical Nazism seems excusable, or at least understandable, because it responds to his own personal psychological issues." While Brody's statement presents an interesting interpretation of the film's management of the characters, *Jojo Rabbit* should be contextualized further within Waititi's filmography as it displays similar, jarring, uncomfortable facets. Waititi's entire filmography contains a "Kiwi" sense of humor. Noted Aotearoa satirist John Clarke once described Kiwi humor as "laconic, understated and self-deprecating." Waititi's film certainly relishes in this form of comedy, generating most laughs with a deadpan approach. Perhaps this was an element that irked Brody as:

> the concept of deadpan satire not only helps in mapping the political work carried out by humor as an aesthetic category, but how it also speaks to the distinctive features of . . . Australasian politics of humor, where the deadpan and the satirical frequently collide and intersect in ways that complicate the conception of satire as a political aesthetic mode, particularly with relation to the attribution of political intention and aggression.
>
> (Holm 104)

Jojo Rabbit is not consistently deadpan, however, and contains broad comedy much in the same way as *The Producers*. This mashup of genres can be argued as "genre-splicing," which refers to "the combination of two or more genres in a way that fragments or contradicts the fictional reality of the work or violates the norms of the genres employed" (Singsen 170). Deadpan, alongside broad comedy and drama, does present contradictions, issues of tone, and directorial approach but, again, this features in much of Waititi's work. The oscillation between drama and comedy is purposely jarring to create an uncomfortable experience. As Berger notes, comedy "generates laughter and feeling of optimism and ebullience, while tragedy generates pity and tears" (82), the combination of the two, at least in *Jojo Rabbit*, create a paradox and multiplicity in terms of our responses. There is no binary or black-and-white answers. This juxtaposition is exemplified in the most devastating scene when Jojo discovers his mother has been killed, hung due to her "treacherous" behavior. Yet, the film, predominately, operates due to the same conventions employed in *Boy*, namely the use of a coming-of-age narrative. Jojo's and Boy's journeys navigate the increasingly hostile world of dangerous adults, lack of parenting, and deconstruction of their adolescences into maturity—which may, in fact, be at too young an age. However, this is not an element Waititi focuses on in either film.

To draw further parallels with *The Producers*, there are commonalities in the performances and depictions of Hitler. It would be appropriate to compare LSD and Adolf as both are similarly buffoonish, but they also utilize "hippy" language. LSD ends nearly every sentence with "Baby" and Adolf adds "Man" when conversing with Jojo. LSD and Adolf "Americanize" Hitler's vernacular. In Adolf's case it is to appeal to Jojo's age, utilizing phrases such as "correctamundo" to placate and preserve their imaginary friendship. "Correctamundo" is a reference to 1950s-set television series *Happy Days* (ABC, 1974–1984), spouted by character Fonzie (Henry Winkler) who is considered the epitome of 1950s "cool." Here, the word is an attempt at "youthification," where the far-right becomes even more dangerous and normalized when language being used is to appeal to younger generations. It indicates the attraction of such extreme groups for a "sense of belonging and identity that they gain from the group, to the male comradeship and bonding

248   *Kyle Barrett*

they gain from insider status and the sense that they are contributing to something bigger than themselves" (Miller-Idriss 29). With the possible exception of Klenzendorf, Adolf is seemingly more supportive of Jojo than any of the real-life adults. However, as the war draws toward its end and as Jojo becomes closer to Elsa, Adolf becomes less integral to the boy's life. The de-indoctrination of Nazi ideology concludes when it is revealed that the real-life Hitler has committed suicide. Jojo decides to help Elsa escape and start a new life with her. While *Boy* had a somber conclusion—the titular character has come to accept that his father is not perfect, and they meet at his mother's grave—*Jojo Rabbit* is more chaotic.

The final interaction with Adolf is a complex scene. Jojo has rejected his former beliefs—no longer a uniform, heil-saluting member of Hitler Youth. Adolf, bullet wound oozing blood from his head, barges in to try and convince Jojo to remain his friend and follow his orders. The scene is intentionally designed for darkly comedic effect. Despite the carnage occurring outside as Allied forces storm the streets, the concluding confrontation is between Jojo and Adolf. Waititi stages the scene in an exaggerated manner, where the tension between comedy and the underlying themes are cemented. In this scene, humor is produced "when an audience finds a text to be both attractive and repulsive; that pairing builds tension, which is released through laughter" (Gournelos and Greene 15). The scene is attractive and repulsive. Jojo rejects the Swastika armband and even tells Adolf to "fuck off." The exchange is cartoonish, especially with the level of desperation of Adolf realizing that his time, and influence, are now over. Jojo sides with Elsa and kicks Adolf out of the window, and out of his life, forever. The rejection of the parent, even in this case an imaginary adult, with a seemingly superhuman kick is an adolescent's fantasy. Tension arises due to the fact it is not just *any* adult but Hitler himself, whose ideology and influence can be dispelled by being kicked out the window. However, in keeping in tone with the film, its mix of fantasy and reality, the ending concludes Jojo's journey toward self-discovery and coming of age. Perhaps, ultimately, *Jojo Rabbit* should be viewed as *The Producers* as an "interstitial film," arriving at a period in political, cultural, and societal upheaval that may one day be reread and accepted.

Conclusion

Jonathan Greenberg states that "realism and satire share the functions of truthtelling and exposure, examining the world closely and unflinchingly" (19). By utilizing comedy to undermine fascism, I believe these films are, to reiterate Ezrahi, building blocks in our reflections of a post-Holocaust world. I further believe that these films recognize the responsibility of approaching a subject such as this, to maintain the Holocaust in our memory, furthering our contemplation and reflection on our inhumanity. They demonstrate cinema and, by extension, Popular Culture as important tools to foster discourses during global political strife and perpetuate empathy. *The Producers* was released at a time of flux in North American cinema; perhaps this is why it did not receive as warm a welcome as it should have. It was "ahead of its time." In the near future, the same could possibly be applied to *Jojo*

Rabbit. Both films attempt to underline the absurdity and hypocrisy of far-right ideology. *The Producers* takes the garishness of fascist paraphernalia and turns it into a musical; *Jojo Rabbit* probes the ridiculousness of intolerance and far-right teachings on children. Ultimately, these filmmakers demonstrate that the satirist is:

> two-faced, at once apocalyptic and re-creative, a king and not a king, a fool whose foolishness fills the vacuum left by the departure of order, and an agent of order whose clowning holds up a funhouse glass to our own distortions of humanity.
>
> (McConnell 210)

Brooks and Waititi are filmmakers who construct narratives that require a certain responsibility on the viewer: It is up to us to make up our minds and either laugh at the jokes or be repelled by them. Yet, we cannot deny that they do reflect the distortions of humanity.

Works Cited

Adorno, Theodor W. *Prisms* (Translated by Samuel and Shierry Weber). MIT Press, 1983.

Alvares, Claudia and Peter Dahlgren. "Populism, extremism and media: Mapping an uncertain terrain." *European Journal of Communication*, vol. 31 no. 1, 2016, pp. 46–57.

Beavis, Matthew. *Comedy: A Very Short Introduction*. Oxford University Press, 2012.

Benigni, Roberto, director. *Life Is Beautiful*. Melampo Cinematografica, 1997.

Berger, Arthur Asa. *Blind Men and Elephants: Perspectives on Humor* (Transaction Publishers), 1995.

Bishop, Ryan. *Comedy and Cultural Critique in American Film*. Edinburgh University Press, 2013.

Brody, Richard. "Springtime for Nazis: How the satire of "Jojo Rabbit" backfires." *The New Yorker*, 22 Oct. 2019, www.newyorker.com/culture/the-front-row/springtime-for-nazis-how-the-satire-of-jojo-rabbit-backfires. Accessed 7 Nov. 2021.

Brooks, Mel, director. *Blazing Saddles*. Warner Bros, 1974.

———. *The Producers*. Metro-Goldwyn-Mayer, 1967.

Brooks, Mel and Carl Reiner, creators. *2,000 Years with Mel Brooks and Carl Reiner*. Rhino Records, 1960.

Chaplin, Charlie, director. *The Great Dictator*. United Artists, 1940.

Clarke, John. "John Clarke: Wit & Humor." *New Zealand Listener* (Archived)/*Noted*, 31 Jul. 2009, www.noted.co.nz/archive/archive-listener-nz-2009/john-clarke-wit-humor. Accessed 24 Jul. 2020.

Cousins, Mark, director. *The Story of Film: An Odyssey*. Hopscotch Films, 2011.

Dawson, Tom. "La Vita è Bella (Life Is Beautiful) (1998)." *BBC*, 6 Jun. 2002, www.bbc.co.uk/films/2002/06/06/la_vita_e_bella_1997_review.shtml. Accessed 18 Feb. 2020.

Dentith, Simon. *Parody*. Routledge, 2000.

Devereaux, Mary. "Beauty and Evil: The case of Leni Riefenstahl's Triumph of the Will." *Aesthetics and Ethics: Essays at the Intersection*, edited by Jerrold Levinson. Cambridge University Press, 1998, pp. 227–256.

Dumazedier, Joffre (Translated by Elaine P. Halperin). "The cinema and popular culture." *Diogenes*, vol. 8, no. 31, 1960, pp. 103–113.

250 *Kyle Barrett*

Ezrahi, Sidra DeKoven. "After such knowledge, what laughter?" *The Yale Journal of Criticism*, vol. 14, no. 1, 2001, pp. 287–313.

Fleischer, Richard, director. *Doctor Doolittle*. Twentieth-Century Fox, 1967.

Fox, Alastair, Barry Keith Grant and Hillary Radner. "Introduction: The historical film in New Zealand cinema." In *New Zealand Cinema: Interpreting the Past*, edited by Fox A., Grant B. K. and Radner H. Intellect, 2011, pp. 15–44.

Gournelos, Ted and Viveca S. Greene. "Introduction popular culture and post-9/11 politics." In *Decade of Dark Humor: How Comedy, Irony, and Satire Shaped Post-9/11 America*, edited by Gournelos T. and Greene V. S. University Press of Mississippi, 2011, pp. 9–27.

Greenberg, Jonathan. *The Cambridge Introduction to Satire*. Cambridge University Press, 2018.

Griffin, Dustin. *Satire: A Critical Reintroduction*. University of Kentucky Press, 1994.

Hake, Sabine. *Popular Cinema of the Third Reich*. University of Texas Press, 2001.

Holm, Nicholas. "The politics of deadpan in Australasian satire." In *Satire and Politics: The Interplay of Heritage and Practice*, edited by Jessica Milner Davis. Palgrave Macmillan, 2017, pp. 103–124.

Ilott, Sarah. *New Postcolonial British Genres: Shifting the Boundaries*. Palgrave Macmillan, 2015.

Jenkins, Henry. "Mel Brooks, vulgar modernism, and comic remediation." In *A Companion to Film Comedy*, edited by Andrew Horton and Joanna E. Rapf. John Wiley & Sons Inc., 2013, pp. 151–174.

Kashner, Sam. "The making of The Producers." *Vanity Fair*, 6 Jan. 2004, www.vanityfair.com/culture/2004/01/making-the-producers. Accessed 14 Jul. 2020.

Kay, Jeremy. "Chris Morris's four lions: A mixed dish that fails to satisfy." *The Guardian*, 25 Jan. 2010, www.theguardian.com/film/2010/jan/25/four-lions-chris-morris. Accessed 8 Nov. 2021.

Kerner, Aaron. *Film and the Holocaust: New Perspectives on Dramas, Documentaries, and Experimental Films*. Bloomsbury Academic, 2010.

King, Geoff. *New Hollywood Cinema: An Introduction*. I. B. Tauris, 2002.

Kohn, Eric. " 'Jojo Rabbit' review: Taika Waititi's Nazi satire is a charming muddle of good intentions." *Indiewire*, 9 Sep. 2019, www.indiewire.com/2019/09/jrabbitreview-taika-waititi-tiff-1202172024/. Accessed 17 Feb. 2020.

Kolker, Robert. *A Cinema of Loneliness* (3rd ed.). Oxford University Press, 2000.

Lachmann, Frank M. *Transforming Narcissism Reflections on Empathy, Humor, and Expectations*. Routledge, 2007.

Lanzoni, Susan. *Empathy: A History*. Yale University Press, 2018.

Leunens, Christine. *Caging Skies*. Random House, 2008.

Magilow, Daniel H. and Lisa Silverman. *Holocaust Representations in History*. Bloomsbury, 2015.

Malick, Terrence, director. *A Hidden Place*. Fox Searchlight Pictures, 2019.

Martin, Rod A. and Ford Thomas E. *The Psychology of Humor: An Integrative Approach*. Academic Press, 2018.

McConnell, Frank. *Storytelling and Myth Making: Images from Film and Literature*. Oxford University Press, 1979.

Meier, Matthew R. "What a meshugenner!: Mel Brooks's politics of Jewish Humor." In *The Political Mel Brooks*, edited by Samuel Boerboom and Beth E. Bonnstetter. Lexington Books, 2019, pp. 135–157.

Meikle, Graham. " 'Find out exactly what to think—Next!': Chris Morris, brass eye, and journalistic authority." *Popular Communication*, vol. 10, nos. 1–2, 2012, pp. 14–26.

Miller-Idriss, Cynthia. *The Extreme Gone Mainstream: Commercialization and Far Right Youth Culture in Germany*. Princeton University Press, 2017.

Mintz, Alan. *Popular Culture and the Shaping of Holocaust Memory in America*. University of Washington Press, 2001.

Mintz, Lawrence E. "Humor and popular culture." In *The Primer of Humor Research*, edited by Victor Raskin. Mouton de Gruyter, 2008.

Morris, Chris, director. *Four Lions*. Film4, 2010.

Naficy, Hamid. *An Accented Cinema: Exilic and Diasporic Filmmaking*. Princeton University Press, 2011.

Nagle, Angela. *Kill All Normies: Online Culture Wars from 4Chan and Tumblr to Trump and the Alt-Right*. Zero Books, 2017.

Nemes, László, director. *Son of Saul*. Laokoon Filmgroup, 2015.

Nichols, Mike, director. *The Graduate*. United Artists, 1967.

Penn, Arthur, director. *Bonnie and Clyde*. Warner Bros., 1967.

Riefenstahl, Leni, director. *Triumph of the Will*. Reichsparteitag-Film, 1935.

Rizvi, Wajiha Raza. "Politics, propaganda and film form: Battleship Potemkin (1925) and Triumph of the Will (1935)." *Journal of International Communication*, vol. 20 no. 1, 2014, pp.77–86.

Shaw, Tony. *Cinematic Terror: A Global History of Terrorism on Film*. Bloomsbury Academic, 2015.

Singsen, Doug. "An alternative by any other name: Genre-splicing and mainstream genres in alternative comics." *Journal of Graphic Novels and Comics*, vol. 5, no. 2, 2014, pp. 170–191.

Symons, Alex. "An audience for Mel Brooks's The Producers: The avant-garde of the masses." *Journal of Popular Film and Television*, vol. 34, no. 1, 2006, pp. 24–32.

Waititi, Taika, director. *Boy*. Transmission Films, 2010.

———. *Jojo Rabbit*. Fox Searchlight, 2019.

Waititi, Taika. "Why humor is a key to creativity." *TEDxDoha*, October 2010, www.ted.com/talks/taika_waititi_why_humor_is_key_to_creativity. Accessed 21Sep. 2021.

Walters, Ben. "Lions for lambs: Four Lions." *Sight & Sound*, vol. 20, no. 6, 2010, pp. 58–59.

Weaver, Sylvester L. Jr., creator. *Your Show of Shows*. NBC, 1950–1954.

Wilson, John K. *The Myth of Political Correctness: The Conservative Attack on Higher Education*. Duke University Press, 1995.

Wright, Andrea. " 'I thought I was like you, but I'm not': Identity, masculinity and make-believe in Taika Waititi's Boy (2010)." *Journal of New Zealand & Pacific Studies*, vol. 4, no. 2, 2016, pp. 153–168.

Wright, Joe, director. *Darkest Hour*. Universal Pictures and Focus Features, 2017.

Zandberg, Eyal. "Critical laughter: Humor, popular culture and Israeli Holocaust commemoration." *Media, Culture and Society*, vol. 28, no. 4, 2006, pp. 561–579.

Zelizer, Barbie, editor. *Visual Culture and the Holocaust*. Bloomsbury Publishing, 2000.

Zimmer, Christian. "All films are political." *Substance*, vol. 3, no. 9, 1974, pp. 123–136.

Notes on Contributors

Navras J. Aafreedi is an assistant professor of history at Presidency University, Kolkata, India, where he teaches courses in Jewish history, genocide studies, interfaith relations and minority studies. He is also a fellow of the Salzburg Global Seminar Holocaust Education and Genocide Prevention Program, Austria, and a research fellow at the Institute for the Study of Global Antisemitism and Policy, New York, USA.

Tiasa Bal is a doctoral candidate in the Department of Humanities and Social Sciences at the Indian Institute of Technology Kanpur, India. Her primary research areas are Holocaust studies, memory studies, and trauma studies with particular interest in the intergenerational transmission of trauma and third-generation fictional accounts of the genocide.

Kyle Barrett is a lecturer at the University of Waikato, New Zealand. His research focuses on global, low-budget production cultures and cinemas, gender representations, and creative practice. He has directed several documentaries that have screened internationally.

Astha Chadha is a PhD candidate at Ritsumeikan Asia Pacific University, Japan. Presently a MEXT Scholar at Ritsumeikan APU, she is a researcher at the University's Center for Democracy Promotion. Her research interests include India-Japan relations, India's foreign policy, national identities, and security of regional powers in the Indo-Pacific. She holds MSc in International Relations (Ritsumeikan APU) and MA in Economics (Jawaharlal Nehru University). Her works have been published in *Global Affairs*, *Contemporary Japan*, *Ritsumeikan Journal of Asia Pacific Studies*, *PacNet*, *The Diplomat*, etc.

Roger Chapman is Professor of History at Palm Beach Atlantic University, Florida, USA. Since 2007 he has been a member of the editorial board of the *Journal of Popular Culture*. He has published on diverse topics, including Special Forces operations, Richard Nixon, the Tea Party movement, hippies, Cold War popular culture, the Red Scare, Ponce de Leon, and Dostoyevsky.

Medha Bhadra Chowdhury is an assistant professor in English at St. Xavier's University, Kolkata, India. Her areas of specialization include gender and memory studies, and she takes an interest in women's writing and feminist theory.

Notes on Contributors 253

Iker Itoiz Ciáurriz is a Teaching Fellow in Modern European History at Durham University. His current research interests lie broadly in the political and intellectual history of twentieth-century Europe, political theory, and historical memory.

Priyanka Das is an assistant professor of English at Presidency University, Kolkata, India. Both pedagogically and research-wise, she is invested in critical theory, Holocaust studies, and Popular Culture (web-series, memes, graphic novels, and videogames). She has published on American, Japanese, and Korean television dramas. Obsessed with "monster theory," she is currently working on zombification in Asian dramas.

Silvia Del Zoppo is a professor of Music History at the Conservatory of Como and adjunct professor at the University of Milan, where she completed her PhD as a cotutelle program with the University of Heidelberg. She has been awarded the "Lucia Forneron" prize, the "Maurizio e Clotilde Pontecorvo" grant for a research project at MEIS (Museo dell'Ebraismo Italiano e della Shoah—Ferrara), Italy, and an Abschlussstipendium der Exzellenzinitiative der Graduiertenakademie Heidelberg.

José Rodolfo Avilés Ernult is a PhD candidate at Ritsumeikan Asia Pacific University, Japan. Presently a JASSO scholar at Ritsumeikan APU, his research interests include transcultural aesthetics and cultural analysis of media in Japan and Latin America. He holds MSc in Society and Culture (Ritsumeikan APU) and BA in Philosophy (University of Guadalajara). His works have been published in *Ritsumeikan Journal of Asia Pacific Studies* and *Kootneeti*.

Adriana Krawiec is a PhD candidate at Jagiellonian University, Poland, in the Faculty of International and Political Studies. She is researching how memory sites such as the United States Holocaust Memorial Museum and Auschwitz-Birkenau State Museum are reflections of their cultural policy as well as how they reflect the official Holocaust remembrance policy carried out by the USA and Poland.

Douglas C. MacLeod, Jr. is Associate Professor of Composition and Communication at SUNY Cobleskill, USA. He has presented on various subjects at conferences, including *Marathon Man*, *The Twilight Zone*, *Alfred Hitchcock*, empathy in the Digital Age, stand-up comedy as a tool for composition writers, and Oliver Stone. He is also widely published on such topics as religion and cinema, and Bonnie and Clyde.

Mahitosh Mandal is an assistant professor of English at Presidency University, Kolkata. He works in the field of literary and cultural studies and specializes in psychoanalytic studies, Dalit studies, and Holocaust studies. His first monograph, titled *Jacques Lacan: From Clinic to Culture* was published by Orient BlackSwan in 2018. He has authored 8 research papers and 6 book chapters and delivered a total of 45 academic presentations as of 14 January 2023.

254 *Notes on Contributors*

Ved Prakash teaches literature in the Department of English at the Central University of Rajasthan. His areas of research interest are Cultural Studies, Life Writing, Film Studies, and Writing from the Margins. He co-edited a book titled *Marginality and Resistance: Cultural and Literary Perspectives* (Rawat Books, 2022). His latest work on cinema and caste came out in *The Routledge Companion to Caste and Cinema in India* (Routledge, 2022).

Diganta Ray is an assistant professor in the Department of English in Falakata College, West Bengal, India. His areas of academic interest include horror literature, popular fiction, and gothic romanticism. He is currently pursuing his PhD on 'Cultural Translation of Fear in Dracula and its Adaptations' from Jadavpur University Dept. of English.

Sucharita Sarkar is associate professor of English at D.T.S.S College of Commerce, Mumbai, India. Her research focuses on intersections of maternity with body, cultures, media, and narrative. She has recently participated in an international collaborative project, *Beyond Mother Goddesses: New Directions for International Scholarship on Motherhood in Religious Studies*, accessible at https://beyondmg.study.

Anisha Sen is a PhD candidate at Jawaharlal Nehru University (JNU), New Delhi, India. She works at The Heritage College as an assistant professor in the Department of English. She has worked extensively on fairy tales and her area of interests include children's literature, fairy tales and adaptation studies.

Craig Smith has research interests which include postcolonial and South African literatures, with particular emphasis on fiction of J.M. Coetzee. In addition to articles on Coetzee, he has also published work on Cetacean personhood in Zakes Mda and on issues of anti-colonial violence and political radicalism in the early fiction of Ngũgĩ wa Thiong'o.

Sarah Spinella is an experienced sworn translator and an independent scholar. Her research interests lie in the area of literary geography, linguistic geography, migration, and diaspora. Her major research paper project challenges the origins and the construction of the totalitarian language in Nazi Germany.

Michaela Weiss is an associate professor at the Institute of Foreign Languages at the Silesian University, Opava, Czech Republic. She teaches courses on American literature, literary theory, and creative reading and writing. Her areas of interest include Jewish literatures and cultures and women's studies.

Index

Aarons, Victoria 52, 185
abdirigieren (to detach) 77
abgang (exit) 77
abschieben (to remove) 77
abtransportieren (to transport) 77
Adams, Jenni 184
Adams, Neal 165
Adorno, Theodor W 4, 12, 28, 69, 145, 164, 176, 177, 184, 227, 232, 239
alternative histories 175, 183
Amazon Series 171
Americanization 9, 24, 26, 27, 132, 161, 168, 197
Améry, Jean 39, 42, 43
Amichai, Yehuda 183
Amritsar 83
Anderson, Wayne 84
Anna Kapplehaum 168–170
Annan, Kofi 89
Anne Frank 8, 102–107, 133, 141, 161, 197, 227
Anne no Nikki (1995) 24, 101–111
Annus mirabilis 72
Anthropology 72, 175, 227
Anti-Defamation League 84, 92
Anti-immigrant 28, 164
antisemitism 2, 8–9, 19, 24, 83, 89–91, 93–96, 108–109, 128, 164, 230
aporia 39
Arabic 84
archival footage 51
Arendt, Hannah 4, 141, 165, 236
Arnds, Peter 198
Aryan 16, 25, 64, 71, 86, 230
From the Ashes (1979) 169
Attentat 1942 (videogame, 2017) 49–53
Aufliebung (abolition) 77
Auflösung (dissolution) 77

Aukhti Hitler 84
Auschwitz 4–6, 10, 12, 43–45, 48, 56, 64, 69, 77, 126–137, 145, 154, 166, 170, 177, 203, 218–219, 222, 236, 239, 241; Auschwitz-Birkenau Museum 26, 127, 130, 135; Liberation Day 17; *Musicians of Auschwitz, The* 63; *Survival in Auschwitz* 42, 45, 222; *Witness Auschwitz* 55–56
Außenseiter (outsider) 73
autobiography 63, 78, 84, 89, 162–164, 183
Avisar, Ilan 220–221
Azara, Daniele 55

Bade und Inhalation sraeume (bath and inhalation rooms) 77
Bangladesh 17, 83
Basile, Giambattista 192
Batman with Robin, the Teen Wonder 167
Baudelaire, Charles 145
Bauernhaeuser (rural cottages) 77
Beautiful Losers (1966) 145
Benigni, Roberto 120, 239
Berger Alan L. 52, 185
Berlin 7, 71, 118, 155–162
Berliner, Todd 220
Bernstein, Michael 93
besteht nicht mehr 77
Bettelheim, Bruno 198
Bhatachar Movement 87
Birmingham School 28, 176
Black holocaust 18, 20
Blacks 90
Blanchot, Maurice 181–182
Blazing Saddles (film, 1974) 243
Blessing on the Moon, A 182
Blitzkrieg 70
Blumental, Nachman 23, 70–78
Bogdanove, Jon 170

256 *Index*

Bombay Press Service 87
Bonnie and Clyde (film, 1967) 241–242
Borges, Jorge Luis 176, 209
Borowski, Tadeusz 39, 42–43
Bose, Subhas Chandra 88, 90
Boswell, Matthew 3–4
Bresheeth, Haim 221
British India 83, 88
Broadway 239, 242
Brody, Richard 246–247
Bronner, Emanuel 141, 146–149
Brooks, Mel 239, 241
Browning, Christopher 178
Buhle, Paul 164
Burke, Peter 49
Butler, Octavia E. 191

cabaret 113, 117
Caging Skies 245
Call of Duty 48–53, 56
Calvary 127, 144
Calypso Connection, The (1980) 168–169
Camera 50, 217, 233
camp: Chelmno 192–193, 199;
    concentration camp 6–7, 10–11, 16,
    25–26, 50–51, 54, 60–65, 76–77,
    104–108, 114–120, 129–135, 141,
    154–155, 157, 178, 180, 182, 189, 192,
    203–208, 215, 222, 224, 234–236;
    Dachau 141, 143, 203; death camp 6,
    48, 119, 143, 168, 215; Diebenwald 168,
    170; Majdanek 5, 216; prisoner camp
    50–55; Sobanek 194–196; Sobibor 126;
    Treblinka 4–5, 126, 171
capitalism 66
Captain America 168–171
Captain Marvel 28, 166–167, 170
Carter, Jimmy 132–133, 136, 168
Caste 16–18, 24
Castlevania 25–26
Catholicism 144
Celan, Paul 4, 39, 42, 119
Center for Holocaust Studies, Jagiellonian
    University 127
Centralna Żydowska Komisja Historyczna
    (The Central Jewish Historical
    Commission) 74
Chabon, Michael 180
Chagall, Marc 27, 141–142, 144–149
Chaplin, Charlie 86, 231, 239, 244
Christians 63, 83, 144
cinema 30, 60–69, 86, 102–103, 227,
    231–232, 238, 240, 244–245, 248

Civil Rights Movement 165, 178
Clarke, John 247
CNN poll 37
Cohen, Abner 176
Cohen, Leonard 27, 141–149
Colditz 55
Cold War 126, 136, 165, 218
Cole, Tim 6–7, 188
Combat Kelly 164
comics 20, 27–28, 31, 51, 107, 153,
    161–172
Congress Party 87
The Cost of Freedom 48, 55–56
Cousins, Mark 240
crypt 181
cultural economy 39; malaise 39, 235;
    reservoir 37
culture 3, 6, 20–21, 30, 37, 41, 45, 49,
    61–63, 69, 79, 103, 119, 129–132, 136,
    161, 176, 184, 188, 203, 206, 210, 227,
    232, 240; high culture 21–22, 49, 214, 240
Czechoslovakia 51–52, 115–116
Czech Republic 49

Dalit 10, 17–18, 87, 253
Dalit holocaust 18
Dark Ascent, The 49
Darkest Hour (film, 2017) 238
Dark Tourism 56, 129
David, Robin 87
Davis, Brian 215–216
DC Comics 171
Dear Friend Hitler 85
Death camp 6, 48, 56, 87, 119, 143, 168,
    198, 215, 224
Death march 50
Dehumanization 64, 122, 180
Dentith, Simon 241
Deportation 6, 25, 71, 117, 120–121, 129
Derrida, Jacques 1–2, 11–13
Devereaux, Mary 243
Devils' Arithmetic, The (1990) 29,
    190–192, 196–198, 202–212
Diary of Anne Frank, The (1959) 102, 107,
    141, 197
Dick, Philip K. 173
dictionary 70, 73–74, 77–78
digital archives 177
Disneyland 133
Disney's Mickey Mouse 162
Doctor Doolittle 241
Documentation 26–27, 66, 113–114, 118,
    129, 153

Index 257

Double meaning 51
Drama 29, 70, 78, 95, 110, 215, 218, 239, 244, 246
Dr. Bronner 141, 146–148
Dreams (1961) 143
Dreifus, Erika 180
Dresden 71, 75
Dr. Gruener 167–168, 170
Dr. Klaus Mendelhaus 169
Dr. Schloss 167
Dumazedier, Joffre 240
dystopia 171

Egorova, Yulia 88, 90–91
Eichmann Trial 4, 165, 178
Eisner, Will 165
Eliach, Yaffa 223
Endlösung (final solution) 76
Entertainment 84, 113
entlassen (to dismiss) 77
ethical responsibility 1–2, 161, 178
euphemism 54, 73, 76, 196
European Jews 89, 128
exodus 101, 108
eyewitness 51, 114, 116, 177
Ezrahi, Sidra DeKoven 241, 248

fabrication 178
Fackler, Guido 114, 116
fairy tales 28–29, 175, 188–199
Fanatismus/fanatische 76
fantastic 166, 181
fantastique-étrange (fantastic-uncanny) 181
fantastique-merveilleux (fantastic-marvellous) 181
fantasy 30, 190, 197, 228–237, 239, 245, 248
Farsi 84
Fascism 88, 92, 126
Feldstein, Al 165, 166
Ferramonti di Tarsia 26, 113, 116
Film 23, 63, 217, 220, 227, 238
Final Solution 19, 24, 26, 30, 142–143, 145, 148, 160, 203, 214, 222, 229
First Infantry Division 50
Flowers for Hitler 145–146
Flowers of Evil 145
Foer, Joanathan Safran 180
Folk songs 7, 115, 118
Frame-gutter 27, 162
Frank, Anne 8–9, 102–107, 133, 141, 161, 197, 227
Franklin, Ruth 198

French 61, 71, 73, 92, 142, 144, 148, 240
Freud, Sigmund 13, 192, 208, 235
Friedan, Betty 168
Friedländer, Saul 178
Fugitive Pieces (1996) 180–181, 183
Führer 72, 84, 244

Gandhi to Hitler (film, 2011) 84–85
Gandhi, M. K. 18, 83, 85, 87–88
Gas chamber 43, 48, 56, 64, 77, 87–89, 94, 130, 143, 170, 182, 207, 211, 219, 234–236
Gasché, Rodolphe 182
Gautier, Francios 92
Geertz, Clifford 175
Gegensprache 70
General Didi 84
Genocide 7, 9, 12–31, 38, 41–42, 69–72, 89, 92–96, 128, 130, 136, 141–149, 154, 161, 165–166, 175–180, 184, 204–206, 210–211, 227–232, 236, 242, 252
German: Germanness/*Deutschtum* 72; Jews 70, 72; language 23, 70–74
German Institute of Bombay 87
Germany 87, 90–94, 104, 109, 115–116, 126, 147, 153, 156, 162, 176, 198, 204–206, 219, 235, 254
Gestapo 51, 104, 114, 128, 189
ghetto: Lodz 77, 194–195; Radom 44; Warsaw 60, 65, 171
Ghosts 166, 180–181, 198, 230
Glas-Larsson, Margareta 222
Goldhagen, Daniel Jonah 204
Goldman, William 218
Gold Rush! (1982) 170
Goldstein, Lisa 193
golem 39, 41–46, 182
Golems of Gotham, The 22, 38–41, 43, 46, 180, 182
Golgotha 127
Golwalkar, M. S. 91
Gonshak, Henry 231
Goodman, David 104
Gothic 40, 44, 181
Grabowski, Jan 53
Graduate, The (film, 1967) 241–242
Gramsci, Antonio 21, 184
graphic narrative 27, 156, 165
Gray, Michael 203
Gray zone 43
Great Depression 164
Great Dictator, The (film, 1940) 86
Great Evasion, The (videogame, 2003) 48, 54

258 *Index*

Greenberg, Jonathan 248
Grimm: Brothers 188, 194; tales 191, 198
Gross, Jan 53
Gross, Tomasz 127–128
Groucho Marx 242
Gujarat 87

Hall, Stuart 28, 176
Hanke, Stefan 131
Hansel and Gretel 189–197, 209
Harijan 85, 88
Hartman, Geoffrey 178, 221, 224
Hashimoto, Akiko 101, 107
Hauntology 181
Hayes, Peter 10, 19–20, 51
Hebrew 19, 55, 73, 142–147, 159, 165
Hedgehog 70
Hedgewar, H. S. 91–92
Heilbrunn, Jacob 231
Herskovits, Jack 140
Hetzfilme (hate films) 245
Heydrich, Reinhard 51–52
Himmler, Heinrich 25, 77
Hindu 9, 16, 18, 84–91, 92, 95
Hinduism 18
Hindukush 92
Hindu Mahasabha 87, 91
Hindutva 15, 17, 18
Hirsch, Marianne 157, 159
historical: memories 48, 53, 85, 92;
  narrative 48, 108, 127, 178; textbook 87
Hitler Adolf 83–90, 95–96, 168, 205,
  230–231, 239, 243–245, 248; hitlerism
  71–72
Hitler Didi 84
Hitler Singh 86
Hitler Youth 229, 245–246, 248
Hole, Jannie 53
Hollywood 101–103, 129, 133, 210,
  214–217, 220, 225, 227–228, 231–232,
  242–244
Holocaust: awareness of 69, 89, 96, 111,
  165, 198; children of 38; denial 9, 14, 39,
  41, 84, 92–94, 177, 203; forgetfulness
  14, 38, 41; inversion 94–95; legacy of
  104, 164, 180, 183, 208, 210; literature
  96, 153, 178, 180; memorialists 42;
  memorialization 15, 40, 237; memory
  1, 5–6, 8, 13–19, 24–31, 38–41, 60,
  62, 69, 93, 145, 175–176, 179, 227,
  237; mimesis 180; misremembrance 37;
  museum 26, 37, 126, 189; remembrance
  9, 17, 24, 27, 30–31, 38, 40, 92, 140,
  148, 178; representation 8, 22, 26–29,

39–41, 49, 113, 119, 122, 162, 165,
  169–170, 181, 210, 221, 224, 232, 240;
  survivor 4, 22, 25, 27–28, 38, 43–44,
  60, 70, 75, 119, 140, 153, 160, 164,
  166–168, 176–177, 180–181, 183,
  189, 192–193, 202, 214, 216, 218, 222;
  survivor-writers 39, 43; testimonies 164;
  victims 20, 24, 30, 39, 90, 104–105, 113,
  142, 161, 168, 219, 222–224, 239; writer
  38, 42, 78
Holocaust Memory Law, the, or Polish
  Memory Law 53
Holokitsch 5, 161, 163
Homo Sapiens 170
Homo Superior 170
Horkheimer, Max 176, 184
humour 86
Hunger Games 171
Hunter, Anna 189
Huyssen, Andreas 179
Hydra 171

identity 61, 64, 72, 78–79
ideology 17–18, 30, 48, 72, 94, 167, 172,
  230, 238–239, 244, 248–249
incompatibility 1–4, 9, 11, 15, 22–24, 31,
  69, 106, 111, 236
Incorrectamundo 238
India 15–21, 24, 83–96, 145
Indian Express, The 95
Indo-German News Exchange of New
  Delhi 87
Institute of National Remembrance 53
institutionalization 177
Interactivity 48, 56
International Center for Education about
  Auschwitz and the Holocaust 127, 135
International Holocaust Remembrance
  Alliance (IHRA) 19, 95
International Railway Information Bureau
  of Madras 87
Intolerance 30, 83–84, 160, 238–240,
  246–249
Iran 84
Islamophobia 91
Israel 87, 90, 93–95, 119, 144, 147, 156, 183
I Survived the Camp (exhibition, 2017) 131
Italy 91–92, 115–118
Itkin, Alan 180

Japan 25, 101–111, 171; Japanese 6, 9, 22,
  25, 101–111; Japanese Pop Culture 24,
  101–104, 108
Jazz 113, 115, 121

Jenkins, Henry 243
Jesus of Nazareth 144
Jewish: diaspora 178; folk beliefs 28, 176,
    222; folklore 183, 191; folktale 180;
    martyrology 142
Jews 10–11, 19, 24, 41, 50–53, 56,
    60–64, 66–67, 86, 109–110, 133, 171,
    180; as accidental victims 7; American
    136; anti-Zionist 95; under Christian
    names 167; dirty 154; European 89,
    101–102, 114–115, 128; extermination
    of 76, 126; German 70, 72, 87,
    91–92, 105, 116; Indian 88, 90–91;
    in Lithuania 108; in medieval times
    18; misrepresentation of 8; myth of
    230; from Nazi Europe 88; under Nazi
    occupation 66; in Nazi vision 20, 84;
    new Jews 16; non-metaphoric 90; Polish
    6, 54, 127, 178, 203, 215; popular culture
    offerings by 27, 141; systemic violence
    against 203; as victims 25, 103; in
    Weimar Germany 71
Jikeli, Gunther 95
Johnson, Alan 94
Jojo Rabbit (film, 2019) 29, 227–232, 236,
    239, 244–249
Judenhaus 71
judeocide 23, 119, 140–141
Judgment at Nuremberg (film, 1961) 141

Kabbalah 39
Kaddish (1945) 143, 146
Kaddish 46, 143, 148
Kansteiner, Wulf 179
Katin, Miriam 27, 153–162
Kent, Clark 170
Kerner, Aaron 11–12
Kertész, Imre 189
khurbn-forshung (destruction research) 73
Khurbn period 71
khurbn-shprakh 74
Kimmel, Eric A. 190
King, Stephen 29, 202, 204
Kirby, Jack 169
Kitty 107
Klemperer, Victor 23, 70–72, 74–76, 78
klezmer 39, 119
Kolkata Partition Museum 83
Kor, Eva 219
Kosinski, Jerzy 39
Kosstrin, Hannah 143
Krauss, Nicole 180
Krigstein, Bernard 165, 166
Krigstein, Bernard 165–166

Lagermusik 26, 114–117, 122
Lammel, Inge 115
Lang, Berel 69
Langer, Lawrence L 211
Langhoff, Wolfgang 114
language 4, 19, 23–24, 31, 42, 45, 49, 67,
    70–79, 84, 89, 93–94, 96, 115–117,
    140, 153, 182–184, 207, 217, 221, 227,
    240, 244, 247
Lanzoni, Susan 240
Laub, Dori 11
Lee, Stan 169
Lerner, Max 224
Leunens, Christine 245
Levi, Primo 10–11, 42–43
Levinas, Emmanuel 69, 71–72
Lexicographical literature 78
lexicography 73, 78
Lieder 115, 118
Life is Beautiful (film, 1997) 6, 12, 45, 120,
    129, 135, 239
Lifton, Robert Jay 224
Lilith's Cave 191, 196
Lingua Tertii Imperii 70
Linguistics 23, 69, 71, 240
Lipski, Jan 128
Lipstadt, Deborah E. 9, 168, 203
Little Nightmares 49
ludic frame 51
Lutheranism 71

Mad Master of the Murder Maze!, The
    (1969) 166
mad scientist trope 166
magic 176, 190, 192; realism 28, 175–177,
    180, 182–184, 207; soaps 141, 146, 148
Magilow, Daniel H. 19, 65, 161
Magneto 170
majoritarianism 83
Man in the High Castle, The 171
manipulation 23, 69, 74, 79, 231, 245
Man of Steel (film, 2013) 171
Marak, Adolf Lu Hitler Rangsa 86
Marathon Man (film, 1976) 29, 214–224
Margalit, Avishai 232
Margins 38, 153–154, 175
Marshman, Sophia 5, 62, 224
Martha Graham Dance Company 143
Martin, Luther King Jr 165
Martin, Scorsese 241
Marxist 184
Mass appeal 39; market 22, 39; murder 22,
    39, 73, 190
Master Race (film, 1955) 165–166

260   *Index*

matricentric 153, 162
Maus 27, 153, 156–156, 166–171
McConnell, Frank 242, 245
Medal of Honor 48
Mein Kampf (1925) 63, 83
memoirs 27, 78, 153–159, 160–164
memorials 15, 39, 132–133, 155
memory: boom 127; collective 23, 48, 61,
  103, 126, 236; culture 37; mediated 38
In Memory . . . 543246 (Dance, 1973) 143
Mendelsohn, Daniel 178
Mengele, Josef 196, 218–219
metahistorical myth 180
Metropolis 171, 215
Michaels, Anne 180, 183
military units 48
Miller, Arthur 63
Mintz, Alan 3, 5, 8–9, 24, 62, 113, 178,
  198, 210, 227–228, 233, 241
Mintz, Lawrence E 240
Miyazawa, Masanori 104
monster 14, 85, 169, 210, 230; monstrosity
  166; monstrous 25, 38, 166, 228
Moonje, B. S. 91–92
Moral ABC 147–148
morality 38, 94, 141
moral reference point 38
Morris, Chris 240–241
Munich 71
Muselmann 10–11
music 20–21, 26, 31, 49, 69, 113–122,
  146, 216–217, 233
Musicologist 115
Muslim holocaust 16
Muslim League 88
Muslims 10–11, 16–18, 83–93
My Memory of Us (videogame, 2018) 49,
  53–54
mythmaking 175

Nagaoka, Akinori 103
Nagarkar, Kiran 95
National Eligibility Test (NET) 90
National Socialism 43, 72, 76, 90
Nazi 203–204, 206, 229–230; armies 54;
  atrocities 2, 19, 20, 177, 180; barbaric
  methods 14; barbarism 51; camp 48,
  55, 56, 114–115, 117, 143; crimes 126,
  129–132, 135–136, 165, 218; Europe
  88; genocide 13, 28, 96; Germany 10, 20,
  53, 55, 79, 90, 104, 108–109; Holocaust
  20; ideology 18, 72, 248; intolerance
  160; invasion 54, 153, 159; language 70,

  73, 76–77; mass murder 73; occupation
  51, 54, 66, 71, 116, 127, 171, 190; party
  62–64, 67, 168, 238–239, 245; policies
  84, 91, 95, 129; propaganda in South
  Asia 86–87; victims 37, 43
Nazi Linguistics 23, 69
Nazism 8, 15–16, 18, 23–24, 28, 31, 37,
  72, 74, 78, 83, 90, 94–95, 119, 147,
  165, 167–168, 170, 221, 245–246;
  neo-Nazism 31, 39
NBC Series *Holocaust* 168
NCERT (National Council of Educational
  Research and Training) 90
Nehru, Jawaharlal 88
Nehru Memorial Museum 91
Neologism 18, 73–74
Neo-Nazism 31, 39
Netanyahu, Benjamin 95
New York City 39, 143
New York Times 84, 231
Nordic Teuton 72
Novel 5–6, 38, 42, 63, 133, 144, 179–181,
  183, 206; biographic 120; Boyne 234;
  Cohen 145; Goldman 218; graphic 31;
  Grossman 119; Leunens 245; Oliver 41;
  Rosenbaum 22, 39, 41, 43–46; Seiffert
  14; Vonnegut 166; Wiesel 142; Yolen 28,
  189–199, 202
Novick, Peter 3

Objective reality 178
O.J. Trial 45
Operation Overlord 50
Orringer, Julie 180
Oskar Schindler 102, 228
OTT Platform Zee5 84
Ozick, Cynthia 197

Pakistan 16–17, 83–84, 86, 93
Palestine 86–87, 95
Parker, Holt N. 21–22
Partisan 71
Partition, of India 16–17, 20, 24, 83, 93
Pawnbroker, The (film, 1964) 141
Pederson, Joshua 185
People's Republic of Poland 128, 135
Peppermint 147
performance 26, 41, 49, 69, 114, 117,
  242, 247
Perrault, Charles 188, 192, 194
persecution 7, 26, 69, 86, 88, 102,
  108–111, 116, 142–144, 154, 158–160,
  165, 183, 193, 195, 204, 229, 236

Index 261

Persona Non Grata: Sugihara Chiune (2015) 24, 101–103, 107–111
phantom 181, 183
Philological antidotism 75
Pick, Alison 180
players 48–52, 54–56
Poland 6, 26, 48–50, 53, 60, 64, 73, 108, 115–116, 126–128, 135, 142, 171, 181, 190, 193, 203
policy 60, 62, 64, 77, 91, 95, 126–129, 133, 136
Polish 48, 53, 54–55, 64–65, 73–75, 78, 118, 126–128, 132–136, 146, 183, 195, 204, 209, 219; Poles 20, 50, 53, 61, 88, 108–109, 126–128, 135; Polish Catholic 8; Polish government 48; Polish Jew 6, 54–55, 64, 127, 128, 178, 215; Polish museum 27; Polish-Ukrainian 48; Polish videogames 53
polyglot 73, 78
popular: consciousness 28, 70, 119, 176; culture 1–31, 45–46, 48–49, 56–57, 61–62, 66, 69–70, 79, 96, 101–104, 108–111, 119–122, 128–130, 132–136, 140–149, 161–162, 164, 166, 172, 175–179, 198, 203, 214, 227, 231–232, 237–240; fiction 22, 37; high culture 21, 214, 240; media 6, 46, 48, 104, 111, 137, 210; music 20, 26, 113–114, 119–120, 122; popularization 24, 37, 96
Popular Front 143
Porat, Dina 89, 93–94
Posen speech 77
post: Holocaust 175, 179–180, 237, 248; memory 27, 38, 158, 162, 179; testimonial era 181, 184
Post-Holocaust: accounts 179; collective consciousness 237; fiction 28, 175; generation 122; lives 42; romance 180; world 180, 249
postmodern: America 39; culture 129–130, 132, 135–136; episteme 130, 132, 135; milieu 39; museum 130; music 122; postmodernism 21, 130, 214; postmodernists 70; world 130
postwar 13, 71, 73, 107, 110, 119, 121, 126, 146, 148, 155, 176, 188, 235
Presidency University Kolkata 15, 96
Prisoner of War (videogame, 2002) 54
Producers, The (film, 1967) 239–249
Promised Land 145
psychoanalysis 45, 71
PTSD 145, 169

publicity 39
Pulitzer Prize 171
Punk 3, 119
Punter, David 181

rabbi 45, 71, 147–148, 190
racism 127, 154
radio 52, 64, 94, 176
Ramachandran, Hema 104
Rashtriya Swayamsevak Sangha (RSS) 90, 91
Rawicz, Piotr 39
Red Riding Hood 191, 197
refugee 17, 88, 102, 109, 142, 184
resistance 21, 28–29, 66, 70–71, 87, 115, 171–172, 176–177, 208, 231
rhetoric 26, 71, 84, 90–95, 184, 230, 243–245
Riefenstahl, Leni 239, 243–244
Robbins, Bret 50
Rorschach test 37
Rosenbaum, Thane 14, 22–23, 28, 37–46, 180, 182
Rosenfeld, Alvin H 84, 86, 92, 96
Rosenzweig, Franz 72
Rothberg, Michael 13, 38–39, 177
Rothe, Anne 49, 62, 90, 210, 232, 236
Ruddick, Sara 160
Russian 48, 54, 64, 154–155, 159, 161, 165, 197

sanitization 25, 101, 107
satire 30, 238–239, 242–249
Satyagraha 85
Savarkar, Vinayak Damodar 88, 91–92
Sawyer, Charles 223
scapegoat 72
Schindler's List (film, 1993) 6, 8–9, 14, 45, 54, 120–121, 128, 135, 228
Schönfelder, Christa 198
Schudson, Michael 175
Secret Empire 171
self-referential 39
semanticide 75
Shapira, Shahak 7
shibboleth 75
Shoah 4, 11–13, 19–20, 55, 69, 78, 89, 122, 128, 140, 142–145, 147–149, 241
Shoah (film, 1985) 3, 5, 135
shoujo 104–111
Silverman, Lisa 19, 65, 161
Sivaraman, Satya 84
Skibell, Joseph 28, 180, 183

262   *Index*

slaughter 17, 86, 120, 131, 197
Slaughterhouse-Five (1969) 166
Sleeping Beauty 189, 192–194
sociolinguistic 71
Sokolow, Anna 27, 141–146, 149
Sonderbehandlung (special treatment) 76
Son of Saul (film, 2015) 238
sound bite 39
Soviet Union 73
Spiegelman, Art 5, 27, 38, 153–157, 161, 166
Spotnitz, Frank 171
Springtime for Hitler 242, 244
SS Guards 25, 48, 62, 215, 219
Stalag Luft 55
Star of David 105, 143–145, 168
State of Israel 90, 93–94
Steps of Silence (dance, 1968) 14
Sterczewski, Piotr 53
Stevens, George 107, 141–142
Storey, John 21–22, 214
Story of Film: An Odyssey, The (film, 2011) 240
Stratton, Jon 27, 119, 140–141, 149
Street, John 176
suicide 39, 42, 44–45, 157, 180–183, 210, 218, 223, 241, 248
sui generis 116
Superhero 27, 28, 165–171; comics 164–165, 166, 169, 172; culture 161
Superman 28
supernatural 175–176, 181–182, 230
Survivor testimony 15, 179, 224
Swastika 86–87, 153, 171, 244, 248
symbiotic relationship 24, 70
synagogue 44, 142, 144
Szolayski House 132

Tattoo 41, 167, 169, 204, 222
Tattooist 44
telepathy 181
television 10, 20, 31, 38, 46, 78, 84, 94, 120, 131, 176, 232, 238, 247; series 5, 8, 69, 148, 231; show 50
testimony 4–6, 10–12, 15, 26, 30, 62, 114, 122, 131–132, 161, 179–180, 183, 211–212, 214–216, 224
Thackeray, Bal 91
third generations 52, 140
Third Reich 53, 70–77, 85, 231, 242
Tikkun olam 147
Todorov, Tzvetan 93, 181, 229, 233
Torah 13, 44, 142

totalitarianism 7–1
tragedy 23, 28–29, 69–72, 89, 96, 126, 133, 146, 164, 177, 185, 190, 203, 206–208, 245–247
Train of Life (film, 1998) 6, 129
trauma: generational 38; intergenerational 28, 175
Triumph of the Will (film, 1935) 244
trivialization 83, 92, 120
Turner, Graeme 217

Uncanny X-Men (1963) 170
Union of Italian Jewish Communities (UCEI) 56
United Nations 89, 92, 95
United States Holocaust Memorial Museum 16, 26, 133–134
unmarketability 42
unspeakable 1, 9, 23, 28, 30, 50, 69, 113, 153, 166, 182, 184, 198, 238–239, 242–246
Urdu 84, 93

Van Pels 103
videogames 20, 23–25, 26, 31, 48–57; Indie games 23, 49, 56; shoot-game 50
Vietnam War 13, 241
Vladek 153, 157
Volk (people) 76
volksbewußt [responsive to the people] 76
volksfremd [an enemy of the people] 76
Volksgenosse [national comrade] 76
Volkskanzler [national chancellor] 76
Volksnah [close to the people] 76
Volksschädling [national pest] 76
Vonnegut, Kurt 166

Waititi, Taika 30, 229, 233, 236, 238–240, 244–249
War Comics 164
war criminals 167
Warsaw 64, 73; ghetto 60, 65, 171; Rising of 53
Webb, Cornelius 166
Weimar 71, 176
Weinberger, Aliza 171
Weiss, Jacob 166–170
Weltsch, Robert 222
White Crucifixion (painting, 1938) 142
White, Hayden 128
Wiesel, Ellie 4–5, 7, 11, 25, 28, 38, 45, 89, 134, 140–143, 145–146, 149, 164, 168, 202

Index 263

Wieviorka, Annette 52
Williams, Raymond 202
Winnicott, D.W. 233
Wistrich, Robert 89, 93
World War II 25, 48, 50–55, 69, 71–75, 88,
  101–104, 107, 110, 116, 119, 126–127,
  142–143, 147–148, 164, 184, 199, 215,
  218, 238, 244–245

xenophobia 24, 96, 127, 184
X-Men 28, 169–170

Yad Vashem 10, 20, 189, 202, 216
Yahweh 143
Yarmulke 170

Yerushalmi, Yosef Hayim 180
Yiddish 71–75, 114, 140, 142, 164
Yishuv 93
Yolen, Jane 28–29, 188–199,
  202–208
Yom Kippur War 144, 147, 223

Zachariah, Benjamin 84
Zandberg, Eyal 240
Zee Alwan 84
Zee Entertainment Enterprises: TV 84
Zelizer, Barbie 56, 66, 221, 224
Zen Buddhism 145
Zionist 87, 93–95, 222
Žižek, Slavoj 11–12, 21, 30

Taylor & Francis eBooks

www.taylorfrancis.com

A single destination for eBooks from Taylor & Francis with increased functionality and an improved user experience to meet the needs of our customers.

90,000+ eBooks of award-winning academic content in Humanities, Social Science, Science, Technology, Engineering, and Medical written by a global network of editors and authors.

TAYLOR & FRANCIS EBOOKS OFFERS:

- A streamlined experience for our library customers
- A single point of discovery for all of our eBook content
- Improved search and discovery of content at both book and chapter level

REQUEST A FREE TRIAL
support@taylorfrancis.com

Printed in the USA
CPSIA information can be obtained
at www.ICGtesting.com
LVHW011835041124
795688LV00004B/529

9 781032 169736